THE PUBLIC DIPLOMACY READER

The Public Diplomacy Reader

J. Michael Waller, Editor

THE INSTITUTE OF WORLD POLITICS PRESS
WASHINGTON

THE INSTITUTE OF WORLD POLITICS PRESS

Published in the United States of America
by The Institute of World Politics Press
1521 16th Street NW, Washington DC 20036 USA

www.iwp.edu

"The Institute of World Politics Press" and "IWP Press" are the academic
publishing imprint of The Institute of World Politics.

ISBN: 978-0-6151-5465-7

080120.1

Revised paperback edition

For Maria

The North Wind and the Sun
Aesop (6th century, B.C.)

The North Wind and the Sun disputed as to which was the most powerful, and agreed that he should be declared the victor who could first strip a wayfaring man of his clothes. The North Wind first tried his power and blew with all his might, but the keener his blasts, the closer the Traveler wrapped his cloak around him, until at last, resigning all hope of victory, the Wind called upon the Sun to see what he could do. The Sun suddenly shone out with all his warmth. The Traveler no sooner felt his genial rays than he took off one garment after another, and at last, fairly overcome with heat, undressed and bathed in a stream that lay in his path.

Moral: Persuasion is better than Force.

Translated by George Fyler Townsend (1814-1900). Not copyrighted.

Contents

Introduction   19

Definitions:
What is Public Diplomacy, and What Is It For?   23

Foundational definition: To influence foreign publics   23
    Edward R. Murrow Center for Public Diplomacy
    (1965)
A basic human right   24
    Universal Declaration of Human Rights (1948)
Transnational government and non-government interaction   24
    Edward R. Murrow Center for Public Diplomacy
    (1965)
Programs to inform and influence   24
    U.S. Department of State (1987)
The open exchange of ideas and information   24
    Advisory Commission on Public Diplomacy (1991)
A promoter of the national interest and national security   24
    Edward R. Murrow, U.S. Information Agency (1963)
A new dimension for foreign policy operations   26
    House Foreign Affairs Committee (1964)
A form of international political advocacy   27
    Paul A. Smith (1989)
To supplement and reinforce traditional diplomacy   27
    Advisory Commission on Public Diplomacy (1985)
At it most successful, it's straightforward   28
    Carnes Lord (2007)
A strategic instrument to shape ideological trends   29
    National Security Decision Directive 130 (1984)
To promote the national interest with information   30
    U.S. Advisory Group on Public Diplomacy for the
    Arab and Muslim World (2003)
A means 'to win support for U.S. foreign policy goals'   31
    U.S. Department of State (2007)
Part of a larger whole   31
    Carnes Lord (2007)

A clear and continuing mission   263
    Radio Free Europe/Radio Liberty
Democracy and security in U.S. foreign policy: 264
    The role of RFE/RL
    Thomas A. Dine (2001)
Communicating to the world's most volatile hotspots   270
    Thomas A. Dine (2004)
Mission, vision, priorities, strategic goals and objectives   279
    Broadcasting Board of Governors (2007)

Words and Language   283

Aphorisms about words   283
    Proverbs, Benjamin Franklin, John Adams,
    Thomas Jefferson, Mark Twain, Pope John Paul II, et al.
Distortion of language in wartime   284
    Thucydides (5th century, B.C.)
Thought corrupts language, and vice-versa   285
    George Orwell (1946)
When a word is true and false   285
    Václav Havel (1989)
Carelessness in adopting the language of our opponents   286
    Fred Charles Iklé (1970s)
Semantic infiltration   286
    Daniel Patrick Moynihan (1979)
Defenses against distortions of language   287
    Advisory Commission on Public Diplomacy (1984)
Take back the language   288
    Ronald Reagan (1983)
Know the traditional meanings of Islamic terms   288
    Layla Sein (2002)
Reclaim the true meanings   289
    Asma Afsaruddin (2002)
Qur'an and Muhammad made emphatic distinctions   289
    Sayyid M. Sayyid (2003)
What we should be saying is . . .   290
    Jim Guirard (2001)
Islamic words, ideas and customs can be our best ally   291
    J. Michael Waller (2007)

We're better at the 'inform' than we are at 'influence'   31
    Charlotte Beers (2002)
As part of post-9/11 strategy   32
    Patricia S. Harrison (2004)
Different from public affairs   32
    U.S. Department of State (1997)
Different from traditional diplomacy   32
    USIA Alumni Association (2002)
A component of strategic communication   33
    Defense Science Board (2004)
An essential element of psychological strategy   34
    Stephen Tanous (2003)
An asset built in fits and starts, and not always seriously   35
    Juliana Geran Pilon (2006)
'It takes two hands to clap'   37
    Karen P. Hughes (2005)
Is 'influence' no longer a core function in new strategy?   39
    U.S. Department of State (2007)

An American Tradition   40

Appeal to the Inhabitants of Quebec   41
    Continental Congress (1774)
Petition to the King   49
    Continental Congress (1774)
Address to the People of Great Britain   55
    Continental Congress (1774)
Letter to the Inhabitants of Canada   63
    Continental Congress (1775)
Declaration of the Causes and Necessity of Taking Up Arms   66
    Continental Congress (1775)
Petition to the King   73
    Continental Congress (1775)
Letter to the Inhabitants of Great Britain   77
    Continental Congress (1775)
Letter to the Lord Mayor of London   85
    John Hancock (1775)
Address to the Assembly of Jamaica   86
    Continental Congress (1775)
To the Inhabitants of the Island of Bermuda   90
    George Washington (1775)

To the Inhabitants of Canada 92
George Washington (1775)
Declaration of Independence 94
Continental Congress (1776)
Dialogue between Britain, France, Spain, Holland, 98
Saxony and America
Benjamin Franklin (1777)

The Power of Ideas and Values 101

The Four Freedoms 101
Franklin D. Roosevelt (1941)
The underlying conflict in the realm of ideas and values 102
Paul Nitze, NSC-68 (1950)
Know the enemy and exploit its weaknesses 111
Paul Nitze, NSC-68 (1950)
'A call to bear the burden of a long twilight struggle' 115
John F. Kennedy (1961)
Human rights as a cornerstone of U.S. foreign policy 118
(The 'inordinate fear of communism' speech)
Jimmy Carter (1977)
'Ash heap of history' – the speech at Westminster 126
Ronald Reagan (1982)
Political action: An ideological thrust 136
Ronald Reagan (1983)
The 'Evil Empire' speech 138
Ronald Reagan (1983)
'Mr. Gorbachev, tear down this wall!' 144
Ronald Reagan (1987)

Truth and Trust 152

Truth-telling liar 152
Aesop (6th century B.C.)
'Act sincerely' 152
Aesop (6th century B.C.)
Biases color the perception of truth 152
Pericles (431 B.C.)
Campaign of Truth 153
Harry S Truman (1950)
Truth is the best form of propaganda 159
Edward R. Murrow (1963)

Voice of America Charter   160
Voice of America (1960)
RFE/RL Code of professional journalism standards   160
Radio Free Europe/Radio Liberty

Cultural Diplomacy   164

An art form since the Bronze Age   164
Richard T. Arndt (2005)
The linchpin of public diplomacy   166
*U.S. Advisory Committee on Cultural Diplomacy
(2005)*
'Rock music helped bring down the Iron Curtain'   191
Andras Simonyi (2003)
Music's role must be part of an idea-based strategy   195
Robert R. Reilly (2007)
Keep the end purpose clear   197
John Lenczowski (2007)

Humanitarian Public Diplomacy   200

'He who does a kindness hath the advantage'   200
Pericles (431 B.C.)
Avoid one-way aid programs: Let the recipients plan   200
George C. Marshall (1947)
USAID could not inform people how it was helping them   204
*U.S. Advisory Group on Public Diplomacy
in the Arab and Muslim World (2003)*
Congress calls on State Department to credit U.S.   206
Public Law 108-468 (2004)
Medical diplomacy generates large-scale goodwill   207
Terror Free Tomorrow (2006)

Religion and Public Diplomacy   210

'Religion and morality' in diplomacy   210
George Washington (1796)
Proposal for Christian-Muslim 'common moral front'   211
U.S. Consulate General, Dharan, Saudi Arabia (1951)
Script for Radio Jidda   213
Dean Acheson (1952)

'Interpret the Moslem religion on the basis of tolerance   214
    and to condemn terrorism'
    American Embassy, Beirut (1952)
Propaganda in Saudi Arabia 'will not be tolerated'   215
    American Embassy, Jeddah (1952)
Country plan for Iran   217
    American Embassy Tehran (1952)
Early public diplomacy funding of Islamic event   218
    U.S. Department of State (1953)
Never fail to stress the spiritual factor   221
    Dwight D. Eisenhower (1958)
A sample of a U.S.-funded religious broadcast   222
    Fr. George Benigsen, Radio Liberty (1988)
An inability or unwillingness to come to terms with religion   224
    Adda Bozeman (1988)
The case for a religion attaché   224
    Douglas M. Johnston (2002)
Effective ideological engagement requires   233
    understanding of religion
    Jennifer A. Marshall (2006)
A civil society approach to public diplomacy   238
    Jennifer A. Marshall (2006)
'Islam is part of America'   243
    Karen P. Hughes (2006)
Engage Muslim communities . . .   245
    U.S. Department of State (2007)
. . . but alienate them if we must   245
    U.S. Agency for International Development (2007)
A model fatwa   247
    Islamic Commission of Spain (2005)

Broadcasting as a Mission   254

RFE/RL Mission Statement   254
    Radio Free Europe/Radio Liberty
Bringing news to people who need it   255
    Radio Free Europe/Radio Liberty
VOA Journalistic Code   257
    Voice of America (1995)
An instrument of national security policy   260
    Ronald Reagan, NSDD-45 (1982)

Psychological Planning and Strategy   293

Every policy can have a psychological dimension   293
    Psychological Strategy Board (1952)
Political and psychological offensives can   295
    outflank us militarily
    Dwight D. Eisenhower (1958)
Wisdom requires the long view   296
    John F. Kennedy (1962)
'Relatively low priority'   298
    House Foreign Affairs Committee (1964)
Origins of U.S. psychological strategy   299
    Stephen Tanous (2003)
Management of public diplomacy relative to national security   316
    Ronald Reagan, NSDD-77 (1983)
U.S. international information policy   319
    Ronald Reagan, NSDD-130 (1984)
Restructuring public diplomacy   324
    Bill Clinton (1998)
Useful reminder: Be there at takeoff,   330
    not just at crash landings
    Edward R. Murrow (1961)

Public Diplomacy and Propaganda   332

U.S. officials disagree on difference   332
    USIA Alumni Association (2002)
Propaganda agency   332
    Edward R. Murrow (1963)
Call it what you want   333
    Richard Holbrooke (2001)
Books are weapons   333
    Franklin D. Roosevelt (1942)
Propaganda battle: from VOA to bulletins to health campaigns   334
    Edward W. Barrett (1951)
Public diplomacy, propaganda and rhetoric   335
    Mark Blitz (1986)

Counterpropaganda: 337
Don't Let the Other Side Control the Story

Keep the enemy in the wrong   337
    Samuel Adams (1775)
Insulate the homefront against foreign intrigue   337
    George Washington (1796)
We need resources to combat covert propaganda   339
    Philip Habib (1986)
Counterpropaganda: An absolute essential   340
    Herbert Romerstein (2006)
How to identify misinformation   341
    U.S. Department of State (2005)
Definitions of misinformation and disinformation   346
    U.S. Department of State (2005)
The interagency Active Measures Working Group: 349
    An eyewitness account of U.S. counterpropaganda strategy
    Herbert Romerstein (2006)
A counterinsurgency approach to counterpropaganda   357
    Andrew Garfield (2006)

Integration of Intelligence, Public Diplomacy   363
and Public Affairs

A model white paper   363
    U.S. Department of State (1981)

Public Diplomacy After 9/11   377

New target: Networks   377
    George W. Bush (2003)
A three-dimensional strategy   377
    National Commission on Terrorist Attacks Upon
    the United States (2002)
A new strategy: 'Beyond elites to strategic communities'   380
    Patricia S. Harrison (2004)
Strategy still needed   389
    Advisory Commission on Public Diplomacy (2004)
Nothing at the top   390
    National Security Council (2005)

'Lack of clarity' in Saudi Arabia – five years after   391
    Office of the Inspector General,
    U.S. Department of State (2006)
'Transformational public diplomacy'   392
    Karen P. Hughes (2006)
2006 Audit: 'Strategic approach still lacking'   402
    Government Accountability Office (2006)
'Guided by our tactics'   411
    U.S. Department of State (2006)
An urgent appeal   423
    Eleven former VOA Directors (2007)
2007 Audit: Still no visible strategy   424
    Government Accountability Office (2007)
A strategy emerges   434
    U.S. Department of State (2007)

Technology Challenges and Opportunities   468

They jammed our satellite. Now what?   468
    Broadcasting Board of Governors (2003)
Uncle Sam's blog   471
    Hampton Stephens (2005)
Enhanced technology initiatives   474
    U.S. Department of State (2006)
Perhaps the State Department should try the Internet   475
    Hampton Stephens (2006)
Virtual Diplomacy Initiative
    U.S. Institute of Peace (1997-)   478

Citizen Public Diplomats   481

Ten things Americans can do to support public diplomacy   481
    U.S. Department of State (2007)
World citizen's guide: Practical advice for Americans   482
    traveling abroad
    Business for Diplomatic Action
Public diplomacy advocacy   486
    Public Diplomacy Council (2007)

What the Law Says   489

Founding law: the Smith-Mundt Act and its amendments   489

Ban on domestic USIA activities   492
    Zorinsky Amendment (1985)
Foreign Affairs Reform & Restructuring Act   492
    U.S. House of Representatives, Report 105-432 (1998)
International Broadcasting Act of 1994   494
    U.S. Senate (1994)
Foreign Affairs Reform and Restructuring Act (broadcasting)   495
    U.S. House of Representatives (1998)
Post 9/11 public diplomacy: what Congress passed into law   495
Federal law calls for public diplomacy offensive   496
    in Saudi Arabia
    Public Law 108-468 (2004)
Federal law calls for ideological campaign in Muslim world   496
    Public Law 108-468 (2004)
Federal law calls for political action against   498
    Islamic dictatorships
    Public Law 108-468 (2004)
Federal law calls for Muslim broadcast programming   499
    Public Law 108-468 (2004)
Public diplomacy responsibilities of the Department of State   500
    Public Law 108-468 (2004)
Public diplomacy training: A top congressional priority   503
    Public Law 108-468 (2004)
Promotion of democracy and human rights   504
    Public Law 108-468 (2004)
Expansion of Islamic scholarship and exchange programs   506
    Public Law 108-468 (2004)
Grants to U.S.-sponsored schools in Muslim countries   508
    Public Law 108-468 (2004)
International Youth Opportunity Fund   510
    Public Law 108-468 (2004)
The use of economic policies to combat terrorism   511
    Public Law 108-468 (2004)
Middle East Partnership Initiative to promote rule of law   512
    Public Law 108-468 (2004)
Toward a comprehensive global strategy against terrorism   512
    Public Law 108-468 (2004)

About the Editor   515
About The Institute of World Politics   517

Acknowledgements

This book began as a simple photocopied reader for my "Public Diplomacy and Political Warfare" course at The Institute of World Politics. When public diplomacy and strategic communication professionals, professors at other schools, and – most importantly – my own students, suggested developing a general purpose public diplomacy reader, this book began to take shape.

The editorial contributions and support of my faculty colleagues at The Institute of World Politics – including IWP President John Lenczowski, Marek Chodakiewicz, Juliana Geran Pilon and Herbert Romerstein – were crucial to the compilation of this book. Jim Holmes was relentless with his copy-editing. I could not have done without the research and editing assistance of IWP student interns Mark Beall, Mike Cohn, Chris Fulford, Bryan Hill, Brooks Sommer, Charles Van Someren and Nicole Villescas. My former students Jennifer Marshall, Director of the Richard and Helen DeVos Center for Religion and Civil Society at the Heritage Foundation; and Hampton Stephens, Publisher and Editor of WorldPoliticsReview.com, contributed their own works for this volume.

Andrew Garfield of Glevum Associates, Professor Carnes Lord of the Naval War College, and former Voice of America Director Robert Reilly are among the many who provided inspiration, commentary and ideas. So are professional foreign service officers, public diplomats, broadcasters and other public servants who offered their quiet support and counsel.

I would also like to thank all those who granted permission for me to reprint their works; each is acknowledged in the appropriate footnotes, but I wish to underscore my gratitude here as well. Since this is an edited collection of works, any errors in these pages are my responsibility alone.

This book would not have been possible without the financial support of benefactors of The Institute of World Politics who provided grants for the purpose of developing *The Public*

Diplomacy Reader and other educational products for the global war of ideas.

Finally, I wish to thank my family most profoundly for their boundless encouragement, tolerance, support and curiosity.

Introduction

This edited volume provides a look at slices of public diplomacy: the art of communicating with foreign publics to influence international perceptions, attitudes and policies. Like any art form, the real definition of public diplomacy is subjective, and can be the source of lively and often bitter debates.

Rather than attempt to create a specific definition of public diplomacy, this book takes some of the most insightful and historically significant writings, statements and official documents, from a variety of professional disciplines and political perspectives, so the reader can develop his or her own sense of what the field is all about.

This book makes no pretensions about completeness. The editor found it challenging to keep it under 500 pages of actual text. Here is how *The Public Diplomacy Reader* is designed to serve the user: To provide in a single volume a useful primer on public diplomacy, straight from some of the leading thinkers and practitioners across time and culture. We begin with a variety of short definitions of public diplomacy and what public diplomacy is for, tackling the matter from various civilian and military perspectives to frame it in the larger context of strategic communication.

Next, we devote considerable space to exploring public diplomacy and the American founding. The Continental Congress, General George Washington and others used public diplomacy with varying degrees of success in their asymmetrical warfare against the militarily superior British. The section on public diplomacy as an American tradition consists of twelve declarations and letters from the Continental Congress and other of the nation's founders, and a satirical piece of diplomatic wit by Benjamin Franklin. Each is different and worth close study for the present-day student and practitioner.

The power of ideas and values is the title of the next section, with passages from Presidents Franklin D. Roosevelt, John F. Kennedy, Jimmy Carter and Ronald Reagan, and from President Truman's foundational NSC-68 penned by Paul Nitze. Here is where we find the core of Cold War public diplomacy and the accompanying political and psychological campaigns that President Kennedy's U.S. Information Agency chief, Edward R. Murrow, called an "arsenal of persuasion."

Public diplomacy fails without trust, and "Truth and Trust" provides some timeless statements of principle and practice from ancient Greek fabler Aesop and Athenian statesman Pericles, President Truman, Murrow, the Voice of America and Radio Free Europe/Radio Liberty.

We then look at three different instruments of global persuasion: cultural diplomacy, humanitarian public diplomacy and international broadcasting. Among those elements we discuss religion and public diplomacy, an especially important issue in recent years. Here we find historical documents from the Truman and Eisenhower administrations, including declassified material about how to deal with militant Islamist ideology from more than a half-century ago. These documents may provide useful precedents for current policymakers.

One of the most basic elements of good political communication is the careful use of words. The collection of items on words and language ranges from brief aphorisms from the Book of Proverbs, the Founding Fathers and Mark Twain, Pope John Paul II and some adages from Arabia; as well as selections on the use and abuse of language, defenses against distortions of language, and Islamic terms, meanings, ideas and customs.

All of the above is of little use unless it fits into a larger strategy. Since the purpose of strategic communication is to influence people's minds – the psyche – we need to focus on psychological planning and strategy. And while the U.S. has not done much of that in the past generation, the study of tried-and-true methods from the Twentieth Century will help practitioners avoid unnecessarily re-inventing through trial and error, and will provide historical precedents. Selections from the Psychological Planning Board of the Truman period, a letter from President Eisenhower and a comment from President Kennedy, a summary of the origins of American psychological strategy by a noted military officer, and declassified National Security Decision Directives from President Reagan round out the picture with primary source material. President Clinton's restructuring of public diplomacy is also included.

Psychological strategy leads us to an even more controversial theme: the relationship between public diplomacy and propaganda.

With propaganda comes the need for counterpropaganda – issues that many public diplomacy practitioners find upsetting, at least in public, but that vital to a sound international communication strategy.

Secret intelligence is a resource for any good public diplomacy strategist, and we reprint, after years of obscurity, a model State Department "white paper" from 1981. That paper concerned the politically charged issue of the conflict then unfolding in El Salvador. It is a masterful piece of public diplomacy and public affairs that is based on multiple sources of human, imagery and electronic intelligence. The white paper hints of other public diplomacy products from the 1980s that would follow in confronting the USSR and its global cadres.

Public diplomacy since the September 11, 2001 attacks is elucidated in a lengthy selection of government documents and official statements that, when arranged chronologically, shows the difficulty the U.S. has had in devising a successful strategy to wage the war of ideas.

Our final three areas are: technological opportunities and challenges for public diplomacy (a topic that cries out for far more discussion than is contained in these pages), citizen public diplomats, and public diplomacy and the law.

A few words about editing: The editor has tried to keep all selections true to their original appearances. Historical documents from the 18th century will contain spelling and syntax that may strike the 21st century reader as odd. A U.S. military translation of an Islamic fatwa, or texts of declassified documents, will also retain the original spellings. Transliterations will vary. These are not typographical errors, but attempts to remain faithful to the original texts. In the case of transliterations, the very style can have political or ideological connotations; they are preserved as-is in the following pages. Conversely, in the interests of consistency of form, the editor has committed the horrible academic crime of removing the footnotes from reprints of scholarly works, but he has attempted to warn the reader in introductory comments when he has made such excisions. All other editorial changes are indicated either as ellipsis (. . .) or as brackets ([ ]) as the cases may be. The editor's own comments that introduce each section, and often introduce specific readings, appear in *Verdana sans serif italic font*.

The editor hopes that this reader will be a useful tool for students of diplomacy, communication and national security, the civilian and military professionals in the field, and the interested public. May it provoke much discussion, reflection and action. Any comments or suggestions for a future edition of *The Public Diplomacy Reader* are welcome at pdreader@iwp.edu.

Definitions: What Is Public Diplomacy, and What Is It For?

At its core, public diplomacy is communication with the publics of foreign countries, as opposed to traditional diplomacy which consists of communication between governments. Beyond that very general definition, views about public diplomacy vary.

Some see public diplomacy as an idealistic means to promote mutual understanding. Others see public diplomacy as a harder-edged policy tool. Many government-funded international broadcasters are adamant that their profession is journalism, not public diplomacy, and at best is a peer partner. Other practitioners see broadcasting as a public diplomacy instrument. Fundamentally, public diplomacy has a purpose to influence the perceptions and attitudes of people abroad, and to influence the policies of foreign governments. In this section, we provide a cross-section of definitions over time and across professional disciplines.

Foundational definition: To influence foreign publics
Edward R. Murrow Center for Public Diplomacy (1965) [1]

Public diplomacy . . . deals with the influence of public attitudes on the formation and execution of foreign policies. It encompasses dimensions of international relations beyond traditional diplomacy; the cultivation by governments of public opinion in other countries; the interaction of private groups and interests in one country with those of another; the reporting of foreign affairs and its impact on policy; communication between those whose job is communication, as diplomats and foreign correspondents; and the processes of inter-cultural communications. Central to public diplomacy is the transnational flow of information and ideas.

---

[1] USIA Alumni Association, "What Is Public Diplomacy?" September 1, 2002, citing Edward R. Murrow Center for Public Diplomacy brochure circa 1965, on publicdiplomacy.org.

A basic human right
Universal Declaration of Human Rights (1948) [2]

Everyone has the right to freedom of opinion and expression; this right includes freedom to hold opinions without interference and to seek, receive and impart information and ideas through any media and regardless of frontiers.

Transnational government and non-government interaction
Edward R. Murrow Center for Public Diplomacy (1965) [3]

[Public diplomacy concerns] the role of the press and other media in international affairs, cultivation by governments of public opinion, the non-governmental interaction of private groups and interests in one country with those of another, and the impact of these transnational processes on the formulation of policy and the conduct of foreign affairs.

Programs to inform and influence
U.S. Department of State (1987) [4]

Public diplomacy refers to government-sponsored programs intended to inform or influence public opinion in other countries; its chief instruments are publications, motion pictures, cultural exchanges, radio and television.

The open exchange of ideas and information
Advisory Commission on Public Diplomacy (1991)

Public diplomacy – the open exchange of ideas and information – is an inherent characteristic of democratic societies. Its global

---

[2] Universal Declaration of Human Rights, Adopted and proclaimed by United Nations General Assembly resolution 217 A (III) of 10 December 1948.
[3] Murrow Center brochure, cited by Hans M. Tuch, *Communicating with the World: U.S. Public Diplomacy Overseas* (St. Martin's, 1990), p. 8.
[4] U.S. Department of State, Dictionary of International Relations Terms, 1987, p. 85. Courtesy publicdiplomacy.org

mission is central to foreign policy. And it remains indispensable to [national] interests, ideals and leadership role in the world.

A promoter of the national interest and national security
Edward R. Murrow, U.S. Information Agency (1963) [5]

Ten years ago the Jackson Committee, established to study our worldwide information programs, stated that, "any program supported by Government funds can only be justified to the extent that it assists in the achievement of national objectives."

I agree – and that is the purpose, the sole purpose, of USIA [U.S. Information Agency] today: to further the achievement of U.S. foreign policy objectives as enunciated by the President and the State Department. We do this in two ways: First, by influencing public attitudes abroad in support of these objectives, and second, by advising the President and the executive branch on the implications of foreign opinion for current and contemplated U.S. policies and programs.

We seek to influence people's thinking through the various means of communication – personal contact, radio broadcasting, libraries, book publication and distribution, the press, motion pictures, television, exhibits, English-language instruction, and others. To do this job successfully, our individual country programs are not scattershot efforts but carefully designed to gain support for established U.S. foreign policy objectives relating to the particular country. This requires imagination, sophistication, and flexibility – and means our programs will vary from country to country depending on U.S. policy needs.

There are, of course, many common denominators. Everywhere we seek to encourage constructive public support for what the President has described as "a peaceful world community of free and independent states, free to choose their own future and their own system so long as it does not threaten the freedom of others." We present the United States as a strong, democratic, dynamic nation qualified to lead world efforts toward that goal. We emphasize ways

---

[5] "Statement of Hon. Edward R. Murrow, Director, U.S. Information Agency," in *Winning the Cold War: The U.S. Ideological Offensive*, Hearings before the Subcommittee on International Organizations and Movements of the Committee on Foreign Affairs, U.S. House of Representatives, 88th Congress, First Session, Part I, March 28, 1963, p. 2.

in which U.S. policies harmonize with those of other peoples and governments, and underline those aspects of American life and culture which facilitate sympathetic understanding of our policies. We endeavor to unmask and counter hostile attempts on the part of Communists and others to distort or frustrate American objectives and policies.

A new dimension for foreign policy operations
Foreign Affairs Committee, U.S. House of Representatives (1964)[6]

The concurrent revolutions of the 20th century – in science, warfare, communications, education and other aspects of life – have in turn revolutionized the practice of diplomacy. Foreign policy operations have acquired a new dimension: the ideological or psychological. This revolution has been recognized only recently by the United States – much later, in fact, than by other countries.

For many years military and economic power, used separately or in conjunction, have served as pillars of diplomacy. They still serve that function today. But the recent increase in influence of the masses of people over governments, together with greater awareness on the part of leaders of the aspirations of the people, brought about by the concurrent revolutions of the 20th century, has created a new dimension for foreign policy operations. Certain foreign policy objectives can be pursued by dealing directly with the people of foreign countries, rather than with their governments. Through the use of modern instruments and techniques of communication it is possible today to reach large or influential segments of national populations – to inform them, to influence their attitudes, and at times perhaps even to motivate them to a particular course of action. These groups, in turn, are capable of exerting noticeable, even decisive, pressures on their governments.

. . . Moscow was quick to grasp and to exploit the new opportunities for working through key groups in foreign countries and through the masses of people in advancing its political objectives. These opportunities were also explored and put to use by

---

[6] *Ideological Operations and Foreign Policy*, Report No. 2 on *Winning the Cold War: The U.S. Ideological Offensive*, by the Subcommittee on International Organizations and Movements of the Committee on Foreign Affairs, U.S. House of Representatives, April 27, 1964, pp. 6-7. Rep. Dante Fascell, Chairman.

other countries. In the United States, however, the need for overseas information and propaganda programs was grudgingly accepted only during times of war. In times of peace, these activities were generally viewed with suspicion and considered unnecessary.

A form of international political advocacy
Paul A. Smith (1989) [7]

Public diplomacy is a form of international political advocacy directed openly by civilians to a broad spectrum of audiences, but usually in support of negotiations through diplomatic channels. It is aimed at civilians and is confined in the main to forms of advocacy available to host governments. . . . It seeks to elicit popular support for solutions of mutual benefit that avoids threats, compulsion, or intimidation. It is not a form of political warfare, although it may be used in combination with political warfare.

To supplement and reinforce traditional diplomacy
U.S. Advisory Commission on Public Diplomacy (1985)[8]

Public diplomacy supplements and reinforces traditional diplomacy by explaining U.S. policies to foreign publics, by providing them with information about American society and culture, by enabling many to experience the diversity of our country personally, and by assessing foreign public opinion for American ambassadors and foreign policy decisionmakers in the United States.

It is not one-shot dramatic efforts that make public diplomacy succeed. Rather, it is the steady, wise use of all of the resources of public diplomacy over time. It is recognition by those who seek disproportionately to enhance educational and cultural exchange that the articulation of U.S. policies is also necessary to mutual understanding and rational international dialogue. It is understanding by those who support the vigorous expression of U.S. policies that the Fulbright and International Visitors programs

---

[7] Paul A. Smith, *On Political War* (National Defense University Press, 1989), p. 7.
[8] United States Advisory Commission on Public Diplomacy, *1985 Report* (February 1985), inside cover.

provide foreign audiences with the background and knowledge of our culture that put those policies in perspective. And it is appreciation by our elected and appointed officials of the importance of foreign public opinion and the power of ideas in international political discourse.

At its most successful, it is straightforward
Carnes Lord (2007)[9]

Public diplomacy has many meanings, but for the purposes of introduction, we will use the official State Department definition from the height of the offensive against the Soviets: "Public diplomacy refers to government-sponsored programs intended to inform or influence public opinion in other countries; its chief instruments are publications, motion pictures, cultural exchanges, radio and television."

There is in this definition, however, a (perhaps calculated) ambiguity that points to a long-standing uncertainty over the nature of public diplomacy. To inform – or to influence? The first alternative implies an approach to international communication not far removed from the venerable "public affairs" function of government agencies, or indeed from the commercial media. The second, however, underlines public diplomacy's character as a strategic instrument of national policy. It is important to understand properly the term "strategic" in this context. The practice of "spinning" the news to create immediate benefit for individuals or organizations (politicians or corporations, for example) is a well-known aspect of the contemporary media environment. Public diplomacy is too often confused with such essentially tactical manipulation of the interpretation of events.

Though it is indeed concerned to place the United States and its policies in a favorable light, public diplomacy achieves its most important effects not by this kind of manipulation, but rather by the cumulative impact of its presentation of news and other information or interpretative commentary over time. Public diplomacy is therefore perfectly compatible with a straightforward approach to presenting the news that is not very different from what many would

---

[9] Carnes Lord, "Public Diplomacy," in J. Michael Waller, ed., *Strategic Influence: Public Diplomacy, Counterpropaganda and Political Warfare* (IWP Press, 2007). Copyright © 2007 by IWP Press.

regard as the model provided by the commercial media. It differs from that model by tailoring the information it provides to the needs and concerns of particular audiences, and by engaging in proactive and sustained efforts to shape foreign perceptions and attitudes in ways supportive of American interests and policy.

A strategic instrument to shape ideological trends
National Security Decision Directive 130 (1984) [10]

International information is an integral and vital part of U.S. national security policy and strategy in the broad sense. Together with the other components of public diplomacy, it is a key strategic instrument for shaping fundamental political and ideological trends around the globe on a long-term basis and ultimately affecting the behavior of government.

While improvements have been made in U.S. international information programs and activities over the last several years, there is a need for sustained commitment over time to improving the quality and effectiveness of U.S. international information efforts, the level of resources devoted to them, and their coordination with other elements of U.S. national security policy and strategy. The role of international information considerations in policy formulation needs to be enhanced, and wider understanding of the role of international information should be sought within the Executive Branch as well as with the Congress and the public.

The fundamental purpose of U.S. international information programs is to affect foreign audiences in ways favorable to U.S. national interests. Such programs can only be credible and effective by respecting accuracy and objectivity. At the same time, the habits, interests, expectations and level of understanding of foreign audiences may differ significantly from those of the domestic American audience, and require different approaches and emphases in the selection and presentation of information. While U.S. international information activities must be sensitive to the concerns of foreign governments, our information programs should be understood to be a strategic instrument of U.S. national policy, not a tactical instrument of U.S. diplomacy.

---

[10] "U.S. International Information Policy," National Security Decision Directive 130, March 6, 1984. Declassified secret document.

To promote the national interest with information
U.S. Advisory Group on Public Diplomacy for the Arab and
Muslim World (2003)[11]

Public Diplomacy is the promotion of the national interest by
informing, engaging, and influencing people around the world.
Public diplomacy helped win the Cold War, and it has the potential
to help win the war on terror.

A means 'to win support for U.S. foreign policy goals'
U.S. Department of State (2007)[12]

The [budget request for fiscal year 2008] provides $359 million in
appropriations for public diplomacy to inform foreign opinion and
win support for U.S. foreign policy goals. In addition to advocating
U.S. policies, public diplomacy communicates the principles that
underpin them and creates a sense of common interests and values.
To help win the war of ideas, funding increases in FY 2008 will
support efforts to combat violent extremism in key countries.
Objectives of the public diplomacy strategy include engaging
Muslim communities, promoting democracy and good governance,
de-legitimizing terror, and isolating terrorist leaders and
organizations.

Part of a larger whole
Carnes Lord (2007)[13]

A major factor contributing to the relative neglect of the study and
practice of public diplomacy in the United States and elsewhere is
the tendency to view it through the prism of the small and often
under-funded and otherwise marginalized agencies that are
responsible for it. From this point of view, it is seen as the last and

---

[11] Edward Djerejian, chair, *Changing Minds, Winning Peace: A New
Strategic Direction for U.S. Public Diplomacy in the Arab and Muslim
World*, Report of the U.S. Advisory Group on Public Diplomacy for the
Arab and Muslim World, 2003, p. 13.
[12] "FY 2008 Budget in Brief," Bureau of Resource Management, U.S.
Department of State, February 5, 2007.
[13] Carnes Lord, in., *Strategic Influence*, op. cit., reprinted with permission.

least of the various instruments of national power. Yet this reflects a fundamental misapprehension.

Public diplomacy derives much of its efficacy from the fact that it forms part of a larger whole. This larger whole encompasses not only public words but public deeds – that is to say, government policies and actions. What is more, it extends beyond the operations of government altogether, to the activities of the private sector and to society and culture at large. A great deal of the work of public diplomacy agencies consists of mobilizing and deploying private sector resources. Public diplomacy is enabled, and its effect enhanced, by the larger society and culture. At the same time, public diplomacy helps to amplify and advertise that society and culture to the world.

We're better at the 'inform' than we are at 'influence'
Charlotte Beers (2002)[14]

. . . our work has to result in measurable action. The charter of the Office of Public Diplomacy and Public Affairs is to inform and influence. We're better at the "inform" than we are at "influence." We inform, often the same day, of key speeches and policies in six languages, later in 30 languages to every country in the world. But we're not as comfortable at what it takes to influence one another, especially when the audience is hostile.

We must master persuasive communication. The principles of persuasive communication hold true whether you find yourself in the world of marketing or foreign affairs. There is a discipline we learned in marketing every kind of product and service that does apply to the presenting of American values and policies. . . .

We first have to even battle our own culture to get to persuasive communication. I'll never forget . . . a sign over a door in the British Embassy: "No one has ever been fired for saying nothing to the press."

That's the antithesis of what I'm talking about. After all, life tells us that sometimes just showing up and taking the heat is the first step in changing attitudes. . . . We certainly don't get rewarded for innovating, either.

---

[14] Charlotte Beers, Under Secretary of State for Public Diplomacy and Public Affairs, Remarks at the National Defense University, September 18, 2002.

As part of post-9/11 strategy
Patricia S. Harrison (2004)[15]

The foundation of our public diplomacy strategy is to engage, inform and influence foreign publics in order to increase understanding for American values, policies and initiatives. Through traditional programs and all the tools of technology, involving both the public and private sectors, we are communicating the principles and values that underpin our policies and define us as a nation. At the same time, we are working to increase mutual understanding and respect between the people of the United States and those of other countries.

Different from public affairs
U.S. Department of State (1997)[16]

Public affairs is the provision of information to the public, press, and other institutions concerning the goals, policies and activities of the U.S. government. The thrust of public affairs is to inform the domestic audience . . . [whereas] public diplomacy seeks to promote the national interest of the United States through understanding, informing, and influencing foreign audiences.

Different from traditional diplomacy
USIA Alumni Association (2002)[17]

Public diplomacy differs from traditional diplomacy in that public diplomacy deals not only with governments but primarily with non-governmental individuals and organizations. Furthermore, public diplomacy activities often present many differing views as represented by private American individuals and organizations in addition to official U.S. Government views.

---

[15] Patricia S. Harrison, Assistant Secretary of State for Educational and Cultural Affairs, Statement Before the House Committee on Government Reform: Subcommittee on National Security, Emerging Threats, and International Relations, Washington, D.C., August 23, 2004.

[16] Planning Group for Integration of USIA into the Dept. of State, June 20, 1997, publicdiplomacy.org.

[17] USIA Alumni Association, Publicdiplomacy.org.

Traditional diplomacy actively engages one government with another government. In traditional diplomacy, U.S. Embassy officials represent the U.S. Government in a host country primarily by maintaining relations and conducting official USG business with the officials of the host government whereas public diplomacy primarily engages many diverse non-government elements of a society.

A component of strategic communication
Defense Science Board (2004)[18]

Strategic communication can be understood to embrace four core instruments.

Public diplomacy seeks through the exchange of people and ideas to build lasting relationships and receptivity to a nation's culture, values, and policies. It seeks also to influence attitudes and mobilize publics in ways that support policies and interests. Its time horizons are decades and news cycles. Public diplomacy is distinguished from traditional diplomatic interactions between governments. In an age of global media, the Internet revolution, and powerful nonstate actors – an age in which almost everything governments do and say is understood through the mediating filters of news frames, culture, memory, and language – no major strategy, policy, or diplomatic initiative can succeed without public support. Fulbright scholarships, youth exchanges, embassy press briefings, official websites in language versions, and televised interviews with ambassadors and military commanders are examples of public diplomacy.

Public affairs is used by the Departments of State and Defense to depict communication activities intended primarily to inform and influence U.S. media and the American people. The White House, the NSC, departments and agencies, and military commands all have public affairs staffs. They focus on domestic media, but their advocacy activities reach allies and adversaries around the world. Distinctions between public affairs and public diplomacy continue to shape doctrine, resource allocations, and organization charts. But public diplomacy and public affairs practitioners employ similar tools and methods; their audiences are global and local. The

---

[18]Defense Science Board, *Strategic Communication: Report of the Defense Science Board* (Department of Defense, 2004).

conceptual distinction is losing validity in the world of global media, global audiences, and porous borders.

International broadcasting services are funded by governments to transmit news, information, public affairs programs, and entertainment to global audiences via AM/FM and shortwave radios, satellite television, and web-based systems. Voice of America, Radio Free Europe/Radio Liberty, Radio/TV Marti, and the Radio Sawa, and Al Hurra Arabic language radio and television services are examples of U.S. international broadcasting.

Information operations (IO) is a term used by the DoD [Department of Defense] to include Computer Network Operations (Computer Network Attack and Defense), Electronic Warfare, Operational Security, Military Deception, and PSYOP [psychological operations] . . . that use selected information and indicators to influence the attitudes and behavior of foreign governments, organizations, groups, and individuals in support of military and national security objectives.

An essential element of psychological strategy
Stephen Tanous (2003)[19]

Public diplomacy is an essential element of a psychological strategy for two reasons. First, the rise in the quantity of information available to large publics everywhere directly affects public opinion and attitudes, which in turn influence the actions and decisions of governments. Second, perceptions are just as important as reality. What appears to be true is assumed to be, more so in parts of the world that do not have access to a free press. The confluence of these two factors makes the job of U.S. public diplomacy – to inform, or to try to correct misinformed or disinformed publics – even more important.

---

[19] Col. Stephen Tanous USAF, "Building a Psychological Strategy for the U.S.: Leveraging the Informational Element of National Power," U.S. Army War College paper, April 2003.

An asset built in fits and starts, and not always seriously
Juliana Geran Pilon (2007)[20]

Better known as "foreign information," the idea of public diplomacy was created in the year the United States entered World War I, during the administration of Woodrow Wilson, who finally decided it worth pursuing systematically, at least for the duration of the conflict. Once the war ended, so did the perception that the U.S. needed to explain itself to the rest of humanity. Having found a messy world shockingly far from "safe for democracy," a nostalgic America tried to retreat to its former insularity and stay out of the international conversation. Remarkably, the United States would not revisit the idea until two decades later in 1938, with the establishment of a Division of Cultural Cooperation inside the State Department. After several identity crises and reorganizations, on the wake of Pearl Harbor the unit became known as Office of the Coordinator of Inter-American Affairs (CIAA). Its unwittingly prescient acronym notwithstanding, the office was quite restricted in both scope and vision. Less than a year later, a more ambitious Office of War Information (OWI) was joined by an Office of Strategic Services whose mission was identified with debatably wise candor as "psychological warfare."

That bellicose resoluteness, however, was short-lived. Weeks after Japan's surrender, President Truman dissolved both OWI and the CIAA, replacing it by the Interim International Information Service, shortly thereafter absorbed into the International Information and Cultural Affairs. Renamed as the Office of International Information and Educational Exchange in the fall of 1947, it finally received at least nominal independence in 1953 as the U.S. Information Agency (USIA). The concept of "public diplomacy" had finally found a home. It was less clear whether it also acquire a clearly formulated or adequately understood mandate.

President Dwight Eisenhower, who understood well the importance of communication to the task of waging war perhaps better than any of his predecessors, did the best he could to set it in motion. Trained to think strategically in battle, he turned his superb military skills to the challenge of waging peace. He knew that the

---

[20] Juliana Geran Pilon is a professor at The Institute of World Politics. Excerpted from her chapter in Waller, ed., *Strategic Influence: Public Diplomacy, Counterpropaganda and Political Warfare* (IWP Press, 2007). Copyright © 2007 by IWP Press.

silence of guns could be – and usually was – deceptive, its comfort potentially dangerous. Eisenhower understood (even better than Harry Truman) that America, having won the Second World War by giving Stalin the benefit of a doubt he didn't deserve, was facing another kind of war, no less daunting for being frigid. The weapons would have to be adapted accordingly; USIA was to articulate the nature of the conflict by reflecting, as deftly as possible, America's belief that its method of government "in the long run will win out." At the new Agency's inauguration, Eisenhower declared our system capable of defeating "all forms of dictatorial government because of its greater appeal to the human soul, the human heart, the human mind." A senior executive reportedly later recalled Eisenhower's private confession that he would have liked to increase USIA's funding "because it was such a force in the Cold War."

By contrast, reports the same executive, President Lyndon Johnson "never took it [USIA] seriously." Curiously, it appears that Americans, among the most productive and innovative people in history, have trouble with diplomacy in general, whether public or private. For example, here is how one senator, Homer W. Caphart, described the job of USIA a few years after its creation: "to sell the United States to the world, just as a sales manager's job is to sell a Buick or a Cadillac or a radio or television set." His good-old American plain talk captures with laconic precision one of the reason for the appalling failure of U.S. efforts in this domain. Even elite advocates of public diplomacy tend to focus on quantitative, institutional, and structural issues, rather than scrutinize the very nature of the vision and strategy. Yet surely America is no Buick, nor are its leaders mere sales managers.

What "product," then, is public diplomacy supposed to deliver? The comforting simplicity of the Manichean struggle that defined the Cold War era was now gone. Defining an informational function for the U.S. government involves not only conceptualizing a new strategic vision, but undertaking a realistic evaluation of the state of the world on both a technical and cultural level. Our rhetoric must be matched by our actions; our policies must synchronize with the rhetoric required to effectively articulate them; and rhetoric itself should be complemented by other means of illustrating the rationale for our policies to other nations seeking to survive in a world that remains as Hobbesian as ever.

'It takes two hands to clap'
Karen Hughes (2005) [21]

At her Senate hearing to be confirmed as under secretary of state for public diplomacy and public affairs in July 2005, Karen P. Hughes gave lawmakers her vision about the mission of public diplomacy in a new age of extremist ideology and terrorism.

I believe there is no more important challenge for our future than the urgent need to foster greater understanding, more respect and a sense of common interests and common ideals among Americans and people of different countries, cultures and faiths throughout the world. The mission of public diplomacy is to engage, inform, and help others understand our policies, actions and values – but I am mindful that before we seek to be understood, we must first work to understand.

During one of my visits to Afghanistan, I heard an old Afghan proverb that I believe sets a good standard for our public diplomacy. The proverb counsels: "It takes two hands to clap." As Secretary Rice has said, public diplomacy is a conversation, not a monologue.

If I had the opportunity to say just one thing to people throughout the world, it would be: I am eager to listen. I want to learn more about you and your lives, what you believe, what you fear, what you dream, what you value most. Should I be confirmed, I plan to travel and reach out to both citizens and leaders of other countries, and I plan to mobilize our government to do more listening. And as I travel, I am eager to share the story of the goodness of the American people. Our country, while far from perfect, has been a tremendous force for good, liberating millions and bringing help and hope to countless lives.

I recognize that the job ahead will be difficult. Perceptions do not change quickly or easily. We are involved in a generational and global struggle of ideas – a struggle that pits the power of hate against the power of hope. As Prime Minister Tony Blair said after the horror of the London bombings, "This is a battle that must be won, a battle not just about the terrorist methods but their views. Not just their barbaric acts, but their barbaric ideas."

In the long run, the way to prevail in this battle is through the power of our ideals; for they speak to all of us, every people in

---

[21] Karen Hughes, Nominee for Under Secretary for Public Diplomacy and Public Affairs, Testimony at confirmation hearing before the Senate Foreign Relations Committee, Washington, D.C., July 22, 2005.

every land on every continent. Given a fair hearing, I am sure they will prevail. People the world over want to be able to speak their minds, choose their leaders and worship freely. People the world over want to be treated with dignity and respect. People everywhere want to feel safe in their homes; parents want a better life for their children. Our adversaries resort to propaganda, myths, intimidation and control because they don't want people to decide for themselves. In contrast, we want to create the connections and conditions that allow people to make up their own minds, because we are confident that given a fair hearing and a free choice, people will choose freedom over tyranny and tolerance over extremism every time.

I will be guided by four strategic pillars that I call the four "E's": engagement, exchanges, education and empowerment.

We need to *engage* more vigorously. We cannot expect people to give a fair hearing to our ideas if we don't advocate them. And research shows, when people know that America is partnering with their governments to improve their lives, it makes a difference in how they think about us. America must improve our rapid response, and, as Secretary Rice has said, we must do much more to confront hateful propaganda, dispel dangerous myths, and get out the truth.

The second E is *exchanges*. People who have the opportunity to come here learn for themselves that Americans are generous, hard-working people who value faith and family. I want to recognize our new Assistant Secretary for Educational and Cultural Affairs, Dina Habib Powell, who will be my deputy if I'm confirmed. She is justifiably proud of her rich Middle Eastern heritage and will bring that valuable perspective to our work every day.

Our exchange programs are responding to the new realities of the post-911 world, reaching out to critical new participants such as clerics and community leaders. We need to make our exchange programs even more strategic, attracting teachers, journalists, youth leaders and others who have the ability to influence a wide circle. We want more American young people to study and travel abroad. And I have a special message for young people across the world: we're improving our visa process, and we want you to come and study in America.

The third pillar is *education* – for we know education is the path to upward mobility and greater opportunity – for boys and girls. Americans must educate ourselves to be better citizens of our world – learning different languages and learning more about other countries and cultures. And through English language training programs, we can give young people a valuable tool that helps them improve their own lives and learn more about our values.

The final "E" is *empowerment* – people cannot give a fair hearing to our ideas if they are unable to consider them. We will take the side of those who advocate greater participation for all, including women. We will create relationships with those who share our values and we will help amplify the voices of those who speak up for them – like the brave young Pakistani woman who spoke out to say that rape is a terrible crime – not a matter of honor.

Is 'influence' no longer a core function in new strategy?
U.S. Department of State (2007)[22]

Influence, according to the State Department's 2007 public diplomacy strategy, is no longer a core function. The post-2005 reforms appear to have demoted or isolated "influence" from the mission, as the conclusion to the "U.S. National Strategy for Public Diplomacy and Strategic Communication" indicates.

Public diplomacy is, at its core, about making America's diplomacy public and communicating America's views, values and policies in effective ways to audiences around the world. Public diplomacy promotes linkages between the American people and the rest of the world by reminding diverse populations of our common interests and values. Some of America's most effective public diplomacy is communicated not through words but through our deeds, as we invest in people through education, health care and the opportunity for greater economic and political participation. Public diplomacy also seeks to isolate and marginalize extremists and their ideology. In all these ways, public diplomacy is "waging peace," working to bring about conditions that lead to a better life for people across the world and make it more difficult for extremism to take root.

---

[22] "U.S. National Strategy for Public Diplomacy and Strategic Communication," Strategic Communication and Public Diplomacy Policy Coordinating Commission (PCC), issued by Under Secretary of State Karen Hughes, May 31, 2007, p., 12.

An American Tradition

Public diplomacy has been an American tradition since before the founding of the republic. The Continental Congress made its case to the world in 1774, and used world opinion as part of its battlespace in what we now call asymmetrical warfare. In this section, we take a lengthy look at the complete texts of Continental Congress declarations. Documents include early appeals to neighbors in Canada, Jamaica and Bermuda; to the British public; petitions to King George III, and the Declaration of Independence of July 4, 1776.

A common technique of the Continental Congress declarations, pioneered by Samuel Adams of Massachusetts, was to combine statements of high principle and reason with relentless attacks on the British government. Such statements showed the reasonableness of the American cause, and the un-reasonableness of the British who had given the colonies no choice but to secede from the empire. It is instructive to study how the tone of the Continental Congress changed over time as appeals to reason became more futile.

These letters and declarations are excellent models for public diplomacy today. They seek to build relations with foreign audiences, combining positive messages designed to support the American cause with relentless attacks on the adversary (or enemy) in combination with traditional diplomacy.

The following collection of pronouncements from the Continental Congress, a public letter from John Hancock, two public letters from General George Washington and a satirical piece by Benjamin Franklin indicate how the American colonists directed their messages at different audiences. The documents show how the thinking evolved from merely demanding the rights of Englishmen to ultimately severing all ties with the country they had considered as their own.

The editor has endeavored to keep the spelling and punctuation faithful to the original documents. Brief editorial comments or clarifications appear in brackets [ ].

Appeal to the Inhabitants of Quebec
Continental Congress (1774)[23]

American colonies' relations with their fellow British subjects in the colonies of Canada were complicated, especially in Quebec. The French and Catholic population there had come under British and Protestant rule just 11 years earlier, after the bitterly fought French and Indian War (known in Europe as the Seven Years' War). New Englanders, especially the Puritans in Massachusetts, were notoriously anti-Catholic and their villages had been victimized by French troops and French-backed Indians until as recently as 1763.

But opposition to unrepresentative and arbitrary rule from London provided a new common cause that would make Quebec a natural ally. Or so the American colonies hoped. The British headed off a Quebec secessionist movement by passing the Quebec Act in June, 1774. Among other things, the Quebec Act granted freedom of worship for Catholics and restored the French civil code in Quebec, allowed Catholics to hold public office in the province without the required Protestant religious test, and extended Canadian borders into territory claimed by New England and other American colonies.

At about the same time, parliament passed what it called the four Coercive Acts designed to smother unrest by closing the port of Boston, bringing the Massachusetts government under direct royal control, enabling colonial officials to evade local justice by being tried in England, and quartering troops in private homes and businesses. American colonial leaders called the Coercive Acts the "Intolerable Acts" and included the Quebec Act among them.

In September, 1774, in its first open message to the people of Quebec, the Continental Congress invited the people of Quebec to send their own representatives to join them in Philadelphia. The message was published in English and French.

---

[23] *Journals of the Continental Congress, 1774-1779*, Vol. I, pp. 105-113. Edited from the original records in the Library of Congress by Worthington Chauncey Ford; Chief, Division of Manuscripts (Washington: Government Printing Office, 1905). Courtesy of the Library of Congress.

Friends and fellow-subjects,

We, the Delegates of the Colonies of New-Hampshire, Massachusetts-Bay, Rhode-Island and Providence Plantations, Connecticut, New-York, New-Jersey, Pennsylvania, the Counties of Newcastle Kent and Sussex on Delaware, Maryland, Virginia, North-Carolina and South-Carolina, deputed by the inhabitants of the said Colonies, to represent them in a General Congress at Philadelphia, in the province of Pennsylvania, to consult together concerning the best methods to obtain redress of our afflicting grievances, having accordingly assembled and taken into our most serious consideration the state of public affairs on this continent, have thought proper to address your province as a member therein deeply interested.

When the fortune of war, after a gallant and glorious resistance, had incorporated you with the body of English subjects, we rejoiced in the truly valuable addition, both on our own and your account; expecting, as courage and generosity are naturally united, our brave enemies would become our hearty friends, and that the Divine Being would bless to you the dispensations of his over-ruling providence, by securing to you and your latest posterity the inestimable advantages of a free English constitution of government, which it is the privilege of all English subjects to enjoy.

These hopes were confirmed by the King's proclamation, issued in the year 1763, plighting the public faith for your full enjoyment of those advantages.

Little did we imagine that any succeeding Ministers would so audaciously and cruelly abuse the royal authority, as to with-hold from you the fruition of the irrevocable rights to which you were thus justly entitled.

But since we have lived to see the unexpected time when Ministers of this flagitious temper have dared to violate the most sacred compacts and obligations, and as you, educated under another form of government, have artfully been kept from discovering the unspeakable worth of *that* form you are now undoubtedly entitled to, we esteem it our duty, for the weighty reasons herein after mentioned, to explain to you some of its most important branches.

"In every human society," says the celebrated Marquis *Beccaria,* "there is an *effort, continually tending* to confer on one part the heighth of power and happiness, and to reduce the other to the extreme of weakness and misery. The intent of good laws is to *oppose this effort,* and to diffuse their influence *universally* and *equally.* "

Rulers stimulated by this pernicious "effort," and subjects animated by the just "intent of opposing good laws against it," have occasioned that vast variety of events that fill the histories of so many nations. All these histories demonstrate the truth of this simple position, that to live by the will of one man, or set of men, is the production of misery to all men.

On the solid foundation of this principle, Englishmen reared up the fabrick of their constitution with such a strength as for ages to defy time, tyranny, treachery, internal and foreign wars: And, as an illustrious author of your nation, hereafter mentioned [Montesquieu] observes, – "They gave the people of their Colonies, the form of their own government, and this government carrying prosperity along with it, they have grown great nations in the forests they were sent to inhabit."

In this form, the first grand right is that of the people having a share in their own government by their representatives chosen by themselves, and, in consequence of being ruled by *laws* which they themselves approve, not by *edicts* of *men* over whom they have no controul. This is a bulwark surrounding and defending their property, which by their honest cares and labours they have acquired so that no portions of it can legally be taken from them, but with their own full and free consent, when they in their judgment deem it just and necessary to give them for public service, and precisely direct the easiest, cheapest, and most equal methods, in which they shall be collected.

The influence of this right extends still farther. If money is wanted by Rulers who have in any manner oppressed the people, they may retain it until their grievances are redressed; and thus peaceably procure relief, without trusting to despised petitions or disturbing the public tranquility.

The next great right is that of trial by jury. This provides that neither life, liberty nor property can be taken from the possessor until twelve of his unexceptionable countrymen and peers of his vicinage, who from that neighbourhood may reasonably be supposed to be acquainted with his character and the characters of the witnesses, upon a fair trial, and full enquiry, face to face in open Court before as many people as chuse to attend, shall pass their sentence upon oath against him; a sentence that cannot injure him without injuring their own reputation and probably their interest also, as the question may turn on points that in some degree concern the general welfare; and if it does not, their verdict may form a precedent that on a similar trial of their own may militate against themselves.

Another right relates merely to the liberty of the person. If a subject is seized and imprisoned, tho' by order of Government, he may by virtue of this right immediately obtain a writ termed a Habeas Corpus, from a Judge whose sworn duty it is to grant it, and thereupon procure any illegal restraint to be quickly enquired into and redressed.

A fourth right is that of holding lands by the tenure of easy rents and not by rigorous and oppressive services, frequently forcing the possessors from their families and their business to perform what ought to be done in all well regulated states by men hired for the purpose.

The last right we shall mention regards the freedom of the press. The importance of this consists, besides the advancement of truth, science, morality, and arts in general, in its diffusion of liberal sentiments on the administration of Government, its ready communication of thoughts between subjects, and its consequential promotion of union among them, whereby oppressive officers are shamed or intimidated into more honourable and just modes of conducting affairs.

These are the invaluable rights that form a considerable part of our mild system of government; that, sending its equitable energy through all ranks and classes of men, defends the poor from the rich, the weak from the powerful, the industrious from the rapacious, the peaceable from the violent, the tenants from the lords, and all from their superiors.

These are the rights without which a people cannot be free and happy, and under the protecting and encouraging influence of which these colonies have hitherto so amazingly flourished and increased. These are the rights a profligate Ministry are now striving by force of arms to ravish from us, and which we are with one mind resolved never to resign but with our lives.

These are the rights *you* are entitled to and ought at this moment in perfection to exercise. And what is offered to you by the late Act of Parliament in their place? Liberty of conscience in your religion? No. God gave it to you; and the temporal powers with which you have been and are connected, firmly stipulated for your enjoyment of it. If laws, divine and human, could secure it against the despotic caprices of wicked men, it was secured before. Are the French laws in *civil* cases restored? *It seems so.* But observe the cautious kindness of the Ministers, who pretend to be your benefactors. The words of the statute are–that those "laws shall be the rule, until they shall be *varied* or *altered* by any ordinances of the Governor and Council." Is the "certainty and lenity of the *criminal* law of England, and its benefits and advantages," commended in the said statute, and said to "have been sensibly felt by you," secured to you and your descendants? No. They too are subjected to arbitrary *"alterations"* by the Governor and Council; and a power is expressly reserved of appointing "such courts of *criminal, civil* and *ecclesiastical* jurisdiction, as shall be thought proper." Such is the precarious tenure of mere *will* by which you hold your lives and religion. The Crown and its Ministers are impowered, as far as they could be by Parliament, to establish even the *Inquisition* itself among you. Have you an Assembly composed of worthy men, elected by yourselves and in whom you can confide, to make laws for you, to watch over your welfare, and to direct in what quantity and in what manner your money shall be taken from you? No. The Power of making laws for you is lodged in the governor and council, all of them dependent upon and removeable at the *pleasure* of a Minister. Besides, another late statute, made without your consent, has subjected you to the impositions of *Excise,* the horror of all free states, thus wresting your property from you by the most odious of taxes and laying open to insolent tax-gatherers, houses, the scenes of domestic peace and comfort and called the castles of English subjects in the books of their law. And in the very act for altering your government, and intended to flatter you, you are not authorized to "assess levy, or apply any *rates* and *taxes,* but for the inferior purposes of *making roads,* and erecting and repairing *public buildings,* or for other *local* conveniences, within your respective towns and districts." Why this degrading distinction? Ought not the property, honestly acquired by *Canadians,* to be held as sacred as that of *Englishmen?* Have not Canadians sense enough to attend to any other public affairs than gathering stones from one place and piling them up in another? Unhappy people! who are not only injured, but insulted. Nay more! With such a superlative contempt of your understanding and spirit has an insolent Ministry presumed to think of you, our respectable fellow-subjects, according to the information we have received, as firmly to persuade themselves that your gratitude for the injuries and insults they have recently offered to you will engage you to take up arms and render yourselves the ridicule and detestation of the world, by becoming tools in their hands, to assist them in taking that freedom from *us* which they have treacherously denied to *you;* the unavoidable consequence of which attempt, if successful, would be the extinction of all hopes of you or your posterity being ever restored to freedom. For idiocy itself cannot believe that, when their drudgery is performed, they will treat you with less cruelty than they have us who are of the same blood with themselves.

What would your countryman, the immortal *Montesquieu,* have said to such a plan of domination as has been framed for you? Hear his words, with an intenseness of thought suited to the importance of the subject. – "In a free state, every man, who is supposed a free agent, *ought to be concerned in his own government:* Therefore the *legislative* should reside in the whole body of the *people,* or their *representatives.*" – "The political liberty of the subject is a *tranquillity of mind,* arising from the opinion each person has of his *safety.* In order to have this liberty, it is requisite the government be so constituted, as that one man need not be *afraid* of another. When the power of *making* laws, and the power of *executing* them, are *united* in the same person, or in the same body of Magistrates, *there can be no liberty;* because apprehensions may arise, lest the same *Monarch* or *Senate,* should *enact* tyrannical laws, to *execute* them in a tyrannical manner."

"The power of *judging* should be exercised by persons taken from the *body of the people,* at certain times of the year, and pursuant to a form and manner prescribed by law. *There is no liberty,* if the power of *judging* be not *separated* from the *legislative* and *executive* powers."

"Military men belong to a profession, which *may be* useful, but *is often* dangerous." – "The enjoyment of liberty, and even its support and preservation, consists in every man's being allowed to speak his thoughts, and lay open his sentiments."

Apply these decisive maxims, sanctified by the authority of a name which all Europe reveres, to your own state. You have a Governor, it may be urged, vested with the *executive* powers or the powers of *administration.* In him and in your Council is lodged the power of *making laws.* You have *Judges* who are to *decide* every cause affecting your lives, liberty or property. Here is, indeed, an appearance of the several powers being *separated* and *distributed* into *different* hands for checks one upon another, the only effectual mode ever invented by the wit of men to promote their freedom and prosperity. But scorning to be illuded by a tinsel'd outside, and exerting the natural sagacity of Frenchmen, *examine* the specious device and you will find it, to use an expression of holy writ, "a whited sepulchre" for burying your lives, liberty and property.

Your Judges and your *Legislative Council,* as it is called, are *dependant* on your Governor, and he is dependant on the servant of the Crown in Great-Britain. The *legislative, executive* and *judging* powers are *all* moved by the nods of a Minister. Privileges and immunities last no longer than his smiles. When he frowns, their feeble forms dissolve. Such a treacherous ingenuity has been exerted in drawing up the code lately offered you, that every sentence, beginning with a benevolent pretension, concludes with a destructive power; and the substance of the whole, divested of its smooth words, is–that the Crown and its Ministers shall be as absolute throughout your extended province as the despots of Asia or Africa. What can protect your property from taxing edicts and the rapacity of necessitous and cruel masters, your persons from Letters de Cachet, goals, dungeons, and oppressive services, your lives and general liberty from arbitrary and unfeeling rulers? We defy you, casting your view upon every side, to discover a single circumstance promising from any quarter the faintest hope of liberty to you or your posterity, but from an entire adoption into the union of these Colonies.

What advice would the truly great man before-mentioned, that advocate of freedom and humanity, give you, was he now living and knew that we, your numerous and powerful neighbours, animated by a just love of our invaded rights and united by the indissoluble bands of affection and interest, called upon you by every obligation of regard for yourselves and your children, as we now do, to join us in our righteous contest, to make common cause with us therein and take a noble chance for emerging from a humiliating subjection under Governor's, Intendants, and Military Tyrants, into the firm rank and condition of English freemen, whose custom it is, derived from their ancestors, to make those tremble who dare to think of making them miserable?

Would not this be the purport of his address? "Seize the opportunity presented to you by Providence itself. You have been conquered into liberty, if you act as you ought. This work is not of man. You are a small people, compared to those who with open arms invite you into a fellowship. A moment's reflection should convince you which will be most for your interest and happiness, to have all the rest of North-America your unalterable friends, or your inveterate enemies. The injuries of Boston have roused and associated every colony, from Nova-Scotia to Georgia. Your province is the only link wanting, to compleat the bright and strong chain of union. Nature has joined your country to theirs. Do you join your political interests? For their own sakes, they never will desert or betray you. Be assured, that the happiness of a people inevitably depends on their liberty, and their spirit to assert it. The value and extent of the advantages tendered to you are immense. Heaven grant you may not discover them to be blessings after they have bid you an eternal adieu."

We are too well acquainted with the liberality of sentiment distinguishing your nation to imagine, that difference of religion will prejudice you against a hearty amity with us. You know that the transcendant nature of freedom elevates those who unite in her cause above all such low-minded infirmities. The Swiss Cantons furnish a memorable proof of this truth. Their union is composed of Roman Catholic and Protestant States, living in the utmost concord and peace with one another and thereby enabled, ever since they bravely vindicated their freedom, to defy and defeat every tyrant that has invaded them.

Should there be any among you, as there generally are in all societies, who prefer the favours of Ministers and their own private interests to the welfare of their country, the temper of such selfish persons will render them incredibly active in opposing all public-spirited measures from an expectation of being well rewarded for their sordid industry, by their superiors; but we doubt not you will be upon your guard against such men, and not sacrifice the liberty and happiness of the whole Canadian people and their posterity to gratify the avarice and ambition of individuals.

We do not ask you, by this address, to commence acts of hostility against the government of our common Sovereign. We only invite you to consult your own glory and welfare, and not to suffer yourselves to be inveigled or intimidated by infamous ministers so far as to become the instruments of their cruelty and despotism, but to unite with us in one social compact, formed on the generous principles of equal liberty and cemented by such an exchange of beneficial and endearing offices as to render it perpetual. In order to complete this highly desirable union, we submit it to your consideration whether it may not be expedient for you to meet together in your several towns and districts and elect Deputies, who afterwards meeting in a provincial Congress, may chuse Delegates to represent your province in the continental Congress to be held at Philadelphia on the tenth day of May, 1775.

In this present Congress, beginning on the fifth of the last month and continued to this day, it has been with universal pleasure and an unanimous vote resolved: That we should consider the violation of your rights, by the act for altering the government of your province, as a violation of our own, and that you should be invited to accede to our confederation, which has no other objects than the perfect security of the natural and civil rights of all the constituent members according to their respective circumstances, and the preservation of a happy and lasting connection with Great-Britain on the salutary and constitutional principles herein before mentioned. For effecting these purposes, we have addressed an humble and loyal petition to his Majesty praying relief of our and your grievances; and have associated to stop all importations from Great-Britain and Ireland, after the first day of December, and all exportations to those Kingdoms and the West-Indies after the tenth day of next September, unless the said grievances are redressed.

That Almighty God may incline your minds to approve our equitable and necessary measures, to add yourselves to us, to put your fate whenever you suffer injuries which you are determined to oppose not on the small influence of your single province but on the consolidated powers of North-America, and may grant to our joint exertions an event as happy as our cause is just, is the fervent prayer of us, your sincere and affectionate friends and fellow-subjects.

Petition to the King
Continental Congress (1774)[24]

King George III was loath to treat the American colonies as a single entity, and viewed the Continental Congress as an unlawful body.

In this first official petition to the king, the members of the Continental Congress deferentially addressed their sovereign as any loyal subject would, politely stating their grievances often in the passive voice and blaming the problems on the king's officers and parliament. They sought the king's intercession to correct those problems. They took pains to state that they were writing as

---

[24] Issued October 25, 1774. Courtesy of the Library of Congress.

individuals and as elected representatives of the people of their respective colonies, and not as an inter-colonial organization.

George III reportedly refused to read the petition, and the letter went unanswered – another sign of royal intransigence that worked to the advantage of the tiny independence movement.

To the Kings Most Excellent Majesty. Most Gracious Sovereign, We your majestys faithful subjects of the colonies of Newhampshire, Massachusetts-bay, Rhode-island and Providence Plantations, Connecticut, New-York, New-Jersey, Pennsylvania, the counties of New-Castle Kent and Sussex on Delaware, Maryland, Virginia, North Carolina, and South Carolina, in behalf of ourselves and the inhabitants of these colonies who have deputed us to represent them in General Congress, by this our humble petition, beg leave to lay our grievances before the throne.

A standing army has been kept in these colonies, ever since the conclusion of the late war, without the consent of our assemblies; and this army with a considerable naval armament has been employed to enforce the collection of taxes.

The Authority of the commander in chief, and, under him, of the brigadiers general has in time of peace, been rendered supreme in all the civil governments in America.

The commander in chief of all your majesty's forces in North-America has, in time of peace, been appointed governor of a colony.

The charges of usual offices have been greatly increased; and, new, expensive and oppressive offices have been multiplied.

The judges of admiralty and vice-admiralty courts are empowered to receive their salaries and fees from the effects condemned by themselves. The officers of the customs are empowered to break open and enter houses without the authority of any civil magistrate founded on legal information.

The judges of courts of common law have been made entirely dependent on one part of the legislature for their salaries, as well as for the duration of their commissions.

Councellors holding their commissions, during pleasure, exercise legislative authority.

Humble and reasonable petitions from the representatives of the people have been fruitless.

The agents of the people have been discountenanced and governors have been instructed to prevent the payment of their salaries.

Assemblies have been repeatedly and injuriously dissolved.

Commerce has been burthened with many useless and oppressive restrictions.

By several acts of parliament made in the fourth, fifth, sixth, seventh, and eighth years of your majesty's reign, duties are imposed on us, for the purpose of raising a revenue, and the powers of admiralty and vice-admiralty courts are extended beyond their ancient limits, whereby our property is taken from us without our consent, the trial by jury in many civil cases is abolished, enormous forfeitures are incurred for slight offences, vexatious informers are exempted from paying damages, to which they are justly liable, and oppressive security is required from owners before they are allowed to defend their right.

Both houses of parliament have resolved that colonists may be tried in England, for offences alleged to have been committed in America, by virtue of a statute passed in the thirty fifth year of Henry the eighth; and in consequence thereof, attempts have been made to enforce that statute. A statute was passed in the twelfth year of your majesty's reign, directing, that persons charged with committing any offence therein described, in any place out of the realm, may be indicted and tried for the same, in any shire or county within the realm, whereby inhabitants of these colonies may, in sundry cases by that statute made capital, be deprived of a trial by their peers of the vicinage.

In the last sessions of the parliament, an act was passed for blocking up the harbour of Boston; another, empowering the governor of the Massachussets-bay to send persons indicted for murder in that province to another colony or even to Great Britain for trial whereby such offenders may escape legal punishment; a third, for altering the chartered constitution of government in that province; and a fourth for extending the limits of Quebec, abolishing the English and restoring the French laws, whereby great numbers of British freemen are subjected to the latter, and establishing an absolute government and the Roman Catholick religion throughout those vast regions, that border on the westerly and northerly boundaries of the free protestant English settlements; and a fifth for the better providing suitable quarters for officers and soldiers in his majesty's service in North-America.

To a sovereign, who "glories in the name of Briton" the bare recital of these acts must we presume, justify the loyal subjects, who fly to the foot of his throne and implore his clemency for protection against them.

From this destructive system of colony administration adopted since the conclusion of the last war, have flowed those distresses, dangers, fears and jealousies, that overwhelm your majesty's dutiful colonists with affliction; and we defy our most subtle and inveterate enemies, to trace the unhappy differences between Great-Britain and these colonies, from an earlier period or from other causes than we have assigned. Had they proceeded on our part from a restless levity of temper, unjust impulses of ambition, or artful suggestions of seditious persons, we should merit the opprobrious terms frequently bestowed upon us, by those we revere. But so far from promoting innovations, we have only opposed them; and can be charged with no offence, unless it be one, to receive injuries and be sensible of them.

Had our creator been pleased to give us existence in a land of slavery, the sense of our condition might have been mitigated by ignorance and habit. But thanks be to his adoreable goodness, we were born the heirs of freedom, and ever enjoyed our right under the auspices of your royal ancestors, whose family was seated on the British throne, to rescue and secure a pious and gallant nation from the popery and despotism of a superstitious and inexorable tyrant. Your majesty, we are confident, justly rejoices, that your title to the crown is thus founded on the title of your people to liberty; and therefore we doubt not, but your royal wisdom must approve the sensibility, that teaches your subjects anxiously to guard the blessings, they received from divine providence, and thereby to prove the performance of that compact, which elevated the illustrious house of Brunswick to the imperial dignity it now possesses.

The apprehension of being degraded into a state of servitude from the pre-eminent rank of English free-men, while our minds retain the strongest love of liberty, and clearly foresee the miseries preparing for us and our posterity, excites emotions in our breasts, which though we cannot describe, we should not wish to conceal. Feeling as men, and thinking as subjects, in the manner we do, silence would be disloyalty. By giving this faithful information, we do all in our power, to promote the great objects of your royal cares, the tranquility of your government, and the welfare of your people.

Duty to your majesty and regard for the preservation of ourselves and our posterity, the primary obligations of nature and society command us to entreat your royal attention; and as your majesty enjoys the signal distinction of reigning over freemen, we apprehend the language of freemen can not be displeasing. Your royal indignation, we hope, will rather fall on those designing and dangerous men, who daringly interposing themselves between your royal person and your faithful subjects, and for several years past incessantly employed to dissolve the bonds of society, by abusing your majesty's authority, misrepresenting your American subjects and prosecuting the most desperate and irritating projects of oppression, have at length compelled us, by the force of accumulated injuries too severe to be any longer tolerable, to disturb your majesty's repose by our complaints.

These sentiments are extorted from hearts, that much more willingly would bleed in your majesty's service. Yet so greatly have we been misrepresented, that a necessity has been alledged of taking our property from us without our consent "to defray the charge of the administration of justice, the support of civil government, and the defence protection and security of the colonies." But we beg leave to assure your majesty, that such provision has been and will be made for defraying the two first articles, as has been and shall be judged, by the legislatures of the several colonies, just and suitable to their respective circumstances: And for the defence protection and security of the colonies, their militias, if properly regulated, as they earnestly desire may immediately be done, would be fully sufficient, at least in times of peace; and in case of war, your faithful colonists will be ready and willing, as they ever have been when constitutionally required, to demonstrate their loyalty to your majesty, by exerting their most strenuous efforts in granting supplies and raising forces. Yielding to no British subjects, in affectionate attachment to your majesty's person, family and government, we too dearly prize the privilege of expressing that attachment by those proofs, that are honourable to the prince who receives them, and to the people who give them, ever to resign it to any body of men upon earth.

Had we been permitted to enjoy in quiet the inheritance left us by our forefathers, we should at this time have been peaceably, cheerfully and usefully employed in recommending ourselves by every testimony of devotion to your majesty, and of veneration to the state, from which we derive our origin. But though now exposed to unexpected and unnatural scenes of distress by a contention with that nation, in whose parental guidance on all important affairs we have hitherto with filial reverence constantly trusted, and therefore can derive no instruction in our present unhappy and perplexing circumstances from any former experience, yet we doubt not, the purity of our intention and the integrity of our conduct will justify us at the grand tribunal, before which all mankind must submit to judgment.

We ask but for peace, liberty, and safety. We wish not a diminution of the prerogative, nor do we solicit the grant of any new right in our favour. Your royal authority over us and our connexion with Great-Britain, we shall always carefully and zealously endeavor to support and maintain.

Filled with sentiments of duty to your majesty, and of affection to our parent state, deeply impressed by our education and strongly confirmed by our reason, and anxious to evince the sincerity of these dispositions, we present this petition only to obtain redress of grievances and relief from fears and jealousies occasioned by the system of statutes and regulations adopted since the close of the late war, for raising a revenue in America – extending the powers of courts of admiralty and vice-admiralty – trying persons in Great Britain for offences alledged to be committed in America – affecting the province of Massachusetts-bay, and altering the government and extending the limits of Quebec; by the abolition of which system, the harmony between Great-Britain and these colonies so necessary to the happiness of both and so ardently desired by the latter, and the usual intercourses will be immediately restored. In the magnanimity and justice of your majesty and parliament we confide, for a redress of our other grievances, trusting, that when the causes of our apprehensions are removed, our future conduct will prove us not unworthy of the regard, we have been accustomed, in our happier days, to enjoy. For appealing to that being who searches thoroughly the hearts of his creatures, we solemnly profess, that our councils have been influenced by no other motive, than a dread of impending destruction.

Permit us then, most gracious sovereign, in the name of all your faithful people in America, with the utmost humility to implore you, for the honour of Almighty God, whose pure religion our enemies are undermining; for your glory, which can be advanced only by rendering your subjects happy and keeping them united; for the interests of your family depending on an adherence to the principles that enthroned it; for the safety and welfare of your kingdoms and dominions threatened with almost unavoidable dangers and distresses; that your majesty, as the loving father of your whole people, connected by the same bands of law, loyalty, faith and blood, though dwelling in various countries, will not suffer the transcendant relation formed by these ties to be farther violated, in uncertain expectation of effects, that, if attained, never can compensate for the calamities, through which they must be gained.

We therefore most earnestly beseech your majesty, that your royal authority and interposition may be used for our relief; and that a gracious answer may be given to this petition.

That your majesty may enjoy every felicity through a long and glorious reign over loyal and happy subjects, and that your descendants may inherit your prosperity and dominions 'til time shall be no more, is and always will be our sincere and fervent prayer.

Address to the People of Great Britain
Continental Congress (1774)[25]

To pressure the British government, and to inform and energize the opposition Whig party in Parliament, the Continental Congress issued a statement for publication in Britain that coincided with the petition to the king. The lively British press could be relied upon to publish the address in its entirety and serve as platforms for public debate across the Atlantic. John Jay was the principal author. The language differs markedly from that of the petition.

WHEN A NATION, led to greatness by the hand of liberty, and possessed of all the glory that heroism, munificence, and humanity can bestow, descends to the ungrateful task of forging chains for her friends and children, and instead of giving support to freedom, turns advocate for slavery and oppression, there is reason to suspect she has either ceased to be virtuous, or been extremely negligent in the appointment of her rulers.

In almost every age, in repeated conflicts, long and bloody wars, as well civil as foreign, against many and powerful nations, against the open assaults of enemies and the more dangerous treachery of friends, have the inhabitants of your island, your great and glorious ancestors maintained their independence, and transmitted the rights of men and the blessings of liberty to you, their posterity.

---

[25] Courtesy of the Library of Congress.

Be not surprised, therefore, that we, who are descended from the same common ancestors, that we, whose forefathers participated in all the rights, the liberties, and the constitution you so justly boast of, and who have carefully conveyed the same fair inheritance to us, guaranteed by the plighted faith of government and the most solemn compacts with British sovereigns, should refuse to surrender them to men who found their claims on no principles of reason, and who prosecute them with a design that, by having our lives and property in their power, they may with the greater facility enslave you.

The cause of America is now the object of universal attention; it has at length become very serious. This unhappy country has not only been oppressed but abused and misrepresented; and the duty we owe to ourselves and posterity, to your interest, and the general welfare of the British empire, leads us to address you on this very important subject.

Know then, that we consider ourselves, and do insist that we are and ought to be, as free as our fellow subjects in Britain, and that no power on earth has a right to take our property from us without our consent.

That we claim all the benefits secured to the subject by the English constitution, and particularly that inestimable one of trial by jury.

That we hold it essential to English liberty that no man be condemned unheard, or punished for supposed offenses without having an opportunity of making his defense.

That we think the legislature of Great Britain is not authorized by the constitution to establish a religion fraught with sanguinary and impious tenets, or to erect an arbitrary form of government in any quarter of the globe. These rights we, as well as you, deem sacred. And yet, sacred as they are, they have, with many others, been repeatedly and flagrantly violated.

Are not the proprietors of the soil of Great Britain lords of their own property? Can it be taken from them without their consent? Will they yield it to the arbitrary disposal of any man or number of men whatever? You know they will not.

Why then are the proprietors of the soil of America less lords of their property than you are of yours? Or why should they submit it to the disposal of your Parliament, or any other parliament or council in the world not of their election? Can the intervention of the sea that divides us cause disparity in rights? Or can any reason be given why English subjects who live 3,000 miles from the royal palace should enjoy less liberty than those who are 300 miles distant from it?

Reason looks with indignation on such distinctions, and freemen can never perceive their propriety. And yet, however chimerical and unjust such discriminations are, the Parliament assert that they have a right to bind us in all cases without exception, whether we consent or not; that they may take and use our property when and in what manner they please; that we are pensioners on their bounty for all that we possess, and can hold it no longer than they vouchsafe to permit. Such declarations we consider as heresies in English politics, and which can no more operate to deprive us of our property, than the interdicts of the pope can divest kings of scepters which the laws of the land and the voice of the people have placed in their hands.

At the conclusion of the late war – a war rendered glorious by the abilities and integrity of a minister to whose efforts the British empire owes its safety and its fame – at the conclusion of this war, which was succeeded by an inglorious peace, formed under the auspices of a minister of principles and of a family unfriendly to the Protestant cause and inimical to liberty; we say, at this period, and under the influence of that man, a plan for enslaving your fellow subjects in America was concerted, and has ever since been pertinaciously carrying into execution.

Prior to this era, you were content with drawing from us the wealth produced by our commerce. You restrained our trade in every way that could conduce to your emolument. You exercised unbounded sovereignty over the sea. You named the ports and nations to which alone our merchandise should be carried, and with whom alone we should trade; and though some of these restrictions were grievous, we nevertheless did not complain. We looked up to you as to our parent state, to which we were bound by the strongest ties; and were happy in being instrumental to your prosperity and grandeur.

We call upon you yourselves to witness our loyalty and attachment to the common interest of the whole empire. Did we not, in the last war, add all the strength of this vast continent to the force which repelled our common enemy? Did we not leave our native shores, and meet disease and death, to promote the success of British arms in foreign climates? Did you not thank us for our zeal, and even reimburse us large sums of money which, you confessed, we had advanced beyond our proportion; and far beyond our abilities? You did.

To what causes, then, are we to attribute the sudden changes of treatment, and that system of slavery which was prepared for us at the restoration of peace?

Before we had recovered from the distresses which ever attend war, an attempt was made to drain this country of all its money by the oppressive Stamp Act. Paint, glass, and other commodities which you would not permit us to purchase of other nations were taxed; nay, although no wine is made in any country subject to the British state, you prohibited our procuring it of foreigners without paying a tax imposed by your Parliament on all we imported. These and many other impositions were laid upon us most unjustly and unconstitutionally for the express purpose of raising a revenue. In order to silence complaint, it was indeed provided that this revenue should be expended in America for its protection and defense. These exactions, however, can receive no justification from a pretended necessity of protecting and defending us. They are lavishly squandered on court favorites and ministerial dependents, generally avowed enemies to America, and employing themselves by partial representations to traduce and embroil the colonies.

For the necessary support of government here, we ever were and ever shall be ready to provide. And whenever the exigencies of the state may require it, we shall, as we have heretofore done, cheerfully contribute our full proportion of men and money. To enforce this unconstitutional and unjust scheme of taxation, every fence that the wisdom of our British ancestors had carefully erected against arbitrary power has been violently thrown down in America, and the inestimable right of trial by jury taken away in cases that touch life and property. It was ordained that whenever offenses should be committed in the colonies against particular acts imposing various duties and restrictions upon trade, the prosecutor might bring his action for the penalties in the Courts of Admiralty; by which means the subject lost the advantage of being tried by an honest, uninfluenced jury of the vicinage, and was subjected to the sad necessity of being judged by a single man, a creature of the Crown, and according to the course of a law which exempts the prosecutor from the trouble of proving his accusation, and obliges the defendant either to evince his innocence or to suffer. To give this new judicatory the greater importance, and as if with design to protect false accusers, it is further provided that the judge's certificate of there having been probable causes of seizure and prosecution shall protect the prosecutor from actions at common law for recovery of damages.

By the course of our law, offenses committed in such of the British dominions in which courts are established and justice duly and regularly administered shall be there tried by a jury of the vicinage. There the offenders and witnesses are known, and the degree of credibility to be given to their testimony can be ascertained.

In all these colonies, justice is regularly and impartially administered; and yet, by the construction of some, and the direction of other acts of Parliament, offenders are to be taken by force, together with all such persons as may be pointed out as witnesses, and carried to England, there to be tried in a distant land, by a jury of strangers, and subject to all the disadvantages that result from want of friends, want of witnesses, and want of money.

When the design of raising a revenue from the duties imposed on the importation of tea into America had in a great measure been rendered abortive by our ceasing to import that commodity, a scheme was concerted by the Ministry with the East India Company, and an act passed enabling and encouraging them to transport and vend it in the colonies. Aware of the danger of giving success to this insidious maneuver, and of permitting a precedent of taxation thus to be established among us, various methods were adopted to elude the stroke. The people of Boston, then ruled by a governor whom, as well as his predecessor Sir Francis Bernard, all America considers as her enemy, were exceedingly embarrassed. The ships which had arrived with the tea were by his management prevented from returning. The duties would have been paid, the cargoes landed and exposed to sale; a governor's influence would have procured and protected many purchasers.

While the town was suspended by deliberations on this important subject, the tea was destroyed. Even supposing a trespass was thereby committed, and the proprietors of the tea entitled to damages, the courts of law were open, and judges appointed by the Crown presided in them. The East India Company, however, did not think proper to commence any suits, nor did they even demand satisfaction either from individuals or from the community in general. The Ministry, it seems, officiously made the case their own, and the great council of the nation descended to intermeddle with a dispute about private property.

Diverse papers, letters, and other unauthenticated *ex parte* evidence were laid before them; neither the persons who destroyed the tea nor the people of Boston were called upon to answer the complaint. The Ministry, incensed by being disappointed in a favorite scheme, were determined to recur from the little arts of finesse to open force and unmanly violence. The port of Boston was blocked up by a fleet, and an army placed in the town. Their trade was to be suspended, and thousands reduced to the necessity of gaining subsistence from charity till they should submit to pass under the yoke, and consent to become slaves by confessing the omnipotence of Parliament and acquiescing in whatever disposition they might think proper to make of their lives and property.

Let justice and humanity cease to be the boast of your nation! Consult your history, examine your records of former transactions, nay, turn to the annals of the many arbitrary states and kingdoms that surround you, and show us a single instance of men being condemned to suffer for imputed crimes, unheard, unquestioned, and without even the specious formality of a trial; and that, too, by laws made expressly for the purpose, and which had no existence at the time of the fact committed; If it be difficult to reconcile these proceedings to the genius and temper of your laws and constitution, the task will become more arduous when we call upon our ministerial enemies to justify not only condemning men untried and by hearsay but involving the innocent in one common punishment with the guilty, and for the act of 30 or 40, to bring poverty, distress, and calamity on 30,000 souls, and those not your enemies but your friends, brethren, and fellow subjects.

It would be some consolation to us if the catalogue of American oppressions ended here. It gives us pain to be reduced to the necessity of reminding you that under the confidence reposed in the faith of government, pledged in a royal charter from a British sovereign, the forefathers of the present inhabitants of the Massachusetts Bay left their former habitations and established that great, flourishing, and loyal colony. Without incurring or being charged with a forfeiture of their rights, without being heard, without being tried, without law, and without justice, by an act of Parliament their charter is destroyed, their liberties violated, their constitution and form of government changed. And all this upon no better pretense than because in one of their towns a trespass was committed on some merchandise said to belong to one of the companies, and because the Ministry were of opinion that such high political regulations were necessary to compel due subordination and obedience to their mandates.

Nor are these the only capital grievances under which we labor. We might tell of dissolute, weak, and wicked governors having been set over us; of legislatures being suspended for asserting the rights of British subjects; of needy and ignorant dependents on great men advanced to the seats of justice and to other places of trust and importance; of hard restrictions on commerce, and a great variety of lesser evils, the recollection of which is almost lost under the weight and pressure of greater and more poignant calamities.

Now mark the progression of the ministerial plan for enslaving us. Well aware that such hardy attempts to take our property from us, to deprive us of the valuable right of trial by jury, to seize our persons and carry us for trial to Great Britain, to blockade our ports, to destroy our charters, and change our forms of government would occasion, and had already occasioned, great discontent in the colonies, which might produce opposition to these measures; an act was passed to protect, indemnify, and screen from punishment such as might be guilty even of murder, in endeavoring to carry their oppressive edicts into execution; and by another act the Dominion of Canada is to be so extended, modeled, and governed, as that by being disunited from us, detached from our interests by civil as well as religious prejudices, that by their numbers daily swelling with Catholic emigrants from Europe, and by their devotion to an administration so friendly to their religion, they might become formidable to us, and, on occasion, be fit instruments in the hands of power to reduce the ancient, free, Protestant colonies to the same state of slavery with themselves.

This was evidently the object of the act; and in this view, being extremely dangerous to our liberty and quiet, we cannot forbear complaining of it as hostile to British America. Superadded to these considerations, we cannot help deploring the unhappy condition to which it has reduced the many English settlers who, encouraged by the royal proclamation promising the enjoyment of all their rights, have purchased estates in that country. They are now the subjects of an arbitrary government, deprived of trial by jury, and when imprisoned, cannot claim the benefit of the Habeas Corpus Act, that great bulwark and palladium of English liberty. Nor can we suppress our astonishment that a British Parliament should ever consent to establish in that country a religion that has deluged your island in blood, and dispersed impiety, bigotry, persecution, murder, and rebellion through every part of the world.

This being a state of facts, let us beseech you to consider to what end they lead. Admit that the Ministry, by the powers of Britain and the aid of our Roman Catholic neighbors, should be able to carry the point of taxation, and reduce us to a state of perfect humiliation and slavery. Such an enterprise would doubtless make some addition to your national debt which already presses down your liberties and fills you with pensioners and placement. We presume, also, that your commerce will somewhat be diminished. However, suppose you should prove victorious, in what condition will you then be? What advantages or what laurels will you reap from such a conquest? May not a Ministry with the same armies enslave you? It may be said you will cease to pay them; but remember, the taxes from America, the wealth, and we may add the men, and particularly the Roman Catholics of this vast continent, will then be in the power of your enemies; nor will you have any reason to expect that after making slaves of us, many among us should refuse to assist in reducing you to the same abject state.

Do not treat this as chimerical. Know that in less than half a century the quitrents reserved to the Crown from the numberless grants of this vast continent will pour large streams of wealth into the royal coffers.

And if to this be added the power of taxing America at pleasure, the Crown will be rendered independent of you for supplies, and will possess more treasure than may be necessary to purchase the remains of liberty in your island. In a word, take care that you do not fall into the pit that is preparing for us.

We believe there is yet much virtue, much justice, and much public spirit in the English nation. To that justice we now appeal. You have been told that we are seditious, impatient of government, and desirous of independence. Be assured that these are not facts, but calumnies. Permit us to be as free as yourselves, and we shall ever esteem a union with you to be our greatest glory, and our greatest happiness; we shall ever be ready to contribute all in our power to the welfare of the empire; we shall consider your enemies as our enemies, and your interest as our own.

But if you are determined that your ministers shall wantonly sport with the rights of mankind; if neither the voice of justice, the dictates of the law, the principles of the constitution, or the suggestions of humanity can restrain your hands from shedding human blood in such an impious cause, we must then tell you that we will never submit to be hewers of wood or drawers of water for any ministry or nation in the world.

Place us in the same situation that we were at the close of the last war, and our former harmony will be restored.

But lest the same supineness and the same inattention to our common interest which you have for several years shown should continue, we think it prudent to anticipate the consequences.

By the destruction of the trade of Boston the Ministry have endeavored to induce submission to their measures. The like fate may befall us all. We will endeavor, therefore, to live without trade, and recur for subsistence to the fertility and bounty of our native soil, which affords us all the necessaries and some of the conveniences of life. We have suspended our importation from Great Britain and Ireland; and in less than a year's time, unless our grievances should be redressed, shall discontinue our exports to those kingdoms and the West Indies.

It is with the utmost regret, however, that we find ourselves compelled by the overruling principles of self-preservation to adopt measures detrimental in their consequences to numbers of our fellow subjects in Great Britain and Ireland. But we hope that the magnanimity and justice of the British nation will furnish a Parliament of such wisdom, independence, and public spirit as may save the violated rights of the whole empire from the devices of wicked ministers and evil counselors, whether in or out of office, and thereby restore that harmony, friendship, and fraternal affection between all the inhabitants of His Majesty's kingdoms and territories so ardently wished for by every true and honest American.

Letter to the Inhabitants of Canada
Continental Congress (1775)

Failing to convince Catholic and French-speaking Quebec to join the thirteen American colonies to assert their rights as British subjects, the Continental Congress took another tack and tried to appeal to all Canadians. By this time, in late May, 1775, hostilities had already erupted in the battles of Lexington and Concord. The elected leaders of the American colonies recognized, as Samuel Adams had been warning for years, that royal violence in one colony was a threat to all.

As with the address to the people of Great Britain from the year before, John Jay wrote the "Letter to the Inhabitants of Canada." Congress ordered a translation into French and distribution of 1,000 copies in Quebec. The Continental Congress recognized the challenge of persuading the Canadians, repeating rather defensively that the Americans are friends and not enemies.

To the oppressed Inhabitants of Canada.

FRIENDS AND COUNTRYMEN,

Alarmed by the designs of an arbitrary Ministry, to extirpate the Rights and liberties of all America, a sense of common danger conspired with the dictates of humanity, in urging us to call your attention, by our late address, to this very important object.

Since the conclusion of the late war, we have been happy in considering you as fellow-subjects, and from the commencement of the present plan for subjugating the continent, we have viewed you as fellow-sufferers with us. As we were both entitled by the bounty of an indulgent creator to freedom, and being both devoted by the cruel edicts of a despotic administration, to common ruin, we perceived the fate of the protestant and catholic colonies to be strongly linked together, and therefore invited you to join with us in resolving to be free, and in rejecting, with disdain, the fetters of slavery, however artfully polished.

We most sincerely condole with you on the arrival of that day, in the course of which, the sun could not shine on a single freeman in all your extensive dominion. Be assured, that your unmerited degradation has engaged the most unfeigned pity of your sister colonies; and we flatter ourselves you will not, by tamely bearing the yoke, suffer that pity to be supplanted by contempt.

When hardy attempts are made to deprive men of rights, bestowed by the almighty, when avenues are cut thro' the most solemn compacts for the admission of despotism, when the plighted faith of government ceases to give security to loyal and dutiful subjects, and when the insidious stratagems and manoeuvres of peace become more terrible than the sanguinary operations of war, it is high time for them to assert those rights, and, with honest indignation, oppose the torrent of oppression rushing in upon them.

By the introduction of your present form of government, or rather present form of tyranny, you and your wives and your children are made slaves. You have nothing that you can call your own, and all the fruits of your labour and industry may be taken from you, whenever an avaritious governor and a rapacious council may incline to demand them. You are liable by their edicts to be transported into foreign countries to fight Battles in which you have no interest, and to spill your blood in conflicts from which neither honor nor emolument can be derived: Nay, the enjoyment of your very religion, on the present system, depends on a legislature in which you have no share, and over which you have no controul, and your priests are exposed to expulsion, banishment, and ruin, whenever their wealth and possessions furnish sufficient temptation. They cannot be sure that a virtuous prince will always fill the throne, and should a wicked or a careless king concur with a wicked ministry in extracting the treasure and strength of your country, it is impossible to conceive to what variety and to what extremes of wretchedness you may, under the present establishment, be reduced.

We are informed you have already been called upon to waste your lives in a contest with us. Should you, by complying in this instance, assent to your new establishment, and a war break out with France, your wealth and your sons may be sent to perish in expeditions against their islands in the West Indies.

It cannot be presumed that these considerations will have no weight with you, or that you are so lost to all sense of honor. We can never believe that the present race of Canadians are so degenerated as to possess neither the spirit, the gallantry, nor the courage of their ancestors. You certainly will not permit the infamy and disgrace of such pusillanimity to rest on your own heads, and the consequences of it on your children forever.

We, for our parts, are determined to live free, or not at all; and are resolved, that posterity shall never reproach us with having brought slaves into the world.

Permit us again to repeat that we are your friends, not your enemies, and be not imposed upon by those who may endeavour to create animosities. The taking the fort and military stores at Ticonderoga and Crown-Point, and the armed vessels on the lake, was dictated by the great law of self-preservation. They were intended to annoy us, and to cut off that friendly intercourse and communication, which has hitherto subsisted between you and us. We hope it has given you no uneasiness, and you may rely on our assurances, that these colonies will pursue no measures whatever, but such as friendship and a regard for our mutual safety and interest may suggest.

As our concern for your welfare entitles us to your friendship, we presume you will not, by doing us injury, reduce us to the disagreeable necessity of treating you as enemies.

We yet entertain hopes of your uniting with us in the defence of our common liberty, and there is yet reason to believe, that should we join in imploring the attention of our sovereign, to the unmerited and unparalleled oppressions of his American subjects, he will at length be undeceived, and forbid a licentious Ministry any longer to riot in the ruins of the rights of Mankind.

Declaration of the Causes and Necessity of Taking Up Arms
Continental Congress (1775)[26]

Within three months of the battles of Lexington and Concord and just three weeks after Bunker Hill and George Washington's commission as Commander of the Continental Army, the Continental Congress issued a declaration on July 6, 1775 to explain to the colonial public and the world why the American colonies had to take up arms. This pronouncement shows how the Congress fundamentally viewed itself as a representative body of British subjects seeking to avoid civil war. Thomas Jefferson and John Dickinson were the primary drafters.

Knowing how the strongly competitive British newspapers operated at the time, the Continental Congress was confident that the declarations would quickly be published in London, as indeed was the case. Here again we see a thematic pattern: a reasonable-sounding list of grievances balancing with positive statements of principle. The language is polite, respectful, reluctant and conciliatory, deferential to the king and seeking to avert a transatlantic civil war – sincere language, as only two or three delegates (among them Samuel and John Adams of Massachusetts) were open advocates of independence at the time.

The document refers to what we now call a public diplomacy mission: "so to sight justice and the opinion of mankind, we esteem ourselves bound by obligations of respect to the rest of the world, to make known the justice of our cause." This theme would later resonate in the Declaration of Independence.

---

[26] *Documents Illustrative of the Formation of the Union of the American States* (Washington: Government Printing Office, 1927), House Document No. 328. Selected, Arranged and Indexed by Charles C. Tansill. Courtesy of the Library of Congress.

If it was possible for men, who exercise their reason to believe, that the divine Author of our existence intended a part of the human race to hold an absolute property in, and an unbounded power over others, marked out by his infinite goodness and wisdom, as the objects of a legal domination never rightfully resistible, however severe and oppressive, the inhabitants of these colonies might at least require from the parliament of Great-Britain some evidence, that this dreadful authority over them, has been granted to that body. But a reverance for our Creator, principles of humanity, and the dictates of common sense, must convince all those who reflect upon the subject, that government was instituted to promote the welfare of mankind, and ought to be administered for the attainment of that end. The legislature of Great-Britain, however, stimulated by an inordinate passion for a power not only unjustifiable, but which they know to be peculiarly reprobated by the very constitution of that kingdom, and desparate of success in any mode of contest, where regard should be had to truth, law, or right, have at length, deserting those, attempted to effect their cruel and impolitic purpose of enslaving these colonies by violence, and have thereby rendered it necessary for us to close with their last appeal from reason to arms. – Yet, however blinded that assembly may be, by their intemperate rage for unlimited domination, so to sight justice and the opinion of mankind, we esteem ourselves bound by obligations of respect to the rest of the world, to make known the justice of our cause.

Our forefathers, inhabitants of the island of Great-Britain, left their native land, to seek on these shores a residence for civil and religious freedom. At the expense of their blood, at the hazard of their fortunes, without the least charge to the country from which they removed, by unceasing labour, and an unconquerable spirit, they effected settlements in the distant and unhospitable wilds of America, then filled with numerous and warlike barbarians. – Societies or governments, vested with perfect legislatures, were formed under charters from the crown, and an harmonious intercourse was established between the colonies and the kingdom from which they derived their origin. The mutual benefits of this union became in a short time so extraordinary, as to excite astonishment. It is universally confessed, that the amazing increase of the wealth, strength, and navigation of the realm, arose from this source; and the minister, who so wisely and successfully directed the measures of Great-Britain in the late war, publicly declared, that these colonies enabled her to triumph over her enemies. – Towards the conclusion of that war, it pleased our sovereign to make a change in his counsels. – From that fatal movement, the affairs of the British empire began to fall into confusion, and gradually sliding from the summit of glorious prosperity, to which they had been advanced by the virtues and abilities of one man, are at length distracted by the convulsions, that now shake it to its deepest foundations. – The new ministry finding the brave foes of Britain, though frequently defeated, yet still contending, took up the unfortunate idea of granting them a hasty peace, and then subduing her faithful friends.

These devoted colonies were judged to be in such a state, as to present victories without bloodshed, and all the easy emoluments of statuteable plunder. – The uninterrupted tenor of their peaceable and respectful behaviour from the beginning of colonization, their dutiful, zealous, and useful services during the war, though so recently and amply acknowledged in the most honourable manner by his majesty, by the late king, and by parliament, could not save them from the meditated innovations. – Parliament was influenced to adopt the pernicious project, and assuming a new power over them, have in the course of eleven years, given such decisive specimens of the spirit and consequences attending this power, as to leave no doubt concerning the effects of acquiescence under it. They have undertaken to give and grant our money without our consent, though we have ever exercised an exclusive right to dispose of our own property; statutes have been passed for extending the jurisdiction of courts of admiralty and vice-admiralty beyond their ancient limits; for depriving us of the accustomed and inestimable privilege of trial by jury, in cases affecting both life and property; for suspending the legislature of one of the colonies; for interdicting all commerce to the capital of another; and for altering fundamentally the form of government established by charter, and secured by acts of its own legislature solemnly confirmed by the crown; for exempting the *"murderers"* of colonists from legal trial, and in effect, from punishment; for erecting in a neighbouring province, acquired by the joint arms of Great-Britain and America, a despotism dangerous to our very existence; and for quartering soldiers upon the colonists in time of profound peace. It has also been resolved in parliament, that colonists charged with committing certain offences, shall be transported to England to be tried.

But why should we enumerate our injuries in detail? By one statute it is declared, that parliament can *"of right make laws to bind us in all cases whatsoever."* What is to defend us against so enormous, so unlimited a power? Not a single man of those who assume it, is chosen by us; or is subject to our control or influence; but, on the contrary, they are all of them exempt from the operation of such laws, and an American revenue, if not diverted from the ostensible purposes for which it is raised, would actually lighten their own burdens in proportion, as they increase ours. We saw the misery to which such despotism would reduce us. We for ten years incessantly and ineffectually besieged the throne as supplicants; we reasoned, we remonstrated with parliament, in the most mild and decent language.

Administration sensible that we should regard these oppressive measures as freemen ought to do, sent over fleets and armies to enforce them. The indignation of the Americans was roused, it is true; but it was the indignation of a virtuous, loyal, and affectionate people. A Congress of delegates from the United Colonies was assembled at Philadelphia, on the fifth day of last September. We resolved again to offer an humble and dutiful petition to the King, and also addressed our fellow-subjects of Great-Britain. We have pursued every temperate, every respectful measure; we have even proceeded to break off our commercial intercourse with our fellow-subjects, as the last peaceable admonition, that our attachment to no nation upon earth should supplant our attachment to liberty. – This, we flattered ourselves, was the ultimate step of the controversy: but subsequent events have shewn, how vain was this hope of finding moderation in our enemies.

Several threatening expressions against the colonies were inserted in his majesty's speech; our petition, tho' we were told it was a decent one, and that his majesty had been pleased to receive it graciously, and to promise laying it before his parliament, was huddled into both houses among a bundle of American papers, and there neglected. The lords and commons in their address, in the month of February, said, that *"a rebellion at that time actually existed within the province of Massachusetts-Bay; and that those concerned with it, had been countenanced and encouraged by unlawful combinations and engagements, entered into by his majesty's subjects in several of the other colonies; and therefore they besought his majesty, that he would take the most effectual measures to inforce due obediance to the laws and authority of the supreme legislature."* – Soon after, the commercial intercourse of whole colonies, with foreign countries, and with each other, was cut off by an act of parliament; by another several of them were intirely prohibited from the fisheries in the seas near their coasts, on which they always depended for their sustenance; and large reinforcements of ships and troops were immediately sent over to general Gage.

Fruitless were all the entreaties, arguments, and eloquence of an illustrious band of the most distinguished peers, and commoners, who nobly and strenuously asserted the justice of our cause, to stay, or even to mitigate the heedless fury with which these accumulated and unexampled outrages were hurried on. – equally fruitless was the interference of the city of London, of Bristol, and many other respectable towns in our favor. Parliament adopted an insidious manoeuvre calculated to divide us, to establish a perpetual auction of taxations where colony should bid against colony, all of them uninformed what ransom would redeem their lives; and thus to extort from us, at the point of the bayonet, the unknown sums that should be sufficient to gratify, if possible to gratify, ministerial rapacity, with the miserable indulgence left to us of raising, in our own mode, the prescribed tribute. What terms more rigid and humiliating could have been dictated by remorseless victors to conquered enemies? In our circumstances to accept them, would be to deserve them.

Soon after the intelligence of these proceedings arrived on this continent, general Gage, who in the course of the last year had taken possession of the town of Boston, in the province of Massachusetts-Bay, and still occupied it a garrison, on the 19th day of April, sent out from that place a large detachment of his army, who made an unprovoked assault on the inhabitants of the said province, at the town of Lexington, as appears by the affidavits of a great number of persons, some of whom were officers and soldiers of that detachment, murdered eight of the inhabitants, and wounded many others. From thence the troops proceeded in warlike array to the town of Concord, where they set upon another party of the inhabitants of the same province, killing several and wounding more, until compelled to retreat by the country people suddenly assembled to repel this cruel aggression. Hostilities, thus commenced by the British troops, have been since prosecuted by them without regard to faith or reputation. – The inhabitants of Boston being confined within that town by the general their governor, and having, in order to procure their dismission, entered into a treaty with him, it was stipulated that the said inhabitants having deposited their arms with their own magistrate, should have liberty to depart, taking with them their other effects. They accordingly delivered up their arms, but in open violation of honour, in defiance of the obligation of treaties, which even savage nations esteemed sacred, the governor ordered the arms deposited as aforesaid, that they might be preserved for their owners, to be seized by a body of soldiers; detained the greatest part of the inhabitants in the town, and compelled the few who were permitted to retire, to leave their most valuable effects behind.

By this perfidy wives are separated from their husbands, children from their parents, the aged and the sick from their relations and friends, who wish to attend and comfort them; and those who have been used to live in plenty and even elegance, are reduced to deplorable distress.

The general, further emulating his ministerial masters, by a proclamation bearing date on the 12th day of June, after venting the grossest falsehoods and calumnies against the good people of these colonies, proceeds to *"declare them all, either by name or description, to be rebels and traitors, to supersede the course of the common law, and instead thereof to publish and order the use and exercise of the law martial."* – His troops have butchered our countrymen, have wantonly burnt Charlestown, besides a considerable number of houses in other places; our ships and vessels are seized; the necessary supplies of provisions are intercepted, and he is exerting his utmost power to spread destruction and devastation around him.

We have received certain intelligence, that general Carelton [sic], the governor of Canada, is instigating the people of that province and the Indians to fall upon us; and we have but too much reason to apprehend, that schemes have been formed to excite domestic enemies against us. In brief, a part of these colonies now feel, and all of them are sure of feeling, as far as the vengeance of administration can inflict them, the complicated calamities of fire, sword and famine. We are reduced to the alternative of chusing an unconditional submission to the tyranny of irritated ministers, or resistance by force. – The latter is our choice. – We have counted the cost of this contest, and find nothing so dreadful as voluntary slavery. – Honour, justice, and humanity, forbid us tamely to surrender that freedom which we received from our gallant ancestors, and which our innocent posterity have a right to receive from us. We cannot endure the infamy and guilt of resigning succeeding generations to that wretchedness which inevitably awaits them, if we basely entail hereditary bondage upon them.

Our cause is just. Our union is perfect. Our internal resources are great, and, if necessary, foreign assistance is undoubtedly attainable. – We gratefully acknowledge, as signal instances of the Divine favour towards us, that his Providence would not permit us to be called into this severe controversy, until we were grown up to our present strength, had been previously exercised in warlike operation, and possessed of the means of defending ourselves. With hearts fortified with these animating reflections, we most solemnly, before God and the world, declare, that, exerting the utmost energy of those powers, which our beneficent Creator hath graciously bestowed upon us, the arms we have been compelled by our enemies to assume, we will, in defiance of every hazard, with unabating firmness and perseverence, employ for the preservation of our liberties; being with one mind resolved to die freemen rather than to live slaves.

Lest this declaration should disquiet the minds of our friends and fellow-subjects in any part of the empire, we assure them that we mean not to dissolve that union which has so long and so happily subsisted between us, and which we sincerely wish to see restored. – Necessity has not yet driven us into that desperate measure, or induced us to excite any other nation to war against them. – We have not raised armies with ambitious designs of separating from Great-Britain, and establishing independent states. We fight not for glory or for conquest. We exhibit to mankind the remarkable spectacle of a people attacked by unprovoked enemies, without any imputation or even suspicion of offence. They boast of their privileges and civilization, and yet proffer no milder conditions than servitude or death.

In our own native land, in defence of the freedom that is our birthright, and which we ever enjoyed till the late violation of it – for the protection of our property, acquired solely by the honest industry of our fore-fathers and ourselves, against violence actually offered, we have taken up arms. We shall lay them down when hostilities shall cease on the part of the aggressors, and all danger of their being renewed shall be removed, and not before.

With an humble confidence in the mercies of the supreme and impartial Judge and Ruler of the Universe, we most devoutly implore his divine goodness to protect us happily through this great conflict, to dispose our adversaries to reconciliation on reasonable terms, and thereby to relieve the empire from the calamities of civil war.

Petition to the King
Continental Congress (1775) [27]

As with the 1774 petition, the 1775 appeal to King George III is reverent and deferential in a tone befitting Englishmen to their sovereign. The delegates again signed as individuals representing the people of their colonies, and not as members of the Continental Congress.

Continental Congress President John Hancock was the lead signer of the petition. Richard Penn, a descendant of Quaker leader William Penn with a trusted name in England, carried this message and other declarations to London on behalf of the Continental Congress. As before, George III refused to receive the appeal. This time, the king called for "loyal subjects" in America to punish the ringleaders for their foul treason. The Continental Congress correctly anticipated that the lively London press would publish the documents in full.

To the King's most excellent Majesty:

MOST GRACIOUS SOVEREIGN,

We, your Majesty's faithful subjects of the colonies new Hampshire, Massachusetts bay, Rhode island and Providence Plantations, Connecticut, New York, New Jersey, Pennsylvania, the counties of New Castle, Kent, and Sussex, on Delaware, Maryland, Virginia, North Carolina, and South Carolina, in behalf of ourselves, and the inhabitants of these colonies, who have deputed us to represent them in general Congress, entreat your Majesty's gracious attention to this our humble petition.

The union between our Mother country and these colonies, and the energy of mild and just government, produced benefits so remarkably important, and afforded such an assurance of their

---

[27] *Journals of the Continental Congress, 1774-1779*, Vol. II, Pages 158-161. Edited from the original records in the Library of Congress by Worthington Chauncey Ford; Chief, Division of Manuscripts (Washington: Government Printing Office, 1905). Courtesy of the Library of Congress.

permanency and increase, that the wonder and envy of other Nations were excited, while they beheld Great Britain riseing to a power the most extraordinary the world had ever known.

Her rivals, observing that there was no probability of this happy connexion being broken by civil dissensions, and apprehending its future effects, if left any longer undisturbed, resolved to prevent her receiving such continual and formidable accessions of wealth and strength, by checking the growth of these settlements from which they were to be derived.

In the prosecution of this attempt, events so unfavourable to the design took place, that every friend to the interests of Great Britain and these colonies, entertained pleasing and reasonable expectations of seeing an additional force and extension immediately given to the operations of the union hitherto experienced, by an enlargement of the dominions of the Crown, and the removal of ancient and warlike enemies to a greater distance.

At the conclusion, therefore, of the late war, the most glorious and advantageous that ever had been carried on by British arms, your loyal colonists having contributed to its success, by such repeated and strenuous exertions, as frequently procured them the distinguished approbation of your Majesty, of the late king, and of parliament, doubted not but that they should be permitted, with the rest of the empire, to share in the blessings of peace, and the emoluments of victory and conquest. While these recent and honorable acknowledgments of their merits remained on record in the journals and acts of that august legislature, the Parliament, undefaced by the imputation or even the suspicion of any offense, they were alarmed by a new system of statutes and regulations adopted for the administration of the colonies, that filled their minds with the most painful fears and jealousies; and, to their inexpressible astonishment, perceived the dangers of a foreign quarrel quickly succeeded by domestic dangers, in their judgment, of a more dreadful kind.

Nor were their anxieties alleviated by any tendency in this system to promote the welfare of the Mother country. For tho' its effects were more immediately felt by them, yet its influence appeared to be injurious to the commerce and prosperity of Great Britain.

We shall decline the ungrateful task of describing the irksome variety of artifices, practiced by many of your Majesty's Ministers, the delusive presences, fruitless terrors, and unavailing severities, that have, from time to time, been dealt out by them, in their attempts to execute this impolitic plan, or of traceing, thro'a series of years past, the progress of the unhappy differences between Great Britain and these colonies, which have flowed from this fatal source.

Your Majesty's Ministers, persevering in their measures, and proceeding to open hostilities for enforcing them, have compelled us to arm in our own defence, and have engaged us in a controversy so peculiarly abhorrent to the affections of your still faithful colonists, that when we consider whom we must oppose in this contest, and if it continues, what may be the consequences, our own particular misfortunes are accounted by us only as parts of our distress.

Knowing to what violent resentments and incurable animosities, civil discords are apt to exasperate and inflame the contending parties, we think ourselves required by indispensable obligations to Almighty God, to your Majesty, to our fellow subjects, and to ourselves, immediately to use all the means in our power, not incompatible with our safety, for stopping the further effusion of blood, and for averting the impending calamities that threaten the British Empire.

Thus called upon to address your Majesty on affairs of such moment to America, and probably to all your dominions, we are earnestly desirous of performing this office, with the utmost deference for your Majesty; and we therefore pray, that your royal magnanimity and benevolence may make the most favourable construction of our expressions on so uncommon an occasion. Could represent in their full force, the sentiments that agitate the minds of us your dutiful subjects, we are persuaded your Majesty would ascribe any seeming deviation from reverence in our language, and even in our conduct, not to any reprehensible intention, but to the impossibility of reconciling the usual appearances of respect, with a just attention to our own preservation against those artful and cruel enemies, who abuse your royal confidence and authority, for the purpose of effecting our destruction.

Attached to your Majesty's person, family, and government, with all devotion that principle and affection can inspire, connected with Great Britain by the strongest ties that can unite societies, and deploring every event that tends in any degree to weaken them, we solemnly assure your Majesty, that we not only most ardently desire the former harmony between her and these colonies may be restored, but that a concord may be established between them upon so firm a basis as to perpetuate its blessings, uninterrupted by any future dissensions, to succeeding generations in both countries, and to transmit your Majesty's Name to posterity, adorned with that signal and lasting glory, that has attended the memory of those illustrious personages, whose virtues and abilities have extricated states from dangerous convulsions, and, by securing happiness to others, have erected the most noble and durable monuments to their own fame.

We beg leave further to assure your Majesty, that notwithstanding the sufferings of your loyal colonists, during the course of the present controversy, our breasts retain too tender a regard for the kingdom from which we derive our origin, to request such a reconciliation as might in any manner be inconsistent with her dignity or her welfare. These, related as we are to her, honor and duty, as well as inclination, induce us to support and advance; and the apprehensions that now oppress our hearts with unspeakable grief, being once removed, your Majesty will find your faithful subjects on this continent ready and willing at all times, as they ever have been, with their lives and fortunes, to assert and maintain the rights and interests of your Majesty, and of our Mother country.

We, therefore, beseech your Majesty, that your royal authority and influence may be graciously interposed to procure us relief from our afflicting fears and jealousies, occasioned by the system before mentioned, and to settle peace through every part of your dominions, with all humility submitting to your Majesty's wise consideration whether it may not be expedient for facilitating those important purposes, that your Majesty be pleased to direct some mode, by which the united applications of your faithful colonists to the throne, in pursuance of their common councils, may be improved into a happy and permanent reconciliation; and that, in the mean time, measures may be taken for preventing the further destruction of the lives of your Majesty's subjects; and that such statutes as more immediately distress any of your Majesty's colonies may be repealed.

For by such arrangements as your Majesty's wisdom can form, for collecting the united sense of your American people, we are convinced your Majesty would receive such satisfactory proofs of the disposition of the colonists towards their sovereign and parent state, that the wished for opportunity would soon be restored to them, of evincing the sincerity of their professions, by every testimony of devotion becoming the most dutiful subjects, and the most affectionate colonists.

That your Majesty may enjoy a long and prosperous reign, and that your descendants may govern your dominions with honor to themselves and happiness to their subjects, is our sincere and fervent prayer.

Letter to the inhabitants of Great Britain
Continental Congress (1775)[28]

As with the 1774 petition to King George III, the Continental Congress on July 8, 1775 issued a companion declaration for the British public. Unlike the above petition to the king, the letter uses graphic language designed to inflame the people's sensibilities and win their sympathy. Still, the letter shows not a hint of sentiment for secession from the crown. Richard Penn brought the letter to London for distribution.

FRIENDS, COUNTRYMEN, AND BRETHREN!

By these, and by every other Appellation that may designate the Ties, which bind us to each other, we entreat your serious Attention to this our second Attempt to prevent their Dissolution. Rememberance of former Friendships, Pride in the glorious Atchievements of our common Ancestors, and Affection for the Heirs of their Virtues, have hitherto preserved our mutual Connexion; but when that Friendship is violated by the grossest Injuries; when the Pride of Ancestry becomes our Reproach, and we are no otherwise allied than as Tyrants and Slaves; when reduced to the melancholy Alternative of renouncing your Favour or our Freedom; can we hesitate about the Choices Let the Spirit of Britons determine.

In a former Address we asserted our Rights, and stated the Injuries we had then received. We hoped, that the mention of our Wrongs would have roused that honest Indignation which has slept too long for your Honor, or the Welfare of the Empire. But we have not been permitted to entertain this pleasing expectation. Every Day brought an accumulation of Injuries, and the Invention of the Ministry has been constantly exercised, in adding to the Calamities of your American Brethren.

After the most valuable Right of Legislation was infringed; when the Powers assumed by your Parliament, in which we are not represented, and from our local and other Circumstances cannot

---

[28] *Journals of the Continental Congress, 1774-1789*, Vol. II, pp. 163-171. Courtesy of the Library of Congress.

properly be represented, rendered our Property precarious; after being denied that mode of Trial, to which we have long been indebted for the safety of our Persons, and the preservation of our Liberties; after being in many instances divested of those Laws, which were transmitted to us by our common Ancestors, and subjected to an arbitrary Code, compiled under the auspices of Roman Tyrants; after those Charters, which encouraged our Predecessors to brave Death and Danger in every Shape, on unknown Seas, in Deserts unexplored, amidst barbarous and inhospitable Nations, were annulled; when, without the form of Trial, without a public Accusation, whole Colonies were condemned, their Trade destroyed, their inhabitants impoverished; when Soldiers were encouraged to embrue their Hands in the Blood of Americans, by offers of Impunity; when new modes of Trial were instituted for the ruin of the accused, where the charge carried with it the horrors of conviction; when a despotic Government was established in a neighbouring Province, and its Limits extended to every of our Frontiers; we little imagined that any thing could be added to this black Catalogue of unprovoked Injuries: but we have unhappily been deceived, and the late Measures of the Brash Ministry fully convince us, that their object is the reduction of these Colonies to Slavery and Ruin.

To confirm this Assertion, let us recal your attention to the Affairs of America, since our last Address. Let us combat the Calumnies of our Enemies; and let us warn you of the hangers that threaten you in our destruction. Many of your Fellow-Subjects, whose situation deprived them of other Support, drew their Maintenance from the Sea; but the deprivation of our Liberty being insufficient to satisfy the resentment of our Enemies, the horrors of Famine were super-added, and a British Parliament, who, in better times, were the Protectors of Innocence and the Patrons of Humanity, have, without distinction of Age or Sex, robbed thousands of the Food which they were accustomed to draw from that inexhaustible Source, placed in their neighbourhood by the benevolent Creator.

Another Act of your Legislature shuts our Ports, and prohibits our Trade with any but those States from whom the great Law of self-preservation renders it absolutely necessary we should at present withhold our Commerce. But this Act (whatever may have been its design) we consider rather as injurious to your Opulence than our Interest. All our Commerce terminates with you; and the Wealth we procure from other Nations, is soon exchanged for your

Superfluities. Our remittances must then cease with our trade; and our refinements with our Affluence. We trust, however, that Laws which deprive us of every Blessing but a Soil that teems with the necessaries of Life, and that Liberty which renders the enjoyment of them secure, will not relax our Vigour in their Defence.

We: might here observe on the Cruelty and Inconsistency of those, who, while they publicly Brand us with reproachful and unworthy Epithets, endeavour to deprive us of the means of defence, by their Interposition with foreign Powers, and to deliver us to the lawless Ravages of a merciless Soldiery. But happily we are not without Resources; and though the timid and humiliating Applications of a Brash Ministry should prevail with foreign Nations, yet Industry, prompted by necessity, will not leave us without the necessary Supplies.

We could wish to go no further, and, not to wound the Ear of Humanity, leave untold those rigorous Acts of Oppression, which are daily exercised in the Town of Boston, did we not hope, that by disclaiming their Deeds and punishing the Perpetrators, you would shortly vindicate the Honour of the British Name, and re-establish the violated Laws of Justice.

That once populous, nourishing and commercial Town is now garrisoned by an Army sent not to protect, but to enslave its Inhabitants. The civil government is overturned, and a military Despotism erected upon its Ruins. Without Law, without Right, Powers are assumed unknown to the Constitution. Private Property is unjustly invaded. The Inhabitants, daily subjected to the Licentiousness of the Soldiery, are forbid to remove in Defiance of their natural Rights, in Violation of the most solemn Compacts. Or if, after long and wearisome Solicitation, a Pass is procured, their Edects are detained, and even those who are most favoured, have no Alternative but Poverty or Slavery. The Distress of many thousand People, wantonly deprived of the Necessaries of Life, is a Subject, on which we would not wish to enlarge.

Yet, we cannot but observe, that a British Fleet (unjustified even by Acts of your Legislature) are daily employed in ruining our Commerce, seizing our Ships, and depriving whole Communities of their daily Bread. Nor will a Regard for your Honour permit us to be silent, while British Troops sully your Glory, by Actions, which the most inveterate Enmity will not palliate among civilized Nations, the wanton and unnecessary Destruction of Charlestown, a large, ancient, and once populous Town, just before deserted by its Inhabitants, who had fled to avoid the Fury of your Soldiery.

If you still retain those Sentiments of Compassion, by which Britons have ever been distinguished, if the Humanity, which tempered the Valour of our common Ancestors, has not degenerated into Cruelty, you will lament the Miseries of their Descendants.

To what are we to attribute this Treatment? If to any secret Principle of the Constitution, let it be mentioned; let us learn, that the Government, we have long revered, is not without its Defects, and that while it gives Freedom to a Part, it necessarily enslaves the Remainder of the Empire. If such a Principle exists, why for Ages has it ceased to operate? Why at this Time is it called into Action? Can no Reason be assigned for this Conducts Or must it be resolved into the wanton Exercise of arbitrary Power? And shall the Descendants of Britons tamely submit to this? – No, Sirs! We never will, while we revere the Memory of our gallant and virtuous Ancestors, we never can surrender those glorious Privileges, for which they fought, bled, and conquered. Admit that your Fleets could destroy our Towns, and ravage our Sea-Coasts; these are inconsiderable Objects, Things of no Moment to Men, whose Bosoms glow with the Ardor of Liberty. We can retire beyond the Reach of your Navy, and, without any sensible Diminution of the Necessaries of Life, enjoy a Luxury, which from that Period you will want-the Luxury of being Free.

We know the Force of your Arms, and was it called forth in the Cause of Justice and your Country, we might dread the Exertion: but will Britons fight under the Banners of Tyranny? Will they counteract the Labours, and disgrace the Victories of their Ancestors? Will they forge Chains for their Posterity? If they descend to this unworthy Task, will their Swords retain their Edge, their Arms their accustomed Vigour? Britons can never become the Instruments of Oppression, till they lose the Spirit of Freedom, by which alone they are invincible.

Our Enemies charge us with Sedition. In what does it consist? In our Refusal to submit to unwarrantable Acts of injustice and Cruelty? If so, shew us a Period in your History, in which you have not been equally Seditious.

We are accused of aiming at Independence; but how is this Accusation supported? By the Allegations of your Ministers, not by our Actions. Abused, insulted, and contemned, what Steps have we pursued to obtain Redress? We have carried our dutiful Petitions to the Throne. We have applied to your Justice for Relief. We have retrenched our Luxury, and withheld our Trade.

The Advantages of our Commerce were designed as a Compensation for your Protection: When you ceased to protect, for what were we to compensate?

What has been the Success of our Endeavours? The Clemency of our Sovereign is unhappily diverted; our Petitions are treated with Indignity; our Prayers answered by Insults. Our Application to you remains unnoticed, and leaves us the melancholy Apprehension of your wanting either the Will, or the Power, to assist us.

Even under these Circumstances, what Measures have we taken that betray a Desire of Independence? Have we called in the Aid of those foreign Powers, who are the Rivals of your Grandeur? When your Troops were few and defenseless, did we take Advantage of their Distress and expel them our Towns? Or have we permitted them to fortify, to receive new Aid, and to acquire additional Strength?

Let not your Enemies and ours persuade you, that in this we were influenced by Fear or any other unworthy Motive. The Lives of Britons are still dear to us. They are the Children of our Parents, and an uninterrupted Intercourse of mutual Benefits had knit the Bonds of Friendship. When Hostilities were commenced, when on a late Occasion we were wantonly attacked by your Troops, though we repelled their Assaults and returned their Blows, yet we lamented the Wounds they obliged us to give; nor have we yet learned to rejoice at a Victory over Englishmen.

As we wish not to colorer our Actions, or disguise our Thoughts, we shall, in the simple Language of Truth, avow the Measures we have pursued, the Motives upon which we have acted, and our future Designs.

When our late Petition to the Throne produced no other Effect than fresh Injuries, and Votes of your Legislature, calculated to justify every Severity; when your Fleets and your Armies were prepared to wrest from us our Property, to rob us of our Liberties or our Lives; when the hostile Attempts of General Gage evinced his Designs, we levied Armies for our Security and Defence. When the Powers vested in the Governor of Canada, gave us Reason to apprehend Danger from that Quarter; and we had frequent Intimations, that a cruel and savage Enemy was to be let loose upon the defenseless Inhabitants of our Frontiers; we took such Measures as Prudence dictated, as Necessity will justify. We possessed

ourselves of Crown Point and Ticonderoga. Yet give us leave most
solemnly to assure you, that we have not yet lost Sight of the Object
we have ever had in View, a Reconciliation with you on
constitutional Principles, and a Restoration of that friendly
Intercourse, which, to the Advantage of both, we till lately
maintained.

The Inhabitants of this Country apply themselves chiefly to
Agriculture and Commerce. As their Fashions and Manners are
similar to yours, your Markets must afford them the Conveniences
and Luxuries, for which they exchange the Produce of their Labours.
The Wealth of this extended Continent centres with you; and our
Trade is so regulated as to be subservient only to your Interest. You
are too reasonable to expect, that by Taxes (in Addition to this) we
should contribute to your Expence; to believe, after diverting the
Fountain, that the Streams can flow with unabated Force.

It has been said, that we refuse to submit to the Restrictions on our
Commerce. From whence is this Inference drawn? Not from our
Words, we have repeatedly declared the Contrary; and we again
profess our Submission to the several Acts of Trade and Navigation,
passed before the Year 1763, trusting, nevertheless, in the Equity
and Justice of Parliament, that such of them as, upon cool and
impartial Consideration, shall appear to have imposed unnecessary
or grievous Restrictions, will, at some happier Period, be repealed or
altered. And we cheerfully consent to the Operation of such Acts of
the British Parliament, as shall be restrained to the Regulation of our
external Commerce, for the Purpose of securing the commercial
Advantages of the whole Empire to the Mother Country, and the
commercial Benefits of its respective Members; excluding every
Idea of taxation internal or external, for raising a Revenue on the
Subjects in America, without their Consent.

It is alledged that we contribute nothing to the common Defence.
To this we answer, that the Advantages which Great Britain receives
from the Monopoly of our Trade, far exceed our Proportion of the
Expence necessary for that Purpose. But should these Advantages be
inadequate thereto, let the Restrictions on our Trade be removed,
and we will cheerfully contribute such Proportion when
constitutionally required.

It is a fundamental Principle of the British Constitution, that every
Man should have at least a Representative Share in the Formation of
those Laws, by which he is bound. Were it otherwise, the Regulation
of our internal Police by a British Parliament, who are and ever will

be unacquainted with our local Circumstances, must be always inconvenient, and frequently oppressive, working our wrong, without yielding any possible Advantage to you.

A Plan of Accommodation (as it has been absurdly called) has been proposed by your Ministers to our respective Assemblies. Were this Proposal free from eatery other Objection, but that which arises from the Time of the Offer, it would not be unexceptionable. Can Men deliberate with the Bayonet at their Breast, Can they treat with Freedom, while their Towns are sacked; when daily instances of Injustice and Oppression disturb the slower Operations of Reason?

If this Proposal is really such as you would offer and we accept, why was it delayed till the Nation was put to useless expence, and we were reduced to our present melancholy Situation a If it holds forth nothing, why was it proposed Unless indeed to deceive you into a Belief, that we were unwilling to listen to any Terms of Accommodation. But what is submitted to our Considerations We contend for the Disposal of our Property. We are told that our Demand is unreasonable, that our Assemblies may indeed collect our Money, but that they must at the same Time offer, not what your Exigencies or ours may require, but so much as shall be deemed sufficient to satisfy the Desires of a Minister and enable him to provide for Favourites and Dependants. A Recurrence to your own Treasury wild convince you how little of the Money already extorted from us has been applied to the Relief of your Burthens. To suppose that we would thus grasp the Shadow and give up the Substance, is adding Insult to Injuries.

We have nevertheless again presented an humble and dutiful Petition to our Sovereign, and to remove every imputation of Obstinacy, have requested his Majesty to direct some Mode, by which the united Applications of his faithful Colonists may be improved into a happy and permanent Reconciliation. We are willing to treat on such Terms as can alone render an accommodation lasting, and we hatter ourselves that our pacific Endeavours will be attended with a removal of ministerial Troops, and a repeal of those Laws, of the Operation of which we complain, on the one part, and a disbanding of our Army, and a dissolution of our commercial Associations, on the other.

Yet conclude not from this that we propose to surrender our Property into the Hands of your Ministry, or vest your Parliament with a Power which may terminate in our Destruction. The great Bulwarks of our Constitution we have desired to maintain by every temperate, by every peaceable Means; but your Ministers (equal Foes to British and American freedom) have added to their former Oppressions an Attempt to reduce us by the Sword to a base and abject submission. On the Sword, therefore, we are compelled to rely for Protection. Should Victory declare in your Favour, yet Men trained to Arms from their Infancy, and animated by the Love of Liberty, will afford neither a cheap or easy Conquest. Of this at least we are assured, that our Struggle will be glorious, our Success certain; since even in Death we shall find that Freedom which in Life you forbid us to enjoy.

Let us now ask what Advantages are to attend our Reduction? the Trade of a ruined and desolate Country is always inconsiderable, its Revenue trifling; the Expence of subjecting and retaining it in subjection certain and inevitable. What then remains but the gratification of an ill-judged Pride, or the hope of rendering us subservient to designs on your Liberty.

Soldiers who have sheathed their Swords in the Bowels of their American Brethren, will not draw them with more reluctance against you. When too late you may lament the loss of that freedom, which we exhort you, while still in your Power, to preserve.

On the other hand, should you prove unsuccessful; should that Connexion, which we most ardently wish to maintain, be dissolved; should your Ministers exhaust your Treasures and waste the Blood of your Countrymen in vain Attempts on our Liberty; do they not deliver you, weak and defenseless, to your natural Enemies?

Since then your Liberty must be the price of your Victories; your Ruin, of your Defeat: What blind fatality can urge you to a pursuit destructive of all that Britons hold dear?

If you have no regard to the Connexion that has for Ages subsisted between us; if you have forgot the Wounds we have received fighting by your Side for the extension of the Empire; if our Commerce is not an object below your consideration; if Justice and Humanity have lost their influence on your Hearts; still Motives are not wanting to excite your Indignation at the Measures now pursued; Your Wealth, your Honour, your Liberty are at Stake.

Notwithstanding the Distress to which we are reduced, we sometimes forget our own Afflictions, to anticipate and sympathize in yours. We grieve that rash and inconsiderate Councils should precipitate the destruction of an Empire, which has been the envy and admiration of Ages, and call God to witness! that we would part with our Property, endanger our Lives, and sacrifice every thing but Liberty, to redeem you front ruin.

A Cloud hangs over your Heads and ours; 'ere this reaches you, it may probably burst upon us; let us then (before the remembrance of former Kindness is obliterated) once more repeat those Appellations which are ever grateful in our Ears; let us entreat Heaven to avert our Ruin, and the Destruction that threatens our Friends, Brethren and Countrymen, on the other side of the Atlantic.

Letter to the Lord Mayor of London
John Hancock (1775)[29]

With the approval of the delegates of the twelve colonies in the Continental Congress (Georgia at the time was not represented), Congress President John Hancock wrote a brief message on July 8, 1775 to the Lord Mayor of London, who openly sympathized with the colonies. Richard Penn delivered the letter.

MY LORD, Permitt the Delegates of the people of twelve ancient colonies, to pay ye Lordship, and the very respectable body of which you are head, the just tribute of gratitude and thanks, for the virtuous and unsolicited resentment you have strewn to the violated rights of a free people. The city of London, my Lord, having in all ages, approved itself the patron of liberty, and the support of just government, against lawless tyranny and oppression, cannot fail to make us deeply sensible of the powerful aid, our cause must receive from such advocates. A cause, my Lord, worthy the support of the first city in the world, as it involves the fate of a great continent, and threatens to shake the foundations of a nourishing, and, until lately, a happy empire.

North America, my Lord, wishes most ardently for a lasting connection with Great Britain on terms of just and equal liberty; less than which generous minds will not offer, nor brave and free ones be willing to receive.

A cruel war has at length been opened age us, and whilst we prepare to defend ourselves like the descendants of Britons, we still hope that the mediation of wise and good citizens, will at length prevail over despotism, and restore harmony and peace, on permanent principles, to an oppressed and divided empire.

---

[29] *Journals of the Continental Congress, 1774-1789*, Vol. II. Courtesy of the Library of Congress.

Address to the Assembly of Jamaica
Continental Congress (1775)[30]

In an effort to reassure Britain's important Caribbean colony of Jamaica, the Continental Congress explained why it had had no choice but to include the island in its embargo of British goods. Legisltors thanked the Jamaicans for their unsuccessful attempt to intervene with the Crown on the American colonies' behalf. The Congress knew it could win no more from Jamaica, given the powerful British presence there.

This July 25, 1775 address reassures Jamaican lawmakers that the Continental Congress expects no further help from the island, but does not blame the islanders for the situation and, indeed, considers Jamaica a friend in mutual peril.

MR. SPEAKER AND GENTLEMEN OF THE ASSEMBLY OF JAMAICA,

We would think ourselves deficient in our duty, if we suffered this Congress to pass over, without expressing our esteem for the assembly of Jamaica.

Whoever attends to the conduct of those who have been entrusted with the administration of the British affairs, during these last twelve years, will discover in it, a deliberate plan to destroy, in every part of the empire, the free constitution, for which Britain has been so long and so justly famed. With a dexterity, artful and wicked, they have varied the modes of attack, according to the different characters and circumstances of those whom they meant to reduce. In the East Indies, where the effeminacy of the inhabitants promised an easy conquest, they thought it unnecessary to veil their tyrannic principles under the thinnest disguise. Without deigning even to pretend a justification of their conduct, they sacrificed the lives of millions to the gratification of their insatiable avarice and lust of power. In Britain, where the maxims of freedom were still known, but where luxury and dissipation had diminished the wonted reverence for them, the attack has been carried on in a more secret and indirect manner: Corruption has been employed to undermine them. The Americans are not enervated by effeminacy, like the inhabitants of India; nor debauched by luxury, like those of Great Britain: It was, therefore, judged improper to assail them by bribery, or by undisguised force. Plausible systems were formed; specious

---

[30] *Ibid*, pp. 204-206.

presences were made: All the arts of sophistry were tried to shew that the British ministry had by law a right to enslave us. The first and best maxims of the constitution, venerable to Britons and to Americans, were perverted and profaned. The power of parliament, derived from the people, to bind the people, was extended over those from whom it was never derived. It is asserted that a standing army may be constitutionally kept among us, without our consent. Those principles, dishonorable to those who adopted them, and destructive to those to whom they were applied, were nevertheless carried into execution by the foes of liberty and of mankind. Acts of parliament, ruinous to America, and unserviceable to Britain, were made to bind us; armies, maintained by the parliament, were sent over to secure their operation. The power, however, and the cunning of our adversaries, were alike unsuccessful. We refused to their parliaments an obedience, which our judgments disapproved of: We refused to their armies a submission, which spirits unaccustomed to slavery, could not brook.

But while we spurned a disgraceful subjection, we were far from running into rash or seditious measures of opposition. Filled with sentiments of loyalty to our sovereign, and of affection and respect for our fellow subjects in Britain, we petitioned, we supplicated, we expostulated: Our prayers were rejected; – our remonstrances were disregarded; – our grievances were accumulated. All this did not provoke us to violence.

An appeal to the justice and humanity of those who had injured us, and who were bound to redress our injuries, was ineffectual: we next resolved to make an appeal to their interests, though by doing so, we knew we must sacrifice our own, and (which gave us equal uneasiness) that of our friends, who had never offended us, and who were connected with us by a sympathy of feelings, under oppressions similar to our own. We resolved to give up our commerce that we might preserve our liberty. We flattered ourselves, that when, by withdrawing our commercial intercourse with Britain, which we had an undoubted right either to withdraw or continue, her trade should be diminished, her revenues impaired, and her manufactures unemployed, our ministerial foes would be induced by interest, or compelled by necessity, to depart from the plan of tyranny which they had so long pursued, and to substitute in its place, a system more compatible with the freedom of America, and justice of Britain. That this scheme of non-importation and non-exportation might be productive of the desired effects, we were obliged to include the islands in it. From this necessity, and from this necessity alone, has our conduct towards them proceeded. By converting your sugar plantations into fields of grain, you can supply yourselves with the necessaries of life: While the present unhappy struggle shall continue, we cannot do more.

But why should we make any apology to the patriotic assembly of Jamaica, who knows so well the value of liberty; who are so sensible of the extreme danger to which ours is exposed; and who foresee how certainly the destruction of ours must be followed by the destruction of their own?

We receive uncommon pleasure from observing the principles of our righteous opposition distinguished by your approbation: We feel the warmest gratitude for your pathetic mediation in our behalf with the crown. It was indeed unavailing – but are you to blame? Mournful experience tells us that petitions are often rejected, while the sentiments and conduct of the petitioners entitle what they offer to a happier fate.

That our petitions have been treated with disdain, is now become the smallest part of our complaint: Ministerial insolence is lost in ministerial barbarity. It has, by an exertion peculiarly ingenious, procured those very measures, which it laid us under the hard necessity of pursuing, to be stigmatized in parliament as rebellious: It has employed additional fleets and armies for the infamous purpose of compelling us to abandon them: It has plunged us in all the horrors and calamities of civil war: It has caused the treasure and blood of Britons (formerly shed and expended for far other ends) to be spilt and wasted in the execrable design of spreading slavery over British America: It will not, however, accomplish its aim: In the worst of contingencies, a choice will still be left, which it never can prevent us from making.

The peculiar situation of your island forbids your assistance. But we have your good wishes. From the good wishes of the friends of liberty and mankind, we shall always derive consolation.

To the Inhabitants of the Island of Bermuda
George Washington (1775) [31]

*The Americans found some popular sympathy for their cause in
Bermuda, a strategically located British territory 640 miles off the
North Carolina coast. Formerly part of the Virginia colony,
Bermuda was an important British shipping supply station,
shipbuilding center and trading hub; prominent Bermudian
families emigrated to the American South and created strong
economic and social bonds between the colonies and the
archipelago.*

*Unlike Jamaica, Bermuda refused London's order to embargo trade
with the colonies, and the Continental Congress exempted
Bermuda from its reciprocal boycott of British goods. Bermuda
housed an important but lightly guarded British fortress and
supply of gunpowder, shot and other weapons. The governor of
Bermuda sympathized with the American colonists.*

*In a July, 1775, meeting in Philadelphia, the Continental Congress
approved a plan by Benjamin Franklin to trade food for the powder
and arms, and the operation succeeded the following month. Gen.
George Washington, who was in Massachusetts and had heard
about the arsenal separately but did not know about the official
operation, authorized a mission on his own and on September 6
wrote a personal letter to the public of Bermuda to seek their
support.*

*As with other pre-1776 writings, Washington does not argue for
independence from Britain, but for avoiding a civil war among
British subjects.*

In the great conflict, which agitates this continent, I cannot doubt
but the assertors of freedom and the rights of the constitution are
possessed of your most favorable regards and wishes for success. As
descendents of freemen, and heirs with us of the same glorious
inheritance, we flatter ourselves, that, though divided by our
situation, we are firmly united in sentiment. The cause of virtue and
liberty is confined to no continent or climate. It comprehends, within

---

[31] General George Washington, "To the Inhabitants of the Island of
Bermuda," September 6, 1775, in John C. Fitzpatrick, ed., *George
Washington: A Collection*, Vol. 3 (Government Printing Office, 1931), p.
475. Courtesy of the Library of Congress.

its capacious limits, the wise and good, however dispersed and separated in space or distance.

You need not be informed that the violence and rapacity of a tyrannic ministry have forced the citizens of America, your brother colonist, into arms. We equally detest and lament the prevalence of those counsels, which have led to the effusion of so much human blood, and left us no alternative but a civil war, or a base submission. The wise Disposer of all events has hitherto smiled upon our virtuous efforts. Those mercenary troops, a few of whom lately boasted of subjugating this vast continent, have been checked in their earliest ravages, and now actually encircled within a small space their arms disgraced, and themselves suffering all the calamities of a siege. The virtue, spirit, and union of the provinces leave them nothing to fear, but the want of ammunition. The application of our enemies to foreign states, and their vigilance upon our coasts, are the only efforts they have made against us with success.

Under these circumstances, and with these sentiments, we have turned our eyes to you, Gentlemen, for relief. We are informed, that there is a very large magazine in your island under a very feeble guard. We would not wish to involve you in an opposition, in which, from your situation, we should be unable to support you; we knew not, therefore, to what extent to solicit your assistance, in availing ourselves of this supply; but, if your favor and friendship to North America and its liberties have not been misrepresented, I persuade myself you may, consistently with your own safety, promote and further this scheme, so as to give it the fairest prospect of success. Be assured that, in this case, the whole power and exertion of my influence will be made with the honorable Continental Congress, that your island may not only be supplied with provisions, but experience every other mark of affection and friendship, which the grateful citizens of a free country can bestow on its brethren and benefactors. I am, Gentlemen,

With much esteem,
Your humble servant,
G. Washington

To the Inhabitants of Canada
George Washington (1775) [32]

On September 6, 1775, the same day he wrote to the people of Bermuda, General Washington penned a similar letter to the citizens of Canada. The declaration coincided with a Continental Congress-approved plan to invade Canada to split British forces there, prevent Britain from invading the colonies from the north and potentially cutting off New England, prevent crown authorities from raising local armies, expand the new American Continental Army, capture British weaponry, and drive out the redcoats.

The officers named in the letter, Maj. Gen. Philip John Schuyler and Col. Benedict Arnold, were preparing to lead the Continental Army forces into Canada: Schuyler in Ticonderoga, New York, to take Montreal and Quebec City; and Arnold to take Quebec City via Maine. Schuyler would fall ill and be replaced by Maj. Gen. Richard Montgomery. The Americans would take Montreal but face defeat at the gates of Quebec City, where Montgomery would die.

Friends and Brethren: The unnatural Contest between the English Colonies, and Great Britain has now risen to such a Height, that Arms alone must decide it.

The Colonies, confiding in the Justice of their Cause and the purity of their intentions, have reluctantly appealed to that Being, in whose hands are all Human Events: He has hitherto smiled upon their virtuous Efforts: The Hand of Tyranny has been arrested in its Ravages, and the British Arms, which have shone with so much Splendor in every part of the Globe, are now tarnished with disgrace and disappointment. Generals of approved experience, who boasted of subduing this great Continent, find themselves circumscribed within the limits of a single City and its Suburbs, suffering all the shame and distress of a Siege. While the Freeborn Sons of America, animated by the genuine principles of Liberty and Love of their Country, with increasing Union, Firmness and discipline, repel every attack and despise every Danger.

Above all we rejoice that our Enemies have been deceived with Regard to you: They have persuaded themselves, they have even dared to say, that the Canadians were not capable of distinguishing

---

[32] George Washington, "To the Inhabitants of Canada," handwritten letter in *George Washington Papers at the Library of Congress, 1741-1799: Series 3d Varick Transcripts*. Courtesy of the Library of Congress.

between the Blessings of Liberty and the Wretchedness of Slavery; that gratifying the Vanity of a little Circle of Nobility would blind the Eyes of the people of Canada. By such Artifices they hoped to bend you to their Views; but they have been deceived: Instead of finding in you that poverty of Soul, and baseness of Spirit, they see with a Chagrin equal to our Joy, that you are enlightened, generous, and Virtuous; that you will not renounce your own Rights, or serve as Instruments to deprive your Fellow subjects of theirs. Come then, my Brethern, Unite with us in an indissoluble Union. Let us run together to the same Goal. We have taken up Arms in Defence of our Liberty, our Property; our Wives and our Children: We are determined to preserve them or die. We look forward with pleasure to that day not far remote (we hope) when the Inhabitants of America shall have one Sentiment and the full Enjoyment of the blessings of a Free Government.

Incited by these Motives and encouraged by the advice of many Friends of Liberty among you, the Great American Congress have sent an Army into your Province, under the command of General Schuyler; not to plunder but to protect you; to animate and bring forth into Action those sentiments of Freedom you have declared, and which the Tools of dispositism would extinguish through the whole Creation. To co-operate with this design and to frustrate those cruel and perfidious Schemes, which would deluge our Frontier with the Blood of Women and Children, I have detached Colonel Arnold into your Country, with a part of the Army under my Command. I have enjoined upon him, and I am certain that he will consider himself, and act as in the Country of his Patrons and best Friends. Necessaries and Accommodations of every kind which you may furnish, he will thankfully receive, and render the full Value. I invite you therefore as Friends and Brethren, to provide him with such supplies as your Country affords; and I pledge myself not only for your safety and security, but for ample Compensation. Let no Man desert his habitation. Let no Man flee as before an Enemy.

The cause of America and of liberty is the cause of every virtuous American Citizen Whatever may be his Religion or his descent, the United Colonies know no distinction, but such as Slavery, Corruption and Arbitrary Domination may create. Come then ye generous Citizens, range yourselves under the Standard of general Liberty, against which all the force and Artifice of Tyranny will never be able to prevail. I am, etc.

G. Washington

The Declaration of Independence
Continental Congress (1776)

*The actual founding document of American independence was
fundamentally intended, in part, as an instrument of public
diplomacy. It was a manifesto to educate the world as much as
the American public. Twice in the declaration, the Continental
Congress made references to international opinion. The first part
of the document is a statement of high principle.*

*No longer does the Congress deflect blame from King George III
and lay it only on his ministers and Parliament. The second main
part reads like a criminal indictment of the king of the British – in
stark contrast to the deferential petitions and comments over the
previous two years. Outlining all the royal offenses against his
subjects in America, the Declaration calls the king a usurper, a
despot and a tyrant, an opponent of the wholesome and an
obstructor of justice; a plunderer an arsonist, an author of
barbaric cruelty and an "unfit" ruler of free people. Faced with
such a ruler, the Founders showed why the American colonies had
no alternative but to declare total independence from Britain.*

IN CONGRESS, July 4, 1776

The unanimous Declaration of the thirteen united States of
America,

When in the Course of human events, it becomes necessary for
one people to dissolve the political bands which have connected
them with another, and to assume among the powers of the earth, the
separate and equal station to which the Laws of Nature and of
Nature's God entitle them, a decent respect to the opinions of
mankind requires that they should declare the causes which impel
them to the separation.

We hold these truths to be self-evident, that all men are created
equal, that they are endowed by their Creator with certain
unalienable Rights, that among these are Life, Liberty and the
pursuit of Happiness. – That to secure these rights, Governments are
instituted among Men, deriving their just powers from the consent of
the governed, – That whenever any Form of Government becomes
destructive of these ends, it is the Right of the People to alter or to
abolish it, and to institute new Government, laying its foundation on
such principles and organizing its powers in such form, as to them
shall seem most likely to effect their Safety and Happiness.

Prudence, indeed, will dictate that Governments long established should not be changed for light and transient causes; and accordingly all experience hath shewn, that mankind are more disposed to suffer, while evils are sufferable, than to right themselves by abolishing the forms to which they are accustomed. But when a long train of abuses and usurpations, pursuing invariably the same Object evinces a design to reduce them under absolute Despotism, it is their right, it is their duty, to throw off such Government, and to provide new Guards for their future security. Such has been the patient sufferance of these Colonies; and such is now the necessity which constrains them to alter their former Systems of Government. The history of the present King of Great Britain is a history of repeated injuries and usurpations, all having in direct object the establishment of an absolute Tyranny over these States. To prove this, let Facts be submitted to a candid world.

He has refused his Assent to Laws, the most wholesome and necessary for the public good.

He has forbidden his Governors to pass Laws of immediate and pressing importance, unless suspended in their operation till his Assent should be obtained; and when so suspended, he has utterly neglected to attend to them.

He has refused to pass other Laws for the accommodation of large districts of people, unless those people would relinquish the right of Representation in the Legislature, a right inestimable to them and formidable to tyrants only.

He has called together legislative bodies at places unusual, uncomfortable, and distant from the depository of their public Records, for the sole purpose of fatiguing them into compliance with his measures.

He has dissolved Representative Houses repeatedly, for opposing with manly firmness his invasions on the rights of the people. He has refused for a long time, after such dissolutions, to cause others to be elected; whereby the Legislative powers, incapable of Annihilation, have returned to the People at large for their exercise; the State remaining in the mean time exposed to all the dangers of invasion from without, and convulsions within.

He has endeavoured to prevent the population of these States; for that purpose obstructing the Laws for Naturalization of Foreigners; refusing to pass others to encourage their migrations hither, and raising the conditions of new Appropriations of Lands.

He has obstructed the Administration of Justice, by refusing his Assent to Laws for establishing Judiciary powers.

He has made Judges dependent on his Will alone, for the tenure of their offices, and the amount and payment of their salaries.

He has erected a multitude of New Offices, and sent hither swarms of Officers to harrass our people, and eat out their substance.

He has kept among us, in times of peace, Standing Armies without the Consent of our legislatures.

He has affected to render the Military independent of and superior to the Civil power.

He has combined with others to subject us to a jurisdiction foreign to our constitution, and unacknowledged by our laws; giving his Assent to their Acts of pretended Legislation:

For Quartering large bodies of armed troops among us:

For protecting them, by a mock Trial, from punishment for any Murders which they should commit on the Inhabitants of these States:

For cutting off our Trade with all parts of the world:

For imposing Taxes on us without our Consent:

For depriving us in many cases, of the benefits of Trial by Jury:

For transporting us beyond Seas to be tried for pretended offences

For abolishing the free System of English Laws in a neighbouring Province, establishing therein an Arbitrary government, and enlarging its Boundaries so as to render it at once an example and fit instrument for introducing the same absolute rule into these Colonies:

For taking away our Charters, abolishing our most valuable Laws, and altering fundamentally the Forms of our Governments:
For suspending our own Legislatures, and declaring themselves invested with power to legislate for us in all cases whatsoever.
He has abdicated Government here, by declaring us out of his Protection and waging War against us.

He has plundered our seas, ravaged our Coasts, burnt our towns, and destroyed the lives of our people.

He is at this time transporting large Armies of foreign Mercenaries to compleat the works of death, desolation and tyranny, already begun with circumstances of Cruelty & perfidy scarcely paralleled in the most barbarous ages, and totally unworthy the Head of a civilized nation.

He has constrained our fellow Citizens taken Captive on the high Seas to bear Arms against their Country, to become the executioners of their friends and Brethren, or to fall themselves by their Hands.

He has excited domestic insurrections amongst us, and has endeavoured to bring on the inhabitants of our frontiers, the merciless Indian Savages, whose known rule of warfare, is an undistinguished destruction of all ages, sexes and conditions.

In every stage of these Oppressions We have Petitioned for Redress in the most humble terms: Our repeated Petitions have been answered only by repeated injury. A Prince whose character is thus marked by every act which may define a Tyrant, is unfit to be the ruler of a free people.

Nor have We been wanting in attentions to our Brittish brethren. We have warned them from time to time of attempts by their legislature to extend an unwarrantable jurisdiction over us. We have reminded them of the circumstances of our emigration and settlement here. We have appealed to their native justice and magnanimity, and we have conjured them by the ties of our common kindred to disavow these usurpations, which, would inevitably interrupt our connections and correspondence. They too have been deaf to the voice of justice and of consanguinity. We must, therefore, acquiesce in the necessity, which denounces our Separation, and hold them, as we hold the rest of mankind, Enemies in War, in Peace Friends.

We, therefore, the Representatives of the united States of America, in General Congress, Assembled, appealing to the Supreme Judge of the world for the rectitude of our intentions, do, in the Name, and by Authority of the good People of these Colonies, solemnly publish and declare, That these United Colonies are, and of Right ought to be Free and Independent States; that they are Absolved from all Allegiance to the British Crown, and that all political connection between them and the State of Great Britain, is and ought to be totally dissolved; and that as Free and Independent States, they have full Power to levy War, conclude Peace, contract Alliances, establish Commerce, and to do all other Acts and Things which Independent States may of right do. And for the support of this Declaration, with a firm reliance on the protection of divine Providence, we mutually pledge to each other our Lives, our Fortunes and our sacred Honor.

Dialogue between Britain, France, Spain, Holland, Saxony and America
Benjamin Franklin (1777)[33]

Now that the United States of America had declared its independence, the new country needed help from Britain's European foes. Gaining European support for the American war effort was the principal reason for the Continental Congress to send Benjamin Franklin to Paris to lead the small diplomatic outpost there in late 1776. Chief among Franklin's assignments was to secure military support and cash loans from non-British powers.

Franklin wrote this "dialogue" shortly after his arrival in France, and had it translated into French, Spanish, Dutch and German as part of his diplomatic campaign to persuade the European powers to provide the United States with military support. Written with Franklin's typical sense of wit, the dialogue caricaturizes Britain as an isolated, cold, double-dealing bully, bereft of friends and undeserving of the same until it changed its ways.

Britain. Sister of Spain, I have a favor to ask of you. My subjects in America are disobedient, and I am about to chastise them; I beg you will not furnish them with any arms or ammunition.

Spain. Have you forgotten, then, that when my subjects in the Low Countries rebelled against me, you not only furnished them with military stores, but joined them with an army and a fleet? I wonder how you can have the impudence to ask such a favor of me, or the folly to expect it!

Britain. You, my dear sister France, will surely not refuse me this favor.

France. Did you not assist my rebel Huguenots with a fleet and an army at Rochelle? And have you not lately aided privately and sneakingly my rebel subjects in Corsica? And do you not at this instant keep their chief, pensioned, and ready to head a fresh revolt there, whenever you can find or make an opportunity? Dear sister, you must be a little silly!

---

[33] Albert Henry Smyth, ed., *The Writings of Benjamin Franklin*, Vol. VII, 1777-1779 (Macmillan, 1906), pp. 82-86. The actual date on which Franklin wrote the dialogue is unknown, but is generally accepted as being in late 1777.

Britain. Honest Holland! You see it is remembered I was once your friend; you will therefore be mine on this occasion. I know, indeed, you are accustomed to smuggle with these rebels of mine. I will wink at that; sell them as much tea as you please, to enervate the rascals, since they will not take it of me; but for God's sake don't supply them with any arms!

Holland. 'Tis true you assisted me against Philip, my tyrant of Spain, but have I not assisted you against one of your tyrants [James 2nd]; and enabled you to expel him? Surely that account, as we merchants say, is *balanced,* and I am nothing in your debt. I have indeed some complaints against *you,* for endeavouring to starve me by your *Navigation Acts;* but, being peaceably disposed, I do not quarrel with you for that. I shall only go on quietly with my own business. Trade is my profession; 'tis all I have to subsist on. And, let me tell you, I shall make no scruple (on the prospect of a good market for that commodity) even to send my ships to Hell and supply the Devil with brimstone. For you must know, I can insure in London against the burning of my sails.

America to Britain. Why, you old bloodthirsty bully! You, who have been everywhere vaunting your own prowess, and defaming the Americans as poltroons! You, who have boasted of being able to march over all their bellies with a single regiment! You, who by fraud have possessed yourself of their strongest fortress, and all the arms they had stored up in it! You, who have a disciplined army in their country, intrenched to the teeth, and provided with every thing! Do *you* run about begging all Europe not to supply those poor people with a little powder and shot? Do you mean, then, to fall upon them naked and unarmed, and butcher them in cold blood? Is this your courage? Is this your magnanimity?

Britain. Oh! you wicked – Whig – Presbyterian – Serpent! Have you the impudence to appear before me after all your disobedience? Surrender immediately all your liberties and properties into my hands, or I will cut you to pieces. Was it for this that I planted your country at so great an expense? That I protected you in your infancy, and defended you against all your enemies?

America. I shall not surrender my liberty and property, but with my life. It is not true, that my country was planted at your expense. Your own records [Journal of the House of Commons, 1640-1642] refute that falsehood to your face. Nor did you ever afford me a man or a shilling to defend me against the Indians, the only enemies I had upon my own account. But, when you have quarrelled with all

Europe, and drawn me with you into all your broils, then you value yourself upon protecting me from the enemies you have made for me. I have no natural cause of difference with Spain, France, or Holland, and yet by turns I have joined with you in wars against them all. You would not suffer me to make or keep a separate peace with any of them, though I might easily have done it to great advantage. Does your protecting me in those wars give you a right to fleece me? If so, as I fought for you, as well as you for me, it gives me a proportionable right to fleece you. What think you of an American law to make a monopoly of you and your commerce, as you have done by your laws of me and mine? Content yourself with that monopoly if you are wise, and learn justice if you would be respected!

Britain. You impudent b—h! Am not I your mother country? Is not that a sufficient title to your respect and obedience?

Saxony. Mother country! Ha! ha! ha! What respect have *you* the front to claim as a mother country? You know that I am *your* mother country, and yet you pay me none. Nay, it is but the other day, that you hired ruffians [Prussians] to rob me on the highway [they enter'd and rais'd contributions in Saxony], and burn my house [and they burnt the fine suburbs of Dresden the capital of Saxony]! For shame! Hide your face and hold your tongue. If you continue this conduct, you will make yourself the contempt of Europe!

Britain. O Lord! Where are my friends?

France, Spain, Holland, and Saxony, all together. Friends! Believe us, you have none, nor ever will have any, till you mend your manners. How can we, who are your neighbours, have any regard for you, or expect any equity from you, should your power increase, when we see how basely and unjustly you have used both your *own mother and your own children?*

The Power of Ideas and Values

America is the first country created on an idea. We saw that idea unfold in the founding documents. In this section, we turn to the institutionalization of public diplomacy in the 20th century as part of the great battleground of ideas. The first half of the century saw the defeat of absolute monarchy in Europe; defeat of Nazism, fascism and Japanese military imperialism; and the beginning of the Cold War with Hitler's former ally in starting World War II, the Soviet Union.

We start with an excerpt from a landmark speech that President Franklin D. Roosevelt gave during the early years of World War II, eleven months before Japan and Germany declared war on the United States. The "four freedoms" that Roosevelt outlined became the basis of the U.S. propaganda campaigns of World War II, the Cold War, and the "War on Terror."

The Four Freedoms
Franklin D. Roosevelt (1941) [34]

In the future days, which we seek to make secure, we look forward to a world founded upon four essential human freedoms.

The first is freedom of speech and expression – everywhere in the world.

The second is freedom of every person to worship God in his way – everywhere in the world.

The third is freedom from want – which, translated into world terms, means economic understandings which will secure to every

---

[34] Franklin D. Roosevelt, Annual Message of the President to the Congress, January 6, 1941. *A Decade of American Policy: Basic Documents, 1941-1941, Prepared at the Request of the Senate Committee on Foreign Relations by the Staff of the Committee and the Department of State* (Washington: Government Printing Office, 1950).

nation a healthy peacetime life for its inhabitants – everywhere in the world.

The fourth is freedom from fear – which, translated into world terms, means a world-wide reduction of armaments to such a point and in such a thorough fashion that no nation will be in a position to commit an act of physical aggression against any neighbor – anywhere in the world.

The Underlying Conflict in the Realm of Ideas and Values
Paul Nitze, NSC-68 (1950)[35]

Considered the founding document of the American Cold War strategy of containment of the Soviet Union, National Security Council Directive 68, commonly called NSC-68, lays out the reasons for the United States to become the world leader in opposition to the Soviet Union. After explaining the aims of the United States and the Soviet Union and the nature of the world conflict, NSC-68 arrays a range of tools, from diplomacy and negotiations to isolation and nuclear war. Notably, it quotes from the Preamble to the Constitution, the Declaration of Independence, and the Federalist Papers.

National Security Council directives are generally credited to the respective president who signs them. However, NSC-68 has been treated as a special case, with credit going to Paul Nitze, head of the Policy Planning office at the Department of State and chairman of the National Security Council Study Group that authored the paper. NSC-68 is dated April 7, 1950. President Harry S Truman officially signed the policy on September 30 of that year. NSC-68 was classified until 1977.

The document consists of eight main parts. Part I gives a background of the world crisis as it was in 1950. Part II defines the "fundamental purposes of the United States." Part III outlines the fundamental grand strategy of the Soviet Union. Part IV describes the underlying conflict of ideas and values between the West and the Kremlin.

Part V covers Soviet intentions and capabilities, including political and psychological. Parts VI through VIII, which are not reprinted

---

[35] "United States Objectives and Programs for National Security: A Report to the President Pursuant to the President's Directive of January 31, 1950," NSC-68. Courtesy of the Truman Presidential Museum and Library.

in this book, respectively concern U.S. capabilities and intentions, present risks in 1950, atomic armaments and possible courses of action, and a conclusion.

The last paragraph of Part I and all of sections II, III and IV appear below. Part V is reprinted in the following section.

I. Background of the present world crisis

. . . The issues that face us are momentous, involving the fulfillment or destruction not only of this Republic but of civilization itself. They are issues which will not await our deliberations. With conscience and resolution this Government and the people it represents must now take new and fateful decisions.

II. Fundamental purpose of the United States

The fundamental purpose of the United States is laid down in the Preamble to the Constitution: ". . . to form a more perfect Union, establish justice, insure domestic Tranquility, provide for the common defence, promote the general Welfare, and secure the Blessings of Liberty to ourselves and our Posterity." In essence, the fundamental purpose is to assure the integrity and vitality of our free society, which is founded upon the dignity and worth of the individual.

Three realities emerge as a consequence of this purpose: Our determination to maintain the essential elements of individual freedom, as set forth in the Constitution and Bill of Rights; our determination to create conditions under which our free and democratic system can live and prosper; and our determination to fight if necessary to defend our way of life, for which as in the Declaration of Independence, "with a firm reliance on the protection of Divine Providence, we mutually pledge to each other our lives, our Fortunes, and our sacred Honor."

III. Fundamental design of the Kremlin

The fundamental design of those who control the Soviet Union and the international communist movement is to retain and solidify their absolute power, first in the Soviet Union and second in the areas now under their control. In the minds of the Soviet leaders, however, achievement of this design requires the dynamic extension of their authority and the ultimate elimination of any effective opposition to their authority.

The design, therefore, calls for the complete subversion or forcible destruction of the machinery of government and structure of society in the countries of the non-Soviet world and their replacement by an apparatus and structure subservient to and controlled from the Kremlin. To that end Soviet efforts are now directed toward the domination of the Eurasian land mass. The United States, as the principal center of power in the non-Soviet world and the bulwark of opposition to Soviet expansion, is the principal enemy whose integrity and vitality must be subverted or destroyed by one means or another if the Kremlin is to achieve its fundamental design.

IV. The underlying conflict in the realm of ideas and values between the U.S. purpose and the Kremlin design

A. Nature of the conflict

The Kremlin regards the United States as the only major threat to the conflict between idea of slavery under the grim oligarchy of the Kremlin, which has come to a crisis with the polarization of power described in Section I, and the exclusive possession of atomic weapons by the two protagonists. The idea of freedom, moreover, is peculiarly and intolerably subversive of the idea of slavery. But the converse is not true. The implacable purpose of the slave state to eliminate the challenge of freedom has placed the two great powers at opposite poles. It is this fact which gives the present polarization of power the quality of crisis.

The free society values the individual as an end in himself, requiring of him only that measure of self-discipline and self-restraint which make the rights of each individual compatible with the rights of every other individual. The freedom of the individual has as its counterpart, therefore, the negative responsibility of the individual not to exercise his freedom in ways inconsistent with the freedom of other individuals and the positive responsibility to make constructive use of his freedom in the building of a just society.

From this idea of freedom with responsibility derives the marvelous diversity, the deep tolerance, the lawfulness of the free society. This is the explanation of the strength of free men. It constitutes the integrity and the vitality of a free and democratic system. The free society attempts to create and maintain an environment in which every individual has the opportunity to realize his creative powers. It also explains why the free society tolerates those within it who would use their freedom to destroy it. By the same token, in relations between nations, the prime reliance of the free society is on the strength and appeal of its idea, and it feels no compulsion sooner or later to bring all societies into conformity with it.

For the free society does not fear, it welcomes, diversity. It derives its strength from its hospitality even to antipathetic ideas. It is a market for free trade in ideas, secure in its faith that free men will take the best wares, and grow to a fuller and better realization of their powers in exercising their choice.

The idea of freedom is the most contagious idea in history, more contagious than the idea of submission to authority. For the breadth of freedom cannot be tolerated in a society which has come under the domination of an individual or group of individuals with a will to absolute power. Where the despot holds absolute power–the absolute power of the absolutely powerful will–all other wills must be subjugated in an act of willing submission, a degradation willed by the individual upon himself under the compulsion of a perverted faith. It is the first article of this faith that he finds and can only find the meaning of his existence in serving the ends of the system. The system becomes God, and submission to the will of God becomes submission to the will of the system. It is not enough to yield outwardly to the system–even Gandhian non-violence is not acceptable–for the spirit of resistance and the devotion to a higher authority might then remain, and the individual would not be wholly submissive.

The same compulsion which demands total power over all men within the Soviet state without a single exception, demands total power over all Communist Parties and all states under Soviet domination. Thus Stalin has said that the theory and tactics of Leninism as expounded by the Bolshevik party are mandatory for the proletarian parties of all countries. A true internationalist is defined as one who unhesitatingly upholds the position of the Soviet Union and in the satellite states true patriotism is love of the Soviet Union. By the same token the "peace policy" of the Soviet Union, described at a Party Congress as "a more advantageous form of fighting capitalism," is a device to divide and immobilize the non-Communist world, and the peace the Soviet Union seeks is the peace of total conformity to Soviet policy.

The antipathy of slavery to freedom explains the iron curtain, the isolation, the autarchy of the society whose end is absolute power. The existence and persistence of the idea of freedom is a permanent and continuous threat to the foundation of the slave society; and it therefore regards as intolerable the long continued existence of freedom in the world. What is new, what makes the continuing crisis, is the polarization of power which now inescapably confronts the slave society with the free.

The assault on free institutions is world-wide now, and in the context of the present polarization of power a defeat of free institutions anywhere is a defeat everywhere. The shock we sustained in the destruction of Czechoslovakia was not in the measure of Czechoslovakia's material importance to us. In a material sense, her capabilities were already at Soviet disposal. But when the integrity of Czechoslovak institutions was destroyed, it was in the intangible scale of values that we registered a loss more damaging than the material loss we had already suffered.

Thus unwillingly our free society finds itself mortally challenged by the Soviet system. No other value system is so wholly irreconcilable with ours, so implacable in its purpose to destroy ours, so capable of turning to its own uses the most dangerous and divisive trends in our own society, no other so skillfully and powerfully evokes the elements of irrationality in human nature everywhere, and no other has the support of a great and growing center of military power.

B. Objectives

The objectives of a free society are determined by its fundamental values and by the necessity for maintaining the material environment in which they flourish. Logically and in fact, therefore, the Kremlin's challenge to the United States is directed not only to our values but to our physical capacity to protect their environment. It is a challenge which encompasses both peace and war and our objectives in peace and war must take account of it.

1. Thus we must make ourselves strong, both in the way in which we affirm our values in the conduct of our national life, and in the development of our military and economic strength.

2. We must lead in building a successfully functioning political and economic system in the free world. It is only by practical

affirmation, abroad as well as at home, of our essential values, that we can preserve our own integrity, in which lies the real frustration of the Kremlin design.

3. But beyond thus affirming our values our policy and actions must be such as to foster a fundamental change in the nature of the Soviet system, a change toward which the frustration of the design is the first and perhaps the most important step. Clearly it will not only be less costly but more effective if this change occurs to a maximum extent as a result of internal forces in Soviet society.

In a shrinking world, which now faces the threat of atomic warfare, it is not an adequate objective merely to seek to check the Kremlin design, for the absence of order among nations is becoming less and less tolerable. This fact imposes on us, in our own interests, the responsibility of world leadership. It demands that we make the attempt, and accept the risks inherent in it, to bring about order and justice by means consistent with the principles of freedom and democracy. We should limit our requirement of the Soviet Union to its participation with other nations on the basis of equality and respect for the rights of others. Subject to this requirement, we must with our allies and the former subject peoples seek to create a world society based on the principle of consent. Its framework cannot be inflexible. It will consist of many national communities of great and varying abilities and resources, and hence of war potential. The seeds of conflicts will inevitably exist or will come into being. To acknowledge this is only to acknowledge the impossibility of a final solution. Not to acknowledge it can be fatally dangerous in a world in which there are no final solutions.

All these objectives of a free society are equally valid and necessary in peace and war. But every consideration of devotion to our fundamental values and to our national security demands that we seek to achieve them by the strategy of the cold war. It is only by developing the moral and material strength of the free world that the Soviet regime will become convinced of the falsity of its assumptions and that the pre-conditions for workable agreements can be created. By practically demonstrating the integrity and vitality of our system the free world widens the area of possible agreement and thus can hope gradually to bring about a Soviet acknowledgement of realities which in sum will eventually constitute a frustration of the Soviet design. Short of this, however, it might be possible to create a situation which will induce the Soviet Union to accommodate itself, with or without the conscious abandonment of its design, to coexistence on tolerable terms with the non-Soviet world. Such a development would be a triumph for the idea of freedom and democracy. It must be an immediate objective of United States policy.

There is no reason, in the event of war, for us to alter our overall objectives. They do not include unconditional surrender, the subjugation of the Russian peoples or a Russia shorn of its economic potential. Such a course would irrevocably unite the Russian people behind the regime which enslaves them. Rather these objectives contemplate Soviet acceptance of the specific and limited conditions requisite to an international environment in which free institutions can flourish, and in which the Russian peoples will have a new chance to work out their own destiny. If we can make the Russian people our allies in the enterprise we will obviously have made our task easier and victory more certain.

The objectives outlined in NSC 20/4 (November 23, 1948) ... are fully consistent with the objectives stated in this paper, and they remain valid. The growing intensity of the conflict which has been imposed upon us, however, requires the changes of emphasis and the additions that are apparent. Coupled with the probable fission bomb capability and possible thermonuclear bomb capability of the Soviet Union, the intensifying struggle requires us to face the fact that we can expect no lasting abatement of the crisis unless and until a change occurs in the nature of the Soviet system.

C. Means

The free society is limited in its choice of means to achieve its ends.

Compulsion is the negation of freedom, except when it is used to enforce the rights common to all. The resort to force, internally or externally, is therefore a last resort for a free society. The act is permissible only when one individual or groups of individuals within it threaten the basic rights of other individuals or when another society seeks to impose its will upon it. The free society cherishes and protects as fundamental the rights of the minority against the will of a majority, because these rights are the inalienable rights of each and every individual.

The resort to force, to compulsion, to the imposition of its will is therefore a difficult and dangerous act for a free society, which is warranted only in the face of even greater dangers. The necessity of the act must be clear and compelling; the act must commend itself to the overwhelming majority as an inescapable exception to the basic idea of freedom; or the regenerative capacity of free men after the act has been performed will be endangered.

The Kremlin is able to select whatever means are expedient in seeking to carry out its fundamental design. Thus it can make the best of several possible worlds, conducting the struggle on those levels where it considers it profitable and enjoying the benefits of a pseudo-peace on those levels where it is not ready for a contest. At the ideological or psychological level, in the struggle for men's minds, the conflict is worldwide. At the political and economic level, within states and in the relations between states, the struggle for power is being intensified. And at the military level, the Kremlin has thus far been careful not to commit a technical breach of the peace, although using its vast forces to intimidate its neighbors, and to support an aggressive foreign policy, and not hesitating through its agents to resort to arms in favorable circumstances. The attempt to carry out its fundamental design is being pressed, therefore, with all means which are believed expedient in the present situation, and the Kremlin has inextricably engaged us in the conflict between its design and our purpose.

We have no such freedom of choice, and least of all in the use of force. Resort to war is not only a last resort for a free society, but it is also an act which cannot definitively end the fundamental conflict in the realm of ideas. The idea of slavery can only be overcome by the timely and persistent demonstration of the superiority of the idea of freedom. Military victory alone would only partially and perhaps only temporarily affect the fundamental conflict, for although the ability of the Kremlin to threaten our security might be for a time destroyed, the resurgence of totalitarian forces and the re-establishment of the Soviet system or its equivalent would not be long delayed unless great progress were made in the fundamental conflict.

Practical and ideological considerations therefore both impel us to the conclusion that we have no choice but to demonstrate the superiority of the idea of freedom by its constructive application, and to attempt to change the world situation by means short of war in such a way as to frustrate the Kremlin design and hasten the decay of the Soviet system.

For us the role of military power is to serve the national purpose by deterring an attack upon us while we seek by other means to create an environment in which our free society can flourish, and by fighting, if necessary, to defend the integrity and vitality of our free society and to defeat any aggressor. The Kremlin uses Soviet military power to back up and serve the Kremlin design. It does not hesitate to use military force aggressively if that course is expedient in the achievement of its design. The differences between our fundamental purpose and the Kremlin design, therefore, are reflected in our respective attitudes toward and use of military force.

Our free society, confronted by a threat to its basic values, naturally will take such action, including the use of military force, as may be required to protect those values. The integrity of our system will not be jeopardized by any measures, covert or overt, violent or non-violent, which serve the purposes of frustrating the Kremlin design, nor does the necessity for conducting ourselves so as to affirm our values in actions as well as words forbid such measures, provided only they are appropriately calculated to that end and are not so excessive or misdirected as to make us enemies of the people instead of the evil men who have enslaved them.

But if war comes, what is the role of force? Unless we so use it that the Russian people can perceive that our effort is directed against the regime and its power for aggression, and not against their own interests, we will unite the regime and the people in the kind of last ditch fight in which no underlying problems are solved, new ones are created, and where our basic principles are obscured and compromised. If we do not in the application of force demonstrate the nature of our objectives we will, in fact, have compromised from the outset our fundamental purpose. In the words of the *Federalist* (No. 28) "The means to be employed must be proportioned to the extent of the mischief." . . .

Know the enemy and exploit its weaknesses
Paul Nitze, NSC-68 (1950)

The following passage is Part V of NSC-68. This section examines the selected adversary's intentions and capabilities, assesses its strengths and weaknesses, and discusses how to exploit the latter through political means.

Part V may be considered a cornerstone of American public diplomacy, as waged against the USSR, its colonies and its political friends; and in support of democracies and other American allies and interests affected by Soviet imperialism.

Soviet Intentions and Capabilities

A. Political and psychological
The Kremlin's design for world domination begins at home. The first concern of a despotic oligarchy is that the local base of its power and authority be secure. The massive fact of the iron curtain isolating the Soviet peoples from the outside world, the repeated political purges within the USSR and the institutionalized crimes of the MVD [the Soviet Ministry of Internal Affairs] are evidence that the Kremlin does not feel secure at home and that "the entire coercive force of the socialist state" is more than ever one of seeking to impose its absolute authority over "the economy, manner of life, and consciousness of people" (Vyshinski, *The Law of the Soviet State,* p. 74). Similar evidence in the satellite states of Eastern Europe leads to the conclusion that this same policy, in less advanced phases, is being applied to the Kremlin's colonial areas.

Being a totalitarian dictatorship, the Kremlin's objectives in these policies is the total subjective submission of the peoples now under its control. The concentration camp is the prototype of the society which these policies are designed to achieve, a society in which the personality of the individual is so broken and perverted that he participates affirmatively in his own degradation.

The Kremlin's policy toward areas not under its control is the elimination of resistance to its will and the extension of its influence and control. It is driven to follow this policy because it cannot, for the reasons set forth in Chapter IV, tolerate the existence of free societies; to the Kremlin the most mild and inoffensive free society is an affront, a challenge and a subversive influence. Given the nature of the Kremlin, and the evidence at hand, it seems clear that the ends toward which this policy is directed are the same as those where its control has already been established.

The means employed by the Kremlin in pursuit of this policy are limited only by considerations of expediency. Doctrine is not a limiting factor; rather it dictates the employment of violence, subversion, and deceit, and rejects moral considerations. In any event, the Kremlin's conviction of its own infallibility has made its devotion to theory so subjective that past or present pronouncements as to doctrine offer no reliable guide to future actions. The only apparent restraints on resort to war are, therefore, calculations of practicality.

With particular reference to the United States, the Kremlin's strategic and tactical policy is affected by its estimate that we are not only the greatest immediate obstacle which stands between it and world domination, we are also the only power which could release forces in the free and Soviet worlds which could destroy it. The Kremlin's policy toward us is consequently animated by a peculiarly virulent blend of hatred and fear. Its strategy has been one of attempting to undermine the complex of forces, in this country and in the rest of the free world, on which our power is based. In this it has both adhered to doctrine and followed the sound principle of seeking maximum results with minimum risks and commitments. The present application of this strategy is a new form of expression for traditional Russian caution. However, there is no justification in Soviet theory or practice for predicting that, should the Kremlin become convinced that it could cause our downfall by one conclusive blow, it would not seek that solution.

In considering the capabilities of the Soviet world, it is of prime importance to remember that, in contrast to ours, they are being drawn upon close to the maximum possible extent. Also in contrast to us, the Soviet world can do more with less – it has a lower standard of living, its economy requires less to keep it functioning, and its military machine operates effectively with less elaborate equipment and organization.

The capabilities of the Soviet world are being exploited to the full because the Kremlin is inescapably militant. It is inescapably militant because it possesses and is possessed by a world-wide revolutionary movement, because it is the inheritor of Russian imperialism, and because it is a totalitarian dictatorship. Persistent crisis, conflict, and expansion are the essence of the Kremlin's militancy. This dynamism serves to intensify all Soviet capabilities.

Two enormous organizations, the Communist Party and the secret police, are an outstanding source of strength to the Kremlin. In the Party, it has an apparatus designed to impose at home an ideological uniformity among its people and to act abroad as an instrument of propaganda, subversion and espionage. In its police apparatus, it has a domestic repressive instrument guaranteeing under present circumstances the continued security of the Kremlin. The demonstrated capabilities of these two basic organizations, operating openly or in disguise, in mass or through single agents, is unparalleled in history. The party, the police and the conspicuous might of the Soviet military machine together tend to create an overall impression of irresistible Soviet power among many peoples of the free world.

The ideological pretensions of the Kremlin are another great source of strength. Its identification of the Soviet system with communism, its peace campaigns and its championing of colonial peoples may be viewed with apathy, if not cynicism, by the oppressed totalitariat of the Soviet world, but in the free world these ideas find favorable responses in vulnerable segments of society. They have found a particularly receptive audience in Asia, especially as the Asiatics have been impressed by what has been plausibly portrayed to them as the rapid advance of the USSR from a backward society to a position of great world power. Thus, in its pretensions to being (a) the source of a new universal faith and (b) the model "scientific" society, the Kremlin cynically identifies itself with the genuine aspirations of large numbers of people, and places itself at the head of an international crusade with all of the benefits which derive therefrom.

Finally, there is a category of capabilities, strictly speaking neither institutional nor ideological, which should be taken into consideration. The extraordinary flexibility of Soviet tactics is certainly a strength. It derives from the utterly amoral and opportunistic conduct of Soviet policy. Combining this quality with the elements of secrecy, the Kremlin possesses a formidable capacity to act with the widest tactical latitude, with stealth, and with speed.

The greatest vulnerability of the Kremlin lies in the basic nature of its relations with the Soviet people.

That relationship is characterized by universal suspicion, fear, and denunciation. It is a relationship in which the Kremlin relies, not only for its power but its very survival, on intricately devised mechanisms of coercion. The Soviet monolith is held together by the iron curtain around it and the iron bars within it, not by any force of natural cohesion. These artificial mechanisms of unity have never been intelligently challenged by a strong outside force. The full measure of their vulnerability is therefore not yet evident.

The Kremlin's relations with its satellites and their peoples is likewise a vulnerability. Nationalism still remains the most potent emotional-political force. The well-known ills of colonialism are compounded, however, by the excessive demands of the Kremlin that its satellites accept not only the imperial authority of Moscow but that they believe in and proclaim the ideological primacy and infallibility of the Kremlin. These excessive requirements can be made good only through extreme coercion. The result is that if a satellite feels able to effect its independence of the Kremlin, as Tito was able to do, it is likely to break away.

In short, Soviet ideas and practices run counter to the best and potentially the strongest instincts of men, and deny their most fundamental aspirations. Against an adversary which effectively affirmed the constructive and hopeful instincts of men and was capable of fulfilling their fundamental aspirations, the Soviet system might prove to be fatally weak.

The problem of succession to Stalin is also a Kremlin vulnerability. In a system where supreme power is acquired and held through violence and intimidation, the transfer of that power may well produce a period of instability.

In a very real sense, the Kremlin is a victim of its own dynamism. This dynamism can become a weakness if it is frustrated, if in its forward thrusts it encounters a superior force which halts the expansion and exerts a superior counterpressure. Yet the Kremlin cannot relax the condition of crisis and mobilization, for to do so would be to lose its dynamism, whereas the seeds of decay within the Soviet system would begin to flourish and fructify.

The Kremlin is, of course, aware of these weaknesses. It must know that in the present world situation they are of secondary significance. So long as the Kremlin retains the initiative, so long as it can keep on the offensive unchallenged by clearly superior counter-force – spiritual as well as material – its vulnerabilities are largely inoperative and even concealed by its successes. The Kremlin has not yet been given real reason to fear and be diverted by the rot within its system.

'A call to bear the burden of a long twilight struggle'
John F. Kennedy (1961)

*Containing some of the most iconic phrases and images of any
modern speech, the inaugural address of President John F.
Kennedy is at once a seamless statement of domestic politics and
an act of international public diplomacy.*

*The speech celebrates freedom, challenging Soviet expansionism
indirectly but unmistakably, announcing during an era of
decolonization that the U.S. would be the primary friend of the
world's poor countries while guaranteeing the independence of the
Western hemisphere in a new Alliance for Progress. Without
accusing Moscow, Kennedy put the onus on the Soviets to behave
and serve humanity. Kennedy's approach changed the American
tone during the Cold War - steadfast as always, but gentler and
more people-oriented. The president called for every citizen to
sacrifice to win what was certain to be a long, protracted
ideological war. He followed his words with action, not only with
his initiative for the Americas, but with a robust public diplomacy
and international broadcasting machine, founding the U.S. Agency
for International Development, and establishing the Peace Corps.*

We observe today not a victory of party but a celebration of
freedom – symbolizing an end as well as a beginning – signifying
renewal as well as change. For I have sworn before you and
Almighty God the same solemn oath our forbears prescribed nearly
a century and three-quarters ago.

The world is very different now. For man holds in his mortal
hands the power to abolish all forms of human poverty and all forms
of human life. And yet the same revolutionary beliefs for which our
forebears fought are still at issue around the globe – the belief that
the rights of man come not from the generosity of the state but from
the hand of God.

We dare not forget today that we are the heirs of that first
revolution. Let the word go forth from this time and place, to friend
and foe alike, that the torch has been passed to a new generation of
Americans – born in this century, tempered by war, disciplined by a
hard and bitter peace, proud of our ancient heritage – and unwilling
to witness or permit the slow undoing of those human rights to

---

[36] President John F. Kennedy, Inaugural Address, January 20, 1961.
Courtesy of the John F. Kennedy Library.

which this nation has always been committed, and to which we are committed today at home and around the world.

Let every nation know, whether it wishes us well or ill, that we shall pay any price, bear any burden, meet any hardship, support any friend, oppose any foe to assure the survival and the success of liberty.

This much we pledge – and more.

To those old allies whose cultural and spiritual origins we share, we pledge the loyalty of faithful friends. United there is little we cannot do in a host of cooperative ventures. Divided there is little we can do–for we dare not meet a powerful challenge at odds and split asunder.

To those new states whom we welcome to the ranks of the free, we pledge our word that one form of colonial control shall not have passed away merely to be replaced by a far more iron tyranny. We shall not always expect to find them supporting our view. But we shall always hope to find them strongly supporting their own freedom – and to remember that, in the past, those who foolishly sought power by riding the back of the tiger ended up inside.

To those people in the huts and villages of half the globe struggling to break the bonds of mass misery, we pledge our best efforts to help them help themselves, for whatever period is required – not because the communists may be doing it, not because we seek their votes, but because it is right. If a free society cannot help the many who are poor, it cannot save the few who are rich.

To our sister republics south of our border, we offer a special pledge – to convert our good words into good deeds – in a new alliance for progress – to assist free men and free governments in casting off the chains of poverty. But this peaceful revolution of hope cannot become the prey of hostile powers. Let all our neighbors know that we shall join with them to oppose aggression or subversion anywhere in the Americas. And let every other power know that this Hemisphere intends to remain the master of its own house.

To that world assembly of sovereign states, the United Nations, our last best hope in an age where the instruments of war have far outpaced the instruments of peace, we renew our pledge of support – to prevent it from becoming merely a forum for invective – to strengthen its shield of the new and the weak – and to enlarge the area in which its writ may run.

Finally, to those nations who would make themselves our adversary, we offer not a pledge but a request: that both sides begin anew the quest for peace, before the dark powers of destruction unleashed by science engulf all humanity in planned or accidental self-destruction.

We dare not tempt them with weakness. For only when our arms are sufficient beyond doubt can we be certain beyond doubt that they will never be employed.

But neither can two great and powerful groups of nations take comfort from our present course – both sides overburdened by the cost of modern weapons, both rightly alarmed by the steady spread of the deadly atom, yet both racing to alter that uncertain balance of terror that stays the hand of mankind's final war.

So let us begin anew – remembering on both sides that civility is not a sign of weakness, and sincerity is always subject to proof. Let us never negotiate out of fear. But let us never fear to negotiate.

Let both sides explore what problems unite us instead of belaboring those problems which divide us.

Let both sides, for the first time, formulate serious and precise proposals for the inspection and control of arms – and bring the absolute power to destroy other nations under the absolute control of all nations.

Let both sides seek to invoke the wonders of science instead of its terrors. Together let us explore the stars, conquer the deserts, eradicate disease, tap the ocean depths and encourage the arts and commerce.

Let both sides unite to heed in all corners of the earth the command of Isaiah – to "undo the heavy burdens . . . (and) let the oppressed go free."

And if a beachhead of cooperation may push back the jungle of suspicion, let both sides join in creating a new endeavor, not a new balance of power, but a new world of law, where the strong are just and the weak secure and the peace preserved.

All this will not be finished in the first one hundred days. Nor will it be finished in the first one thousand days, nor in the life of this Administration, nor even perhaps in our lifetime on this planet. But let us begin.

In your hands, my fellow citizens, more than mine, will rest the final success or failure of our course. Since this country was founded, each generation of Americans has been summoned to give testimony to its national loyalty. The graves of young Americans who answered the call to service surround the globe.

Now the trumpet summons us again – not as a call to bear arms, though arms we need – not as a call to battle, though embattled we are – but a call to bear the burden of a long twilight struggle, year in and year out, "rejoicing in hope, patient in tribulation" – a struggle against the common enemies of man: tyranny, poverty, disease and war itself.

Can we forge against these enemies a grand and global alliance, North and South, East and West, that can assure a more fruitful life for all mankind? Will you join in that historic effort?

In the long history of the world, only a few generations have been granted the role of defending freedom in its hour of maximum danger. I do not shrink from this responsibility – I welcome it. I do not believe that any of us would exchange places with any other people or any other generation. The energy, the faith, the devotion which we bring to this endeavor will light our country and all who serve it – and the glow from that fire can truly light the world.

And so, my fellow Americans: ask not what your country can do for you – ask what you can do for your country.

My fellow citizens of the world: ask not what America will do for you, but what together we can do for the freedom of man.

Finally, whether you are citizens of America or citizens of the world, ask of us here the same high standards of strength and sacrifice which we ask of you. With a good conscience our only sure reward, with history the final judge of our deeds, let us go forth to lead the land we love, asking His blessing and His help, but knowing that here on earth God's work must truly be our own.

Human rights as a cornerstone of U.S. foreign policy, or 'We are now free of that inordinate fear of Communism'
Jimmy Carter (1977) [37]

In a June, 1977 commencement speech at the University of Notre Dame, President Jimmy Carter announced what he considered a radical departure from traditional American foreign policy. Under his leadership, the U.S. would place human rights first in its dealings with other nations. That was Carter's stated intention,

---

[37] Jimmy Carter, *Public Papers of the Presidents of the United States: Jimmy Carter*, vol.1 (1977), p. 954.

anyway; though high in principle, the policy, to his opponents and even to members of his party, was naïve and even dangerous, as the Soviets would take advantage and install even worse and more aggressive regimes. In the speech, Carter decried what he called "that inordinate fear of communism."

That policy led some members of his party, such as Jeane Kirkpatrick, to break ranks and, in 1980, join Ronald Reagan at the core of his foreign policy team. Reagan largely continued Carter's human rights agenda, but tempered it to fight Soviet communist expansionism first, and promote democracy once Soviet forces had been routed. The speech below is titled "Human Rights and Foreign Policy."

Nation: to provide more efficiently for the needs of our people, to demonstrate – against the dark faith of our times – that our Government can be both competent and more humane.

But I want to speak to you today about the strands that connect our actions overseas with our essential character as a nation. I believe we can have a foreign policy that is democratic, that is based on fundamental values, and that uses power and influence, which we have, for humane purposes. We can also have a foreign policy that the American people both support and, for a change, know about and understand.

I have a quiet confidence in our own political system. Because we know that democracy works, we can reject the arguments of those rulers who deny human rights to their people.

We are confident that democracy's example will be compelling, and so we seek to bring that example closer to those from whom in the past few years we have been separated and who are not yet convinced about the advantages of our kind of life.

We are confident that the democratic methods are the most effective, and so we are not tempted to employ improper tactics here at home or abroad.

We are confident of our own strength, so we can seek substantial mutual reductions in the nuclear arms race.

And we are confident of the good sense of American people, and so we let them share in the process of making foreign policy decisions. We can thus speak with the voices of 215 million, and not just of an isolated handful.

Democracy's great recent successes – in India, Portugal, Spain, Greece – show that our confidence in this system is not misplaced. Being confident of our own future, we are now free of that inordinate fear of communism which once led us to embrace any dictator who joined us in that fear. I'm glad that that's being changed.

For too many years, we've been willing to adopt the flawed and erroneous principles and tactics of our adversaries, sometimes abandoning our own values for theirs. We've fought fire with fire, never thinking that fire is better quenched with water. This approach failed, with Vietnam the best example of its intellectual and moral poverty. But through failure we have now found our way back to our own principles and values, and we have regained our lost confidence.

By the measure of history, our Nation's 200 years are very brief, and our rise to world eminence is briefer still. It dates from 1945, when Europe and the old international order lay in ruins. Before then, America was largely on the periphery of world affairs. But since then, we have inescapably been at the center of world affairs.

Our policy during this period was guided by two principles: a belief that Soviet expansion was almost inevitable but that it must be contained, and the corresponding belief in the importance of an almost exclusive alliance among non-Communist nations on both sides of the Atlantic. That system could not last forever unchanged. Historical trends have weakened its foundation. The unifying threat of conflict with the Soviet Union has become less intensive, even though the competition has become more extensive.

The Vietnamese war produced a profound moral crisis, sapping worldwide faith in our own policy and our system of life, a crisis of confidence made even more grave by the covert pessimism of some of our leaders.

In less than a generation, we've seen the world change dramatically. The daily lives and aspirations of most human beings have been transformed. Colonialism is nearly gone. A new sense of national identity now exists in almost 100 new countries that have been formed in the last generation. Knowledge has become more widespread. Aspirations are higher. As more people have been freed from traditional constraints, more have been determined to achieve, for the first time in their lives, social justice.

The world is still divided by ideological disputes, dominated by regional conflicts, and threatened by danger that we will not resolve the differences of race and wealth without violence or without drawing into combat the major military powers. We can no longer separate the traditional issues of war and peace from the new global questions of justice, equity, and human rights.

It is a new world, but America should not fear it. It is a new world, and we should help to shape it. It is a new world that calls for a new American foreign policy – a policy based on constant decency in its values and on optimism in our historical vision.

We can no longer have a policy solely for the industrial nations as the foundation of global stability, but we must respond to the new reality of a politically awakening world.

We can no longer expect that the other 150 nations will follow the dictates of the powerful, but we must continue – confidently – our efforts to inspire, to persuade, and to lead.

Our policy must reflect our belief that the world can hope for more than simple survival and our belief that dignity and freedom are fundamental spiritual requirements. Our policy must shape an international system that will last longer than secret deals.

We cannot make this kind of policy by manipulation. Our policy must be open; it must be candid; it must be one of constructive global involvement, resting on five cardinal principles.

I've tried to make these premises clear to the American people since last January. Let me review what we have been doing and discuss what we intend to do.

First, we have reaffirmed America's commitment to human rights as a fundamental tenet of our foreign policy. In ancestry, religion, color, place of origin, and cultural background, we Americans are as diverse a nation as the world has even seen. No common mystique of blood or soil unites us. What draws us together, perhaps more than anything else, is a belief in human freedom. We want the world to know that our Nation stands for more than financial prosperity.

This does not mean that we can conduct our foreign policy by rigid moral maxims. We live in a world that is imperfect and which will always be imperfect – a world that is complex and confused and which will always be complex and confused.

I understand fully the limits of moral suasion. We have no illusion that changes will come easily or soon. But I also believe that it is a mistake to undervalue the power of words and of the ideas that words embody. In our own history, that power has ranged from Thomas Paine's "Common Sense" to Martin Luther King, Jr.'s "I Have a Dream."

In the life of the human spirit, words are action, much more so than many of us may realize who live in countries where freedom of expression is taken for granted. The leaders of totalitarian nations understand this very well. The proof is that words are precisely the action for which dissidents in those countries are being persecuted.

Nonetheless, we can already see dramatic, worldwide advances in the protection of the individual from the arbitrary power of the state. For us to ignore this trend would be to lose influence and moral authority in the world. To lead it will be to regain the moral stature that we once had.

The great democracies are not free because we are strong and prosperous. I believe we are strong and influential and prosperous because we are free.

Throughout the world today, in free nations and in totalitarian countries as well, there is a preoccupation with the subject of human freedom, human rights. And I believe it is incumbent on us in this country to keep that discussion, that debate, that contention alive. No other country is as well-qualified as we to set an example. We have our own shortcomings and faults, and we should strive constantly and with courage to make sure that we are legitimately proud of what we have.

Second, we've moved deliberately to reinforce the bonds among our democracies. In our recent meetings in London, we agreed to widen our economic cooperation, to promote free trade, to strengthen the world's monetary system, to seek ways of avoiding nuclear proliferation. We prepared constructive proposals for the forthcoming meetings on North-South problems of poverty, development, and global well-being. And we agreed on joint efforts to reinforce and to modernize our common defense.

You may be interested in knowing that at this NATO meeting, for the first time in more than 25 years, all members are democracies. Even more important, all of us reaffirmed our basic optimism in the future of the democratic system. Our spirit of confidence is spreading. Together, our democracies can help to shape the wider architecture of global cooperation.

Third, we've moved to engage the Soviet Union in a joint effort to halt the strategic arms race. This race is not only dangerous, it's morally deplorable. We must put an end to it. I know it will not be easy to reach agreements. Our goal is to be fair to both sides, to produce reciprocal stability, parity, and security. We desire a freeze on further modernization and production of weapons and a continuing, substantial reduction of strategic nuclear weapons as well. We want a comprehensive ban on all nuclear testing, a prohibition against all chemical warfare, no attack capability against space satellites, and arms limitations in the Indian Ocean.

We hope that we can take joint steps with all nations toward a final agreement eliminating nuclear weapons completely from our arsenals of death. We will persist in this effort.

Now, I believe in detente with the Soviet Union. To me it means progress toward peace. But the effects of detente should not be limited to our own two countries alone. We hope to persuade the Soviet Union that one country cannot impose its system of society upon another, either through direct military intervention or through the use of a client state's military force, as was the case with Cuban intervention in Angola.

Cooperation also implies obligation. We hope that the Soviet Union will join with us and other nations in playing a larger role in aiding the developing world, for common aid efforts will help us build a bridge of mutual confidence in one another.

Fourth, we are taking deliberate steps to improve the chances of lasting peace in the Middle East. Through wide-ranging consultation with leaders of the countries involved – Israel, Syria, Jordan, and Egypt – we have found some areas of agreement and some movement toward consensus. The negotiations must continue.

Through my own public comments, I've also tried to suggest a more flexible framework for the discussion of the three key issues which have so far been so intractable: the nature of a comprehensive peace – what is peace; what does it mean to the Israelis; what does it mean to their Arab neighbors; secondly, the relationship between security and borders – how can the dispute over border delineations be established and settled with a feeling of security on both sides; and the issue of the Palestinian homeland.

The historic friendship that the United States has with Israel is not dependent on domestic politics in either nation; it's derived from our common respect for human freedom and from a common search for permanent peace.

We will continue to promote a settlement which all of us need. Our own policy will not be affected by changes in leadership in any of the countries in the Middle East. Therefore, we expect Israel and her neighbors to continue to be bound by United Nations Resolutions 242 and 338, which they have previously accepted.

This may be the most propitious time for a genuine settlement since the beginning of the Arab-Israeli conflict almost 30 years ago. To let this opportunity pass could mean disaster not only for the

Middle East but, perhaps, for the international political and economic order as well.

And fifth, we are attempting, even at the risk of some friction with our friends, to reduce the danger of nuclear proliferation and the worldwide spread of conventional weapons.

At the recent summit, we set in motion an international effort to determine the best ways of harnessing nuclear energy for peaceful use while reducing the risks that its products will be diverted to the making of explosives.

We've already completed a comprehensive review of our own policy on arms transfers. Competition in arms sales is inimical to peace and destructive of the economic development of the poorer countries.

We will, as a matter of national policy now in our country, seek to reduce the annual dollar volume of arms sales, to restrict the transfer of advanced weapons, and to reduce the extent of our coproduction arrangements about weapons with foreign states. And just as important, we are trying to get other nations, both free and otherwise, to join us in this effort.

But all of this that I've described is just the beginning. It's a beginning aimed towards a clear goal: to create a wider framework of international cooperation suited to the new and rapidly changing historical circumstances.

We will cooperate more closely with the newly influential countries in Latin America, Africa, and Asia. We need their friendship and cooperation in a common effort as the structure of world power changes.

More than 100 years ago, Abraham Lincoln said that our Nation could not exist half slave and half free. We know a peaceful world cannot long exist one-third rich and two-thirds hungry.

Most nations share our faith that, in the long run, expanded and equitable trade will best help the developing countries to help themselves. But the immediate problems of hunger, disease, illiteracy, and repression are here now.

The Western democracies, the OPEC nations, and the developed Communist countries can cooperate through existing international institutions in providing more effective aid. This is an excellent alternative to war.

We have a special need for cooperation and consultation with other nations in this hemisphere – to the north and to the south. We do not need another slogan. Although these are our close friends and neighbors, our links with them are the same links of equality that we forge for the rest of the world. We will be dealing with them as part of a new, worldwide mosaic of global, regional, and bilateral relations.

It's important that we make progress toward normalizing relations with the People's Republic of China. We see the American and Chinese relationship as a central element of our global policy and China as a key force for global peace. We wish to cooperate closely with the creative Chinese people on the problems that confront all mankind. And we hope to find a formula which can bridge some of the difficulties that still separate us.

Finally, let me say that we are committed to a peaceful resolution of the crisis in southern Africa. The time has come for the principle of majority rule to be the basis for political order, recognizing that in a democratic system the rights of the minority must also be protected.

To be peaceful, change must come promptly. The United States is determined to work together with our European allies and with the concerned African States to shape a congenial international framework for the rapid and progressive transformation of southern African society and to help protect it from unwarranted outside interference.

Let me conclude by summarizing: Our policy is based on an historical vision of America's role. Our policy is derived from a larger view of global change. Our policy is rooted in our moral values, which never change. Our policy is reinforced by our material wealth and by our military power. Our policy is designed to serve mankind. And it is a policy that I hope will make you proud to be Americans.

'Ash heap of history' – the speech at Westminster
Ronald Reagan (1982)[38]

President Reagan's June 8, 1982 speech to the British parliament at Westminster set the stage for the new ideological strategy being laid out to force the Soviet Union to collapse on itself. The speech parallels the development of a series of National Security Decision Directives that set the pieces in place to hasten the demise of the Soviet Union in an integrated strategy to attack Soviet power on all fronts without actually going to war with Moscow.

The journey of which this visit forms a part is a long one. Already it has taken me to two great cities of the West, Rome and Paris, and to the economic summit at Versailles. And there, once again, our sister democracies have proved that even in a time of severe economic strain, free peoples can work together freely and voluntarily to address problems as serious as inflation, unemployment, trade, and economic development in a spirit of cooperation and solidarity.

Other milestones lie ahead. Later this week, in Germany, we and our NATO allies will discuss measures for our joint defense and America's latest initiatives for a more peaceful, secure world through arms reductions.

Each stop of this trip is important, but among them all, this moment occupies a special place in my heart and in the hearts of my countrymen – a moment of kinship and homecoming in these hallowed halls.

Speaking for all Americans, I want to say how very much at home we feel in your house. Every American would, because this is, as we have been so eloquently told, one of democracy's shrines. Here the rights of free people and the processes of representation have been debated and refined.

It has been said that an institution is the lengthening shadow of a man. This institution is the lengthening shadow of all the men and women who have sat here and all those who have voted to send representatives here.

This is my second visit to Great Britain as President of the United States. My first opportunity to stand on British soil occurred almost

---

[38] Ronald Reagan, "Address to the British Parliament," June 8, 1982. Text courtesy of the Ronald Reagan Presidential Library and Foundation.

a year and a half ago when your Prime Minister graciously hosted a diplomatic dinner at the British Embassy in Washington. Mrs. Thatcher said then that she hoped I was not distressed to find staring down at me from the grand staircase a portrait of His Royal Majesty King George III. She suggested it was best to let bygones be bygones, and in view of our two countries' remarkable friendship in succeeding years, she added that most Englishmen today would agree with Thomas Jefferson that "a little rebellion now and then is a very good thing."

Well, from here I will go to Bonn and then Berlin, where there stands a grim symbol of power untamed. The Berlin Wall, that dreadful gray gash across the city, is in its third decade. It is the fitting signature of the regime that built it.

And a few hundred kilometers behind the Berlin Wall, there is another symbol. In the center of Warsaw, there is a sign that notes the distances to two capitals. In one direction it points toward Moscow. In the other it points toward Brussels, headquarters of Western Europe's tangible unity. The marker says that the distances from Warsaw to Moscow and Warsaw to Brussels are equal. The sign makes this point: Poland is not East or West. Poland is at the center of European civilization. It has contributed mightily to that civilization. It is doing so today by being magnificently unreconciled to oppression.

Poland's struggle to be Poland and to secure the basic rights we often take for granted demonstrates why we dare not take those rights for granted. Gladstone, defending the Reform Bill of 1866, declared, "You cannot fight against the future. Time is on our side." It was easier to believe in the march of democracy in Gladstone's day – in that high noon of Victorian optimism.

We're approaching the end of a bloody century plagued by a terrible political invention – totalitarianism. Optimism comes less easily today, not because democracy is less vigorous, but because democracy's enemies have refined their instruments of repression. Yet optimism is in order, because day by day democracy is proving itself to be a not-at-all-fragile flower. From Stettin on the Baltic to Varna on the Black Sea, the regimes planted by totalitarianism have had more than 30 years to establish their legitimacy. But none – not one regime – has yet been able to risk free elections. Regimes planted by bayonets do not take root.

The strength of the Solidarity movement in Poland demonstrates the truth told in an underground joke in the Soviet Union. It is that the Soviet Union would remain a one-party nation even if an opposition party were permitted, because everyone would join the opposition party.

America's time as a player on the stage of world history has been brief. I think understanding this fact has always made you patient with your younger cousins – well, not always patient. I do recall that on one occasion, Sir Winston Churchill said in exasperation about one of our most distinguished diplomats: "He is the only case I know of a bull who carries his china shop with him."

But witty as Sir Winston was, he also had that special attribute of great statesmen – the gift of vision, the willingness to see the future based on the experience of the past. It is this sense of history, this understanding of the past that I want to talk with you about today, for it is in remembering what we share of the past that our two nations can make common cause for the future.

We have not inherited an easy world. If developments like the Industrial Revolution, which began here in England, and the gifts of science and technology have made life much easier for us, they have also made it more dangerous. There are threats now to our freedom, indeed to our very existence, that other generations could never even have imagined.

There is first the threat of global war. No President, no Congress, no Prime Minister, no Parliament can spend a day entirely free of this threat. And I don't have to tell you that in today's world the existence of nuclear weapons could mean, if not the extinction of mankind, then surely the end of civilization as we know it. That's why negotiations on intermediate-range nuclear forces now underway in Europe and the START talks – Strategic Arms Reduction Talks – which will begin later this month, are not just critical to American or Western policy; they are critical to mankind. Our commitment to early success in these negotiations is firm and unshakable, and our purpose is clear: reducing the risk of war by reducing the means of waging war on both sides.

At the same time there is a threat posed to human freedom by the enormous power of the modern state. History teaches the dangers of government that overreaches – political control taking precedence over free economic growth, secret police, mindless bureaucracy, all combining to stifle individual excellence and personal freedom.

Now, I'm aware that among us here and throughout Europe there is legitimate disagreement over the extent to which the public sector should play a role in a nation's economy and life. But on one point all of us are united – our abhorrence of dictatorship in all its forms, but most particularly totalitarianism and the terrible inhumanities it has caused in our time – the great purge, Auschwitz and Dachau, the Gulag, and Cambodia.

Historians looking back at our time will note the consistent restraint and peaceful intentions of the West. They will note that it was the democracies who refused to use the threat of their nuclear monopoly in the forties and early fifties for territorial or imperial gain. Had that nuclear monopoly been in the hands of the Communist world, the map of Europe – indeed, the world – would look very different today. And certainly they will note it was not the democracies that invaded Afghanistan or suppressed Polish Solidarity or used chemical and toxin warfare in Afghanistan and Southeast Asia.

If history teaches anything it teaches self-delusion in the face of unpleasant facts is folly. We see around us today the marks of our terrible dilemma – predictions of doomsday, antinuclear demonstrations, an arms race in which the West must, for its own protection, be an unwilling participant. At the same time we see totalitarian forces in the world who seek subversion and conflict around the globe to further their barbarous assault on the human spirit. What, then, is our course? Must civilization perish in a hail of fiery atoms?

Must freedom wither in a quiet, deadening accommodation with totalitarian evil?

Sir Winston Churchill refused to accept the inevitability of war or even that it was imminent. He said, "I do not believe that Soviet Russia desires war. What they desire is the fruits of war and the indefinite expansion of their power and doctrines. But what we have to consider here today while time remains is the permanent prevention of war and the establishment of conditions of freedom and democracy as rapidly as possible in all countries."

Well, this is precisely our mission today: to preserve freedom as well as peace. It may not be easy to see; but I believe we live now at a turning point.

In an ironic sense Karl Marx was right. We are witnessing today a great revolutionary crisis, a crisis where the demands of the economic order are conflicting directly with those of the political order. But the crisis is happening not in the free, non-Marxist West, but in the home of Marxist-Leninism, the Soviet Union. It is the Soviet Union that runs against the tide of history by denying human freedom and human dignity to its citizens. It also is in deep economic difficulty. The rate of growth in the national product has been steadily declining since the fifties and is less than half of what it was then.

The dimensions of this failure are astounding: A country which employs one-fifth of its population in agriculture is unable to feed its own people. Were it not for the private sector, the tiny private sector tolerated in Soviet agriculture, the country might be on the brink of famine. These private plots occupy a bare 3 percent of the arable land but account for nearly one-quarter of Soviet farm output and nearly one-third of meat products and vegetables. Overcentralized, with little or no incentives, year after year the Soviet system pours its best resource into the making of instruments of destruction. The constant shrinkage of economic growth combined with the growth of military production is putting a heavy strain on the Soviet people. What we see here is a political structure that no longer corresponds to its economic base, a society where productive forces are hampered by political ones.

The decay of the Soviet experiment should come as no surprise to us. Wherever the comparisons have been made between free and closed societies – West Germany and East Germany, Austria and Czechoslovakia, Malaysia and Vietnam – it is the democratic countries what are prosperous and responsive to the needs of their people. And one of the simple but overwhelming facts of our time is this: Of all the millions of refugees we've seen in the modern world, their flight is always away from, not toward the Communist world. Today on the NATO line, our military forces face east to prevent a possible invasion. On the other side of the line, the Soviet forces also face east to prevent their people from leaving.

The hard evidence of totalitarian rule has caused in mankind an uprising of the intellect and will. Whether it is the growth of the new schools of economics in America or England or the appearance of the so-called new philosophers in France, there is one unifying thread running through the intellectual work of these groups – rejection of the arbitrary power of the state, the refusal to subordinate the rights of the individual to the superstate, the realization that collectivism stifles all the best human impulses.

Since the exodus from Egypt, historians have written of those who sacrificed and struggled for freedom – the stand at Thermopylae, the revolt of Spartacus, the storming of the Bastille, the Warsaw uprising in World War II. More recently we've seen evidence of this same human impulse in one of the developing nations in Central America. For months and months the world news media covered the fighting in El Salvador. Day after day we were treated to stories and film slanted toward the brave freedom-fighters battling oppressive government forces in behalf of the silent, suffering people of that tortured country.

And then one day those silent, suffering people were offered a chance to vote, to choose the kind of government they wanted. Suddenly the freedom-fighters in the hills were exposed for what they really are – Cuban-backed guerrillas who want power for themselves, and their backers, not democracy for the people. They threatened death to any who voted, and destroyed hundreds of buses and trucks to keep the people from getting to the polling places. But on election day, the people of El Salvador, an unprecedented 1.4 million of them, braved ambush and gunfire, and trudged for miles to vote for freedom.

They stood for hours in the hot sun waiting for their turn to vote. Members of our Congress who went there as observers told me of a women who was wounded by rifle fire on the way to the polls, who refused to leave the line to have her wound treated until after she had voted. A grandmother, who had been told by the guerrillas she would be killed when she returned from the polls, and she told the guerrillas, ``You can kill me, you can kill my family, kill my neighbors, but you can't kill us all.'' The real freedom-fighters of El Salvador turned out to be the people of that country – the young, the old, the in-between.

Strange, but in my own country there's been little if any news coverage of that war since the election. Now, perhaps they'll say it's — well, because there are newer struggles now.

On distant islands in the South Atlantic young men are fighting for Britain. And, yes, voices have been raised protesting their sacrifice for lumps of rock and earth so far away. But those young men aren't fighting for mere real estate. They fight for a cause – for the belief that armed aggression must not be allowed to succeed, and the people must participate in the decisions of government – [applause] – the decisions of government under the rule of law. If there had been firmer support for that principle some 45 years ago, perhaps our generation wouldn't have suffered the bloodletting of World War II.

In the Middle East now the guns sound once more, this time in Lebanon, a country that for too long has had to endure the tragedy of civil war, terrorism, and foreign intervention and occupation. The fighting in Lebanon on the part of all parties must stop, and Israel should bring its forces home. But this is not enough. We must all work to stamp out the scourge of terrorism that in the Middle East makes war an ever-present threat.

But beyond the troublespots lies a deeper, more positive pattern. Around the world today, the democratic revolution is gathering new strength. In India a critical test has been passed with the peaceful change of governing political parties. In Africa, Nigeria is moving into remarkable and unmistakable ways to build and strengthen its democratic institutions. In the Caribbean and Central America, 16 of 24 countries have freely elected governments. And in the United Nations, 8 of the 10 developing nations which have joined that body in the past 5 years are democracies.

In the Communist world as well, man's instinctive desire for freedom and self-determination surfaces again and again. To be sure, there are grim reminders of how brutally the police state attempts to snuff out this quest for self-rule – 1953 in East Germany, 1956 in Hungary, 1968 in Czechoslovakia, 1981 in Poland. But the struggle continues in Poland. And we know that there are even those who strive and suffer for freedom within the confines of the Soviet Union itself. How we conduct ourselves here in the Western democracies will determine whether this trend continues.

No, democracy is not a fragile flower. Still it needs cultivating. If the rest of this century is to witness the gradual growth of freedom and democratic ideals, we must take actions to assist the campaign for democracy.

Some argue that we should encourage democratic change in right-wing dictatorships, but not in Communist regimes. Well, to accept this preposterous notion – as some well-meaning people have – is to invite the argument that once countries achieve a nuclear capability, they should be allowed an undisturbed reign of terror over their own citizens.

We reject this course.

As for the Soviet view, Chairman Brezhnev repeatedly has stressed that the competition of ideas and systems must continue and that this is entirely consistent with relaxation of tensions and peace.

Well, we ask only that these systems begin by living up to their own constitutions, abiding by their own laws, and complying with the international obligations they have undertaken. We ask only for a process, a direction, a basic code of decency, not for an instant transformation.

We cannot ignore the fact that even without our encouragement there has been and will continue to be repeated explosions against repression and dictatorships. The Soviet Union itself is not immune to this reality. Any system is inherently unstable that has no peaceful means to legitimize its leaders. In such cases, the very repressiveness of the state ultimately drives people to resist it, if necessary, by force.

While we must be cautious about forcing the pace of change, we must not hesitate to declare our ultimate objectives and to take concrete actions to move toward them. We must be staunch in our conviction that freedom is not the sole prerogative of a lucky few, but the inalienable and universal right of all human beings. So states the United Nations Universal Declaration of Human Rights, which, among other things, guarantees free elections.

The objective I propose is quite simple to state: to foster the infrastructure of democracy, the system of a free press, unions, political parties, universities, which allows a people to choose their own way to develop their own culture, to reconcile their own differences through peaceful means.

This is not cultural imperialism, it is providing the means for genuine self-determination and protection for diversity. Democracy already flourishes in countries with very different cultures and historical experiences. It would be cultural condescension, or worse, to say that any people prefer dictatorship to democracy. Who would voluntarily choose not to have the right to vote, decide to purchase government propaganda handouts instead of independent newspapers, prefer government to worker-controlled unions, opt for land to be owned by the state instead of those who till it, want government repression of religious liberty, a single political party instead of a free choice, a rigid cultural orthodoxy instead of democratic tolerance and diversity?

Since 1917 the Soviet Union has given covert political training and assistance to Marxist-Leninists in many countries. Of course, it also has promoted the use of violence and subversion by these same forces. Over the past several decades, West European and other Social Democrats, Christian Democrats, and leaders have offered open assistance to fraternal, political, and social institutions to bring about peaceful and democratic progress. Appropriately, for a vigorous new democracy, the Federal Republic of Germany's political foundations have become a major force in this effort.

We in America now intend to take additional steps, as many of our allies have already done, toward realizing this same goal. The chairmen and other leaders of the national Republican and Democratic Party organizations are initiating a study with the bipartisan American political foundation to determine how the United States can best contribute as a nation to the global campaign for democracy now gathering force. They will have the cooperation of congressional leaders of both parties, along with representatives of business, labor, and other major institutions in our society. I look forward to receiving their recommendations and to working with these institutions and the Congress in the common task of strengthening democracy throughout the world.

It is time that we committed ourselves as a nation – in both the pubic and private sectors – to assisting democratic development.

We plan to consult with leaders of other nations as well. There is a proposal before the Council of Europe to invite parliamentarians from democratic countries to a meeting next year in Strasbourg. That prestigious gathering could consider ways to help democratic political movements.

This November in Washington there will take place an international meeting on free elections. And next spring there will be a conference of world authorities on constitutionalism and self-government hosted by the Chief Justice of the United States. Authorities from a number of developing and developed countries – judges, philosophers, and politicians with practical experience – have agreed to explore how to turn principle into practice and further the rule of law.

At the same time, we invite the Soviet Union to consider with us how the competition of ideas and values – which it is committed to support – can be conducted on a peaceful and reciprocal basis. For example, I am prepared to offer President Brezhnev an opportunity to speak to the American people on our television if he will allow me the same opportunity with the Soviet people. We also suggest that panels of our newsmen periodically appear on each other's television to discuss major events.

Now, I don't wish to sound overly optimistic, yet the Soviet Union is not immune from the reality of what is going on in the world. It has happened in the past – a small ruling elite either mistakenly attempts to ease domestic unrest through greater repression and foreign adventure, or it chooses a wiser course. It begins to allow its people a voice in their own destiny. Even if this latter process is not realized soon, I believe the renewed strength of the democratic movement, complemented by a global campaign for freedom, will strengthen the prospects for arms control and a world at peace.

I have discussed on other occasions, including my address on May 9th, the elements of Western policies toward the Soviet Union to safeguard our interests and protect the peace. What I am describing now is a plan and a hope for the long term – the march of freedom and democracy which will leave Marxism-Leninism on the ash-heap of history as it has left other tyrannies which stifle the freedom and muzzle the self-expression of the people. And that's why we must continue our efforts to strengthen NATO even as we move forward with our Zero-Option initiative in the negotiations on intermediate-range forces and our proposal for a one-third reduction in strategic ballistic missile warheads.

Our military strength is a prerequisite to peace, but let it be clear we maintain this strength in the hope it will never be used, for the ultimate determinant in the struggle that's now going on in the world will not be bombs and rockets, but a test of wills and ideas, a trial of spiritual resolve, the values we hold, the beliefs we cherish, the ideals to which we are dedicated.

The British people know that, given strong leadership, time and a little bit of hope, the forces of good ultimately rally and triumph over evil. Here among you is the cradle of self-government, the Mother of Parliaments. Here is the enduring greatness of the British contribution to mankind, the great civilized ideas: individual liberty, representative government, and the rule of law under God.

I've often wondered about the shyness of some of us in the West about standing for these ideals that have done so much to ease the plight of man and the hardships of our imperfect world. This reluctance to use those vast resources at our command reminds me of the elderly lady whose home was bombed in the Blitz. As the rescuers moved about, they found a bottle of brandy she'd stored behind the staircase, which was all that was left standing. And since she was barely conscious, one of the workers pulled the cork to give her a taste of it. She came around immediately and said, ``Here now – there now, put it back. That's for emergencies.''

Well, the emergency is upon us. Let us be shy no longer. Let us go to our strength. Let us offer hope. Let us tell the world that a new age is not only possible but probable.

During the dark days of the Second World War, when this island was incandescent with courage, Winston Churchill exclaimed about Britain's adversaries, ``What kind of a people do they think we are?'' Well, Britain's adversaries found out what extraordinary people the British are. But all the democracies paid a terrible price for allowing the dictators to underestimate us. We dare not make that mistake again. So, let us ask ourselves, "What kind of people do we think we are?" And let us answer, "Free people, worthy of freedom and determined not only to remain so but to help others gain their freedom as well."

Sir Winston led his people to great victory in war and then lost an election just as the fruits of victory were about to be enjoyed. But he left office honorably, and, as it turned out, temporarily, knowing that the liberty of his people was more important than the fate of any single leader. History recalls his greatness in ways no dictator will ever know. And he left us a message of hope for the future, as timely now as when he first uttered it, as opposition leader in the Commons nearly 27 years ago, when he said, "When we look back on all the perils through which we have passed and at the mighty foes that we have laid low and all the dark and deadly designs that we have frustrated, why should we fear for our future? We have," he said, "come safely through the worst."

Well, the task I've set forth will long outlive our own generation. But together, we too have come through the worst. Let us now begin a major effort to secure the best – a crusade for freedom that will engage the faith and fortitude of the next generation. For the sake of peace and justice, let us move toward a world in which all people are at last free to determine their own destiny.

Political action: An ideological thrust
Ronald Reagan (1983) [39]

President Reagan's National Security Decision Directive number 75, "U.S. Relations with the USSR," outlines a strategy for confronting the Soviets and hastening the collapse of the Soviet Union through a combination of military, economic, diplomatic, and ideological pressure. In some ways, NSDD-75 resembles NSC-68 under President Truman more than 30 years before, and it

---

[39] Ronald Reagan, "U.S. Relations with the USSR," National Security Decision Directive 75, January 17, 1983. Declassified secret document.

renews the call for a systematic political-psychological campaign against the Kremlin. But NSDD-75 goes even further, not merely to contain Soviet expansionism but to reverse it even within the borders of the USSR.

The timing was crucial: as the NSDD was being drafted, longtime Communist Party General Secretary Leonid Brezhnev was dying and a generational succession was underway. By the time Reagan signed the document in January 1983, Brezhnev was dead and ailing KGB Chairman Yuri Andropov was in power. President Reagan called the moment "a particularly opportune time for external forces to affect the policies of Brezhnev's successors." NSDD-75 defined three functional areas of engagement: military strategy, economic policy and political action. The latter area includes public diplomacy and international broadcasting, as the following excerpt shows.

U.S. policy must have an ideological thrust which clearly affirms the superiority of U.S. and Western values of individual dignity and freedom, a free press, free trade unions, free enterprise, and political democracy over the repressive features of Soviet Communism. We need to review and significantly strengthen U.S. interests of political action including: (1) The President's London initiative [see the 1982 speech, above] to support democratic forces; (b) USG efforts to highlight Soviet human rights violations; and (c) U.S. radio broadcasting policy. The U.S. should:

- Expose at all available fora the double standards employed by the Soviet Union in dealing with difficulties within its own domain and the outside ('capitalist') world (e.g., treatment of labor, policies toward ethnic minorities, use of chemical weapons, etc.).
- Prevent the Soviet propaganda machine from seizing the semantic high-ground in the battle of ideas through appropriation of such terms as 'peace.'

The 'Evil Empire' speech
Ronald Reagan (1983)[40]

As his National Security Council designed the new U.S. strategy to confront the Soviet Union and roll back Soviet power, President Reagan intensified his carefully calibrated rhetoric.

By early 1983, momentum was building in favor of a Soviet-sponsored "nuclear freeze" that would have frozen U.S. and Soviet nuclear weapons modernization and arguably end the arms race. The Soviet propaganda campaign was designed to stop the superpowers' nuclear weapons programs in-place – after Moscow had undergone a massive strategic nuclear modernization effort, and before the U.S. could catch up. The freeze also would prevent the U.S. from deploying Pershing II and cruise missiles in Western Europe to counter the Soviet SS-20 missiles already deployed there.

In a last-minute move that alarmed the State Department and some of his own top officials, Reagan used a March 8, 1983 forum before a Christian evangelical group to frame the debate in the terms of a struggle between good and evil, giving what quickly became known as the "Evil Empire speech." Excerpts from that speech follow.

... So, I tell you there are a great many God-fearing, dedicated, noble men and women in public life, present company included. And yes, we need your help to keep us ever mindful of the ideas and the principles that brought us into the public arena in the first place. The basis of those ideals and principles is a commitment to freedom and personal liberty that, itself, is grounded in the much deeper realization that freedom prospers only where the blessings of God are avidly sought and humbly accepted.

The American experiment in democracy rests on this insight. Its discovery was the great triumph of our Founding Fathers, voiced by William Penn when he said, "If we will not be governed by God, we must be governed by tyrants."

Explaining the inalienable rights of men, Jefferson said, "The God who gave us life, gave us liberty at the same time."

---

[40] Ronald Reagan, "Remarks to the National Association of Evangelicals," Orlando, Florida, March 8, 1983. Courtesy of the Ronald Reagan Presidential Museum and Library.

And it was George Washington who said that "of all the dispositions and habits which lead to political prosperity, religion and morality are indispensable supports."

And finally, that shrewdest of all observers of American democracy, Alexis de Tocqueville, put it eloquently after he had gone on a search for the secret of America's greatness and genius – and he said, "Not until I went into the churches of America and heard her pulpits aflame with righteousness did I understand the greatness and the genius of America. America is good. And if America ever ceases to be good, America will cease to be great."

Well, I'm pleased to be here today with you who are keeping America great by keeping her good. Only through your work and prayers and those of millions of others can we hope to survive this perilous century and keep alive this experiment in liberty – this last, best hope of man.

I want you to know that this administration is motivated by a political philosophy that sees the greatness of America in you, her people, and in your families, churches, neighborhoods, communities – the institutions that foster and nourish values like concern for others and respect for the rule of law under God.

Now, I don't have to tell you that this puts us in opposition to, or at least out of step with, a prevailing attitude of many who have turned to a modern-day secularism, discarding the tried and time-tested values upon which our very civilization is based. No matter how well intentioned, their value system is radically different from that of most Americans. And while they proclaim that they're freeing us from superstitions of the past, they've taken upon themselves the job of superintending us by government rule and regulation. Sometimes their voices are louder than ours, but they are not yet a majority....

Freedom prospers when religion is vibrant and the rule of law under God is acknowledged. When our Founding Fathers passed the First Amendment, they sought to protect churches from government interference. They never intended to construct a wall of hostility between government and the concept of religious belief itself.

The evidence of this permeates our history and our government. The Declaration of Independence mentions the Supreme Being no less than four times. "In God We Trust" is engraved on our coinage. The Supreme Court opens its proceedings with a religious invocation. And the members of Congress open their sessions with a prayer. I just happen to believe the schoolchildren of the United

States are entitled to the same privileges as Supreme Court Justices and Congressmen....

Now, I'm sure that you must get discouraged at times, but you've done better than you know, perhaps. There's a great spiritual awakening in America, a renewal of the traditional values that have been the bedrock of America's goodness and greatness.

One recent survey by a Washington-based research council concluded that Americans were far more religious than the people of other nations; 95 percent of those surveyed expressed a belief in God and a huge majority believed the Ten Commandments had real meaning in their lives. And another study has found that an overwhelming majority of Americans disapprove of adultery, teenage sex, pornography, abortion, and hard drugs. And this same study showed a deep reverence for the importance of family ties and religious belief.

I think the items that we've discussed here today must be a key part of the Nation's political agenda. For the first time the Congress is openly and seriously debating and dealing with the prayer and abortion issues – and that's enormous progress right there. I repeat: America is in the midst of a spiritual awakening and a moral renewal. And with your Biblical keynote, I say today, "Yes, let justice roll on like a river, righteousness like a never-failing stream.

"Now, obviously, much of this new political and social consensus I've talked about is based on a positive view of American history, one that takes pride in our country's accomplishments and record. But we must never forget that no government schemes are going to perfect man. We know that living in this world means dealing with what philosophers would call the phenomenology of evil or, as theologians would put it, the doctrine of sin.

There is sin and evil in the world, and we're enjoined by Scripture and the Lord Jesus to oppose it with all our might. Our nation, too, has a legacy of evil with which it must deal. The glory of this land has been its capacity for transcending the moral evils of our past. For example, the long struggle of minority citizens for equal rights, once a source of disunity and civil war, is now a point of pride for all Americans. We must never go back. There is no room for racism, anti-Semitism, or other forms of ethnic and racial hatred in this country.

I know that you've been horrified, as have I, by the resurgence of some hate groups preaching bigotry and prejudice. Use the mighty voice of your pulpits and the powerful standing of your churches to denounce and isolate these hate groups in our midst. The commandment given us is clear and simple: "Thou shalt love thy neighbor as thyself." But whatever sad episodes exist in our past, any objective observer must hold a positive view of American history, a history that has been the story of hopes fulfilled and dreams made into reality. Especially in this century, America has kept alight the torch of freedom, but not just for ourselves but for millions of others around the world.

And this brings me to my final point today. During my first press conference as President, in answer to a direct question, I pointed out that, as good Marxist-Leninists, the Soviet leaders have openly and publicly declared that the only morality they recognize is that which will further their cause, which is world revolution. I think I should point out I was only quoting Lenin, their guiding spirit, who said in 1920 that they repudiate all morality that proceeds from supernatural ideas – that's their name for religion – or ideas that are outside class conceptions. Morality is entirely subordinate to the interests of class war. And everything is moral that is necessary for the annihilation of the old, exploiting social order and for uniting the proletariat.

Well, I think the refusal of many influential people to accept this elementary fact of Soviet doctrine illustrates an historical reluctance to see totalitarian powers for what they are. We saw this phenomenon in the 1930's. We see it too often today. This doesn't mean we should isolate ourselves and refuse to seek an understanding with them. I intend to do everything I can to persuade them of our peaceful intent, to remind them that it was the West that refused to use its nuclear monopoly in the forties and fifties for territorial gain and which now proposes 50-percent cut in strategic ballistic missiles and the elimination of an entire class of land-based, intermediate-range nuclear missiles.

At the same time, however, they must be made to understand we will never compromise our principles and standards. We will never give away our freedom. We will never abandon our belief in God. And we will never stop searching for a genuine peace. But we can assure none of these things America stands for through the so-called nuclear freeze solutions proposed by some.

The truth is that a freeze now would be a very dangerous fraud, for that is merely the illusion of peace. The reality is that we must find peace through strength.

I would agree to a freeze if only we could freeze the Soviets' global desires. A freeze at current levels of weapons would remove any incentive for the Soviets to negotiate seriously in Geneva and virtually end our chances to achieve the major arms reductions which we have proposed. Instead, they would achieve their objectives through the freeze.

A freeze would reward the Soviet Union for its enormous and unparalleled military buildup. It would prevent the essential and long overdue modernization of United States and allied defenses and would leave our aging forces increasingly vulnerable. And an honest freeze would require extensive prior negotiations on the systems and numbers to be limited and on the measures to ensure effective verification and compliance. And the kind of a freeze that has been suggested would be virtually impossible to verify. Such a major effort would divert us completely from our current negotiations on achieving substantial reductions.

A number of years ago, I heard a young father, a very prominent young man in the entertainment world, addressing a tremendous gathering in California. It was during the time of the Cold War, and communism and our own way of life were very much on people's minds. And he was speaking to that subject. And suddenly, though, I heard him saying, "I love my little girls more than anything – "And I said to myself, "Oh, no, don't. You can't – don't say that."

But I had underestimated him. He went on: "I would rather see my little girls die now, still believing in God, than have them grow up under communism and one day die no longer believing in God."

There were thousands of young people in that audience. They came to their feet with shouts of joy. They had instantly recognized the profound truth in what he had said, with regard to the physical and the soul and what was truly important.

Yes, let us pray for the salvation of all of those who live in that totalitarian darkness – pray they will discover the joy of knowing God. But until they do, let us be aware that while they preach the supremacy of the state, declare its omnipotence over individual man, and predict its eventual domination of all peoples on the Earth, they are the focus of evil in the modern world.

It was C.S. Lewis who, in his unforgettable *Screwtape Letters*, wrote: "The greatest evil is not done now in those sordid 'dens of crime' that Dickens loved to paint. It is not even done in concentration camps and labor camps. In those we see its final result. But it is conceived and ordered (moved, seconded, carried and minuted) in clear, carpeted, warmed, and well-lighted offices, by quiet men with white collars and cut fingernails and smooth-shaven cheeks who do not need to raise their voice."

Well, because these "quiet men" do not "raise their voices"; because they sometimes speak in soothing tones of brotherhood and peace; because, like other dictators before them, they're always making "their final territorial demand," some would have us accept them at their word and accommodate ourselves to their aggressive impulses. But if history teaches anything, it teaches that simple-minded appeasement or wishful thinking about our adversaries is folly. It means the betrayal of our past, the squandering of our freedom.

So, I urge you to speak out against those who would place the United States in a position of military and moral inferiority. You know, I've always believed that old Screwtape reserved his best efforts for those of you in the church. So, in your discussions of the nuclear freeze proposals, I urge you to beware the temptation of pride – the temptation of blithely declaring yourselves above it all and label both sides equally at fault, to ignore the facts of history and the aggressive impulses of an evil empire, to simply call the arms race a giant misunderstanding and thereby remove yourself from the struggle between right and wrong and good and evil.

I ask you to resist the attempts of those who would have you withhold your support for our efforts, this administration's efforts, to keep America strong and free, while we negotiate real and verifiable reductions in the world's nuclear arsenals and one day, with God's help, their total elimination.

While America's military strength is important, let me add here that I've always maintained that the struggle now going on for the world will never be decided by bombs or rockets, by armies or military might. The real crisis we face today is a spiritual one; at root, it is a test of moral will and faith.

Whittaker Chambers, the man whose own religious conversion made him a witness to one of the terrible traumas of our time, the Hiss-Chambers case, wrote that the crisis of the Western World exists to the degree in which the West is indifferent to God, the degree to which it collaborates in communism's attempt to make man stand alone without God. And then he said, for Marxism-Leninism is actually the second oldest faith, first proclaimed in the Garden of Eden with the words of temptation, "Ye shall be as gods."

The Western world can answer this challenge, he wrote, "but only provided that its faith in God and the freedom He enjoins is as great as communism's faith in Man."

I believe we shall rise to the challenge. I believe that communism is another sad, bizarre chapter in human history whose last pages even now are being written. I believe this because the source of our strength in the quest for human freedom is not material, but spiritual. And because it knows no limitation, it must terrify and ultimately triumph over those who would enslave their fellow man. For in the words of Isaiah: "He giveth power to the faint; and to them that have no might He increased strength But they that wait upon the Lord shall renew their strength; they shall mount up with wings as eagles; they shall run, and not be weary."

Yes, change your world. One of our Founding Fathers, Thomas Paine, said, "We have it within our power to begin the world over again." We can do it, doing together what no one church could do by itself.

'Mr. Gorbachev, tear down this wall!'
Ronald Reagan (1987)[41]

Six years into his presidency, Ronald Reagan saw his strategy come to fruition. His 1982 strategy to open up closed societies in the Soviet bloc, his 1983 NSDD declaring political warfare on the Soviet Union, and his other public diplomacy improvements, integrated with an economic warfare campaign and a military buildup to challenge the Soviets, were credited with forcing the USSR to open itself up to reforms.

And though he was on friendly personal terms with Soviet Communist Party leader Mikhail Gorbachev, Reagan continued to challenge the Russian to do more – so much more that it would mean the unraveling of the Soviet empire. On June 12, 1987, Reagan appeared at the Brandenburg Gate in West Berlin with Chancellor Helmut Kohl. Connecting directly with the German people, Reagan reminisced about President Kennedy's "Ich bin ein Berliner" speech of nearly two-and-a-half decades before, and noted the 40th anniversary of the Marshall Plan and all the

[41] Ronald Reagan, "Remarks at Brandenburg Gate," West Berlin, West Germany, June 12, 1987. Courtesy of the Ronald Reagan Presidential Foundation and Library.

prosperity the U.S.-led effort had brought to Germans in the free West.

Berliners in the communist eastern sector of the city could hear Reagan's speech as the American president challenged the Soviet leader to tear down the Berlin Wall. The event would mark the culmination of Reagan's public diplomacy and political warfare campaign to force the USSR to collapse and encourage the Soviet people to organize for democracy.

Some in the State Department thought Reagan's challenge, at the very symbol of Soviet occupation of Eastern Europe, was unnecessarily provocative. Speechwriter Peter Robinson recalls that Secretary of State George P. Shultz, White House Chief of Staff Howard Baker, and Deputy National Security Advisor Colin Powell tried and failed to have the "tear down this wall" challenge removed from the speech for fear the words would offend the Kremlin.

But the public diplomacy professionals at the U.S. Information Agency were with the program. The Voice of America and RFE/RL broadcast the speech live, translated into various languages, to amplify the president's voice in denied areas. Because the speech so masterfully combines aggressive challenge with positive vision, identification with a local foreign audience in remarks meant for the world, and references to history as guides to build a brighter future, the text appears here in full.

Chancellor Kohl, Governing Mayor Diepgen, ladies and gentlemen: Twenty-four years ago, President John F. Kennedy visited Berlin, speaking to the people of this city and the world at the City Hall. Well, since then two other presidents have come, each in his turn, to Berlin. And today I, myself, make my second visit to your city.

We come to Berlin, we American presidents, because it's our duty to speak, in this place, of freedom. But I must confess, we're drawn here by other things as well: by the feeling of history in this city, more than 500 years older than our own nation; by the beauty of the Grunewald and the Tiergarten; most of all, by your courage and determination. Perhaps the composer Paul Lincke understood something about American presidents. You see, like so many presidents before me, I come here today because wherever I go, whatever I do: *Ich hab noch einen Koffer in Berlin.* [I still have a suitcase in Berlin.]

Our gathering today is being broadcast throughout Western Europe and North America. I understand that it is being seen and heard as well in the East. To those listening throughout Eastern Europe, a special word: Although I cannot be with you, I address my remarks to you just as surely as to those standing here before me. For I join you, as I join your fellow countrymen in the West, in this firm, this unalterable belief: *Es gibt nur ein Berlin.* [There is only one Berlin.]

Behind me stands a wall that encircles the free sectors of this city, part of a vast system of barriers that divides the entire continent of Europe. From the Baltic, south, those barriers cut across Germany in a gash of barbed wire, concrete, dog runs, and guard towers. Farther south, there may be no visible, no obvious wall. But there remain armed guards and checkpoints all the same – still a restriction on the right to travel, still an instrument to impose upon ordinary men and women the will of a totalitarian state. Yet it is here in Berlin where the wall emerges most clearly; here, cutting across your city, where the news photo and the television screen have imprinted this brutal division of a continent upon the mind of the world. Standing before the Brandenburg Gate, every man is a German, separated from his fellow men. Every man is a Berliner, forced to look upon a scar.

President von Weizsacker has said, "The German question is open as long as the Brandenburg Gate is closed." Today I say: As long as the gate is closed, as long as this scar of a wall is permitted to stand, it is not the German question alone that remains open, but the question of freedom for all mankind. Yet I do not come here to lament. For I find in Berlin a message of hope, even in the shadow of this wall, a message of triumph.

In this season of spring in 1945, the people of Berlin emerged from their air-raid shelters to find devastation. Thousands of miles away, the people of the United States reached out to help. And in 1947 Secretary of State – as you've been told – George Marshall announced the creation of what would become known as the Marshall Plan. Speaking precisely 40 years ago this month, he said: "Our policy is directed not against any country or doctrine, but against hunger, poverty, desperation, and chaos."

In the Reichstag a few moments ago, I saw a display commemorating this 40th anniversary of the Marshall Plan. I was struck by the sign on a burnt-out, gutted structure that was being rebuilt. I understand that Berliners of my own generation can remember seeing signs like it dotted throughout the western sectors of the city. The sign read simply: "The Marshall Plan is helping here to strengthen the free world." A strong, free world in the West, that dream became real. Japan rose from ruin to become an economic giant. Italy, France, Belgium – virtually every nation in Western Europe saw political and economic rebirth; the European Community was founded.

In West Germany and here in Berlin, there took place an economic miracle, the *Wirtschaftswunder*. Adenauer, Erhard, Reuter, and other leaders understood the practical importance of liberty – that just as truth can flourish only when the journalist is given freedom of speech, so prosperity can come about only when the farmer and businessman enjoy economic freedom. The German leaders reduced tariffs, expanded free trade, lowered taxes. From 1950 to 1960 alone, the standard of living in West Germany and Berlin doubled.

Where four decades ago there was rubble, today in West Berlin there is the greatest industrial output of any city in Germany–busy office blocks, fine homes and apartments, proud avenues, and the spreading lawns of parkland. Where a city's culture seemed to have been destroyed, today there are two great universities, orchestras and an opera, countless theaters, and museums. Where there was want, today there's abundance – food, clothing, automobiles – the wonderful goods of the Ku'damm. From devastation, from utter ruin, you Berliners have, in freedom, rebuilt a city that once again ranks as one of the greatest on earth. The Soviets may have had other plans. But my friends, there were a few things the Soviets didn't count on – *Berliner Herz, Berliner Humor, ja, und Berliner Schnauze*. [Berliner heart, Berliner humor, yes, and a Berliner Schnauze.]

In the 1950s, Khrushchev predicted: "We will bury you." But in the West today, we see a free world that has achieved a level of prosperity and well-being unprecedented in all human history. In the Communist world, we see failure, technological backwardness, declining standards of health, even want of the most basic kind–too little food. Even today, the Soviet Union still cannot feed itself. After these four decades, then, there stands before the entire world one great and inescapable conclusion: Freedom leads to prosperity. Freedom replaces the ancient hatreds among the nations with comity and peace. Freedom is the victor.

And now the Soviets themselves may, in a limited way, be coming to understand the importance of freedom. We hear much from Moscow about a new policy of reform and openness. Some political prisoners have been released. Certain foreign news broadcasts are no longer being jammed. Some economic enterprises have been permitted to operate with greater freedom from state control.

Are these the beginnings of profound changes in the Soviet state? Or are they token gestures, intended to raise false hopes in the West, or to strengthen the Soviet system without changing it? We welcome change and openness; for we believe that freedom and security go together, that the advance of human liberty can only strengthen the cause of world peace. There is one sign the Soviets can make that would be unmistakable, that would advance dramatically the cause of freedom and peace.

General Secretary Gorbachev, if you seek peace, if you seek prosperity for the Soviet Union and Eastern Europe, if you seek liberalization: Come here to this gate! Mr. Gorbachev, open this gate! Mr. Gorbachev, tear down this wall!

I understand the fear of war and the pain of division that afflict this continent – and I pledge to you my country's efforts to help overcome these burdens. To be sure, we in the West must resist Soviet expansion. So we must maintain defenses of unassailable strength. Yet we seek peace; so we must strive to reduce arms on both sides.

Beginning 10 years ago, the Soviets challenged the Western alliance with a grave new threat, hundreds of new and more deadly SS-20 nuclear missiles, capable of striking every capital in Europe. The Western alliance responded by committing itself to a counter-deployment unless the Soviets agreed to negotiate a better solution; namely, the elimination of such weapons on both sides. For many months, the Soviets refused to bargain in earnestness. As the alliance, in turn, prepared to go forward with its counter-deployment, there were difficult days – days of protests like those during my 1982 visit to this city – and the Soviets later walked away from the table.

But through it all, the alliance held firm. And I invite those who protested then – I invite those who protest today – to mark this fact: Because we remained strong, the Soviets came back to the table. And because we remained strong, today we have within reach the possibility, not merely of limiting the growth of arms, but of eliminating, for the first time, an entire class of nuclear weapons from the face of the earth.

As I speak, NATO ministers are meeting in Iceland to review the progress of our proposals for eliminating these weapons. At the talks in Geneva, we have also proposed deep cuts in strategic offensive weapons. And the Western allies have likewise made far-reaching proposals to reduce the danger of conventional war and to place a total ban on chemical weapons.

While we pursue these arms reductions, I pledge to you that we will maintain the capacity to deter Soviet aggression at any level at which it might occur. And in cooperation with many of our allies, the United States is pursuing the Strategic Defense Initiative – research to base deterrence not on the threat of offensive retaliation, but on defenses that truly defend; on systems, in short, that will not target populations, but shield them. By these means we seek to increase the safety of Europe and all the world. But we must remember a crucial fact: East and West do not mistrust each other because we are armed; we are armed because we mistrust each other. And our differences are not about weapons but about liberty. When President Kennedy spoke at the City Hall those 24 years ago, freedom was encircled, Berlin was under siege. And today, despite all the pressures upon this city, Berlin stands secure in its liberty. And freedom itself is transforming the globe.

In the Philippines, in South and Central America, democracy has been given a rebirth. Throughout the Pacific, free markets are working miracle after miracle of economic growth. In the industrialized nations, a technological revolution is taking place–a revolution marked by rapid, dramatic advances in computers and telecommunications.

In Europe, only one nation and those it controls refuse to join the community of freedom. Yet in this age of redoubled economic growth, of information and innovation, the Soviet Union faces a choice: It must make fundamental changes, or it will become obsolete.

Today thus represents a moment of hope. We in the West stand ready to cooperate with the East to promote true openness, to break down barriers that separate people, to create a safe, freer world. And surely there is no better place than Berlin, the meeting place of East and West, to make a start. Free people of Berlin: Today, as in the past, the United States stands for the strict observance and full implementation of all parts of the Four Power Agreement of 1971. Let us use this occasion, the 750th anniversary of this city, to usher in a new era, to seek a still fuller, richer life for the Berlin of the future. Together, let us maintain and develop the ties between the

Federal Republic and the Western sectors of Berlin, which is permitted by the 1971 agreement.

And I invite Mr. Gorbachev: Let us work to bring the Eastern and Western parts of the city closer together, so that all the inhabitants of all Berlin can enjoy the benefits that come with life in one of the great cities of the world.

To open Berlin still further to all Europe, East and West, let us expand the vital air access to this city, finding ways of making commercial air service to Berlin more convenient, more comfortable, and more economical. We look to the day when West Berlin can become one of the chief aviation hubs in all central Europe.

With our French and British partners, the United States is prepared to help bring international meetings to Berlin. It would be only fitting for Berlin to serve as the site of United Nations meetings, or world conferences on human rights and arms control or other issues that call for international cooperation.

There is no better way to establish hope for the future than to enlighten young minds, and we would be honored to sponsor summer youth exchanges, cultural events, and other programs for young Berliners from the East. Our French and British friends, I'm certain, will do the same. And it's my hope that an authority can be found in East Berlin to sponsor visits from young people of the Western sectors.

One final proposal, one close to my heart: Sport represents a source of enjoyment and ennoblement, and you may have noted that the Republic of Korea – South Korea – has offered to permit certain events of the 1988 Olympics to take place in the North. International sports competitions of all kinds could take place in both parts of this city. And what better way to demonstrate to the world the openness of this city than to offer in some future year to hold the Olympic games here in Berlin, East and West? In these four decades, as I have said, you Berliners have built a great city. You've done so in spite of threats – the Soviet attempts to impose the East-mark, the blockade. Today the city thrives in spite of the challenges implicit in the very presence of this wall. What keeps you here? Certainly there's a great deal to be said for your fortitude, for your defiant courage. But I believe there's something deeper, something that involves Berlin's whole look and feel and way of life–not mere sentiment. No one could live long in Berlin without being completely disabused of illusions. Something instead, that has seen the difficulties of life in Berlin but chose to accept them, that continues to build this good and proud city in contrast to a surrounding totalitarian presence that refuses to release human energies or aspirations. Something that speaks with a powerful voice of affirmation, that says yes to this city, yes to the future, yes to freedom. In a word, I would submit that what keeps you in Berlin is love – love both profound and abiding.

Perhaps this gets to the root of the matter, to the most fundamental distinction of all between East and West. The totalitarian world produces backwardness because it does such violence to the spirit, thwarting the human impulse to create, to enjoy, to worship. The totalitarian world finds even symbols of love and of worship an affront. Years ago, before the East Germans began rebuilding their churches, they erected a secular structure: the television tower at Alexander Platz. Virtually ever since, the authorities have been working to correct what they view as the tower's one major flaw, treating the glass sphere at the top with paints and chemicals of every kind. Yet even today when the sun strikes that sphere – that sphere that towers over all Berlin – the light makes the sign of the cross. There in Berlin, like the city itself, symbols of love, symbols of worship, cannot be suppressed.

As I looked out a moment ago from the Reichstag, that embodiment of German unity, I noticed words crudely spray-painted upon the wall, perhaps by a young Berliner: "This wall will fall. Beliefs become reality." Yes, across Europe, this wall will fall. For it cannot withstand faith; it cannot withstand truth. The wall cannot withstand freedom.

And I would like, before I close, to say one word. I have read, and I have been questioned since I've been here about certain demonstrations against my coming. And I would like to say just one thing, and to those who demonstrate so. I wonder if they have ever asked themselves that if they should have the kind of government they apparently seek, no one would ever be able to do what they're doing again.

Thank you and God bless you all.

Truth and Trust

Truth-telling liar
Aesop (6th century, B.C.)[42]

There is no believing a liar, even when he speaks the truth.

'Act sincerely'
Aesop (6th century, B.C.)[43]

A Hound, having started a Hare on the hillside, pursued her for some distance, at one time biting her with his teeth as if he would take her life, and at another fawning upon her, as if in play with another dog. The Hare said to him, "I wish you would act sincerely by me, and show yourself in your true colors. If you are a friend, why do you bite me so hard? If an enemy, why do you fawn on me?'

Moral: No one can be a friend if you know not whether to trust or distrust him.

Biases color the perception of truth
Pericles (431 B.C.)[44]

Difficult, indeed, it is, judiciously to handle a subject where even probable truth will hardly gain assent. The hearer, enlightened by a long acquaintance, and warm in his affection, may quickly

---

[42] Aesop, "The Shepherd's Boy and the Wolf," trans. George Fyler Townsend. There is no copyright on the Townsend translation.
[43] Aesop, "The Dog and the Hare," trans. George Fyler Townsend.
[44] Pericles, "Funeral Oration," 431 B.C., in Lewis Copeland, et al., eds., *The World's Great Speeches*, 4th ed. (Dover, 1999), p. 3. Pericles was an Athenian statesman who gave the classic funeral oration to memorialize the first Athenian soldiers who died in the Peloponnesian War.

pronounce everything unfavorably expressed in respect to what he wishes and what he knows – while the stranger pronounces all exaggerated through envy of those deeds which he is conscious are above his own achievement. For the praises bestowed upon others are then only to be endured, when men imagine they can do those feats they hear to have been done; they envy what they cannot equal, and immediately pronounce it false.

Campaign of Truth
President Harry S Truman (1950)[45]

Shortly after the writing of NSC-68 in 1950, President Harry S Truman addressed journalists in a speech to the National Society of Newspaper Editors. He exhorted them to be part of a "campaign of truth" against Soviet propaganda. The full text appears below.

I am happy to be here today with this group of editors. You and I have a great many important problems in common, and one of the most important of these is the responsibility we share in helping to make the foreign policy of the United States of America. That is why I am going to take this opportunity to discuss with you some of the aspects of that policy.

No group of men in this country is of greater importance to our foreign policy than the group your society represents.

In a democracy foreign policy is based on the decisions of the people.

One vital function of a free press is to present the facts on which the citizens of a democracy can base their decisions. You are a link between the American people and world affairs. If you inform the people well and completely, their decisions will be good. If you misinform them, their decisions will be bad; our country will suffer and the world will suffer.

You cannot make up people's minds for them. What you can do is to give them the facts they need to make up their own minds. Now that is a tremendous responsibility.

Most of you are meeting that responsibility well – but I am sorry to say a few are meeting it very badly. Foreign policy is not a matter for partisan presentation. The facts about Europe or Asia should not

---

[45] President Harry S Truman, speech to the National Society of Newspaper Editors, April 20, 1950. Courtesy of the Truman Museum and Library.

be twisted to conform to one side or the other of a political dispute. Twisting the facts might change the course of an election here at home, but it would certainly damage our country's program abroad.

In many other countries today, the papers print about foreign affairs only what their governments tell them to print. They can't add anything, or cut anything. In the democracies, the papers have a free hand. Only in a democracy is there such mutual trust and confidence among citizens that a private group is given such an all-important role in determining what the Nation as a whole shall do. There is too much nonsense about striped trousers in foreign affairs. Far more influence is exerted at home by the baggy pants of the managing editor than ever is exerted by the striped pants in the State Department.

There never has been a time in our history when there was so great a need for our citizens to be informed and to understand what is happening in the world.

The cause of freedom is being challenged throughout the world today by the forces of imperialistic communism. This is a struggle, above all else, for the minds of men. Propaganda is one of the most powerful weapons the Communists have in this struggle. Deceit, distortion, and lies are systematically used by them as a matter of deliberate policy.

This propaganda can be overcome by the truth – plain, simple, unvarnished truth – presented by the newspapers, radio, newsreels, and other sources that the people trust. If the people are not told the truth, or if they do not have confidence in the accuracy and fairness of the press, they have no defense against falsehoods. But if they are given the true facts, these falsehoods become laughable instead of dangerous.

We can have confidence that the free press of the United States and most of the other free nations will keep us from being deceived by Communist propaganda. But in other parts of the world the struggle between falsehood and truth is far more intense and far more dangerous.

Communist propaganda is so false, so crude, so blatant, that we wonder how men can be swayed by it. We forget that most of the people to whom it is directed do not have free access to accurate information. We forget that they do not hear our broadcasts or read impartial newspapers. We forget that they do not have a chance to learn the truth by traveling abroad or by talking freely to travelers in their own countries.

All too often the people who are subject to Communist propaganda do not know Americans, or citizens of other free nations, as we really are. They do not know us as farmers and as workers. They do not know us as people having hopes and problems like their own. Our way of life is something strange to them. They do not even know what we mean when we say "democracy."

This presents one of the greatest tasks facing the free nations today. That task is nothing less than to meet false propaganda with truth all around the globe. Everywhere that the propaganda of the Communist totalitarianism is spread, we must meet it and overcome it with honest information about freedom and democracy.

In recent years there has been tremendous progress all over the world in education and the exchange of ideas. This progress has stirred men everywhere to new desires and new ambitions. They want greater knowledge, they want better lives, they want to be masters of their own affairs. We have helped and encouraged these people, but the Communists have seized upon their desires and ambitions and are seeking to exploit them for their own selfish purposes.

In the Far East, for example, millions are restlessly seeking to break away from the conditions of poverty and misery that have surrounded them in the past. The Communists understand this situation very well. They are trying to move in and take advantage of these aspirations. They are making glittering promises about the benefits of communism. They reach directly to the peasant or the villager in these vast areas, and talk to him directly in his own tongue about the things he has learned to desire. They say that they can get these things for him. And too often he hears no voice from our side to that dispute.

We know how false these Communist promises are. But it is not enough for us to know this. Unless we get the real story across to the people in other countries, we will lose the battle for men's minds by pure default.

The Communist propaganda portrays the Soviet Union as the world's foremost advocate of peace and the protector of defenseless peoples. The contradiction between what the Communist leaders have promised and what they have actually done is so startling that we are amazed that anyone can be deceived. In Berlin, in Czechoslovakia, in the Balkans, in the Far East, they have proved, time after time, that their talk about peace is only a cloak for imperialism. But their intended victims will not learn these facts from Soviet propaganda. We are the ones who must make sure that the truth about communism is known everywhere.

At the same time, we must overcome the constant stream of slander and vilification that the Communists pour out in an effort to discredit the United States and other free nations.

Soviet propaganda constantly reviles the United States as a nation of "warmongers" and "imperialists." You and I know how absurd this is. We know that the United States is wholly dedicated to the cause of peace. We have no purpose of going to war except in the defense of freedom. Our actions demonstrate that we mean exactly what we say. But when men throughout the world are making their choice between communism and democracy, the important thing is not what we know about our purposes and our actions–the important thing is what they know.

Communist propaganda also seeks to destroy our influence in the world by saying the American economy is weak and about to collapse. We know this is preposterous. The industrial production of the United States is equal to that of all the rest of the world combined. Our agricultural production is more than adequate for our needs. Our people enjoy the highest standard of living in the history of the world. Our economic strength is the bulwark of the free world.

From every standpoint, our free way of life is vastly superior to the system of oppression which the Communists seek to impose upon mankind. In many parts of the world, however, where men must choose between freedom and communism, the story is going untold.

We cannot run the risk that nations may be lost to the cause of freedom, because their people do not know the facts.

I am convinced that we should greatly extend and strengthen our efforts to make the truth known to people in all the world.

Most of us have recognized for years, of course, how important it is to spread the truth about freedom and democracy. We are already doing some very good work – through the "Voice of America" and the United States information offices and libraries in many parts of the world, through the exchange of students, through the United Nations and its affiliated organizations, and in many other ways. But events have shown, I believe, that we need to do much more, both ourselves and in cooperation with the other free nations. We must use every means at our command, private as well as governmental, to get the truth to other peoples.

Private groups and organizations have an important part to play. Our labor unions have already done fine work in communicating with labor in Europe, in Latin America, and elsewhere. The story of free American labor, told by American trade unionists, is a better weapon against Communist propaganda among workers in other countries than any number of speeches by Government officials.

The same principle applies to other groups. The best way for farmers in other countries to find out about us is to talk directly with our own farmers. Our businessmen can speak directly to businessmen abroad. We need to promote much more direct contact between our people and those of other countries.

We should encourage many more people from other countries to visit us here, to see for themselves what is true and what is not true about this great country of ours. We should find more opportunities for foreign students to study in our schools and universities. They will learn here the skills and techniques needed in their own countries. They will also see at first hand the rights and duties of citizens in our land of democratic institutions.

Our colleges should train more Americans to go abroad as teachers, especially to teach modern methods of farming, industry, and public health – and, by example, to teach our concepts of democracy. The notable record of our many charitable and religious organizations who send teachers abroad is a proof of what can be done.

Another major part of our effort must be carried out through our great public information channels – newspapers and magazines, radio, and motion pictures. We must strive constantly to break down or leap over barriers to free communication wherever they exist. We must make full use of every effective means of communicating information, in simple, understandable form, to people whose backgrounds and cultures are different from our own.

This poses an enormous challenge to groups such as yours, a challenge which can be met only by extraordinary inventiveness and enterprise. I am confident that the American press can and will make a tremendously useful contribution toward finding new solutions.

The Government's programs for telling the truth about the United States to the peoples of the world also need constant improvement. Our present overseas information and educational exchange program is getting results. For example, the "Voice of America" has been carrying to people behind the Iron Curtain the true story of world events. It has been so successful that the Soviet government is using a vast amount of costly equipment in an attempt to drown out our broadcasts by jamming. We must devise ways to break through that jamming and get our message across. And we must improve and strengthen our whole range of information and educational services.

This is not a conclusion reached by Government officials alone. We have had the valuable aid of the United States Advisory Commission on Information created by the Congress. Your own society is ably represented on that commission by Mr. Mark Ethridge and Mr. Erwin D. Canham. The members of the Commission have given intensive study to the overseas information program and have made repeated recommendations that it be substantially expanded. Similar recommendations for the exchange program have been made by the Advisory Commission on Education, headed by Dr. Harvie Branscomb. I have been glad to see that many members of the Congress have urged an improved and expanded program in these fields – as shown, for example, by the resolution introduced recently by Senator Benton for himself and a number of his colleagues.

Because of the pressing need to increase our efforts along this line, I have directed the Secretary of State to plan a strengthened and more effective national effort to use the great power of truth in working for peace. This effort will require the imagination and energies of private individuals and groups throughout the country. We shall need to use fully all the private and governmental means that have proved successful so far-and to discover and employ a great many new ones.

Our task is to present the truth to millions of people who are uninformed or misinformed or unconvinced. Our task is to reach them in their daily lives, as they work and learn. We must be alert, ingenious, and diligent in reaching peoples of other countries, whatever their educational and cultural backgrounds may be. Our task is to show them that freedom is the way to economic and social advancement, the way to political independence, the way to strength, happiness, and peace.

This task is not separate and distinct from other elements of our foreign policy. It is a necessary part of all we are doing to build a peaceful world. It is as important as armed strength or economic aid. The Marshall plan, military aid, point 4 – these and other programs depend for their success on the understanding and support of our own citizens and those of other countries.

We must make ourselves known as we really are – not as Communist propaganda pictures us. We must pool our efforts with those of other free peoples in a sustained, intensified program to promote the cause of freedom against the propaganda of slavery. We must make ourselves heard round the world in a great campaign of truth.

We have tremendous advantages in the struggle for men's minds and loyalties. We have truth and freedom on our side. The appeal of free institutions and self-government springs from the deepest and noblest aspirations of mankind. It is based on every man's desire for liberty and opportunity. It is based on every man's wish to be self-reliant and to shape his own destiny.

As we go forward with our campaign of truth, we will make lasting progress toward the kind of world we seek – a world in which men and nations live not as enemies but as friends and brothers.

Truth is the Best Propaganda
Edward R. Murrow (1963)[46]

We operate on the basis of truth. Voice of America news broadcasts are balanced and objective. They cover all the news, even when it hurts.

American traditions and the American ethic require us to be truthful, but the most important reason is that truth is the best propaganda and lies are the worst. To be persuasive we must be believable; to be believable we must be credible; to be credible we must be truthful. It is as simple as that.

---

[46] "Statement of Hon. Edward R. Murrow, Director, U.S. Information Agency," in *Winning the Cold War: The U.S. Ideological Offensive*, Hearings before the Subcommittee on International Organizations and Movements, Committee on Foreign Affairs, U.S. House of Representatives, 88th Congress, First Session, Part I, March 28, 1963, pp. 3-4. Murrow was a prolific news broadcaster whom President Kennedy appointed to direct USIA.

Voice of America Charter
Voice of America (1960) [47]

The Voice of America (VOA) is the official international broadcast voice of the United States government, but it is not a government mouthpiece. VOA maintains its editorial independence. This independence can be an annoyance to policymakers, but has been the Voice's main strength over the decades, earning the confidence of generations of people around the world. The VOA strives to be accurate as a news organization, presenting many American sides to issues, but with a general approach consistent with the national interest. The charter defines VOA's role.

The long-range interests of the United States are served by communicating directly with the peoples of the world by radio. To be effective, the Voice of America must win the attention and respect of listeners. These principles will therefore govern Voice of America (VOA) broadcasts.

1. VOA will serve as a consistently reliable and authoritative source of news. VOA news will be accurate, objective, and comprehensive.
2. VOA will represent America, not any single segment of American society, and will therefore present a balanced and comprehensive projection of significant American thought and institutions.
3. VOA will present the policies of the United States clearly and effectively, and will also present responsible discussions and opinion on these policies.

RFE/RL Code of professional journalism standards
Radio Free Europe/Radio Liberty[48]

While maintaining their objectivity and journalistic integrity, Radio Free Europe and Radio Liberty also have a set of principles that reinforces a mission to promote the spread of freedom among

---

[47] Authored in 1960, the VOA Charter was codified into federal law as Public Law 94-350 on July 12, 1976. Courtesy of Alan L. Heil, Jr.
[48] Copyright © 2007. RFE/RL, Inc. Reprinted with the permission of Radio Free Europe/Radio Liberty, 1201 Connecticut Ave. N.W., Washington DC 20036.

their listeners. RFE/RL radios are not voices of the United States, but serve as "surrogate radios," or free voices of the people in their respective broadcast areas, usually where freedom is new, threatened or repressed. RFE/RL's Code of Professional Journalism Standards sets the practice.

All RFE/RL journalists and journalistic contributors must observe the following principles:

Accuracy

RFE/RL journalists will do their utmost to ensure that all broadcasts and publications (including those transmitted via the Internet) are factually accurate. Where doubt or controversy may exist on significant points of fact, information must be based on at least two independent sources.

RFE/RL journalists will not broadcast or publish material that is based on rumor or unsubstantiated information.

Factual errors will be corrected as soon as possible.

Impartiality

Information will be presented in a factual context that enhances understanding of the events and issues and provides clarity without distortion or bias.

Journalists will present opposing or differing views accurately and in a balanced manner on all issues. When groups or individuals whose views are important for balanced programming decline to comment, it is appropriate to note this in the story or article.

RFE/RL shall be independent from any political party, ruling or opposition group, émigré organization, commercial or other special-interest organization, or religious body, whether inside or outside the set of countries to which RFE/RL broadcasts radio or television programming (the "Broadcasting Area"); and shall not endorse or advocate any specific political, economic, or religious viewpoint.

Analysis, Commentary, and Editorials

All broadcasts and publications should contain elements of background information and explanation that help the audience better understand the significance and consequences of the information being reported. Journalists must not insert their personal opinions or judgments in factual reports.

Commentaries should generally be avoided. RFE/RL prefers assessment to personal points of view. Commentaries may be written by RFE/RL staffers only in very exceptional cases and only if approved in advance by the Director of Broadcasting; or an Associate Director of Broadcasting. Commentaries provided by an outside expert must meet RFE/RL's professional standards.

Tone of Moderation and Respect

Broadcasts and publications shall at all times maintain a calm and moderate tone and project a model of civilized, reasoned discourse and a respect for the human rights of all persons. Broadcasts and publications shall not contain religious, ethnic, socio-economic, or cultural slurs upon any person or groups and shall observe common standards of etiquette and taste.

Broadcasts and publications shall not contain material that could be construed as inflammatory or as incitement to violence. Programming on disturbances or other tense situations must be balanced and factual.

Avoidance of Advocacy

RFE/RL supports democracy and the human rights common to democratic states. However, RFE/RL shall not advocate the adoption of specific policies or legislation; nor shall programming endorse or oppose candidates for elective or appointed office.

RFE/RL supports the right of all peoples to self-determination as stated in the Helsinki Final Act of the Conference on Security and Cooperation in Europe. However, broadcasts and publications shall not advocate or endorse separatist or secessionist causes.

RFE/RL supports freedom of travel and migration for all peoples in accordance with internationally recognized norms. However, RFE/RL broadcasts and publications shall not incite the act of defection or encourage emigration.

Ethical Conduct

RFE/RL staff and contributors to programs and publications shall maintain the highest ethical standards in all conduct, taking particular care to avoid any conflict of interest, or the appearance thereof, in their relations with individuals, groups, political or commercial interests inside or outside the Broadcast Area. RFE/RL staff and contributors shall in no way abuse their status as public figures or the good reputation of RFE/RL to promote personal interest or gain. See policy on Conflict of Interest.

Cultural Diplomacy

An art form since the Bronze Age
Richard T. Arndt (2005) [49]

[A] few selective glimpses into three thousand years of history, lingering here and there, will remind us that the well-read American Founders, however gifted, did not invent the diplomacy of cultures. For at least three millennia before them, cultural diplomacy had been the first resort of kings.

Recorded since the Bronze Age, cultural diplomacy has been a norm for humans intent upon civilization. By the third millennium B.C.E. [sic], diplomacy had evolved, in parallel with language, to permit cooperation between large groups. Moving beyond rituals and ceremonies, chants and dance, language conveyed ideas and permitted forward planning, self-awareness, and reflection. While brute force could still destroy civilization, diplomacy tried to preserve it by linking cultures to cultures.

Diplomats were the king's surrogates. They carried messages, and the best of them also brought back learning. Wise adaptive cultures like the Persians and the Greeks eagerly assimilated foreign information and technologies. They were told Arnold Toynbee's "Herodians," who fared better than closed-minded and bullying "Zealots" like the Assyrians or the Chinese of the later T'ang.

Every diplomacy meant relations not between nation-states but between cultures. Adaptive language-cultures, defining themselves over time by custom, then adopted rules, codified them, and turned them into laws, designed to minimize disputes and maximize cooperation. Rules sprang from the metaphors of the family: fatherhood defined dominance, equals were "brothers," and

---

migratory tribes around the globe still boast of hospitality in welcoming "a cousin off the plains," in the classic Arab greeting.

Ritual and ceremony helped measure time and mark seasons. Raymond Cohen notes of Bronze Age intergroup relations that "ceremony was of the essence, enacting men's reverence for the gods, exalting the king over his subjects, sanctifying the conclusion of treaties." Groups exchanged first gifts, then information, then goods and people, including mates; they sent their children to live among the Celts as fosterage – such "exchanges" are as old as time. When trade succeeded raid, plunder and tribute gave way to tariffs and duties. . . .

Culture in fact was power: with the library and its adjoining Museum, a center for scholars like Euclid, Alexandria overtook Pergamum and Athens to become the major center of learning in the Mediterranean world.

Cultural interchange meant a complex and balanced give-and-take of learning and teaching, export and import, weakness and strength, humility and self-confidence. The Greeks' ethical code *paideia* set the tone of a diplomacy in which humility, modesty, and respect for others were key ideas. Approaching other cultures as learning opportunities, the Greeks continually refreshed their minds and launched a golden age of literature, art, science, and philosophy.

Intellect mattered. While earlier groups had stolen sacred fire, new leaders literally competed for scholars and poets. Philip of Macedon lured Aristotle away from Athens to his court. Theater and mass spectacles served political purposes, forged the group's identity, and, according to Aristotle, kept public passions in check. The Greeks sent their best men – poets and philosophers – abroad as ambassadors, especially when Greek power began to wane. Having drawn from earlier civilizations, they gave freely to others.

The linchpin of public diplomacy
Advisory Committee on Cultural Diplomacy (2005)[50]

The Advisory Committee on Cultural Diplomacy issued a report in 2005, calling cultural diplomacy a core element of public diplomacy and describing in detail what it is meant to accomplish, what it has accomplished in the past, and what its future role should be. The committee is an independent, presidentially appointed body appointed in 2004, with bipartisan membership, to advise the secretary of state. The following report thus represents a bipartisan approach to cultural diplomacy.

Executive Summary

Cultural diplomacy is the linchpin of public diplomacy; for it is in cultural activities that a nation's idea of itself is best represented. And diplomacy can enhance our national security in subtle, wide-ranging, and sustainable ways. Indeed history may record that America's cultural riches played no less a role than military action in shaping our international leadership, including the war on terror. For the values embedded in our artistic and intellectual traditions form a bulwark against the forces of darkness.

The ideals of the Founding Fathers, enshrined in the Declaration of Independence, the Constitution, the Federalist Papers, and the Bill of Rights, take on new life in the vibrant traditions of American art, dance, film, jazz, and literature, which continue to inspire people the world over despite our political differences. But in the wake of the invasion of Iraq, the prisoner abuse scandal at Abu Ghraib, and the controversy over the handling of detainees at Bagram and Guantánamo Bay, America is viewed in much of the world less as a beacon of hope than as a dangerous force to be countered. This view diminishes our ability to champion freedom, democracy, and individual dignity – ideas that continue to fuel hope for oppressed peoples everywhere. The erosion of our trust and credibility within the international community must be reversed if we hope to use

---

[50] Advisory Committee on Cultural Diplomacy, *Cultural Diplomacy: The Linchpin of Public Diplomacy*, April 15, 2005. The editor of this volume has removed the footnotes from the reprinted text. For the footnotes, the reader may refer to the original document, available at: www.state.gov/documents/organization/54374/pdf.

more than our military and economic might in the shaping of world opinion. Culture matters.

Cultural diplomacy reveals the soul of a nation, which may explain its complicated history in American political life: when our nation is at war, every tool in the diplomatic kit bag is employed, including the promotion of cultural activities. But when peace returns, culture gets short shrift, because of our traditional lack of public support for the arts. Now that we are at war again, interest in cultural diplomacy is on the rise. Perhaps this time we can create enduring structures within which to practice effective public diplomacy and articulate a sustaining vision of the role that culture can play in enhancing the security of this country. And if, as Secretary of State Condoleezza Rice suggests, America's involvement in Iraq requires "a generational commitment," then our cultural diplomacy efforts require a similar commitment of funds, expertise, courage, and time.

Cultural Diplomacy

- Helps create "a foundation of trust" with other peoples, which policy makers can build on to reach political, economic, and military agreements;
- Encourages other peoples to give the United States the benefit of the doubt on specific policy issues or requests for collaboration, since there is a presumption of shared interests;
- Demonstrates our values, and our interest in values, and combats the popular notion that Americans are shallow, violent, and godless;
- Affirms that we have such values as family, faith, and the desire for education in common with others;
- Creates relationships with peoples, which endure beyond changes in government;
- Can reach influential members of foreign societies, who cannot be reached through traditional embassy functions;
- Provides a positive agenda for cooperation in spite of policy differences;
- Creates a neutral platform for people-to-people contact;
- Serves as a flexible, universally acceptable vehicle for rapprochement with countries where diplomatic relations have been strained or are absent;
- Is uniquely able to reach out to young people, to non-elites, to broad audiences with a much reduced language barrier;

- Fosters the growth of civil society;
- Educates Americans on the values and sensitivities of other societies, helping us to avoid gaffes and missteps;
- Counterbalances misunderstanding, hatred, and terrorism;
- Can leaven foreign internal cultural debates on the side of openness and tolerance.

The Advisory Committee on Cultural Diplomacy urges the Secretary of State to consider the following recommendations:

- To increase funding and staffing for cultural diplomacy and, in a larger sense, for public diplomacy.
- To provide advanced training and professional development opportunities for FSOs, who are public affairs officers and have responsibility for public diplomacy and cultural diplomacy throughout their careers, with particular attention to research, polling, and the uses of new media.
- To create an independent clearinghouse, in the manner of the British Council, to promote the national interest; support missions in their efforts to bring the best artists, writers, and other cultural figures, to their audiences; develop public-private partnerships; and raise funds, with separate housing from the embassies so that cultural events can attract wider audiences.
- To set aside funds for translation projects, into and out of English, of the most important literary, intellectual, philosophical, political, and spiritual works from this and other countries.
- To streamline visa issues, particularly for international students.
- To implement the recommendations issued by the Center for Arts and Culture in *Cultural Diplomacy and Research* (www.culturalpolicy.org).
- To revamp Al Hurra, the Arabic-language television station, in keeping with the highest traditions of American broadcasting.
- To expand international cultural exchange programs, inviting more Arab and Muslim artists, performers, and writers to the United States, and sending their American counterparts to the Islamic world. Effective cultural diplomacy requires a long-term commitment to winning the hearts and minds of reasonable people everywhere. Now is the time to create a cultural diplomacy infrastructure and policy for the twenty-first century.

I. Introduction

History may record that America's cultural riches played no less a role than military action in shaping our international leadership, including the war on terror. For the values embedded in our artistic and intellectual traditions form a bulwark against the forces of darkness. And cultural diplomacy, which presents the best of what American artists, performers, and thinkers have to offer, can enhance our national security in subtle, wide-ranging, and sustainable ways. But limited resources and a lack of government-wide focus restrict our efforts in the battle for the hearts and minds of people everywhere.

It is time for change: time to articulate a vision of cultural diplomacy congruent with our position as what former Secretary of State Madeline Albright called "the indispensable nation," time to show how the values we preach in the political arena are embodied in our culture – and time to listen to what the cultures of the rest of world are saying about us.

"There's a worldwide debate about the relationship between Islam and the West," said an American official, "and we don't have a seat at that table."

Indeed, the Defense Science Board on Strategic Communications issued a report, in September 2004, asserting that "[t]he contest of ideas [within Islam] is taking place not just in Arab and other Islamic countries but in the cities and villages of Europe, Asia, Africa, and the Western Hemisphere." Further, "U.S. policies on Israeli-Palestinian issues and Iraq in 2003-2004 have damaged America's credibility and power to persuade." Cultural diplomacy is a means by which we may engage and influence that debate.

The stakes have never been higher. Anecdotal evidence and opinion surveys conducted by a range of organizations, including Zogby International, the Pew Research Center, and Gallup (CNN/USA Today), testify to widespread hostility toward the United States and its policies, particularly in the wake of the war in Iraq. This is brought into sharpest relief in the Arab/Muslim world, where large majorities in Egypt, Morocco, and Saudi Arabia, for example, view George W. Bush as a greater threat to the world order than Osama bin Laden; favorability ratings in Turkey, Pakistan, and Jordan steadily declined in 2002, 2003, and 2004; a poll taken in ten countries in October 2004 – in Canada, France, Britain, Spain, Japan, South Korea, Australia, Mexico, Israel, and Russia: some of our closest allies – revealed the same trend. And while recent polling suggests that American relief efforts after the tsunami in Southeast Asia, in December 2004, have at least temporarily mitigated the damage to our international standing, notably in the world's most populous Muslim nation, Indonesia, the fact remains that for much of the rest of the world the United States has lost its luster. What happened?

It is an axiom of international relations that the more power a country acquires, the more suspicions it provokes when it uses that power. Certainly this was the case with the U.S.-led invasion and occupation of Iraq, when large majorities of people around the world came to believe that the United States will impose its will where- and whenever it chooses, without what Thomas Jefferson called "a decent respect to the opinions of mankind." But a country can accumulate so much power that in the end it will have no friends at all. And history demonstrates that friendless nations fall to ruin.

Cultural diplomacy, which has been defined as "the exchange of ideas, information, art, and other aspects of culture among nations and their peoples in order to foster mutual understanding," is the linchpin of public diplomacy; for it is in cultural activities that a nation's idea of itself is best represented. Indeed the ideals of the Founding Fathers, enshrined in the Declaration of Independence, the Constitution, the Federalist Papers, and the Bill of Rights, take on new life in the vibrant traditions of American art, dance, film, jazz, and literature, which continue to inspire people the world over despite our political differences; the glories of our higher educational system, which remains the envy of the world despite the difficulties that foreign students face in securing visas to matriculate in this country, testify to the ingenuity, support (public and private), and solid intellectual foundations integral to the American experiment in democracy.

What people throughout the world love about American culture – the idea of America, if you will – is the sense of freedom coursing through the writings of Emerson and Thoreau, of Hemingway and Fitzgerald; the music of Duke Ellington, Charlie Parker, and John Coltrane; the paintings of Jackson Pollock, Willem de Kooning, and Robert Motherwell; the choreography of Martha Graham, Merce Cunningham, and Paul Taylor; the films of Woody Allen and Martin Scorsese. But as an American official said of the government's declining support for cultural programming: "It's like sucking the air out of a bell jar: if there's no other way to engage us except in political terms, then we lose."

With the end of the Cold War and the subsequent abolishment of the U.S. Information Agency (USIA) in 1999, official American cultural presence abroad was significantly reduced; cultural programming was slashed even before the dispersal of USIA personnel through the U.S. Department of State (DOS) destroyed the institutional memory necessary for the maintenance of cultural ties. What remains is an ad hoc congeries of programs, administered largely through the Bureau of Education and Cultural Affairs (ECA) at the DOS, with a reduced budget and staff, a diminished position in the hierarchy of diplomatic values, and a vision of cultural diplomacy incommensurate with American ideals and foreign policy objectives.

Cultural diplomacy is a two-way street: for every foreign artist inspired by an American work of art, there is an American waiting to be touched by the creative wonders of other traditions. Culture spreads from individual to individual, often by subterranean means; in exchange programs like Fulbright, Humphrey, and Muskie, in person-to-person contacts made possible by international visitor and student exchange programs, ideas that we hold dear – of family, education, and faith –cross borders, creating new ways of thinking.

Listening is central to this effort. To practice effective cultural diplomacy, we must first listen to our counterparts in other lands, seeking common ground with curators and writers, filmmakers and theater directors, choreographers and educators – that is, with those who are engaged in exploring the universal values of truth and freedom. The quest for meaning is shared by everyone, and every culture has its own way of seeking to understand our walk in the sun. We must not imagine that our attempts to describe reality hold for everyone. Indeed the history of art and literature is an essay in cross-fertilization.

And American culture gains from its dialogue with the artistic and intellectual riches of other cultures. American artists who travel abroad, in official and unofficial capacities, are cultural diplomats who make incalculable contributions to the body politic. As Joan Channick notes: "Artists engage in cross-cultural exchange not to proselytize about their own values but rather to understand different cultural traditions, to find new sources of imaginative inspiration, to discover new methods and ways of working and to exchange ideas with people whose worldviews differ from their own. They want to be influenced rather than to influence."

Which is to say: they listen. And so they offset the impression that America is a monolithic society defined solely by its foreign policy.

For what can be heard around the world, in the wake of the invasion of Iraq, the prisoner abuse scandal at Abu Ghraib, and the controversy over the handling of detainees at Bagram and Guantánamo Bay, is that America is less a beacon of hope than a dangerous force to be countered. This assertion, repeated in newspaper columns, on radio and television broadcasts, and via the Internet, diminishes our ability to champion freedom, democracy, and individual dignity – ideas that continue to fuel hope for oppressed peoples everywhere. The erosion of our trust and credibility within the international community must be reversed if we hope to use more than our military and economic might in the shaping of world opinion. Culture matters.

Thus, if, as Secretary of State Condoleezza Rice suggests, America's involvement in Iraq will require "a generational commitment," then our cultural diplomacy efforts require a similar commitment of funds, expertise, courage, and time.

This report synthesizes the findings of several academic studies, independent task forces, and various commissions and committees on public and cultural diplomacy; incorporates insights gleaned by this committee on a fact-finding mission to Oman, Egypt, and the United Kingdom, in the summer of 2004, as well as from separate DOS-sponsored visits by one committee member to Greece, Malaysia, and Norway; interviews with artists, choreographers, cultural activists, educators, film makers, theater directors, and writers in this country and abroad; discussions with American diplomats, program officers at the DOS, and a range of foreign officials, journalists, and experts. A sense of crisis was everywhere apparent, first in the growing perception of the United States as a hostile force, then in the scale of the diplomatic problem that must be solved: bridges rebuilt and new links forged. Put simply, we have lost the goodwill of the world, without which it becomes ever more difficult to execute foreign policy. "We Who Loved America," the title of a bitter panel discussion at an international literary festival in Molde, Norway, has in the last three years become a common sentiment around the world. The question, now, is how to regain that love, which was rooted in the promise of America.

Authorized by Congress and PL 107-228, the Advisory Committee on Cultural Diplomacy (ACCD) was appointed in March 2004. It was charged with advising the Secretary of State on programs and policies to advance the use of cultural diplomacy in U.S. foreign policy, paying particular attention to: 1) increasing the presentation abroad of America's finest creative, visual, and performing artists; and 2) developing strategies for increasing public-private sector partnerships to sponsor cultural exchange programs that promote the national interest of the United States.

II. Background

If diplomacy, as former Secretary of State George P. Shultz suggests, can be likened to gardening – "You get the weeds out when they are small. You also build confidence and understanding. Then, when a crisis arises, you have a solid base from which to work." Then the role of cultural diplomacy is to plant seeds – ideas and ideals; aesthetic strategies and devices; philosophical and political arguments; spiritual perceptions; ways of looking at the world – which may flourish in foreign soils. Cultural diplomacy reveals the soul of a nation, which may explain its complicated history in American political life: when our nation is at war, every tool in the diplomatic kit bag is employed, including the promotion of cultural activities. But when peace returns, culture gets short shrift, because of our traditional lack of public support for the arts. Now that we are at war again, interest in cultural diplomacy is on the rise. Perhaps this time we can create enduring structures within which to practice effective cultural diplomacy and articulate a sustaining vision of the role that culture can play in enhancing the security of this country.

The first efforts in U.S cultural diplomacy date from World War I, though it was not until 1938, in the face of Nazi Germany's cultural activities in Latin America, that a division of cultural relations was created in the DOS. The government agreed to support exchange programs for students and artists under the 1936 Convention for the Promotion of Inter-American Cultural Relations – the model for the numerous exchange programs integral to public diplomacy during the Cold War.

It is worth recalling some of the language included in the founding legislation of U.S. cultural diplomacy – the Information and Educational Exchange Act of 1948 – and in the program policies for one of the most successful Cold War initiatives: The purpose and objectives of this program are "to enable the Government of the United States to promote a better understanding of the United States in other countries and to increase mutual understanding between the people of the United States and the people of other countries." Among the means to be used in achieving these objectives is the international exchange of persons, knowledge, and skills.

International exchange of persons and projects constitute an integral and essential technique in attaining the general objectives of this educational exchange program. Persons participating in such projects carry to other countries, and bring back to their own, information, knowledge, and attitudes which through personal experience and personal influence promote a better understanding of the United States abroad and increase mutual understanding between the people of the United States and the people of other countries. These programs play a leading and direct, personalized role in contributing to the exchange of technical services, of knowledge and skills, and of information regarding developments in education, the arts, and sciences.

The spread of American knowledge, skills, and ideals –our success in the war of ideas with the Soviet Union – may be traced to the vitality of these programs. The late Anwar Sadat, Prime Minister Tony Blair, Chancellor Gerhard Schroeder, former Prime Minister Margaret Thatcher, Afghan President Harmid Karzai – these are some of the many world leaders who benefited from international visitor programs. Meantime, countless people were introduced to our cultural traditions at American libraries and information centers, which after 1953 were administered by the USIA. The Central Intelligence Agency even entered the cultural fray in the 1950s, covertly supporting exhibitions of American art, performing arts tours, and the publication of *Encounter*, one of the more dynamic journals in its time – a practice that was stopped in 1967.

But after the Cold War, when cultural diplomacy ceased to be a priority, funding for its programs fell dramatically. "Since 1993, budgets have fallen by nearly 30%, staff has been cut by about 30% overseas and 20% in the U.S., and dozens of cultural centers, libraries and branch posts have been closed," Juliet Antunes Sablosky reports. The abolishment of the USIA in 1999 marked the end of a formal cultural diplomacy policy – and the beginning of a retreat from the war of ideas raging around the world. For example, "between 1995 and 2001 the number of exchange participants in ECA programs fell from about 45,000 to 29,000."

And the waning of American cultural presence abroad left a gap in public perception eagerly filled by those with political agendas diametrically at odds with ours – particularly extremists in the Islamic world. In *The First Resort of Kings*, a history of American cultural diplomacy, Richard T. Arndt argues that "the sharp rise in foreign non-understanding" is a function of this policy. "Yet few have suggested that a crippled cultural diplomacy might have anything to do with either cause or cure. Cultural diplomacy's decline has thus passed unnoticed, leaving a nation baffled by its apparent defenselessness against the cultural onslaught of an enraged Islamic fragment."

Moreover, tightening visa restrictions since the events of 9/11 threatens our most successful, albeit underrated, exchange program – access to higher education and exposure to America. If in the 1990s the number of foreign students at American universities increased by 10 percent a year, restrictive entry requirements reduced that increase to less than 1 percent in 2002 and 2003; the difficulties of securing visas are prompting more foreign students to attend universities in Australia and the European Union. "In an effort to exclude a dangerous few," Joseph S. Nye, Jr. writes, "we are keeping out the helpful many."

Indeed foreign students not only fill important gaps in science and engineering, teaching undergraduates, for example, and embarking upon cutting-edge research (the National Science Board reports that 38 percent of the doctorates in our engineering and scientific workforce are foreign-born), but those who return home are grateful for their education and often serve as informal ambassadors for this country. They embody America ideals, creating reserves of goodwill. (Mexican President Vicente Fox and U.N. Secretary General Kofi Anan hold degrees from American colleges.) But as Nye writes, "Last year, the number of foreign students at American colleges and universities fell for the first time since 1971. Recent reports show that total foreign student enrollment in our 2,700 colleges and universities dropped 2.4 percent, with a much sharper loss at large research universities."

Nor should we minimize the economic consequences of these declining enrollments: NAFSA, the Association of International Educators, reports that foreign students and their families add nearly $13 billion per year to the economy; the losses to the economy in 2003 (the last year for which data is available) were more than $300 million.

As former Secretary of State Colin Powell said, "I can think of no more valuable asset to our country than the friendship of future world leaders who have been educated here."

No doubt the most pressing issue is funding. The DOS budget for public diplomacy in 2003 totaled $600 million, 40 percent of which was spent on educational and cultural programs – 4 percent of the department's overall international affairs budget or about three-tenths of 1 percent of the Pentagon's annual budget. ECA, with an annual budget of $245 million (of which approximately $3 million is earmarked for cultural activities), offers a variety of programs, including academic, youth, and professional exchanges; support for traveling exhibits of paintings, sculpture, photographs, and film; tours of performing artists; lectures and workshops by cultural specialists. Among the highlights: CultureConnect, which brings eminent cultural figures like Yo-Yo Ma, Wynton Marsalis, and Frank McCourt to foreign audiences, focusing on ages 12-25, to promote cross-cultural understanding; the Ambassador's Fund for Cultural Preservation, which helps countries preserve historic sites and manuscripts, museum collections, and traditional forms of music, dance, and language; the International Partnerships Among Museums program, which develops linkages between museums in this country and abroad; the Jazz

Ambassadors program, which sends quartets on four-to-six-week tours abroad, featuring performances, workshops, and lecture-demonstrations; and the Performing Arts Calendar, a database web site listing information about American performing artists touring abroad, which posts can use to extend the tours to their regions – and which is no longer funded.

Of course this represents but a fraction of the international cultural activities undertaken by the private sector. American popular culture, prominently film and music, is one of the most powerful forces at work in the world today. But American culture takes many forms, each of which enhances the image of this country, and ECA, which according to a report from the U.S. Government Accountability Office "is the primary focus for public-private partnerships within State," plays an important role in forging connections between artists, writers, and intellectuals in this country and abroad. Some 1,500 private sector organizations, academic institutions, and NGOs manage the majority of exchanges and cultural programs in ECA, which also maintains a network, through the National Council of International Visitors, of 80,000 American volunteers who help to show this country to foreign guests. They work, with considerably less show than their counterparts in the entertainment industry, to influence perceptions of America, and vice versa. And the fruits of these public-private partnerships endure: visitors to this country gain deeper views of a vast and changing society, while Americans broaden their understanding of the world beyond our shores. Cultural exchanges counteract the stereotypes that inform the attitudes of people everywhere, revealing the common ground.

A Malaysian NGO's effort to document and preserve the traditional ceremonies of Kelantan, a province in northern Malaysia, against the strictures of the local Islamic authorities (PAS), is a fine example of cultural diplomacy in action. With a small grant from the Ambassador's Fund for Cultural Preservation, this NGO has helped to maintain the ancient traditions of dance, shadow puppetry, and healing rites, training a new generation of local artists. These practices, which mix Islamic, Buddhist, Hindu, and animist elements, fly in the face of the purifying doctrines of the Islamists. The political consequences cannot be ignored: after more than a decade of banning such ceremonies, in the recent elections PAS lost many seats because, as a political commentator noted, the Islamists only know how to ban things; they have nothing to offer to replace them. What the NGO promotes, then, is a foil to Islamic extremism. And this small investment has paid off handsomely, clearing a space in the uncommitted middle of the political spectrum for more moderate voices to get a hearing.

III. Fact-Finding Mission

In June 2004, six members of the ACCD went on a fact-finding mission to Muscat, Cairo, and London to study the role of the arts and culture in the conduct of foreign policy; to assess the impact of arts and cultural programming; to review the value to field posts of arts and cultural offerings; to examine how arts and cultural programs can be coordinated at the mission level; to learn how the DOS can best support the missions in implementing arts and cultural programming; to see possible structural impediments to increased arts and cultural programming; to explore how the arts and culture can enhance America's image abroad; and to discuss ways to collaborate with the American private sector.

The ACCD's discussions confirmed the message conveyed by recent polling – America's image and reputation abroad could hardly be worse. There is deep and abiding anger toward U.S. policies and actions. It is essential, though, not to see our audiences, Islamic or otherwise, as monolithic or their opinions as undiscriminating. Our interlocutors in Oman and Egypt carefully distinguished between different aspects of America, roundly condemning, on the one hand, our policies in the Middle East and praising, on the other, our higher educational system, science, technology, and values – freedom, democracy, and individual dignity. America is still seen as a place where things can happen, where change is not feared: a land of diversity, openness, candor, and generosity.

Which is to say: the door is open – even if the welcome mat is not always prominently displayed – for cooperation on a broad range of endeavors, including culture and the arts.

In fact, a common frustration voiced was that on the cultural front America had vanished.

One woman said it seemed as if America was "under the veil." Another speaker said the

Arab world was ready to cooperate with America but that America had gone missing.

Several speakers urged us not to be afraid, but to please rejoin the cultural scene. The rest are here, they said – the British, French, Germans, Italians – but where are you?

In Muscat, a senior official raised an issue the committee was to hear repeatedly: that the idea of an American ideal is drowned out by Arab media coverage of the Israeli-Palestinian impasse and the war in Iraq; the fallout from the Abu Ghraib prison scandal – the photographs, broadcast repeatedly and circulated continuously on the Web, of hooded prisoners attached to electrodes, of leering American soldiers, and so on—would long haunt the image of the United States. And in a country as small as Oman (population 2.3 million) cultural diplomacy efforts are perforce small: a concert by Mary Wilson, a CultureConnect ambassador; micro-scholarships for the study of English; the opening of a fifth American Corner, the public-private initiative designed to replace the American libraries closed after the Cold War, in which aspects of American culture are represented; support for exhibits; exchanges in the International Visitor Leadership Program, etc.

"The problem is sustainability," said another official, echoing a story told by a diplomat in Southeast Asia, who was at the opening of an American library in the 1960s.

"Aren't you pleased to finally have an American library," he said to his host.

"Actually, this is our sixth library," said the host. "During every international crisis, you open a library, and then, when the crisis passes, you close it down and disburse the books. When you close this library, don't bother to distribute the books," he concluded. "We have plenty already."

This official also raised the issue of translation, mourning the fact that so few English titles exist in Arabic translation, and vice versa. Indeed translation lies at the heart of any cultural diplomacy initiative; some misunderstandings between peoples may be resolved through engagement with each other's literary and intellectual traditions; the poverty of insight displayed by American policy makers and pundits in their view of other lands may in some cases be mediated by contact, in translation, with thinkers from abroad. It was a Frenchman, after all, Alexis de Tocqueville, who wrote the classic work on American democracy. And translation can lead to cultural cross-fertilization.

But it is important to note that, according to *Publisher's Weekly*, while translated works make up 25-45 percent of the books published annually in many countries, the figure in this country is 3 percent; of 185,000 titles published here in English in 2004, only 874 were works of literary translation. In a word, we are not privy to the conversations—literary, philosophical, political, and spiritual—taking place in much of the world. And the same is true for many Arabs.

The 2002 *Arab Human Development Report* issued by the UN noted that, "Translation is one of the most important channels for the dissemination of information and communication with the rest of the world. The translation movement in the Arab world, however, remains static and chaotic. On average, only 4.4 translated books per million people were published in the first five years of the 1980s (less that one book per million people per year), while the corresponding rate in Hungary was 519 books per one million people and in Spain 920 books." Translation is an inexpensive form of exchange, the fruits of which—the dissemination of information and ideas, the inculcation of nuanced views of foreign cultures, increased empathy and understanding, the recognition of our common humanity – will be on display for a very long time.

A theme emerged from a luncheon in Muscat with members of the Omani Fine Arts Society, which we would hear throughout our travels: the need for more exchanges of actors, animators, artists, directors, writers, stage technicians, and web designers. This is a form of what Joseph S. Nye, Jr. calls "soft power," which he defines as "the ability to get what you want by attracting and persuading others to adopt your goals," and which he argues is as essential to the war on terrorism as the carrots and sticks of economic and military might – and considerably less expensive.

"If we can relate to each other on a cultural basis," said a photographer, "we can transcend our political differences."

This theme was reinforced at a meeting, in Cairo, with a senior Egyptian official.

He had just published a book about the Arabic language, in which he asserted that reforms – political and spiritual – must begin in the language – an idea which had earned him the wrath of an MP seeking to ban the book.

"We need more than ever to open ourselves to ideas from abroad, because we are facing a wave of intolerance and religious intolerance," he said defiantly.

Like everyone we met in the region, he dismissed the Middle East Project (MEP), believing that reform could not be imposed from without. Instead, he called on the United States to concentrate on training young artists: to send special effects specialists, say, or theater consultants. He mourned the fact that he could not attract famous American actors and directors to the Cairo Film Festival: the appearance of Sean Penn or Spike Lee, he said, would have a dramatic impact on Egyptian popular opinion.

"There is a basic misunderstanding between the West and the Islamic world," he continued. "Your prejudices are cultural – that we are a backward people. Our prejudices are political – that you are very biased toward Israel." And because the United States has cut back on its cultural programming, Arabs only see American political machinations; hence there is no cultural counterweight to our foreign policy.

At the National Cultural Center, a dazzling $60 million complex of theaters, music halls, exhibition spaces, and offices built for the Egyptian people by the Japanese government, we saw the results of cultural diplomacy: 700 performances a year, attended by 300,000 people, each of whom, in some small corner of his or her mind, remembers the benefactors of the space in which they take such pleasure.

The seven members of the Ministry of Culture were eager to meet the committee, even if, as they said, they feared this was just another attempt to refurbish our image in the region. They insisted that culture was the answer to the Islamists. "We want to oppose the Islamic groups with good artworks," said one official. "The Islamists are very good at talking, but culture can oppose the extremists." And so they requested training in several fields –technicians (sound, light, décor), stage directors (artistic and technical), singers, dancers, musicians; support for their musical library, instruments, and scores; funding for a year-long residency of an American conductor; and help with preserving the heritage of Arabic music, a project undertaken with the help of the Dutch Embassy. They hoped for exchanges of American and Egyptian troupes. And they complained about the haphazard nature of our efforts in the cultural sphere: how the embassy will ask them to collaborate on an event with only two days' notice, when their calendars have been set for months.

In a meeting the next day at our embassy we learned why there was often a lack of coordination between Washington, the post, and Egyptian cultural institutions.

"You reach the people through arts and culture," said an official. "But our cultural presence in this country no longer exists. The French Cultural Ministry can give you a monthly calendar. We can't do anything, because we don't know when anything will happen. We put on a circus act to keep things running until the money arrives. We're not speaking to anyone anymore. People ask, Where's your culture? Where are you?"

The missing link, it seemed, was in Washington. Several people said that more funding at ECA would make cultural programming more cost-effective.

"Then you can send troupes on to other countries," said an official, who thought the embassy had to offer a variety of cultural programs – books in translation, performers, teachers. "In a country of 71 million people you can't just shotgun things all the time."

Especially when anti-American feelings are running so high. "To win the war of ideas," said a senior American official, "we should wake up each day with more friends than enemies. But it's the other way around—which is fertile ground for our enemies."

He described a new phenomenon – the instantaneousness of Arab media, MTV, and cultural programming – which gives us an opportunity to get our story out, not least because an Arab version of the culture wars is on: "They're asking, Is it okay for a female singer to have a pierced belly button? Which is to say: this is a vibrant place. It isn't a barren cultural landscape with a monolithic view of America."

Nevertheless, he took a dim view of Washington's forays into the regional media markets. Al Hurra, the Arab-language television station launched in the wake of 9/11, is outperformed by Al Jazeera, Al Arabiya, and other satellite stations.

"We want to be on the cutting edge of their cultural wars," he argued. "So we need new instruments to play here. People-to-people exchanges. American teachers in the schools. And a sounding board – perhaps a group of wise Muslims who can tell us where they see things heading in the Middle East."

To get such a reading the committee met with a group of independent artists, dancers, directors, film makers, musicians, and writers, whose disdain for American military assistance to Egypt was palpable. They said in no uncertain terms that they had no interest in improving America's image in the Arab world; moreover, it was probably too late to remedy the situation. But they welcomed technical assistance.

"Interaction is the only way to make friends," said a filmmaker. "One hundred soldiers make Egyptians angry; one workshop makes friends."

"Art is the mirror of the people," said a woman wearing a veil. "It is the perfect medium to bring people together."

But the very existence of the ACCD evoked some humor and sarcasm among Egyptian artists and officials alike. Several said that America seems to launch cultural initiatives, and tries to explain itself, only when it is in trouble. Cultural engagement must be consistent though, if it is to be successful. Thus, the story later told to the ACCD at the British Council of an American tourist who, on a visit to Oxford, asks the gardener the secret of the green lawns. It's very simple, the gardener replies. You prepare the bed, plant seeds, water, and then cut it for five hundred years.

"Cultural diplomacy emerges at times of crisis," said a senior Egyptian official. "But this should be a process of building bridges, not a one-way street. Developing respect for others and their ways of thinking – this is what cultural diplomacy does. Let there be a dialogue. We've had a cultural agreement with the United States since 1962: why not implement it? We want people to know about real Americans. You have the right to be different, and I have the right to be different. Let your people know that Egyptians are not just fanatics – Islam is one religion, but there are many ways of applying it. I won't let what happened in Abu Ghraib change my feelings for the American people. My idea of America is the Statue of Liberty opening her arms, not turning away. Americans should build bridges, they shouldn't be afraid, they need to open up again. Don't go into a shell."

This speech led inevitably to the question of accountability. But no metric or language exists by which to gauge the success of a cultural initiative. As Milton Cummings notes, "a certain degree of faith is involved in cultural diplomacy."

How to quantify, for example, the effect of the thirty essays, articles, and poems that a Vietnamese writer, participating in the International Writing Program at the University of Iowa, published after 9/11, in the largest daily newspaper in Hanoi, detailing American reactions to the tragedy? This writer, who as a child had lived through the U.S. bombardment of his city, proved to be an empathetic witness to the trials of the American people. As Juliet Antunes Sablosky writes, "some of the fundamental goals of cultural diplomacy appear to be like the value of the arts. They are not easy to measure." She goes on to note, however, that it was a USIA-sponsored visit to America that changed F.W. DeKlerk's ideas about blacks and whites living together. His decision, as President of South Africa, to release Nelson Mandela from prison and start his country on the path to a multiracial democracy became a victory for American cultural diplomacy – and the people of South Africa.

More fruits of American exchange programs were on display in a meeting at our embassy in London, where alumni of the International Writing Program, the Fulbright Program, and the International Visitor Leadership Program detailed their experiences in the United States. A curator praised the openness of the curators and museum directors who readily shared financial information and operational strategies with him.

A composer from Belfast, who premiered a work in New York City just weeks after 9/11, said that cultural dialogue can achieve things that political dialogue cannot. A writer, grateful for the space and time in which to complete his new novel, was pleased to discover no political agenda operating in his program. Each was impressed by American volunteerism, inspired by the variety of American culture, and came away with a more complex understanding of America. They proved, in the words of one diplomat, that culture, a point of access and interest, opens doors when certain doors are closed for political reasons. This is why cultural diplomacy requires long-term thinking – five, ten, twenty years.

"Our cultural contacts have long memories," said the diplomat. "They remember the good things we do for them. Our political contacts don't remember for very long."

On the last stop of our fact-finding mission we visited the British Council, which as an independent institution (funded by the government and by revenues from the teaching of English) promotes Britain's national interests through cultural programming. For seventy years, one official said, the British Council has drawn on various resources to cast different angles of vision on the United Kingdom. He said it was hugely important for the Council not to be viewed as a mouthpiece for the government, particularly in places where they need to make the most progress.

"We're not prepared to accept the Foreign Office's message for short-term political gain," he said, "because that would undermine our credibility."

A semi-autonomous institution thus offers a means for those who wish to participate in British cultural activities but who, for a variety of reasons, wish to keep their distance from the trappings of the British government. The local chapters of the Council also provide congenial settings for events – away from the embassies, which for the sake of security increasingly resemble fortresses.

"Access is everything to us," said the official.

Presence, engagement, reciprocity – these are the watchwords of their work. And their confidence-building measures in troubled regions depend upon subtle interventions and an enduring commitment to the truth.

"You've got to underpin your credibility by not engaging in propaganda but by showing the rough and the smooth," said the curator of an exhibit by a group of Islamic photographers from Indonesia and Malaysia invited to work in the United Kingdom.

Indeed, the photographers were encouraged to portray Islamic life without concern for the feelings of the British government. "Design answers questions,' said the curator. "Art asks questions."

The courage to entertain those questions, hard as they may be, lies at the heart of cultural diplomacy, which works subtly, by indirection, and over a long period of time.

Hence the need for an enduring commitment to soft power, to winning hearts and minds in the cultural arena. The most generous estimate of U.S. spending on cultural diplomacy, though, is 65 cents per capita – the lowest in a recent survey of nine countries.

Richard T. Arndt observes that "A decent cultural diplomacy costs amazingly little, a shadow of the cost of one wing of fighter aircraft."

Now is the time to create a cultural diplomacy infrastructure and policy for the twenty-first century.

What did we learn from our fact-finding mission? cultural diplomacy:

- Helps create "a foundation of trust" with other peoples, which policy makers can build on to reach political, economic, and military agreements;
- Encourages other peoples to give the United States the benefit of the doubt on specific policy issues or requests for collaboration, since there is a presumption of shared interests;
- Demonstrates our values, and our interest in values, and combats the popular notion that Americans are shallow, violent, and godless;
- Affirms that we have such values as family, faith, and the desire for education in common with others;
- Creates relationships with peoples, which endure beyond changes in government;
- Can reach influential members of foreign societies, who cannot be reached through traditional embassy functions;
- Provides a positive agenda for cooperation in spite of policy differences;
- Creates a neutral platform for people-to-people contact;
- Serves as a flexible, universally acceptable vehicle for rapprochement with countries where diplomatic relations have been strained or are absent;
- Is uniquely able to reach out to young people, to non-elites, to broad audiences with a much reduced language barrier;
- Fosters the growth of civil society;
- Educates Americans on the values and sensitivities of other societies, helping us to avoid gaffes and missteps;

- Counterbalances misunderstanding, hatred, and terrorism;
- Can leaven foreign internal cultural debates on the side of openness and tolerance.

But what this mission also revealed is that increasing cultural diplomacy is not just a matter of political will. The infrastructure in Washington and in the field to support cultural and artistic activities is inadequate. Likewise, funding for the programs, as well as for human resources in Washington and at our embassies abroad, is insufficient.

With the severe personnel cuts in Washington staff in the 1990s, our embassies were largely thrown on their own resources if they wished to continue cultural programming.

Modest increases in Washington staff would bring economies of scale and improvements in coordination. A larger Washington staff would have a greater capacity to contact artists and agents, obtain or prepare promotional materials, and coordinate multi-country tours.

Public diplomacy field staff has been particularly hard hit by the budget cuts in the 1990s and the subsequent merger with the DOS. Our embassies lost public diplomacy FSO and FSN positions (there are now 614 public diplomacy FSO staff in the DOS; in the 1960s, there were some 1,200 FSO staff in the USIA).

They had administrative staff transferred to centralized embassy offices and public diplomacy positions downgraded, and they saw an enormous growth in desk work. Public diplomacy officers, who used to spend their time out of the office, cultivating contacts and promoting American culture, are now "chained to their desks." They need to return to the field.

IV. Recommendations

The following compilation of recommendations, drawn from various reports, interviews, and discussions, for the Secretary of State to consider, is divided into three categories, the first of which the ACCD regards as its highest priority:

- To increase funding and staffing for cultural diplomacy and, in a larger sense, for public diplomacy.
- To provide advanced training and professional development opportunities for FSOs, who are public affairs officers and have responsibility for public diplomacy and cultural diplomacy

throughout their careers, with particular attention to research, polling, and the uses of new media.

- To create an independent clearinghouse, in the manner of the British Council, to promote the national interest; support missions in their efforts to bring the best artists, writers, and other cultural figures to their audiences; develop public-private partnerships; and raise funds, with separate housing from the embassies so that cultural events can attract wider audiences.

- To set aside funds for translation projects, into and out of English, of the most important literary, intellectual, philosophical, political, and spiritual works from this and other countries. A recommendation of the Djerejian report on public diplomacy – to create the American Knowledge Library, translating thousands of the best American books in many fields of education into local languages and making them available to libraries, American Studies centers, universities, and American Corners – should be coupled with a recommendation to the National Endowment for the Arts – to create a fund for international literature to "ensure that the American reading public has access to a broad array of contemporary international literature by assisting publishers to pay translation fees for international titles they accept for publication, thereby increasing the number of literary works in translation they can afford to publish each year, and by helping publishers with the marketing of these titles once they are produced." Put these two ideas together to establish a secure base from which to inspire and sustain the dialogue among all nations, which is essential to cultural diplomacy.

- To streamline visa issues, particularly for international students. Specific recommendations from the Association of American Universities and other academic groups: 1) establish a timely process by which exchange visitors holding F and J visas can revalidate their visas, or at least begin the renewal process, before they leave the United States to attend academic and scientific conferences, visit family, or attend to personal business; 2) create a mechanism by which visa applicants and their sponsors can inquire about the status of pending visa applications and establish a process by which applications pending for more than 30 days are given priority processing; 3) revise visa reciprocity agreements between the United states and key sending countries, such as China and Russia, to extend the duration of visas each country grants citizens of the other, thereby reducing the number of times that visiting international students, scholars, and scientists must renew their visas; and 4) implement a fee-collection system for the Student and Exchange Visitor Information System (SEVIS) that allows for a variety of simple fee payment methods that are quick, safe, and secure, including payment after the individual arrives in the United States.

- To implement the recommendations issued by the Center for Arts and Culture in *Cultural Diplomacy: Recommendations and Research* (www.culturalpolicy.org).
- To revamp Al Hurra, the Arabic-language television station, in keeping with the highest traditions of American broadcasting.
- To expand international cultural exchange programs, inviting more Arab and Muslim artists, performers, and writers to the United States, and sending their American counterparts to the Islamic world.

The following recommendations, while smaller in scope, are nonetheless vital to effective cultural diplomacy, and the ACCD urges the Secretary of State to consider implementing as many of these as possible:

- To negotiate reciprocal arrangements for exchange programs in developed countries, through bi-national foundations, which can raise money and send people in both directions, freeing funds for programs in less-developed countries.
- To maintain momentum established in exchange programs by creating a formal mechanism through which to keep track of alumni and involve them in embassy activities—web sites, newsletters, surveys, etc. Encourage missions to seek local corporate sponsorship for events using returned exchange people.
- To highlight the importance of cultural diplomacy at every level of the DOS, encouraging ambassadors and FSOs to promote cultural activities; to build, in the words of Richard T. Arndt, "a corps of authentic cultural diplomats."
- To create more American Corners, with links to digital libraries and online books. The WiderNet Project (www.widernet.org), which is developing and distributing a digital library to

developing countries, provides a model for breaking down the
digital divide between the First and Third Worlds.
- To increase funding for World Affairs Councils and the National
  Council for International Visitors and encourage them to seek
  more public-private partnerships.
- To widen CultureConnect to include young artists, creating a
  corps of emerging cultural figures willing to spend longer
  periods of time abroad.
- To make greater use of available assets, notably closer
  cooperation with the Department of Defense and its assets, such
  as military bands. Explore the possibility of collaboration with
  the USO and its performing arts tours. Interactive videos and
  video-streaming of master classes with performing artists,
  writers, and thinkers could reach large number of people at
  minimal cost.
- To re-establish an office dedicated to the acquisition of private
  sector television and film media for official overseas use, and to
  export some of the excellent documentaries produced by PBS
  explaining different aspects of American culture.
- To expand the Sister Cities program to form more and stronger
  relationships between American communities and people and
  places around the world.
- To incorporate medical outreach into cultural diplomacy,
  coordinating visits to the home countries of foreign-born doctors
  now practicing in the United States (approximately 200,000 or
  nearly one-quarter of our physician work force) to treat patients
  and train local doctors.
- To expand the process of surveying alumni of the International
  Visitor Leadership Program to gauge their success in "moving
  the needle" of public opinion in favor of the United States.
- To require American officials abroad to participate in embassy
  outreach activities and add such a requirement to annual
  performance forms.
- To encourage U.S. cultural organizations to sponsor internships
  for young men and women from the Islamic world.
- To encourage U.S. museums to sponsor tours of artworks and
  artifacts from museums in the Middle East. Finally, some of the
  public diplomacy recommendations of the 9/11 Commission,
  urging the government to engage in the struggle of ideas
  underway in the Islamic world, dovetail with the imperatives of
  cultural diplomacy: "Just as we did in the Cold War, we need to

defend our ideals abroad vigorously. America does stand up for its values. The United States defended, and still defends, Muslims against tyrants and criminals in Somalia, Bosnia, Kosovo, Afghanistan, and Iraq. If the United States does not act aggressively to define itself in the Islamic world, the extremists will gladly do the job for us.

- Recognizing that Arab and Muslim audiences rely on satellite television and radio, the government has begun some promising initiatives in television and radio broadcasting to the Arab world, Iran, and Afghanistan. These efforts are beginning to reach large audiences. The Broadcasting Board of Governors has asked for much larger resources. It should get them.

- The United States should rebuild the scholarship, exchange, and library programs that reach out to young people and offer them knowledge and hope. Where such assistance is provided, it should be identified as coming from the citizens of the United States.

V. Summary

It was Zhuge Liang, a Chinese military advisor during the period of the Three Kingdoms, who told a general that even in war, "Above all else is culture" – a useful axiom for understanding the practice and place of cultural diplomacy in a nation's political life. For it is through culture that a nation defines itself, and the cultural riches of the United States have won us many friends and admirers over the centuries. But Patricia Sharpe's lament captures something essential about our current predicament: "When I was a press officer working for the U.S. Information Agency," she writes, "I spent a good deal of time refuting Soviet disinformation – and taking pride in the fact that we in the USIA had a mandate to tell the whole American story, warts and all. Warts or no, we didn't have to lie to look good. But in those days we didn't have to explain away the shockingly cruel and illegal treatment of prisoners at Guantánamo, at Abu Ghraib, in Afghanistan. Who in the world can look at scenes of torture and associate America with 'democratic ideals'? And once a campaign of disinformation is underway, nothing the U.S. government says will be trusted by anyone with good sense for a long time to come.... Soft power is what American used to have in spades. Soft power doesn't need propaganda or a hard sell. And the America I used to love never needed a hard sell either.

The task now is to present the enduring truth of the American experience – that we are a people capable not only of espousing, enacting, and spreading our noblest values but also of self-correction. It was no accident that the first flowering of American literature – the essays of Ralph Waldo Emerson, Henry David Thoreau's *Walden*, the stories of Edgar Allan Poe, Nathaniel Hawthorne's *The Scarlet Letter*, Herman Melville's *Moby Dick*, Walt Whitman's *Leaves of Grass* – occurred in the run-up to the Civil War, when the constitutional crisis destined to tear the country apart came into focus; nor that the most eloquent witness to the ensuing carnage was Emily Dickinson, the reclusive poet from Amherst, Massachusetts, who knew that many of her countrymen would not survive "the Hour of Lead" that had befallen our land. But her poetry, her witness, has sustained millions of people the world over. And it is this tradition of facing the truth that may inspire American artists and writers to come to terms with our latest fall from grace – a tradition upon which to build a permanent structure of cultural diplomacy.

'Rock music helped to bring down the Iron Curtain'
Andras Simonyi (2003)[51]

Just as when Radio Liberty broadcasts of jazz music fueled an underground cultural rebellion movement in the Soviet Union, rock music was an American and British cultural phenomenon in its own right that inspired young people in totalitarian societies. Hungarian Ambassador Andras Simonyi, who plays the electric guitar, spoke at the Rock and Roll Hall of Fame in Cleveland, Ohio, to describe in very personal ways how rock helped tear down the Iron Curtain. Excerpts follow.

I used to play in a rock band when I was younger and we used to do this stuff so I can tell when it's quality. . . . I'm not here to pretend that I'm a rock artist. I'm here to tell you that I'm an ambassador of a country that is closely tied together with the United States today. We work hard to maintain our relationship. And there is a pillar that has been so important to me all my life when I was a

---

[51] Andras Simonyi was Hungary's ambassador to the United States. Andras Simonyi, Speech at the Rock and Roll Hall of Fame, Cleveland, Ohio, November 8, 2003.

kid, when I grew older, and now, which I think is one of the real ties between us. . . .

[I was asked a question,] "Do you really think that rock and roll brought down the Iron Curtain?" And I said no, I don't because the Iron Curtain was pulled down by efforts on both sides, government and people on your side and people trying to influence things on our side. But I do believe that rock and roll played a key role.

This is what I am going to be explaining to you, why I think so. And I'm sorry if I will be too personal but I do think that the things we're doing, you know, diplomacy, is not made by diplomats, it's made by people. Successful diplomacy is about people. So therefore I'll try to get close to your hearts and your minds and probably the best way to do it is to tell you my personal story and how I got here.

. . . . I was four when Russian tanks rolled down the streets of Budapest. It's a strong memory I have. I was just a kid and I didn't really understand what was happening. But it did leave a strong mark in my mind. I must say that I had a great family – a great father, mother, a brother and a sister, who helped preserve a life for me. That was pretty much like yours; they were very protective. This family took me to Denmark in 1960 where my father was trade representative, I had the luck to go to an American school – that's probably why I picked up some English and Danish, and I had the honor to just live the ordinary life of an ordinary guy on the streets of Copenhagen. Here is how it all started. Let me just write this on the blackboard. [Writes "All My Loving" on the blackboard.]

You know this too? This was the first Beatles song that I ever heard, at a party at school. It caught me and I said, this is my music. And it hasn't let go since. While I was in Denmark, particularly in '66 and '67, like the Danes embraced the rock music at its best, like the Danes got to know Cream, Jimmy Hendrix, Zappa, Jefferson Airplane, Janis Joplin and you name it, I got to know them as well. I was listening to this kind of music day and night. I didn't know what the underlying message was and I didn't care. I just thought this was something that I had to embrace.

. . . I had a great time until in '67 we moved back to Budapest. Budapest at that time was not a very funny place. It was a pretty tough, dark, and gloomy place. It was just ten years after the 1956 revolution which was broken by the Soviets. Still, society was quietly and slowly coming alive. But it was a very tough place to be, especially for me who'd got used to freedom – freedom in the way I dressed, freedom in the way I communicated, freedom in the way I talked to people, and freedom in the way I picked up my music.

The music that I thought so much of was simply not available in Hungary. I stayed a year with an aunt and uncle of mine who turned out to be a very conservative communist. And honestly, they didn't get it when I started to explain about Good Vibrations and the Four Tops and the Spencer Davis group. She didn't understand. And my brother and I, we had a big old Bakelite radio that I got from my father so we could listen to Western radio stations and we used to listen to that at night. Listening to that music at night was very important to us to keep track of what was going on in the West. One night as we were listening to some real nice stuff, the old man came in, very angry, and took away the radio. Next day we asked for an audience and we said "Sorry for having listened to this music so loud," and he said "The problem was not that it was loud. The problem was that you were listening to a Western radio station."

That was something that really hurt us – I was 14 and my brother was 16 – being told you're not allowed to listen to music on a Western radio station that we always listened to. That was real tough. And we got to understand very quickly that this Hungary is not very similar to the Denmark where we used to live.

Still, you had to keep going and it was so important for me, my continuing to keep in touch with the music scene in the West. It kept us sane and kind of made us part of the free world. We would listen to Radio Free Europe, Voice of America, and above all, to Radio Luxemburg. We used to listen to this stuff at night and as we listened to this radio, as we listened to Radio Luxemburg, we were suddenly out of our bodies and our soul was part of the free world. We would join our peers in the West. We would be part of the scene that was so natural for all of you here in the United States or in England or Denmark or Holland or elsewhere in the free world. . . .

Hungarians didn't understand the text [of any of the rock tunes]. And I just suddenly realized that it was not the text but the power of music, the power of a couple of guys standing on stage with a Stratocaster, with a Fender bass, a guy playing on organ, a drummer playing a Gretsch drum set, that really made Hungarians think this was something very important.

So while the authorities tried to limit through the propaganda machinery the impact of this on Hungarians and obviously also on other Central Eastern Europeans, there was no way to stop the onslaught of the message of freedom through rock and roll. That was the most powerful instrument to convey the message to my generation about the free world. I do believe today, what the satellite and VHS was for the '80s and what the Internet is today, was rock and roll and rock music in the '60s and the early '70s. It was about sending a strong message of freedom through the Berlin Wall to us who were living behind the Iron Curtain. . . .

You remember, in 1975 the Helsinki Conference happened and I think we Hungarians were the ones who really tried to push it to the limits. This was pretty much about opening up to the free world. It was about East and West slowly growing together, and it was the guys who had grown up on this music that slowly began to infiltrate the ranks of power. And I seriously believe they opened us to the world, them wanting to end the Cold War, them wanting to hold hands with Americans, with Brits, with Germans, with Danes, with Norwegians. They were the ones with whom I had spent so many years walking in the streets of Budapest, talking about this music, and talking about us being part of the free world.

In 1988 – and that's a big jump; I am not trying to give you history lesson, just trying to tell you what this whole thing meant to me – so in 1988, Amnesty International was on a world tour, and that was the year when I knew the [Berlin] Wall will be torn down and we will put an end to the Cold War and Hungary will soon be free. Amnesty International was brought to Hungary by Sting, Peter Gabriel, Tracy Chapman, and Bruce Springsteen. Just imagine the powerful message of Bruce Springsteen singing "Born in the USA" at the stadium in Budapest and 80,000 Hungarian kids roaring and saying, yes, we're together. That was the year when I was 100 percent convinced that [Communism] will be over soon. My friends in the West reacted in disbelief, but I was right. What stronger message than the message that came through rock music can you imagine?

In 1989, the world moved on and Hungary was free again. You might wonder, what next? My personal life, the music that I embraced all my life has played an incredible role of since. I have a very easy rapport with my friends and colleagues in the West, primarily in the United States. I got to know friends who are working for the U.S. government when we suddenly figured out that we were listening to the same kind of music. I name one song, you name the band. That's how I met your ambassador to Moscow [Alexander Vershbow], who used to be my friend and colleague in NATO, and he used to be a rock musician when he was a kid, still plays. And as we grew closer, as Hungary started to move into NATO, the closer this friendship grew. We jammed together and this really made our friendship close. We both agree that this is something that has to continue to glue us together. . . .

Music's role must be part of an idea-based strategy
Robert R. Reilly (2007)[52]

From a national level, international broadcasting must fit within the broad parameters of a coherent message strategy. After the 1998 public diplomacy reforms that abolished the U.S. Information Agency, the federal government placed international broadcasting in the hands of a new independent, bipartisan Broadcasting Board of Governors (BBG). The BBG decided to shut down high-end broadcasting aimed at small elite audiences abroad, and take the commercial approach of reaching large audiences with music and other pop culture. The zero-sum approach meant that the quality broadcasting to decision-making elites would be sacrificed for new media aimed at "the street."

One of the flagship new stations is the Arabic-language Radio Sawa, which broadcasts American and Arab pop music as well as light news programs. Former Voice of America Director Robert Reilly looks at the problem in this excerpt from an op-ed he wrote for the Washington Post.

Is MTV winning the "war of ideas"? After years of the United States broadcasting Britney Spears to the Levant, the average radical mullah has not exactly succumbed to apoplexy or come to love democracy. A State Department inspector general's draft report on Radio Sawa (the final report was never issued) found that "it is difficult to ascertain Radio Sawa's impact in countering anti-American views and the biased state-run media of the Arab world." Or, as one expert panel assembled to assess its value concluded, "Radio Sawa failed to present America to its audience."

The BBG has achieved part of its objective in gaining large youth audiences in some areas of the Middle East, such as in Amman,

---

[52] Robert R. Reilly was the 25th director of the Voice of America and was a senior advisor to the Iraqi Ministry of Information during Operation Iraqi Freedom. Robert R. Reilly, "Britney vs. the Terrorists," *Washington Post*, February 9, 2007. Copyright © Robert R. Reilly. Reprinted with permission.

Jordan, where it has an FM transmitter. But as the Jordanian journalist Jamil Nimri told me: "Radio Sawa is fun, but it's irrelevant." We do not teach civics to American teenagers by asking them to listen to pop music, so why should we expect Arabs and Persians to learn about America or democracy this way? The condescension implicit in this nearly all-music format is not lost on the audience that we should wish to influence the most – those who think.

Some, of course, suspect that the United States is consciously attempting to subvert the morals of Arab youth. Undersecretary of State Karen Hughes told columnist Cal Thomas in December that our "view of freedom is sometimes seen as licentiousness. . . . And that is only exacerbated by the movies and the television and some of the music and the lyrics that they see exported from America." Especially, Hughes might have added, since the BBG, on which she sits as an ex officio member, promotes this very image.

Becoming a caricature of ourselves is bad policy and bad public diplomacy. The job of U.S. international broadcasting is to present, before we are attacked, what much of the world saw only after Sept. 11 – the sacrifice, bravery and piety of the American people – as part of a complete picture. By presenting this aspect of our culture, we might even prevent the miscalculations of those who believe they should attack the United States or can do so with impunity because we are a weak, irreligious, morally corrupt country.

We need radio broadcasting in the "war of ideas," but it has to deal in ideas to be effective. The "MTV message" is something that commercial broadcasting can do and would do better than government-funded radio. Government broadcasting is needed when the United States must communicate a message to a key audience that that audience otherwise would not hear.

Music may have a role in this kind of broadcast mission, but only if it is part of a larger, idea-based strategy. Where are the ideas that will help us win this war, and why are they not being deployed by all available means to the places that most need to hear them? Isn't it time to change our tune?

Keep the end purpose clear
John Lenczowski (2007)[53]

Cultural diplomacy may be defined as the use of various elements of culture to influence foreign publics, opinion makers, and even foreign leaders. These elements comprehend the entire range of characteristics within a culture: including the arts, education, ideas, history, science, medicine, technology, religion, customs, manners, commerce, philanthropy, sports, language, professional vocations, hobbies, etc., and the various media by which these elements may be communicated. Cultural diplomacy seeks to harness these elements to influence foreigners in several ways: to have a positive view of the United States, its people, its culture, and its policies; to induce greater cooperation with the United States; to change the policies of foreign governments; to bring about political or cultural change in foreign lands; and to prevent, manage, mitigate, and prevail in conflicts with foreign adversaries. It is designed to encourage Americans to improve their understanding of foreign cultures so as to lubricate international relations (including such activities as commercial relations), enhance cross-cultural communication, improve one's intelligence capabilities, and understand foreign friends and adversaries, their intentions and their capabilities. Cultural diplomacy may also involve efforts to counter hostile foreign cultural diplomacy at home and abroad.

In short, cultural diplomacy, being designed not only for mutual understanding but for these other purposes as well, has as its proper end the enhancement of national security and the protection and advancement of other vital national interests.

Note that the this definition, in addition to those cited earlier, contains enough references to foreign publics, foreign opinion makers, foreign cultures, and "Americans" in general, that cultural diplomacy fits principally within the sphere of public diplomacy, which involves principally relations with, and influence over,

[53] John Lenczowski was a senior public diplomacy official at the Department of State and served as Director of European and Soviet Affairs on the White House National Security Council. He is founder and President of The Institute of World Politics. Excerpted from John Lenczowski, "Cultural Diplomacy," in Waller, ed., *Strategic Influence: Public Diplomacy, Counterpropaganda and Political Warfare* (IWP Press, 2007). Copyright © IWP Press.

foreign publics, with a result being greater understanding by Americans of foreign cultures and policies as well. While it does comprehend influence and relations with governments, the primacy of its public diplomatic effects is worth stressing because some cultural diplomats, as discussed below, have been known to subordinate cultural diplomacy to the exigencies of traditional government-to-government diplomacy.

Integration with other arts of statecraft

Properly speaking, cultural diplomacy is an element of national security policy in general and public diplomacy in particular. Cultural diplomacy can be integrated with other elements of these activities whether they be in the realm of information policy, ideological competition, countering hostile propaganda, foreign aid policy, religious diplomacy, or establishing relationships of trust. In these capacities, cultural diplomacy can have positive effects on foreign cooperation with U.S. policy.

Foreigners who trust the United States, Americans in general, or even merely certain individual Americans, and who feel that Americans respect them and are willing to listen to their point of view, are more likely to help those whom they trust with sustenance, safe haven, information, and communications in wartime. They are more likely to help establish relations with others, build coalitions, collaborate with U.S.-sponsored political arrangements, and so forth during times of peace making and peace keeping. They are also more likely to do business with Americans.

Cultural diplomacy is an important ingredient in the collection of secret intelligence and open-source information of a political, diplomatic, or other national security-oriented nature. This is not to say that participants in cultural diplomatic activities are, or should be, intelligence collectors. In fact, as in the case with Peace Corps volunteers, it is more effective that such participants should stay clear of intelligence activities precisely in order to maximize the beneficial effects of their activity. Nevertheless, cultural diplomats and participants in cultural diplomatic activities often have insights into foreign political conditions and foreign public attitudes that embassy political officers do not. Yet, rare is the occasion when they are debriefed by our traditional diplomats or policymakers for these insights.

Cultural diplomatic participants also establish and develop relationships with individuals who are not likely to be sources of intelligence or other information, but whose networks of personal relationships can lead to such sources. The best human intelligence collection and operations are accomplished through the broadening of personal relationships. Collection is also successful when there are significant numbers of foreigners who sympathize with American ideas and ideals. Insofar as cultural diplomacy involves the effective promulgation of those ideas and ideals, it increases the pool of potential sources.

Cultural diplomacy can also be integrated with political action, political warfare, and subversion. It can be part of strategic psychological operations.

It can be integrated with these other arts and dimensions of statecraft by being overtly political or, in most cases – and most effectively – by avoiding association with politics altogether. Its effectiveness in the latter case results from the fact that many forms of cultural activities do not have political or strategic strings attached and are authentically aboveboard. And yet, paradoxically, they have tremendous positive political effect. Thus, cultural diplomacy, like other forms of public diplomatic outreach such as Peace Corps volunteerism, foreign medical assistance, disaster relief, and the like, can be undertaken effectively by various governmental and non-governmental participants in many cases without their being aware of strategic integration or the political/psychological methods and effects associated with it.

Humanitarian Public Diplomacy

'He who does a kindness hath the advantage'
Pericles (431 B.C.)[54]

In acts of beneficence . . . we differ from the many. We preserve friends not by receiving, but by conferring, obligations. For he who does a kindness hath the advantage over him who, by the law of gratitude, becomes a debtor to his benefactor. The person obliged is compelled to act the more insipid part, conscious that a return of kindness is merely a payment and not an obligation. And we alone are splendidly beneficient to others, not so much from interested motives as for the credit of pure liberality. I shall sum up what yet remains by only adding that our Athens in general is the school of Greece; and that every single Athenian amongst us is excellently formed, by his personal qualification, for all the various scenes of active life, acting with a most graceful demeanor and a most ready habit of despatch.

Avoid one-way aid programs: Let the recipients plan
George C. Marshall (1947)[55]

The Marshall Plan to revive Europe's shattered economies after World War II was at its heart an effort to win the minds and the hearts of Europeans. Secretary of State George C. Marshall outlined the plan in his short commencement speech at Harvard University on June 5, 1947. The complete text follows.

---

[54] Pericles, "Funeral Oration," 431 B.C., in Lewis Copeland, et al., eds., *The World's Great Speeches*, 4th ed. (Dover, 1999), p. 3. Pericles was an Athenian statesman who gave the classic funeral oration to memorialize the first Athenian soldiers who died in the Peloponnesian War.
[55] Secretary of State George C. Marshall, Commencement Address at Harvard University, June 5, 1947. Text courtesy of the U.S. Agency for International Development.

I need not tell you, gentlemen, that the world situation is very serious. That must be apparent to all intelligent people. I think one difficulty is that the problem is one of such enormous complexity that the very mass of facts presented to the public by press and radio make it exceedingly difficult for the man in the street to reach a clear appraisement of the situation. Furthermore, the people of this country are distant from the troubled areas of the earth and it is hard for them to comprehend the plight and consequent reactions of the long-suffering peoples, and the effect of those reactions on their governments in connection with our efforts to promote peace in the world.

In considering the requirements for the rehabilitation of Europe, the physical loss of life, the visible destruction of cities, factories, mines and railroads was correctly estimated but it has become obvious during recent months that this visible destruction was probably less serious than the dislocation of the entire fabric of European economy. For the past 10 years conditions have been highly abnormal. The feverish preparation for war and the more feverish maintenance of the war effort engulfed all aspects of national economies. Machinery has fallen into disrepair or is entirely obsolete. Under the arbitrary and destructive Nazi rule, virtually every possible enterprise was geared into the German war machine. Long-standing commercial ties, private institutions, banks, insurance companies, and shipping companies disappeared, through loss of capital, absorption through nationalization, or by simple destruction. In many countries, confidence in the local currency has been severely shaken. The breakdown of the business structure of Europe during the war was complete. Recovery has been seriously retarded by the fact that two years after the close of hostilities a peace settlement with Germany and Austria has not been agreed upon. But even given a more prompt solution of these difficult problems the rehabilitation of the economic structure of Europe quite evidently will require a much longer time and greater effort than had been foreseen.

There is a phase of this matter which is both interesting and serious. The farmer has always produced the foodstuffs to exchange with the city dweller for the other necessities of life. This division of labor is the basis of modern civilization. At the present time it is threatened with breakdown. The town and city industries are not producing adequate goods to exchange with the food producing farmer. Raw materials and fuel are in short supply. Machinery is lacking or worn out. The farmer or the peasant cannot find the goods for sale which he desires to purchase. So the sale of his farm produce for money which he cannot use seems to him an unprofitable transaction. He, therefore, has withdrawn many fields from crop cultivation and is using them for grazing. He feeds more grain to stock and finds for himself and his family an ample supply of food, however short he may be on clothing and the other ordinary gadgets of civilization.

Meanwhile people in the cities are short of food and fuel. So the governments are forced to use their foreign money and credits to procure these necessities abroad. This process exhausts funds which are urgently needed for reconstruction. Thus a very serious situation is rapidly developing which bodes no good for the world. The modern system of the division of labor upon which the exchange of products is based is in danger of breaking down.

The truth of the matter is that Europe's requirements for the next three or four years of foreign food and other essential products – principally from America – are so much greater than her present ability to pay that she must have substantial additional help or face economic, social, and political deterioration of a very grave character.

The remedy lies in breaking the vicious circle and restoring the confidence of the European people in the economic future of their own countries and of Europe as a whole. The manufacturer and the farmer throughout wide areas must be able and willing to exchange their products for currencies the continuing value of which is not open to question.

Aside from the demoralizing effect on the world at large and the possibilities of disturbances arising as a result of the desperation of the people concerned, the consequences to the economy of the United States should be apparent to all. It is logical that the United States should do whatever it is able to do to assist in the return of normal economic health in the world, without which there can be no political stability and no assured peace. Our policy is directed not against any country or doctrine but against hunger, poverty, desperation and chaos. Its purpose should be the revival of a working economy in the world so as to permit the emergence of political and social conditions in which free institutions can exist. Such assistance, I am convinced, must not be on a piecemeal basis as various crises develop. Any assistance that this Government may render in the future should provide a cure rather than a mere palliative. Any government that is willing to assist in the task of recovery will find full co-operation I am sure, on the part of the United States Government. Any government which maneuvers to block the recovery of other countries cannot expect help from us. Furthermore, governments, political parties, or groups which seek to perpetuate human misery in order to profit there from politically or otherwise will encounter the opposition of the United States.

It is already evident that, before the United States Government can proceed much further in its efforts to alleviate the situation and help start the European world on its way to recovery, there must be some agreement among the countries of Europe as to the requirements of the situation and the part those countries themselves will take in order to give proper effect to whatever action might be undertaken by this Government. It would be neither fitting nor efficacious for this Government to undertake to draw up unilaterally a program designed to place Europe on its feet economically. This is the business of the Europeans. The initiative, I think, must come from Europe. The role of this country should consist of friendly aid in the drafting of a European program and of later support of such a program so far as it may be practical for us to do so. The program should be a joint one, agreed to by a number, if not all European nations.

An essential part of any successful action on the part of the United States is an understanding on the part of the people of America of the character of the problem and the remedies to be applied. Political passion and prejudice should have no part. With foresight, and a willingness on the part of our people to face up to the vast responsibility which history has clearly placed upon our country, the difficulties I have outlined can and will be overcome.

USAID could not inform people how it was helping them
Djerejian Commission (2003)[56]

*Legalistic policies and regulations effectively censored the U.S.
Agency for International Development (USAID) from informing
people abroad how it was helping the world's needy. An
independent, bipartisan panel led by Ambassador Edward P.
Djerejian noted in 2003 how the U.S. - by design - was not
earning much goodwill for its $13 billion annual aid programs. The
report called for USAID to be re-integrated immediately into the
public diplomacy system. An excerpt from the report follows.*

When we asked the Administrator of the U.S. Agency for
International Development (AID) how much of his budget of $13
billion goes to public diplomacy, he answered, "Almost none." He
explained that AID is generally prohibited from using program
funds to disseminate information about its activities – a restriction
that the Advisory Group recommends be ended immediately. But, in
a broad sense, a great deal of AID's work is public diplomacy at its
best. AID's programs, in the words of one of its top officials, are
"American values in action."

For example, AID funds nongovernmental organizations like the
International Human Rights Law Group, which before the fall of the
Taliban was active in helping Afghan women refugees. AID has
brought tens of thousands of students to U.S. universities on
scholarships. It has helped establish community radio stations "with
civic education and moderation mandates" in Mali and other African
countries. In Iraq, AID has put into place 14 major contracts and
grants for reconstruction work, including partnerships between U.S.
and Iraqi educational institutions and assistance in improving
agriculture. In addition, of course, AID food, health, and
infrastructure assistance helps spread universal values, as practiced
by generous Americans, throughout the developing world.

How many people in the Arab and Muslim world, or anywhere
else for that matter, know the extent of AID's activities? Too few.

---

[56] Edward P. Djerejian, Chairman, *Changing Minds, Winning Peace: A
New Strategic Direction for U.S. Public Diplomacy in the Arab & Muslim
World*, Report of the Advisory Group on Public Diplomacy for the Arab
and Muslim World, Submitted to the Committee on Appropriations, U.S.
House of Representatives, October 1, 2003, pp. 66-67.

The Administrator of AID reports to the Secretary of State, and its officers are part of country teams at our missions abroad. Still, AID operates largely outside the current public diplomacy framework. Our recommendation for providing new strategic direction of public diplomacy through a White House-based architecture would help bring AID into closer coordination with other government agencies. An AID representative, for example, would take active part in the NSC/PCC, and top AID officials would assist in setting overall goals.

As noted, we recommend that AID – which, like many other government agencies, is subject to extensive Congressional earmarking (more than 90 percent of its programs) – be free from burdensome legal restrictions on publicizing its work. A portion of funding from every major project should be devoted to communicating the project's benefits to the public. "We *are* the message," one AID official said to us, but "we get people saying, 'Why don't you publicize what you do?'"

AID has taken an important first step with a corps of new development information officers, mainly foreign service nationals, in 20 countries. AID has also become more forthright about branding its activities, so recipients know that they are receiving contributions from the American people. This outreach is a vital piece of public diplomacy, although we were reminded on our travels in the region that many recipients of aid of any sort sometimes react with resentment at needing it.

Finally, we strongly urge that AID officials be included in the enhanced public diplomacy training that we have recommended for our missions throughout the world. In short, there must be greater recognition, government-wide, that AID must be an integral and conscious part of implementing the public diplomacy strategy of the United States.

Congress calls on State Department to credit U.S.
Public Law 108-468 (2004)[57]

The State Department, in the process of absorbing USAID, was not sufficiently responsive to the Djerejian Commission's recommendation that it inform the recipients of foreign aid that the help came from America. Congress passed a law to address the problem, as the following passage of Public Law 108-468 indicates.

At times it can be beneficial to the U.S. not to take credit for certain forms of aid, especially in the interests of supporting and strengthening third parties who can promote U.S. goals most effectively without an overt American connection. Hence the language in the law - the word "should" instead of "shall," and "to the extent possible" – permits exceptions.

In practice, however, many bureaucrats have misinterpreted the law and reportedly have insisted on counterproductive branding, as if Congress had not allowed for exceptions to be made.

The relevant section of the law follows:

Identification of United States Foreign Assistance – In cooperation with the United States Agency for International Development (USAID) and other public and private assistance organizations and agencies, the Secretary [of State] should ensure that information relating to foreign assistance provided by the United States, nongovernmental organizations, and private entities of the United States is disseminated widely, and particularly, to the extent practicable, within countries and regions that receive such assistance. The Secretary should ensure that, to the extent possible, projects funded by USAID not involving commodities, including projects implemented by private voluntary organizations, are identified as provided by the people of the United States.

---

[57] Public Law 148-468, Title VII, § 7109(d), amendment to the State Department Basic Authorities Act of 1956 (22 U.S.C. 2651a et seq.), Sec. 60(d).

Medical diplomacy generates large-scale goodwill
Terror Free Tomorrow (2006) [58]

*As the quick U.S. Navy response to the 2004 tsunami disaster in
Indonesia proved, the American military can have highly visible
and productive public diplomacy roles. So can the private sector.
When the resources are combined, the results arguably are the
most productive of any single public diplomacy activity. What
follows is from the executive summary of a 2006 report by Terror
Free Tomorrow, surveying public opinion after a U.S. Navy
hospital ship and private volunteers from Project HOPE visited two
of the world's largest Muslim countries.*

In unprecedented public opinion surveys by Terror Free
Tomorrow, Indonesians and Bangladeshis overwhelmingly approve
the U.S. Navy's recent humanitarian mission of the *USNS Mercy* to
their shores.

Mercy is a fully equipped 1,000-bed floating hospital, staffed by
Navy medical personnel and volunteer doctors and nurses from
Project HOPE, which recently provided free medical services and
training to the people of Indonesia and Bangladesh, among others.
And by its mission, *Mercy* helped favorably change public opinion
toward the United States in both Indonesia and Bangladesh – the
world's first and third largest Muslim countries.

In a nationwide poll of Indonesians conducted after the mission, of
those who had heard of the *Mercy*'s visit, a remarkable 85 percent
had a favorable opinion. In a similar survey throughout Bangladesh,
95 percent of the people of Bangladesh were favorable to the
Mercy's mission.

The consensus approval of the Mercy mission cut across every
demographic group and political view. Whether respondents were
unfavorable toward the Untied States and opposed to the U.S. war
on terrorism, or even supporters of Bin Laden and approve suicide
terrorist attacks – whatever their views or demographic category –
every group had a favorable opinion of the Mercy's mission. Indeed,
87 percent of those surveyed in Bangladesh stated that the activities
of *Mercy* made their overall view of the United States more positive.

---

[58] Executive Summary, "Unprecedented Terror Free Tomorrow Polls:
World's Largest Muslim Countries Welcome U.S. Navy: New Results from
Indonesia and Bangladesh" Terror Free Tomorrow, Inc., 2006. Copyright
© Terror Free Tomorrow, Inc.

In fact, having been questioned on terrorism, the United States, humanitarian relief, various types of foreign assistance and the *Mercy* mission, those surveyed were asked to rank what in the future would make their opinion of the United States more favorable. Respondents were given a choice of comparable and concrete activities the United States could undertake.

The first choice of respondents in Indonesia and Bangladesh was educational scholarships. But the number two priority was additional and expanded visits of the hospital ship *Mercy* to their countries. Next came concluding a free trade treaty with the United States and finally, stronger American support for resolving the Palestinian-Israeli conflict and for establishing a Palestinian state.

"The National Military Strategic Plan for the War on Terrorism" by the Pentagon's Joint Chiefs of Staff concludes that American humanitarian assistance is "often key to demonstrating benevolence and goodwill abroad . . . countering ideological support for terrorism [which is] the enemy's center of gravity."

The recent mission of the Mercy proves that ongoing humanitarian missions by the U.S. military will continue to reap demonstrable and measurable gains in popular esteem. Indeed, the near universal approval of the *Mercy* is a striking testament to the ability of tangible humanitarian aid to win favorable public opinion for the United States in the Muslim world.

The surveys also demonstrate that if the United States Navy itself delivers humanitarian assistance, as in the case of the Mercy, people overwhelmingly approve. The fact that the *Mercy* is a U.S. Navy ship makes Indonesians more positive by a striking six to one margin – no doubt a reflection of the continuing goodwill toward the U.S. Navy from tsunami relief.

American humanitarian assistance can make a significant and long-term difference to building goodwill toward the United States and eroding popular support for global terrorists. The mission of the *Mercy* by the United States Navy, in partnership with the volunteer assistance of Project HOPE doctors and medical personnel, sets a stellar example of the kind of actions the United States must take to win popular support, which is essential to winning the long-term struggle against extremism and terrorism.

When *Mercy* is joined by Hope, medical diplomacy succeeds in changing the opinion of the United States in the most populous Muslim countries of the world.

Surveys on the *Mercy* mission were part of a broader inquiry on attitudes in the most populous Muslim countries. A complete analysis of those findings can be accessed at www.terrorfreetomorrow.org. ...

Religion and Public Diplomacy

Since 9/11, the United States has been squeamish about using public diplomacy and international broadcasting to deliver religious messages. Many in the public diplomacy community argue that the U.S. has no business or authority to discuss religion, or that the U.S. should simply avoid the issue. In reality, however, U.S. public diplomacy and broadcasting has featured religious programming for decades.

Linkage of religion and diplomacy dates to the American founding. In his Farewell Address, President George Washington told the nation that "religion and morality" demand that the United States pursue peace and harmony with all nations, and warned against too much favoritism or antipathy toward any nation or group.

The selections that follow the excerpt from Washington's Farewell Address illustrate the American use of religious messages in the war of ideas. That official use includes the explicit discussion of theological trends within Islam and means of influencing positive trends in cooperation with Muslim scholars and leaders from abroad.

'Religion and morality' in diplomacy
George Washington, Farewell Address (1796)

Observe good faith and justice towards all nations; cultivate peace and harmony with all; religion and morality enjoin this conduct; and can it be that good policy does not equally enjoin it? It will be worthy of a free, enlightened, and, at no distant period, a great nation, to give to mankind the magnanimous and too novel example of a people always guided by an exalted justice and benevolence. Who can doubt that, in the course of time and things, the fruits of such a plan would richly repay any temporary advantages that might be lost by a steady adherence to it? Can it be, that Providence has not connected the permanent felicity of a nation with its virtue? The experiment, at least, is recommended by every sentiment which ennobles human nature. Alas! is it rendered impossible by its vices?

In the execution of such a plan, nothing is more essential than that permanent, inveterate antipathies against particular nations, and passionate attachment for others, should be excluded; and that in place of them, just and amicable feelings towards all should be cultivated. The nation, which indulges towards another in habitual hatred, or an habitual fondness, is in some degree a slave. It is a slave to its animosity or to its affection, either of which is sufficient to lead it astray from its duty and its interest. Antipathy in one nation against another, disposes each more readily to offer insult and injury, to lay hold of slight causes of umbrage, and to be haughty and intractable, when accidental or trifling occasions of dispute occur.

Proposal for Christian-Muslim 'common moral front'
U.S. Consulate General, Dharan, Saudi Arabia (1951)[59]

Faced with a common ideological enemy – Soviet communism – the U.S. found common cause with many Muslim leaders in the Middle East. The following letter by William A. Eddy of the Consulate General in Dharan, Saudi Arabia, shows in unusually clear language how U.S. officials openly worked with Muslim leaders on religious grounds for public diplomacy and related purposes. The letter also shows the complexities in dealing with certain leaders who had sided with America's enemies in wartime, but who had become natural allies.

I referred to the possible strategy of the Christian democratic West joining with the Muslim world in a common moral front against communism. Since then my secretary in Washington has sent to you some extracts from my correspondence from others who showed a genuine interest in this possibility, the value of which would be not only to strengthen support for the democratic West in the Muslim world, but also to constitute a recognition by the West of the moral strength and historical significance of Islam. As you know, there have been very few signs that the Western Powers place any value upon Muslims and from the point of view of psychological warfare alone, we need desperately some common

---

[59] William A. Eddy, U.S. Consulate General, Dharan, Saudi Arabia, letter to Dorothy Thompson, June 7, 1951. Courtesy of the National Security Archive, George Washington University.

ground to which we welcome the Muslims and the Arabs as respected and valued friends.

I am glad to say that since writing to you I have had new proof that such a moral alliance would be welcomed by Muslim leaders who would, I think, come more than half-way in responding to a friendly overture from the Christian West.

I. As I wrote to you before, the Secretary-General of the Arab League, Abdul Rahman Pasha, promoted this idea in a conference with high ranking officials of the U.S. Army and Navy in Washington last December. On his way back to the Near East, Azzam Pasha was invited to a private audience with the Pope with whom the same subject was cordially discussed. Azzam Pasha told me in Damascus, May 19, that he was greatly encouraged by the audience with the Pope who may make some official pronouncement in this field, and who recently welcomed Muslim diplomatic representatives at the Vatican contrary to Vatican policy of the past which required Muslim countries to designate a Christian.

II. When in Damascus on May 19, I had a private conference with a man who, no matter how low his political fortunes may have fallen, is still a great influence in Islamic religious circles, the Grand Mufti of Jerusalem, Al Hajji Amin Al Husseini. The Mufti spoke of Russia and of Communism with the deepest hate; insisted that we were on the wrong side in the last war and should have been allied with Germany against Russia. He claims that his actions at the time are now being vindicated in the arming of Germany by the Allies against Russia. The Mufti has no interest in the shifting alliances between the Powers intended to maintain a balance of power but he stated emphatically that all historic religion will be destroyed if Russia conquers the world. He spoke cordially of the cooperation which would be offered by Muslims to promote a joint propaganda with Christians to make this danger clear.

III. While in an audience with the King of Saudi Arabia, Abdul Aziz al Sa'ud, this week, the King addressed himself strongly to the same point. He affirmed that both Christianity and Islam are threatened by Communism, their common enemy. Christians and Muslims both worship the one true God and Russia is determined to destroy the worship of God. Therefore, Muslims in the East, and Christians in the West, should be allies in this trouble to defend their historic faith. I feel sure that a statement along these lines, or quotation, could be secured formally from the King if a way were found to quote a number of other representative persons at the same time who could speak for large numbers of believers among Christians and Muslims. As the ruler of the land of the Holy Cities, Mecca and Medina, to which over 100,000 of the faithful from Morocco to China travel every year, and as head of the puritanical Wahhabi movement to restore the pure faith and practices of Islam, the King is without a doubt the most representative and influential Muslim in the world today.

IV. Finally, I enclose translation of portion of an address made at Cairo, late in March of this year, by Muhammad Ali Allouba Pasha, formerly Minister of Education in Egypt and a recognized leader of Islamic and Arab movements. A few years ago it would have been inconceivable that a Muslim, prominent in public life, would stand on the platform of an American university and speak in public so reverently of Jesus and so respectfully of the Christian religion. What makes this address even more significant is that the lecturer and author requested the noted Egyptian writer, Fuad Sarruf Bey, to please bring the speaker's views to responsible and sympathetic circles in the USA. Perhaps you will find some way to have this done or some publication in which Allouba Pasha's remarks may be published.

Script for Radio Jidda
Dean Acheson (1952) [60]

The following excerpt from a cable from Secretary of State Dean Acheson to the American Embassy in Jidda (Jeddah), Saudi Arabia, shows the importance the U.S. placed on its sponsorship of Islamic and Armenian Orthodox religious programming.

. . . 30 religious program[s] packaged in Tatar, Uzbek, and Azerbaijani, for placement on radio Jidda air pouched to EMB Jidda to be held for you. You [should] review scripts before attempting to place. While Beirut contact Antranik Dzaroukian, care of Vratzian, Armenian Seminary, and inquire status lyrics for Saheg and Mesrop Oratorio. Oratorio being written by Alan Hovhannes.

Phone NY on arrival Cairo. Acheson

---

[60] Secretary of State Dean Acheson, Department of State Cable to the American Embassy in Jidda (Jeddah), Saudi Arabia, Outgoing Telegram, February 11, 1952. Declassified restricted document. Courtesy of the National Security Archive, George Washington University.

'Interpret the Moslem religion on the basis of tolerance and to condemn terrorism'

American Embassy, Beirut (1952) [61]

The current problem of Islamic-inspired terrorism dates back more than a half-century ago. In the early 1950s, the United States found itself struggling to isolate pro-terrorist tendencies in Muslim Arab societies. Today, the issue is mainly extreme forms of Islam or political interpretations thereof. In the early 1950s, the U.S. Britain and their Arab friends battled a form of political Islamism that made common cause with Stalin's Communism.

One of the most important points in this document concerns how U.S. diplomats tried at the time to help friendly Muslims shape and promote their civilized interpretations of Islam.

. . . there is a proposal (1) to create a healthy public opinion in Iraq, Lebanon and Pakistan to interpret the Moslem religion on the basis of tolerance and to condemn terrorism, Communist or otherwise, by close cooperation mainly among Moslem religious societies or with any other cultural societies, including Christian organizations, in those areas. This is to be informal, non-political, and without any undue publicity or reference to the Arab League. (2) to interchange information from time to time between the three countries as appropriate on Communist activities in those countries, including consultation on ways and means of combating terrorism.

According to Mr. Haddad [a former Iraqi military attaché to Washington], Sami Bey Solh [Prime Minister of Lebanon] agreed most heartily with all this and had a talk along these lines with Dr. Fadl Jamali, ex-Foreign Minister and present head of the Iraqi delegation to the UN, who happened to be in Beirut over the past weekend. Zaffarula Khan, Foreign Minister of Pakistan, also was in Beirut over the past weekend and is on his way to Baghdad and Cairo. Jamali has returned to Baghdad. All of these, according to Mr. Haddad, were fully in accord with the idea, as well as the minister of Finance, Emile Lahoud (Maronite [Christian]), who somehow was drawn into the conversation.

---

[61] John H. Bruins, Counselor of Legation, Memorandom for Files, American Legation, Beirut, Lebanon, February 26, 1952. Declassified confidential document. Courtesy of the National Security Archive, George Washington University.

Furthermore, Sami Bey Solh expressed the opinion that economic improvement of the population is the best way to combat Communism in Lebanon and other countries, and he is especially anxious to get early action on (1) electricity and water projects; (2) model homes for slum dwellers (for which he hoped the Americans could use the old aerodrome site); and (3) he said the Arts et Metiors have some government-owned land which they would like to sell to any American company, American Government or UN activity so that they could use the money thus gained for other productive projects in Lebanon. Sami Bey said he had been looking into the American Point Four project and is impatient that it does not get out of the talking stage and wants to do something at once. Mr. Haddad expressed the opinion that he not only wants this for the benefit of the country but also to consolidate his own political situation.

U.S. propaganda in Saudi Arabia will 'not be tolerated'
American Embassy, Jidda (1952) [62]

This 1952 memorandum from the U.S. embassy in Saudi Arabia to the State Department in Washington shows how difficult it has been to conduct public diplomacy in the Wahhabi kingdom. In the case below, which occurred early in the Cold War while Stalin was still alive, an American diplomat cables home that the Saudis do not "need" anti-communist propaganda and would not welcome information with a democratic message.

. . . As previously reported, it is our belief that a propaganda program in this country [Saudi Arabia] would be resented by the Saudi Government and would not be tolerated. Further, there is no need to convince the Saudis of the evils of communism. For these reasons the Embassy would not recommend distribution of cartoon narratives, political pamphlets or the items listed under the heading "Pamphlet Material for Optional Post Production." Certain of the "American" material might be welcomed by the Saudi Department of Education. A post-developed pamphlet program is not planned.

---

[62] Raymond A. Hare, American Embassy, Jidda, Saudi Arabia, to Department of State, Ref: Dept's Circ. Airgram, Dec. 13, 1951, Control 1371, 2:50 P.M., Subj: Proposed Pamphlet Program, January 8, 1952. Declassified confidential document, courtesy of the National Security Archive, George Washington University.

. . . The Embassy does not believe that alteration or adaption [sic] could make these pamphlets palatable in Saudi Arabia.

. . . Since shipment will not be made until the Mission has had an opportunity to review pilot models, the Embassy would prefer to wait for this review before estimating the number of copies required. It would be most unwise to attempt any disguised attribution in this country.

. . . It appears that this material has the double objective of promoting and encouraging democratic government on the one hand while presenting the dangers of communism on the other. Since Saudi Arabia is an absolute monarchy its Government cannot be expected to welcome propaganda of the first category. There is no need for anti-communist propaganda and the pamphlets described in the airgram would be incomprehensible to the average Saudi. Pamphlets of a more factual and non-propaganda nature such as those listed below may serve to present the United States and its citizens in a favorable light to Saudis and will at least teach them something of that country. This is the only specific propaganda purpose which should be attempted.

It is believed that the following pamphlets listed in the reference airgram would be of interest to the Saudis but the Embassy would prefer to review the pilot models before making any specific requests: Cartoon History of the United States, U.S. Guide, TVA, Creative America Series.

Country plan for Iran
American Embassy Tehran (1952)[63]

Iran became an ideological battleground in the early Cold War when Stalin targeted the country for Communist takeover. The Soviets had tried to take Iran during World War II, but were kept out by the British and Americans. By 1952, it was clear that the Soviets were back, using the Iranian Communist (Tudeh) Party as its main political agent. The U.S. devised political means to prevent a Soviet takeover of Iran through infiltration of an anti-

---

[63] American Embassy, Tehran, Foreign Service Despatch to the Department of State, Washington, "Ref. Dept. Instr. 61, Feb. 4, 1952," April 28, 1952. Authored by C. Edward Wells, Public Affairs Officer. Declassified confidential document. Courtesy of the National Security Archive, George Washington University.

U.S. government or through a possible coup. The following is a declassified memorandum sent in the name of the U.S. Ambassador to Tehran to Washington, relating to a public diplomacy "country plan" to blunt the Soviet political offensive by working with Iranian "molders of opinion."

Enclosed herewith is an edited copy of the Country Plan. The changes made were based on extensive discussions between the Public Affairs Officer and the Ambassador, Counselor of Embassy, and head of the Political Section. The delay in replying is regretted. It largely arose out of the fact that some of the suggested changes were controversial and so, were well debated before reaching a final conclusion.

Through Sections 1 to 9 [unavailable], only minor changes were suggested.

Section 10 – Priority Target Groups – the suggested revision rests on the following basis:

Target Group 1 – The Shah, Royal Court, and wealthy land-owners represent a conservative group vitally interested in preserving Iran's integrity, which if they could be stirred to more positive action would represent the strongest possible rallying point for all anti-communist elements. By reason of the strength of their position, they should be able to orient the country toward our direction. The extent to which USIE [U.S. Information and Educational Exchange, the precursor to USIA] can directly reach this group is limited. However, it is felt that working through and with the Ambassador, a great deal can be accomplished.

Target Group 2 – University professors and students, secondary school teachers and students, professional men, including government employees – are a most important group as they represent the public opinion molders, leading the multiplicity of movements now current in Iran. Soviet agents and workers are more active amongst this group than any other in the country.

Happily, they are a group which are readily accessible and can be served by all USIE media output.

Target Group 3 – Leaders of public opinion amongst illiterate masses, Mullahs (Priests), village headmen, tribal chiefs, etc. – The importance of this group lies in the fact that, although the rural population is currently quiescent, there are indications that as Point Four activities extend throughout the country, Tudeh [Iranian Communist Party] forces will become increasingly active in stirring up dissatisfaction and disorder amongst the rural population. It is hoped that by a concentration on these molders of village opinion, much may be accomplished in offsetting this infiltration.

This group is somewhat less accessible than Group #2, however, they can be and are being reached through our mobile unit operation as well as the dissemination of our media material through Point Four.

> Note: This distribution of media material through Point Four will necessarily be confined to a type which demonstrates American techniques and develops American prestige. It is considered that the use of any obviously propaganda material may react against Point Four rural activities.

Target Group 4 – Labor leaders and Army officers – The Soviet agents are working on both of these groups sporadically but with a slow yet perceptible increase in tempo. It is a fertile field for their activities because of bad labor conditions and in the Army, because of inequities and low pay.

It is again intended to limit our audience in this field to the leaders are molders of opinion.

Early public diplomacy funding of Islamic event
Department of State (1953) [64]

This declassified document shows how U.S. public diplomacy strategy engaged Muslim leaders in the 1950s. At the time, the U.S. was trying to influence Muslim movements and trends.

As a result of steps taken by the International Information Administration (IIA) [the precursor to the U.S. Information Agency], the Library of Congress and Princeton University are

---

[64] Wilson Compton, memorandum to Mr. Bruce, Subject: Colloquium on Islamic Culture to be held in September, 1953, under the Joint Sponsorship of the Library of Congress and Princeton University, declassified State Department memorandum, and accompanying "Summary of Salient Facts," January 13, 1953. Courtesy of the National Security Archive, George Washington University.

jointly sponsoring a meeting in September, 1953, between leading intellectuals of the Islamic world and of the United States. . . known as the Colloquium on Islamic culture. . . . On the surface, this colloquium looks like an exercise in pure learning. This in effect is the impression that we desire to give. IIA promoted the colloquium along these lines and has given it financial and other assistance because we consider that this psychological approach is an important contribution at this time to both short term and long term United States political objectives in the Moslem arena.

. . . The Library of Congress and Princeton University are jointly sponsoring a meeting between leading Islamic intellectuals and Americans interested in the Moslem world. . . . Of the 50 to 60 delegates, approximately half will be Moslems.

The colloquium was promoted by the International Information Administration (IIA) and receives extensive financial and other support from IIA. Personnel of other office of the Department [of State] are also contributing generously in time and advice.

The purpose of the colloquium is to further good will and mutual understanding between Islamic peoples and the United States. Since two or three outstanding intellectual leaders are being selected from each Islamic country, the colloquium is expected to bring together persons exerting great influence in formulating Moslem opinion in fields such as education, science, law and philosophy and inevitably, therefore, on politics.

Publicizing the colloquium is a matter requiring constant attention and study. The problem is to gain favorable response among the Moslem peoples without arousing the various elements hostile to the West. Clearly, this is a delicate matter which each embassy will have to handle according to the requirements and specifics of the situation in its country. IIA hopes that Moslem intellectual leaders will themselves promote favorable reactions from indigenous publicity sources.

Among the various results expected from the colloquium are the impetus and direction that may be given to the Renaissance movement within Islam itself. To further this end, the Exchange of Persons program of the IIA is giving leader grants to the delegates from Islamic countries so that they can spend a total of three months in the United States and can visit educational and other institutions either before or after the two weeks of the conference. Many of the delegates will doubtless also be invited to lecture. This important part of the plan will be coordinate by private organizations such as The Middle East Institute or The Governmental Affairs Institute.

It is also expected that the discussions between intellectual leaders of the Islamic world and of the United States will stimulate interest in and research on the Islamic world within American educational circles.

The three major areas defined for discussion are (a) classical elements in Islamic culture, (b) Islamic law and society, and (c) intellectual and spiritual movements in Islam today. More than half of the papers presented at the discussions will, it is hoped, be prepared by Moslem scholars. Every effort is being made, in fact, to ensure that the visitors from Islamic countries feel that the conference is an honor and tribute to their culture and position.

In addition to the American delegates, the majority of whom will be oriental scholars and all of whom will have a connection with the Moslem world, there will be meetings, luncheons and special lectures during the colloquium at which internationally famous American intellectuals will be invited to participate. The Islamic scholars will thereby have an opportunity to become acquainted with a wide range of thought and opinion in the United States. . . .

In addition to taking the initiative in promoting the colloquium, IIA has contributed most of the funds for its conduct. . . . IIA expects also to contribute toward the costs of publication of the papers and discussions.

Since the nature of the expenditures that can be made with monies that the IIA has contributed are limited by legislation and since the exchange program cannot give grants to some individuals whose presence at the colloquium would be desirable, it is hoped that outside sources may provide a small amount of financial assistance. The sponsors would thereby have more flexibility of operation, particularly for entertainment and other amenities that mean a great deal to persons from the Moslem world.

An interesting development in connection is the possibility that the Islamic Institute, an organization in Washington sponsored by the governments of eleven Moslem countries, may be dedicated while the colloquium meetings are taking place in Washington. In any event, the Institute has indicated a desire to cooperate. [65]

---

65 The Islamic Institute in this instance is not to be confused with an organization known by the same name that was founded, with Saudi funds, as an influence operation in Washington in the late 1990s.

It is hoped that the Secretary [of State] and possibly the President may wish to entertain the delegates and that the Secretary will be able to participate in the program of the colloquium.

Never fail to stress the spiritual factor
Dwight D. Eisenhower (1958)[66]

In his often very complicated and difficult dealings in the Middle East – which included Soviet subversion in the region, the consolidation of the State of Israel, the 1953 coup in Iran, the rise of pan-Arab nationalism, the 1956 Arab-Israeli war and the increasing security ties with Saudi Arabia - President Dwight D. Eisenhower found that a common spiritual purpose among American and Arab leaders could bridge even the toughest political impasses.

Below is an excerpt of a letter that Eisenhower wrote late in his presidency to a Presbyterian minister about the importance of religion in American diplomacy.

I assure you that I never fail in any communication with Arab leaders, oral or written, to stress the importance of the spiritual factor in our relationships. I have argued that belief in God should create between them and us the common purpose of opposing atheistic communism. However, in a conversation of this kind with King Saud, he remarked that while it was well to remember that the Communists are no friends of ours, yet Arabs are forced to realize that Communism is a long way off, Israel is a bitter enemy in our own back yard. But the religious approach offers, I agree, a direct path to Arab interest.

. . . I feel that all of us must do more, here at home, if we are to be successful abroad. I have made speeches on this subject, three or four of them on nation-wide television. But I believe teachers, business leaders, labor leaders and, indeed, including and especially the clergy, ought to be active in this work.

---

[66] President Dwight D. Eisenhower, letter to the Rev. Edward L. R. Elson, The National Presbyterian Church, 1764 N Street NW, Washington DC, July 31, 1958. Courtesy of the National Security Archive, George Washington University.

A sample of a U.S.-funded religious broadcast
Fr. George Benigsen (1988)[67]

For decades, Radio Liberty and other U.S.-funded outlets regularly broadcast religious programming into target audiences. Until 1991, Radio Liberty sponsored religious content, including religious services, in its broadcasts to the Soviet Union. What follows is an English translation of a representative sample of one such broadcast, an Easter, 1988 message to the Russian people by Father George Benigsen, marking the millennium of Christianity in Russia.

"If Christ has not been raised from the dead, then we have nothing to preach and you have nothing to believe." (1 Cor 15:14). Thus the Apostle Paul, in his epistle to the young church of Corinth, places the fact of Christ's resurrection from the dead as the very foundation of the Gospel teaching, the very foundation of our entire Christian faith. What some are inclined to consider a "myth," or "invention," the apostle affirms as unshakable fact, without which both faith and the church become the inventions of human fantasy. This apostolic witness, which is sacred for us, is preceded in the same epistle with the following words: "Christ died for our sins, as written in the scriptures. He was buried and raised to life on the third day, as written in the scriptures." (1 Cor 15:3,4) These words, "as written in the Scriptures," serve as apostolic documentation, as we would say today: the documentation of the facts of Christ's death, His burial, His resurrection from the dead. The First Ecumenical Council used this witness in the text of the Creed, the Symbol of Faith, which we so often and so conscientiously repeat during our services and in our personal prayers.

We are affirming faith in Christ, who was "crucified for us under Pontius Pilate, suffered, and was buried, and rose again on the third day according to the scriptures." "Scriptures" is that Old Testamental chain of the divine promises, of human faith, of righteous aspiration, of prophetic insight which binds together in one whole the entire Old Testamental history of all humanity from Adam and Eve until Christ's coming into the world. Christ, who by another witness of the same apostle, "was given over to die because of our sins, and was raised to life to put us right with God." (Rom 4:25)

---

[67] Translation courtesy of the Holy Trinity Orthodox Cathedral of San Francisco, California.

Christ, who will come again into this world, not in the image of humility in which He was incarnated in the cave of Bethlehem, but who will "come in glory to judge the living and the dead, and His kingdom shall have no end." Thus we affirm our faith in the Creed, repeating the witness of the apostle Paul: "Because Christ, therefore, died and rose again and became alive to rule over the living and the dead."

This is why such great joy, faith, expectation, and hope overfill our celebration of the radiant resurrection of Christ. This is why every seventh day of the week is dedicated by the Church to the fullness of the Paschal joy. Our entire faith, our entire worship is founded on this joy – from the day of Christ's resurrection from the dead even till now. It is precisely this Pascal faith, this Pascal joy which sounded from the lips of the first Christian martyr, the Apostle and Archdeacon Stephen, when from under the hail of stones thrown on him by the hands of his murderers, "he looked up to heaven and saw God's glory, and Jesus standing at the right hand of God." (Acts 7:55)

Without faith in Christ's resurrection, holiness is impossible. Impossible is true Christian witness, impossible is martyrdom for Christ. That martyrdom on whose blood the Church of Christ was built from the earliest centuries of Christianity to the very recent victories of the Church of Russia in the last decades of its now millennial existence.

"Christ is risen from the dead, trampling down death by death." Already for centuries this victorious hymn, the hymn of triumph and victory of life over death, has sounded beneath the domes of our churches. It thunders under the domes of our cathedrals, it victoriously rings out in our parish churches and in modest village churches. It sounds in the hearts of the faithful as it sounded in the catacombs of the Roman empire in the early days of Christian martyrdom, so it sounded in a subdued way in the contemporary catacombs of a persecuted faith: in the jails, in the camps, in the solitary cells. It was never silenced and as always, it sounded most victoriously in the believing human heart.

"Christ is risen from the dead, trampling down death by death, and upon those in the tombs bestowing life." "O death, where is your sting? O hell where is your victory?" This challenge was thrown to death and hell by the great father of the church St. John Chrysostom in the fourth century. The words that we hear every Easter night read in all churches, are the words of his Paschal sermon. Whatever progress a mind deprived of God may announce, whatever kingdoms of freedom, equality and brotherhood it may promise in the future of humanity, the logical end result of all these promises is a constantly strengthened hell on earth. And personal existence ends with the one inescapable fact of our life, senseless and completely unjustifiable death. Death which can find its justification only in this "trampling death by death." In the death of Christ, "giving life to those in the tombs." In the death of Christ which opens to all those who believe the gates to the Kingdom of God, "whose kingdom shall have no end."

Christ is risen, dear friends. May the light of His resurrection shine in your hearts, remain in your life, and bring you freedom and new life in our Holy Church.

An inability or unwillingness to come to terms with religion
Adda Bozeman (1988)[68]

The most critical aspect of American disposition toward non-Western societies ... is a pronounced inability or unwillingness to come to terms with religions, philosophies, ideologies, and other bodies of beliefs that have decisively shaped the foreign mind-sets but which continue to baffle Americans.... America's failures in the conduct of foreign affairs must thus be ascribed in no small measure to slipshod treatment of values.

The case for a religion attaché
Douglas M. Johnston (2002)[69]

Aside from the steps that are being taken to eradicate terrorism, is there anything comparable that the U.S. could do to address such motives before they give rise to violent expression?

One of the most helpful steps we could take in this regard would be to elevate the consideration of religious factors within the U.S policy-makers' calculus, a step that is long-overdue. Reluctance to

---

[68] Adda B. Bozeman, "Knowledge and Method in Comparative Intelligence Studies," in *Strategic Intelligence & Statecraft*, (Brassey's, 1992), p. 191.
[69] Douglas M. Johnston, "The Case for a Religion Attaché," *Foreign Service Journal*, February 2002. Copyright © 2002 by the American Foreign Service Association.

consider religious factors cost the U.S. dearly in Iran and Lebanon a quarter-century ago, to name just two countries where we simply did not understand or respond to the religious dynamics.

In the case of Iran, President Carter and his top policy-makers in Washington were caught unaware by the Islamic revolution, even though Embassy Tehran's own reporting at the time noted that the Ayatollah Khomeini had emerged as the most outspoken critic of the government, that the Shah's Islamic opponents were in a strong position, and that the Shah's days were probably numbered. These observations were effectively suppressed at higher levels by the combined influence of economic determinism and dogmatic secularism.

It is entirely possible that a greater recognition and accommodation of the religious dimension may not have significantly altered the outcome in either of those situations. On the other hand, if the religious factors had been properly considered, the resulting improvements in our ability to anticipate and react could conceivably have spared us untold national embarrassment in Iran (and the embassy staff in Tehran 444 days of anguish). The same could also be said for Lebanon (and the loss of 241 U.S. Marines) several years later.

A more recent example of Western indifference to religious imperatives was the NATO decision to bomb Serbia on Orthodox Easter in 1999. Although the issue was intensely debated at the time, the choice to bomb was apparently taken out of a concern that if the bombing were to stop even for a day, it might prove difficult to get the Allies to reengage the following day. Whatever the rationale, it is a decision the Serbs will never forget. As they were quick to point out, the only others to have bombed them on this holy day were the Germans in World War II.

Proper consideration of the religious factors in political conflicts, however, will not necessarily ensure a predictable outcome. In the aftermath of Sept. 11, for example, there was considerable hand-wringing in U.S. policy circles on whether or not to continue the bombing of Afghanistan during Ramadan. The concern was well placed, but in this instance, historical precedent suggested a greater room for maneuver.

The first consideration in such a decision is understanding exactly what it is that the religious observance is celebrating. Then it becomes instructive to examine how Muslims themselves have dealt with this same kind of issue. During the Iran-Iraq War, for example, both sides fought through Ramadan every year of the conflict (although Saddam Hussein once offered a Ramadan cease-fire, only to have it rejected by the Ayatollah Khomeini). In 1973, Egypt and Syria attacked Israel during Ramadan. While commonly referred to in the West as the Yom Kippur War, among Muslims it is known as the Ramadan War. Finally, in 624 AD, Mohammed himself conquered the holy city of Mecca during Ramadan. While none of this should be viewed as a license to do as one pleases, it does provide a helpful context for determining how to deal with such questions.

More Now Than Ever

It is particularly strange that religion has yet to be incorporated as a major consideration in U.S. foreign policy since it is central to much of the strife that is taking place in the world today. Almost anywhere one turns – Macedonia, Indonesia, Nigeria, Chechnya, Kashmir, Sudan or Sri Lanka, for example – one finds a religious dimension to the hostilities. Whether it is the root cause of a conflict, as it is in the Middle East where there are competing religious claims to the same piece of real estate, or merely a mobilizing vehicle for nationalist and ethnic passions, as has traditionally been the case in the Balkans, religion's potential to cause instability at all levels of the global system is arguably unrivaled. And as the Sept. 11 attacks brought home all too vividly, we must face the very real possibility of weapons of mass destruction falling into the hands of religious extremists.

Without the Cold War to suppress its influence, religious conflict has become widespread, virulent and inimical to vital U.S. national interests. South Asia is replete with ethno-religious challenges that are being dealt with along traditional secularist lines. Muslims and Hindus in Kashmir stare nervously at one another through the cross-hairs of their rifle sights or, more ominously, their nuclear delivery systems – ever susceptible to the flames of nationalism and religious unrest. In Sri Lanka, the tenets of Buddhism have been perverted to justify a never-ending stream of military atrocities between the Buddhist majority and the Tamil separatists.

Further east, there is Indonesia, an immense archipelago straddling a number of the world's vital shipping lanes. Once considered a rock of stability, it is periodically wracked with religious violence so severe that some fear it may lead to outright disintegration of the country. And back to the west, Muslims and Jews continue to square off in the Middle East over their mutual religious claims to Jerusalem, as terrorists find continuing inspiration to play their deadly game.

In all likelihood, religion's importance will only continue to increase in response to the growing threat to traditional values posed by economic globalization and the uncertainties stemming from the revolutionary pace of technology change. To underestimate these realities in the formulation of U.S. foreign policy is to tempt the gods, so to speak.

A New Approach

One effective way to give the religious factor its just due as a defining element of national power would be to create a new position within the Foreign Service – that of the religion attaché. These attachés would be assigned to diplomatic missions in those countries where religion has a particular salience. Included in their portfolio of responsibilities would be the tasks of developing relationships of trust with local religious leaders and groups, reporting on relevant religious movements and developments, and helping the mission to deal more effectively with complex religious issues.

The religion attaché's role would not differ dramatically from that of the cultural officer in his or her performance of public diplomacy, except for its narrower focus on religion and its requirement for special aptitudes and training to deal with the non-rational complexities of many religious issues. Like the cultural officer, the religion attaché's mandate would require a penetration of the local culture and a greater focus on people than on institutions. As currently configured, consideration of religious factors typically resides with the cultural attaché or a political officer (or, in some instances, the ambassador). But regardless of where the responsibility lies, the reality is that religious concerns often get squeezed out by other seemingly more pressing matters; hence the need for a new position.

Fortunately, the new religion attaché would not have to begin the process from ground zero. Some exposure will have already taken place in the natural scheme of things, particularly in conjunction with the relatively new reporting requirements of the International Religious Freedom Act. The new attaché could take over the management of these contacts (as well as the religious freedom reporting requirements) and work to deepen them, in addition to developing others. Needless to say, the religion attaché would have to work closely with the political and cultural officers in the sharing of pertinent information and contacts. Configured in this manner, a religion attaché would relieve already overburdened embassy staffs, help improve America's image with important religious groups and leaders, and provide valuable insights into their motives and objectives.

There are a number of characteristics a successful religion attaché would need to have. First, an ability to understand and deal with the specific language of local religious expression would be essential. Second would be a sensitivity to religious motives and priorities, coupled with a keen understanding of how faith inspires action. And finally, the religion attaché should have a gift for foreign languages and dialects, since local religious figures often do not have the same English skills normally found among government officials and the intelligentsia, with whom other FSOs commonly interact.

Obvious places to search for recruits who would have such qualifications would be from among seminary graduates or religion majors as well as from within the ranks of the Foreign Service itself (where those already possessing such skills might welcome the new challenge). With the necessary skills and strong support from the top, the religion attaché could go far in closing the existing gap in religious understanding.

Prime Assignments

A conservative estimate of global requirements suggests the need for a cadre of 30 such attachés at an initial total annual cost of $10 million. This figure is based on a State Department budget office estimate of $250,000 to $300,000 per year to field a person in a new position (including salary, benefits, transportation to and from the post, shipping of household effects, outfitting of a new office, and any allowances for hardship, danger pay, cost of living adjustments, and housing). The total also includes an increment for the added training that would be required. Annual recurring costs would be somewhat less, so even a slight shift from the reactive to the preventive side of the ledger in our budget priorities would more than suffice to fund this initiative.

The new corps of attachés could most usefully be distributed as follows:

The Arab World and Turkey (approx. 8): Because of the unquestioned importance of religion in this region, there should be some coverage of every country in this part of the world. The missions in Israel, Saudi Arabia, Egypt, Lebanon, Algeria, Sudan, and Turkey would all benefit from a full-time religion attaché. For others like Bahrain and Kuwait, shared coverage might suffice.

South Asia (at least 3): Separate religion attachés would be required in both Pakistan and India. As alluded to earlier, religion and religious nationalism are particularly powerful forces in these two countries. That, combined with their historic animosity over Kashmir and the fact that both countries are nuclear powers, makes a very compelling case for individual coverage. Because of the religious dimension to the conflict in Sri Lanka, an attaché should be stationed there as well.

Central Asia (1-2): Religious fundamentalism is a growing concern in this region and a significant factor in any number of conflicts. While there may not yet be a need for coverage in some countries, it would be advisable to have at least one, if not two, attachés to collectively cover Uzbekistan, Turkmenistan, Tajikistan, Kyrgyzstan, and Kazakhstan.

China and Southeast Asia (4): China's repression of the Falun Gong, Tibetan Buddhists, Christians and its Muslim Uighur minority suggests a deep-seated insecurity to which the West should be closely attuned. As already discussed, Indonesia has a compelling need for a religion attaché owing to its strategic importance and the religious aspects of its internal conflicts. The Philippines qualifies for a resident attaché based on the extended conflict there with Muslim insurgents and the strong influence of the Catholic Church. The rest of the region could possibly be covered by a single regional attaché.

Russia (1): Like China, Russia is too strategic and too involved with religion to remain unmonitored. Beyond the situational influence of the Russian Orthodox Church, there are important questions relating to the rights of other religions and religious denominations to actively practice their faith and the prospective impact of Islam on the country's internal stability (as manifested in Chechnya, the Crimea, and certain Central Asian Republics).

Latin America (5): Catholicism is an important part of life in Latin America and has at times played a crucial role in politics, including involvement in the removal of several dictators. The corresponding rise and increasing influence of evangelical Protestantism also suggests a need for some degree of coverage. Here, regional coverage would probably suffice, with one attaché each for the Southern Cone (including Brazil), the Andes, Central America, Mexico, and the Caribbean.

Sub-Saharan Africa (4): Religion plays an underappreciated role in Africa. Like Indonesia, Nigeria has suffered from repeated riots stemming from animosity between Muslim and Christian communities. In South Africa, religious actors were crucial in the movement to dismantle apartheid and to prevent civil war from breaking out in its aftermath. In other African countries like Sierra Leone, where governments have failed to meet the needs of their people, religious institutions have stepped in to provide basic services. As with Latin America, Africa could be split up into southern, western and eastern regions for purposes of this coverage, with individual coverage for Nigeria.

The Balkans (4): Having been coopted earlier by the forces of nationalism, religion has a crucial role to play in peacemaking, conflict prevention, and the rebuilding of civil society in the former Yugoslavia. Religion attachés should be assigned to Bosnia, Croatia, and Serbia/Kosovo, with one additional to cover the rest of the Balkans.

Central and Eastern Europe (1): Although Catholicism played an instrumental role in the fall of communism in Eastern Europe, particularly in such countries as Poland, East Germany, and Romania, it no longer has the influence that it once did. Thus, the region could probably be adequately covered with a single regional attaché.

Possible Problems

To be sure, the idea of establishing this new position comes with a host of concerns that must be carefully thought through. The following are representative:

1. Without adequate support from the ambassador, the traditional political and economic mission sectors could push the newcomer to the side and effectively "ghettoize" religion. Instead of giving religion a higher profile, such a development

could have the reverse effect and actually downgrade its importance. Internal politics are key.

2. The mission assignments of the new attachés might be driven less by need than by political influence and budget.

3. There might be a tendency for the religion attaché to become preoccupied with the major religious traditions to the exclusion of smaller but nevertheless important traditional faiths, such as African animists.

4. The State Department's practice of rotating personnel will result in an ongoing need tore-equip these attachés with an in-depth understanding of the religious complexities he or she will confront with each new posting.

5. The logistical burden of adding additional staff to the smaller missions must be taken into account.

6. Most missions may not want another staff position unless that person comes with a budget to support his or her programs.

7. Some countries may take offense at the presence of a religion attaché on the grounds that it will create an unwanted intrusion in their internal affairs (in much the same way that the annual report on religious freedom has been viewed with some degree of resentment).

None of these concerns, however, are insurmountable. To begin with, the position would, in all likelihood, have the prestige to stand on its own (in terms of its priority in the hierarchy of mission concerns). Second, creation of the position would represent an opening wedge through which religious considerations could begin to balance the influence of the rational-actor model of decision-making that has so dominated U.S. foreign policy over the past 50 years. Through this wedge, the flow of religious reporting over time would sensitize others to religion's importance, as would the presence in the mission of someone specifically assigned to the topic.

The remaining concerns are largely structural in nature and not particularly worrisome. A quick review of the proposed mission assignments reveals that few of the smaller missions would require a religion attaché. Most of the new positions would already be intended for those missions having the larger budgets and greater political clout. Most of those working out of smaller missions would be providing regional coverage (in which several missions would be able to pool their resources in support of a single position). The position itself might also come with a small budget to support religious-related activities, such as inter-faith seminars and the like.

In those countries where the mere assignment of a religion attaché could cause consternation – such as China – the position could technically be given a different label. The remaining concerns generally fall into a category where "forewarned is forearmed;" i.e., if those involved proceed with their eyes open, there should be no problem.

Meeting the New Challenge

It would appear from the foregoing that the benefits of creating the religion attaché position would outweigh the possible liabilities. Increased contact with the local religious communities would provide added insights on (1) what is going on in this critical area at the grass-roots and national levels, (2) concerns that religious leaders may have about U.S. decisions that are either being taken or contemplated, and (3) concerns these leaders might have with regard to local demagogues who attempt to manipulate religion for their own political purposes. Any such information would be highly valuable, as would the greater general understanding of religious imperatives that would accrue.

For far too long, the United States has focused the bulk of its energy and resources on reacting to events, usually in the form of picking up the pieces following the outbreak of hostilities in some near or distant part of the globe. That could be expected in a democracy where a crisis is often required to achieve the necessary political consensus for taking action. But in the post-Sept. 11 world, this approach will no longer suffice.

Other considerations aside, the looming marriage of religious extremism with weapons of mass destruction demands a markedly different approach, one that is both proactive in nature and that gives overriding priority to the task of conflict prevention. Establishing a corps of religion attachés would constitute a meaningful first step in this regard. It would give the United States an added capability for engaging on a preventive basis, while enhancing its ability to deal with a long-overlooked element of national security. The challenge now is to muster the political will to make the adjustment.

Effective ideological engagement requires understanding of religion
Jennifer A. Marshall (2006)[70]

Effective ideological engagement requires an accurate concept of the role of religion in the United States as well as accurate perceptions about the beliefs that motivate foreign publics. That begins with mustering the full force of the ideas on which the United States is founded. A hallmark of the U.S. constitutional order has been its success in balancing the dual allegiances of spiritual and temporal realms without emptying either's authority or significance. Today, however, the religious roots of the American order and the role of religion in the continued success of the American experiment are poorly understood by the general public and policymakers alike.

This leads to a lack of facility in grappling with cultures in which religion plays a dominant role, and an even greater difficulty in communicating with such audiences. America's official awkwardness with religion and ambivalence about its significance hinder U.S. policymakers from reaching and winning hearts and minds abroad.

"Our failure to take seriously religious motivations for public human behavior, at least as seriously as we do the incentives of power, politics and material gain, has placed at risk the security of the American people," says former Foreign Service officer Thomas F. Farr, who directed the State Department's Office of International Religious Freedom.

Among the many disciplines of statecraft, public diplomacy in particular must grapple with religion as a fact of life. Religion is one of the strongest determinants in both the life of the community and the life of the individual; hearts and minds are never more deeply affected than by religious belief. Religion defines the worldview of many whom U.S. public diplomacy seeks to influence. For public diplomacy, finding the appropriate means to appeal to these

---

[70] Jennifer A. Marshall, an IWP alumna, is Director of the Richard and Helen DeVos Center for Religion and Civil Society at the Heritage Foundation and a graduate of The Institute of World Politics. This passage is excerpted from her chapter, "Mediators of the Message: The Role of Religion and Civil Society in Public Diplomacy," in Waller, ed., *Strategic Influence: Public Diplomacy, Counterpropaganda and Political Warfare* (IWP Press, 2007). Copyright © IWP Press.

touchstones and to employ the services of those who can engage on these levels is essential.

To overcome this deficit, American foreign policymakers in general and public diplomats in particular must systematically analyze and address religious factors as a powerful motivating force in human behavior, from the individual to the community, nation and culture. Specifically, U.S. policymakers must:

- understand the role of religion and civil society in the American constitutional order;
- improve articulation of the essential elements of religious liberty and civil society both at home and abroad;
- guard against the distortion of such ideas (whether by friends or foes);
- recognize the perceptual barriers, including religious beliefs and traditions that prevent more widespread understanding of the ideals we hold to be universal;
- identify and confront (and where possible, influence) the sources of opposition to these ideals.

Understanding the role of religion in the American order

The United States can expect to be engaged endlessly in cold wars of ideas. America is a nation built on an idea, specifically, the principle "that all men are created equal, that they are endowed by their Creator with certain unalienable Rights, that among these are Life, Liberty, and the pursuit of Happiness." That idea had its enemies in 1776, and it continues to have them today.

Cold "wars of ideas are fought in terms of ideas and for the sake of ideas. It follows that ideas ... must be in good fighting shape," wrote Adda Bozeman. Today, a number of the ideas essential to the American order are not in prime "fighting shape," including those about the importance of religion and civil society in relation to freedom. That leaves the United States vulnerable in its ideological engagements abroad.

If U.S. public diplomacy aims to impart to foreign audiences an understanding and appreciation of American founding principles, institutions and policy, it must begin with an adequate self-concept of the same. This is not merely the task of public diplomacy; it is also the task of self-government in general. Democracy demands a high degree of social self-consciousness when it comes to the ideas that sustain the order: the principles and institutions of a free society are inherently more susceptible to corruption of purpose and meaning than are those of more authoritarian states.

Despite this imperative of self-government, Americans have not been consistently diligent in defending the ideas at the heart of the American order. Americans' disinclination to study their own history and founding principles, or the history of foreign cultures and thought, has "gradually made for a crippled, decidedly unconvincing national self-image," exposing America's defining attributes to mischaracterization at home and abroad.

Such a vague, "unconvincing" national identity makes it difficult to build a foreign policy, let alone a rhetorical defense for that foreign policy and national identity. It follows that confusion about foreign policy goals is linked to confusion about who we are as an American nation.

Civil society in America has been marked by a strong tradition of religious belief and practice and by active civic associations. These features characterize the American order as much as its political system or market economy and serve to sustain them. Religion has been a dominant theme in American civic life, from the earliest 17th century settlements founded for religious reasons to the great social justice causes led by religious congregations in the late 19th century to the current day charitable giving of religious individuals. This has not translated, however, into an adequate comprehension of American religious freedom and practice in U.S. foreign policy and public diplomacy.

Part of the confusion stems from prevailing assumptions about the direction of the Western world and of modernity in general. It has widely been assumed that over time, scientific knowledge tends to displace faith resulting in a society becoming less religious. While evidence from around the world as well as emerging data on religious belief and practice in the U.S. suggest that secularization is not the trend of history, official secularism has been the inclination of policy for some time. This has led to an expansive "separationist" mentality in which the constitutional idea of non-establishment of religion is interpreted to mean that the government must have nothing to do with religion – to the extent that religion is perceived as a personal, private affair, inconsequential for the purposes of public policy, and of negligible social significance. In addition to the moral framework that religion offers for understanding human motivation in the political sphere, this conception overlooks the wealth of data indicating that religious practice yields significant positive goods for society, including high levels of civic engagement. Still, according to veterans, "secular myopia" dominates at the State Department.

"While most American and European foreign-policy elites may hold a secular worldview, much of the rest of the world lives in one of the great religious traditions," according to Andrew Natsios, former chief of the U.S. Agency for International Development (USAID). By contrast, faith-based organizations "have much more in common with the rest of the world and thus may understand ethnic and religious conflicts, political movements driven by religious devotion, and the way in which the religious mind functions, better than secularized foreign-policy practitioners."

Understanding the role of religion in world politics

The lack of acknowledgement and understanding of religion's relevance domestically contributes to the failure to recognize religion's importance as a motivating factor in world politics. Increasing secularization in the West has also resulted in a greater psychological distance from societies dominated by religious institutions, traditions, and symbols. Without the capacity to conceive of the beliefs and motivations of the religious individual, policymakers will be ill-equipped to imagine how to communicate with him most effectively.

Both the realist and idealist traditions have underappreciated the power of values and beliefs. Realism, as George Weigel has noted, needs "a more comprehensive theory of moral reasoning applied to world politics [to] take more seriously ... the truth that ideas have consequences." On the other hand, a foreign policy that simply repeats an "unresearched trust in the universal validity of such basically Western values as law, democracy, and peace," overlooks the foreign belief systems that hinder the reception of and resonance with American rhetoric on universal ideals.

The religion deficit in U.S. public diplomacy is nowhere more apparent than in the case of Islam. "Western policymakers have let their dedication to a vigorous separation of church and state become an excuse for failing to comprehend – and understand how to deal with – the worldview of Islam," writes Douglas Johnston of the International Center for Religion and Diplomacy.

Strict separationism combined with the "mirror-imaging" tendency result in a failure to perceive the need to more deeply investigate the interaction of religion and politics in Muslim societies. Without adequate appreciation of the role of religion, one cannot begin to comprehend the complexity of Muslim experience with concepts Westerners take for granted, including the state and the notion of a political space (as distinct from the religious or personal). Nor can one proceed to make critical distinctions between Muslim (religious) and Islamist (political ideological) thought.

Religious analysis helps to illuminate such differences and avoid the trap of thinking of Islam as a monolithic faith and culture. Just as sharp domestic political strategists understand the American electorate well enough to know that a national candidate's message must reach Baptists in Oklahoma as well as Roman Catholics in Massachusetts, the challenge of public diplomacy is to develop methods and messages that discern among the sects of Islam and its various cultural and political contexts from Iran to Iraq to Indonesia to Pakistan.

Individuals who understand the religious mindset are best equipped to tackle that challenge. While a secularist viewpoint is antithetical to the Muslim worldview, Western religious believers – evangelicals, conservative Catholics, and Orthodox Jews, for example – can understand and appreciate Muslims' belief in a supernatural reality, adherence to a comprehensive moral code, and concept of a well-ordered interior life. This appreciation is what diplomats, intelligence officers, and policy practitioners operating from a secular viewpoint lack. "As the rising evangelical establishment gains experience in foreign policy, it is likely to prove a valuable – if not always easy – partner for the mostly secular or liberal Christian establishment," observes Walter Russell Mead. One way in which that cooperation could prove beneficial is in encouraging a richer understanding of democratic order in the United States as well as abroad.

A civil society approach to public diplomacy
Jennifer A. Marshall (2006)[71]

Democracy is more than electoral machinery. It is the governmental expression of civil society. Civil society is the network of mediating structures – like family, neighborhood, religious congregation, or clubs – that link the individual in his private life to the state and major institutions of public life. These mediating structures generate and sustain values in a society. As mediating structures are eroded or eliminated, values are increasingly determined by the state. As a state tends toward the extreme of totalitarianism, civil society institutions are under siege or wiped out; the religious faithful are often persecuted and private associations are typically outlawed or highly suspect. The constriction of civil society is one of the most striking differences between an authoritarian state and free society.

In America, civil society has been marked by a strong tradition of religious belief and practice. The moral authority exercised by religious congregations, family, and other private associations is fundamental to maintaining limited government. The American Founders frequently asserted that virtue and religion are essential to maintaining a free society because they preserve "the moral conditions of freedom." Man is capable of both justice and evil, they believed, and he needs to be inspired to love his neighbors and be restrained from harming them by a moral authority beyond government edict.

U.S. foreign policy that aims at democratization or advancing freedom globally must include strategies for cultivating civil society institutions that are adequately robust to support those ends. "Without institutionally reliable processes of mediation," write Peter L. Berger and Richard John Neuhaus,

> the political order becomes detached from the values and realities of individual life. Deprived of its moral foundation, the political order is 'delegitimated.' When that happens, the political order must be secured by coercion rather than by consent. And when that happens, democracy disappears.

---

[71] Ibid.

The context of Berger's and Neuhaus' comments is the United States, but these and other lessons from domestic discussions of civil society have international relevance as well. Domestically, the civil society dialogue arose out of a concern for cultural erosion in American society. Not only were government programs unable to stop it, they seemed often to contribute to the erosion. The civil society movement focused attention on the limits of government and, by contrast, the power of private sector institutions – including family, religious congregations, and other community-based organizations – in creating social stability. Religious congregations and faith-based groups in particular have offered solutions to seemingly intransigent problems like prisoner recidivism, gang warfare, and welfare dependency. Where government programs have failed, religious groups have been effective in dealing with matters of the heart. In short, religious groups have won hearts and minds where the welfare state was unsuccessful.

Could religious groups also have a strategic advantage in the contest for hearts and minds internationally? What would a civil society approach to public diplomacy look like?

A civil society approach to public diplomacy would begin with greater clarity about the role of religion and private associations in the continued success of the American experiment in ordered liberty. It would accurately assess the persistent significance of religious belief and practice and display a deferential rather than dismissive attitude toward religion in America and abroad. Government spokesmen, public diplomats and others would be less visibly awkward in discussing religion and religious issues.

This approach would highlight America's network of mediating structures as a distinguishing feature of the American constitutional order and as an essential support for its system of democratic capitalism. Such a strategy would tap the potential of civil society groups, including religious groups, to communicate and model civil society to their counterparts abroad who could fill similar functions. It would aim to transform hearts and minds among foreign audiences by targeting those cultural and religious gatekeepers who influence community sentiment and allegiance.

This civil society approach to public diplomacy would look beyond both government and market for its message as well as its method. It would contest the idea that global mass communications through corporate marketing or the news media are an adequate substitute for strategic communication about American ideals. From

Madison Avenue and Wall Street to Hollywood and Silicon Valley, American businesses and their marketers have global communications agendas that serve their own ends. These are not inherently at cross-purposes with strategic public diplomacy messaging; marketing messages about the "American way of life" can portray aspects of the civil society ideals that a public diplomacy campaign might aim to communicate.

The proliferation of global communications does pose challenges for a civil society-focused public diplomacy strategy. The distaste of many Americans for some of the sexually explicit or crass mass media messages can serve as a warning system for similar responses on the part of foreign audiences. Such cases demand, at minimum, a more representative portrayal of American life through public diplomacy projects. Not everyone lives like the characters on popular television shows.

Winning the war of ideas is more than a marketing challenge. A corporate model for public diplomacy will not adequately sustain U.S. foreign policy objectives. Selling "brand America" is insufficient. When Condoleezza Rice took the helm at the State Department in 2004, one commentator highlighted the need to remake public diplomacy away from this corporate model. The secretary of state, he argued, "must reinvent our public diplomacy, articulating abroad the values for which the U.S. stands, using not the techniques of Madison Avenue executives (one of the failures of the first part of the administration) but speech rooted in America's history and politics."

When public diplomacy is enlisted in support of democratization, a civil society approach is imperative: civil society is a prerequisite of democracy. Public diplomacy aimed at promoting democracy should be strenuously focused on explaining the role of religious liberty and freedom of conscience as the cornerstone of limited government while cultivating the civil society support system necessary to sustain the consent for the emerging democracy.

Freedom of conscience is a means of preserving the integrity of religion. Far from demoting religion to a lesser status, constitutional religious liberty frees religious institutions, leaders, and individual believers to exercise their "prophetic voice," appraising government actions for their attention to morality and justice without fear of reprisal. In this way, religious institutions and individuals can exercise a check on government claims and actions.

Where civil society has been stifled or never existed, such a model of religious engagement will be quite foreign. Therefore, another element of this approach to public diplomacy should be the identification of religious intermediaries, both individuals and groups, who can model and teach civil society functions or who have already undertaken such projects. In addition to the technical skills they impart, these religious believers' endorsement of civil society processes conveys an important message to religious communities in the target audience.

Finally, a civil society approach to public diplomacy should target leaders of mediating structures in the foreign culture. This approach would look beyond state structures and political leaders to actual or potential civil society leaders, including religious and community leaders. Robert L. Woodson, Sr., founder of the Center for Neighborhood Enterprise, has this to say about domestic civil society strategy: "because their constituents trust them and seek them as a source of support and guidance, indigenous community leaders should be considered the primary vehicle for the delivery of services and resources to their neighborhoods." Just as domestic community leadership efforts have looked beyond formally titled roles to detect the indigenous authorities in a neighborhood – the pastors or matriarchal activists of the inner-city, for example – such an approach applied to foreign policy would seek to identify the culturally authoritative figures in a society.

In his book, *What Went Wrong?* Bernard Lewis discusses the notion of civil society in the Muslim world:

> In the Islamic context, the independence and initiative of the civil society may best be measured not in relation to the state, but in relation to religion, of which in the Muslim perception, the state itself is a manifestation and instrument. In this sense, the primary meaning of civil is non-religious, and the civil society is one in which the organizing principle is something other than religion, that being a private affair of the individual.

This assessment challenges the Westphalian concept of nation-state that provides the framework for U.S. diplomacy and most international politics. It argues for a civil society strategy for public diplomacy that is centered around a clear understanding of religious liberty based on freedom of conscience. Such a campaign must be waged not *against* religion, but *in the interest of* the integrity of religious belief. In other words, public diplomacy directed to Muslim audiences should not be based on a crusade of secularization or Westernization. Both can serve to exacerbate extremism and give occasion or protest against the United States.

In assessing Islam's record of tolerating non-Muslim minorities, Lewis finds greater accommodation prior to the end of the 17th century, from which time Islam has been in retreat. "The emergence of some form of civil society would therefore seem to offer the best hope for decent coexistence based on mutual respect."

A former Iraqi government official advocated the same in a 2006 speech: "Civil society in Iraq … is a question of reconfiguring the age-old structures that kept society intact." Major differences "were resolved in history by smoothing out the edges that allowed for a large common space between Arabs and Kurds, between Shiites and Sunnis, between various minorities and the majoritarian perspective of Islam." Dictatorship cut off this tradition and the insurgency in Iraq represents "an attempt to re-write the history of Islam and its sects by a narrow group of people who have perverted the idea of modernism and have perverted the ideal of the identity of Islam."

'Islam is a part of America'
Karen P. Hughes (2006)[72]

Senior U.S. officials frequently participate in religious events for public diplomacy purposes. Among her outreach activities, Under Secretary of State for Public Diplomacy Karen Hughes joined a Muslim group to celebrate the holiday of Eid in 2006. And while her speech showed friendliness on the part of the U.S. government toward Muslims, it also showed how senior officials can recycle unsubstantiated propaganda from pressure groups. In the excerpted comments from her speech, Hughes echoed estimates from the Council on American-Islamic Relations (CAIR),

---

[72]"Under Secretary Hughes' Eid ul-Fitr Remarks," transcript, U.S. Department of State, October 23, 2006. Coincidentally, the remarks occurred on the 23rd anniversary of the 1983 Hezbollah attack in Beirut, Lebanon, that killed more than 220 U.S. Marines and 20 other American servicemen – the deadliest day for the U.S. Marines since the Battle of Iwo Jima and the highest one-day death toll for the U.S. military since the Tet Offensive of 1968. The State Department is not known to have issued a statement marking the occasion.

a radical Islamist group, which claims that an estimated six to
seven million Muslims live in the United States. Hughes' office
declined this editor's written request to provide the data or source
to back up the statistics. The Pew Research Center estimates that
the actual number is about a third of the Hughes figure, or 2.35
million Muslims in America. [73]

Nevertheless, the speech shows how U.S. officials may graciously
participate in religious events without creating a constitutional
crisis about separation of church and state.

Assalamu alaikum. I am delighted to be here to share this greatly awaited and joyous holiday. I wish all of you *Eid Mubarak*!

Today is an important day – a joyful celebration for Muslims across the world that marks not only the end of Ramadan, but also the opportunity to look forward with hope and gratitude, renewed by the past month of self-denial, self-control, fasting, and prayer.

As I join you this morning, I notice many of you are wearing a colorful and wonderful array of traditional dress, from so many countries, and I am reminded that people from Muslim communities are an important part of what makes America a vibrant mosaic of cultures. Islam is a part of America. As a government official, I represent an estimated six to seven million American Muslims who live, work and worship freely in our country, and are both American and Muslim. Our country is strengthened by the diversity of our people's faiths and traditions.

I am honored to be with you today and grateful for the warm expressions of hospitality and community that I have experienced the last few weeks in sharing Iftar celebrations, breaking bread together, listening and learning more about Islam, during the month of Ramadan.

Many of our government agencies have hosted Iftar dinners. Last Monday the President celebrated an Iftar at the White House and I had the honor of meeting accomplished Muslim women and men from all over the world at our own Department of State Iftaar [sic]. American Embassies throughout the world also opened their doors to welcome Muslims and to publicly celebrate the holy month of Ramadan together. I see friends here today that I made at an Iftar

---

[73] Alan Cooperman, "Survey: U.S. Muslims Assimilated, Opposed to Extremism," *Washington Post*, May 23, 2007, p. A3. For the full report, see "Muslim Americans: Middle Class and Mostly Mainsream," Survey Report, Pew Research Center for the People and the Press, May 22, 2007.

that brought together people of different faiths at a private home and I am grateful for the partnership of individual Muslim Americans who are leaders in fostering understanding and peace.

For me, this holy day is a reminder of the values that Americans share with people across the world: the importance of family and community, and a profound gratitude for the precious gift of life.

Looking around this morning I am delighted to see so many families – it highlights our shared appreciation of the family values that bind and sustain us, individually and as a nation.

Strong families and communities are built on a foundation of trust and respect, and are only strengthened as we connect and learn to rely on one another.

In celebrating Eid, we also celebrate community, coming together, just as we are today, from many backgrounds, heritages and walks of life. At this time of conflict, war and uncertainty, as we come together today, I hope each of us with make a new commitment to do everything each of us can to foster greater respect and understanding – as the Imam said, to reach out to others in a spirit of kindness and mercy that is so needed in today's world.

I am here today to affirm America's respect, partnership and connection with Muslim communities here in the US and across the world. Our goal as Americans is to reach out to other nations and peoples in a spirit of partnership, to be partners for peace and progress.

Today is also a day of gratitude, a day to thank our Creator for the blessings we have received: the freedoms and opportunity we enjoy in this country – freedom to worship as our conscience dictates, the opportunity to live in a country where every person is equal, and equally deserving of dignity and respect. Today is a day for all of us to be reminded of the abundance in which we live.

It is inspiring to see so many beautiful children here, and I was delighted to learn about their acts of kindness in preparing food for the homeless. Now if the children here are anything like mine were, I'm sure they are eager to celebrate the festivities by receiving money, gifts and sweets over the next three days, but as we look into their precious faces, we are also reminded of how important it is to continue to build bridges of understanding and respect across differences of faith or ethnicity, and between countries around the world. By doing so, we help ensure that our children grow up in a safer and better world, not a more divided and dangerous one.

I commend the All Dulles Area Muslim Society today, for leading by example in sharing the rich traditions and significance of Islam with guests. Thank you so much for welcoming me to join you this morning. *Eid Mubarak*!

Engage Muslim communities . . .
U.S. Department of State (2007) [74]

Objectives of the public diplomacy strategy include engaging Muslim communities, promoting democracy and good governance, de-legitimizing terror, and isolating terrorist leaders and organizations.

. . . but alienate them if we must
U.S. Agency for International Development (2007)[75]

Many Islamist extremists have said that their hatred of the United States has as much if not more to do with its export of offensive cultural values than with foreign policy issues. While official U.S. policy very carefully treats issues that might offend religious people's sensibilities in some areas, government agencies sometimes choose to give greater importance to certain politically correct forms of social expression that many people of faith, not merely extremists, find unduly offensive.

The following USAID notice from June, 2007 illustrates wartime policies that can alienate the very people we are trying to de-fuse and attract.

USAID/Notice EOP/OD 06/05/2007
SUBJECT: Celebration of Gay and Lesbian Pride Month

Each June, we acknowledge the contributions of gay, lesbian, bisexual, and transgender (GLBT) employees through the celebration of Pride Month. The observance of Gay and Lesbian

---

[74] "FY 2008 Budget in Brief," Bureau of Resource Management, U.S. Department of State, February 5, 2007.
[75] U.S. Agency for International Development, "USAID/Notice EOP/OD," June 5, 2007. Parts of the memorandum were published in the June, 2007 issue of the GLIFAA newsletter.

Pride Month in June offers each of us a chance to reaffirm our commitment to promoting tolerance, understanding, and communication in our communities and in the workplace.

In observance of Pride Month, Gays and Lesbians in Foreign Affairs Agencies (GLIFAA) invites all employees at the Department of State, USAID, other foreign affairs agencies and their families, friends, and allies to participate in the following events during Pride Month, celebrated in Washington, D.C. as Capital Pride during June 1-10, 2007. Other cities throughout the U.S. and world celebrate through their own events and parades throughout June (information forwarded by GLIFAA members and colleagues for Mexico City, New Delhi, and Riga are listed below)....

American Center New Delhi

June's Saturday Cinema films series will focus on gender and sexuality. Schedule: *Philadelphia* - (June 2, 2007), *Brokeback Mountain* (June 9, 2007), *Far from Heaven* (June 16, 2007), *Boys Don't Cry* (June 23, 2007), and *Kissing Jessica Stein* (June 30, 2007).

U.S. Embassy Riga

Colleagues at post recommend the following link to learn about Pride activities in Latvia . . . GLIFAA is the officially recognized organization representing the concerns of gay and lesbian personnel and their families in the U.S. Department of State, U.S. Agency for International Development (USAID), Foreign Commercial Service, Foreign Agricultural Service, and other foreign affairs agencies and offices in the U.S. Government. GLIFAA members represent Foreign and Civil Service personnel, gay and straight. GLIFAA works to advance the fundamental principle of non-discrimination on the basis of sexual orientation and was formed in 1992 in order to challenge a security clearance process that discriminated against gay men and lesbians. Since that time, GLIFAA has grown to include more than 500 Foreign Service, Civil Service and associated members who serve in Washington, D.C. and at numerous U.S. diplomatic, consular posts and USAID missions worldwide....

A model fatwa
Islamic Commission of Spain (2005)[76]

American policymakers say they are at a loss about how or even whether to spread the messages of Muslim leaders around the world whose interests coincide with those of the United States. Officials often say the U.S. has no authority to issue statements about Muslim affairs. Yet many Muslim affairs are public events or statements that invite public comment, and therefore constitute news. Since the U.S. government operates global news organizations, one could reason that its radios, TV channels and Internet services should report the news – and, like any professional news organization, provide the full text of the statements that make the news.

So it was with the March 11, 2005 edict or fatwa issued by the Islamic Commission of Spain on the first anniversary of the al Qaeda transit bombings in Madrid. No known fatwa against terrorism has been as comprehensive and as absolute as the Spanish one (not even those issued by British and American Muslim leaders), yet U.S. public diplomacy and international broadcasting leaders failed to report on it. News about the fatwa, along with the original texts in Spanish and Arabic, and translations into English, French, Farsi, Urdu, Indonesian and other languages, could have informed target audiences of the nature and quality of the declaration.

For the record, U.S. public diplomacy and international broadcasting officials did not publicize this fatwa or translate it into other languages, even when it was brought to the attention of senior officials at the State Department's public diplomacy office. The following English translation was made by the U.S. Army.

In the name of God, the almighty and merciful.

Fatwa against Osama bin Laden, Al Qaida and many that pretend to justify terrorism based on the sacred Koran or the beliefs of the prophet Muhammad, may God save them.

---

[76] Mansur Escudero Bedate, Secretary General of the Islamic Commission of Spain, Córdova, March 11, 2005. Translation into English by the U.S. Army. The editor acknowledges Jim Guirard for furnishing the translation for this book.

On the 1st anniversary of the terrorist attacks on the 11-M in Madrid, the Islamic Commission of Spain has approved a fatwa (legal religious opinion) in which it declares its strong condemnation of terrorism and emphasizes the impossibility, from an Islamic point of view, that any type or demonstration of terrorism can be justified. God willing, the fatwa will serve as a foundation for the next antiterrorist conference held, God willing, next autumn in Madrid.

Doctrinal foundation

In the Koran, the Book revealed as a guide to humanity, God orders the Muslims to acquire excellence in ethical and moral behavior. Islamic morals are based on values such as: peace, tolerance, mercy and compassion.

The Koran reminds Muslims that they are accountable to God for all their behavior and the way they treat other people, either Muslims or non-Muslims.

In this sense, the Muslim is obligated to seek good for himself, his family, the people around him, and society in general.

"Do good to others as God has done good to you; and do not seek to sow corruption in the land, for certain, God does not love those who sow corruption'. (28:77).

The term 'corruption' includes any form of anarchy and terrorism that undermines peace and security.

The Muslim, therefore, not only cannot commit crimes against innocent people but is also responsible before God to stop those people that have the intention to do it, since they 'sow corruption in the land.'

As one speaks about the treatment toward non-Muslims, so says in the *aleya* (passage?) 60:8: "As for those that do not combat you because of their religion and do not expel you from your homes, you are not prohibited to treat the greater deference (*birr*) or justice, for certainly God loves the just."

The concept of "birr" in this aleya refers to the manner in which someone should treat parents and relatives. Likewise, it comes enclosed in the two principal collections of hadices (Bujari and Muslim) that the Prophet said: "By God, one is not a true believer whose neighbors fear him for his malice."

The prophet encouraged the believers to be kind even with the animals, and prohibited doing them harm or overworking them. A hadiz indicates that the Prophet said about a man who gave water to a thirsty dog, that all his sins were forgiven just for that action.

It was asked then: "Oh Messenger of God, shall we be rewarded for our kindness toward animals?" The prophet responded: "There is a reward for the kindness toward any animal or any human being." (Sahih Muslim, 2244, y Sahih Al-Bujari, 2466).

The Koran does not urge Muslims to return evil with evil; on the contrary, it calls the believers to respond to evil with good deeds.

"But, as good and evil cannot go together, repel evil with something better. Therefore if enmity exists between you and somebody else, he shall become a true friend." (41:34).

In the Koran, God also indicates that the Garden (Paradise) has been prepared for those that spend time in His Cause, in times of prosperity and times of famine, restraining their anger and forgiving others, because God loves those who do good (3:135).

"To those that persevere in doing good, the supreme good awaits them. Their faces will not be darkened by the darkness or humiliation (in judgment day). They are the ones destined for paradise, where they will live for eternity." (10:26).

"Remember that in an attempt to be compensated for something bad, it can become bad at the same time. Therefore, whoever forgives his enemy and makes peace with him, will receive a reward from God, as certainly he does not love the wicked." (42:40).

The loathing of God towards murder is manifest in the aleyas that speak of Abel in the *Surah de La Mesa Servida* [statement unclear – *de La Mesa Servida* means from the served table].

"And Cain said: Be sure that I'll kill you!" (5:27). Abel responded: "Even if you raise your hand to kill me, I won't raise my hand to kill you: in truth, I fear God, the sustainer of the entire world."

After the murder of Abel, God says: 'We decree to the sons of Israel that whoever kills a human being, not being for punishment of murder or for sowing corruption in the land, will be as if to kill all humanity; and whoever saves a life will be as if to save all humanity."

One might point out that the reference to the children of Israel does not affect the universal validity of the message.

The Prophet also remembered that the murder was the second of the great sins than can be committed (Sahih Al-Bujari: 6871, and Sahih Muslim: 88), and said that on Judgment Day the first cases that have to be heard will be those that have to do with bloodshed (Sahih Muslim: 1678, and Sahih Al-Bujari: 6533).

The proper concept of war that is established in the Koran has an exclusively defensive nuance: 'And fight for the cause of God against those that fight you, but do not commit aggressions, for certainly God does not love aggressors." (2:190).

As Muhammad Asad says in his *tafsir* [interpretation of the Koran]: 'the majority of commentators are in agreement that the expression 'the taatadu' means, in this context, "do not commit aggressions." The defensive character in combat 'for God's cause' - that is to say, because of the ethical principles ordered by God- is evident by the reference to 'those that combat you'.... and it is clarified still in aleya 22:39: "For them it is permitted [to fight] that have been unjustly attacked" is, according to all the traditions of which we have the first [and therefore the fundamental one] Koranical reference to the question jihad."

Within the context of defensive warfare, the Prophet imposed strict limits destined to safeguard lives and property. Thus, the Prophet Muhammad prohibited killing, in case of warlike conflict, women and children and civilians in general (Sahih Muslim: 1744, and Sahih Al-Bujari: 3015).

Also he said that a person who killed a person whom had a contract or an agreement with the Muslims would not smell the fragrance of the Paradise (Sahih Al-Bujari: 3166, and Ibn Mayah: 2686).

In light of these and other Islamic texts, the terrorist acts of Osama ben Laden and his organization, Al Qaeda, that look to fill the hearts of defenseless people with fear, that entail the destruction of buildings or properties, that entail the death of civilians, like women and children, or other similar things, they are prohibited and they are the subject of a full sentence within Islam.

Therefore, the accomplishment of terrorist acts under the pretext of 'defending the oppressed nations of the world or the rights of Muslims' has no justification in Islam.

There is no doubt that the Muslims have a legitimate right to react to an aggression or a situation of oppression. Nevertheless, such reaction does not have to give rise to a blind or irrational hatred: "Do not let your hatred towards those which prevent access to the Inviolable House of Adoration (that is to say, the accomplishment of the religious obligations) lead you to transgress (the limits), but on the contrary, you collaborate in fomenting the virtue and the conscience of God, and you do not collaborate in the foment of badness and animosity" (5:2).

Also, the Koran indicates, in reference to which they hypocritically say to follow the Bible, that whenever they ignite the fire of war, God extinguishes it (5:64). God also condemns those nations that violate international treaties and initiate the wars (8:56) and requests that they are reunited by all means possible to defeat them (8:60), but if they incline to peace, the Muslims will have to also do it (8:61).

By it all, it is necessary to show that terrorism and the extremism contradict proper human nature and the lessons of Islam.

Muslims must know that terrorism is a threat against Islam and damages our religion and the Muslims. Correct Islamic training in the madrasas and Islamic universities will allow all to understand that Islam is a peaceful religion, and renounces all acts of terrorism and indiscriminate death.

The presence of signs like arrogance, fanaticism, extremism or religious intolerance in a person or group shows that these have broken away with Islam and the tradition of Muhammad the Prophet.

The commission of terrorist acts supposes a rupture of such magnitude with Islamic lessons that allows affirming that the people or groups who have made them have stopped being Muslim and have located themselves outside the sphere of Islam. Such groups distort and manipulate basic Islamic concepts, such as the one of jihad, putting under them their particular interpretation and criterion.

These groups that use names and languages relative to Islam, discredit, in fact, with their performance, the image of Islam and serve the interests of their enemies. Their performance urges Islamophobia in the countries in which Muslims are a minority, and destroy the relations of cooperation between non-Muslims and Muslims. Their actions provide a false image of Islam that is indeed the one that the enemies of Islam try to offer to the world.

These extremist groups cause death indiscriminately, including the death of other Muslims. We have to remember here that the Prophet expressed that a Muslim that kills another Muslim becomes a *kafir* [unbeliever]. In this same thought, if one Muslim or a group of Muslims commit an act of terrorism, this group is violating the laws of Islam, and is abandoning God's guidance and the path of Din. "God does not give his guidance to those that deliberately do wrong" (9:109). For this, it is necessary to declare:

1. That Islam rejects terrorism in all its forms, whether it's the death of innocents or damage to their property.
2. That Islam is the main victim of terrorist acts performed by some groups that falsely call themselves "Islamic", as such attempts not only cost the lives of many Muslims, but also damage the image of Islam, cause growth in anti-Islamic sentiment, and serve the interests of their enemies.
3. That these groups try to cover their acts by false interpretations of the holy writings, in the effort to gain support of Muslims or gain new converts. This fraud needs to be strongly denounced by the educated and Islamic leaders worldwide.
4. That those that commit terrorist acts violate the basic teachings of the Koran, and become apostate, abandoning Islam.
5. That it is the duty of every Muslim to fight against terrorism, in unison, with the mandate by the Koran that establishes that corruption should not spread in the world.

That according to the Sharia, all that declare that it is permissible to do the things that God has declared should not be done, such as the slaying of innocent people in terrorist acts, becomes *Kafir Murtadd Mustahlil*, or an apostate, for having declared that the killing of innocents is permitted under Islam, crimes which the prophet and the Koran expressly prohibit.

In that Osama Bin Laden and his organization defend the legality of terrorism, saying that it is based on the teachings of the Koran, they are committing a crime and have become apostate, which should not be considered Muslims, or treated as such.

We also declare that Osama Bin laden and his organization, Al Qaeda, who are responsible for horrific crimes against the innocent people that were murdered during the terrorist acts of Mar 11 in Madrid, are outside the parameters of Islam, as are all who proclaim the Koran and the teachings of the Prophet as basis for such terrorist acts.

In addition, we declare that the political vindication attempts of Osama bin Laden and his organization over the recovery of Al Andalus public actions, and therefore notorious and known by all, totally contradict the divine will that has been clearly expressed throughout history, in that God is the Master of History and everything that happens, has happened or will happen, it is design and divine favor and must always be considered in any event by those Muslims for whom God is the giver of goods and the greatest of the conspirators, not having the creature capacity to judge nor question that which divine will has decreed.

The tragedy of Al Andalus, the genocide of Muslims and their expulsion from Spain, their homeland, is an act that God will himself judge, and it is the duty of the created to accept His divine will and be thankful. In reference to the breach of the Santa Fe Capitulations signed by Catholic Kings and the King of the Islamic Kingdom of Granada, we declare that with the signing of the Cooperation Agreements of 1992 between the Spanish State and the legal representatives of the Spanish Muslims, known as the Islamic Commission of Spain, can be given final vindication, legal or political, in so much as the Agreement recognizes in its introduction that "Islam is part the identity of Spain." This recognition, together with the stipulated Agreements, definitively settles the question from the legal or political point of view.

The Cooperation Agreement of 1992 is the new framework that we have given the Spanish State and the Spanish Muslims to reunite us. The Agreement represents the explicit will of the Spanish Muslims and no unknown person in this community, calling himself Bin Laden or calling themselves Al Qaeda, or anyone else, has the right to interfere in the internal issues of our Islamic community.

In line with this fatwa, we requested to the national government and the Spanish media, to stop using the word Islam or Islamic to identify these wrongdoers, as they are not Muslim nor have any relation to our Umma or Islamic Community, they must be called Al Qaeda terrorists or something similar, but without using adjective Islamic, which, as has been stated above, is not appropriate.

Also, we asked the people in charge of the media to lend credence to what is stated here and that from now on, with the criterion expressed above, not to tie Islam or Muslims with any type of terrorist act and especially if it comes disguised with Islamic claims or language.

Mansur Escudero Bedate
Secretary General of the Islamic Commission of Spain
Córdova, 11 March 2005

Broadcasting as a Mission

Government-sponsored international broadcasting serves two principal roles: to serve as the voice of the broadcasting nation (hence the Voice of America), and to act as "free" or "surrogate" media in countries without free journalism with programming about the target audiences' respective countries. The Voice of America has served as a source of objective news and information, and of commentary and opinion from all mainstream U.S. political views. At its most effective, the VOA is not a mouthpiece of the government, but an independent voice that attempts to speak for all Americans.

Surrogate media has a sharply distinct role. Surrogate media programming concerns the specific targeted country or region. News, commentary, cultural programming and entertainment generally pertain to the country of each radio station's target audience. Surrogate media will attempt to report news that is censored or heavily spun by ruling regimes. Radio Free Europe, Radio Liberty, Radio Free Iraq, Radio Free Asia, and Radio Marti are considered surrogate media.

Media such as Radio Farda and Radio Sawa, which provide a news and popular entertainment mix, are generally neither a "voice" of the U.S. nor a surrogate – though this unfortunate situation began to change in mid-2007 under new RFE/RL leadership. In this section, we look at the mission statements of surrogate radios at various points in their histories.

RFE/RL Mission Statement
Radio Free Europe/Radio Liberty[77]

The mission of Radio Free Europe/Radio Liberty is to promote democratic values and institutions by disseminating factual information and ideas.

---

[77] Copyright © 2007. RFE/RL, Inc. Reprinted with the permission of Radio Free Europe/Radio Liberty, 1201 Connecticut Ave., N.W. Washington DC 20036.

From Central Europe to the Pacific, from the Baltic to the Black Sea, from Russia to Central Asia to the Persian Gulf, countries are struggling to overcome autocratic institutions, violations of human rights, centralized economies, ethnic and religious hostilities, regional conflicts, and controlled media.

Stability – based on democracy and free-market economies – throughout this region is essential to global peace. Based on the conviction that the first requirement of democracy is a well informed citizenry, and building on nearly a half century of surrogate broadcasting to this region:

1. RFE/RL provides objective news, analysis, and discussion of domestic and regional issues crucial to successful democratic and free-market transformations.
2. RFE/RL strengthens civil societies by projecting democratic values.
3. RFE/RL combats ethnic and religious intolerance and promotes mutual understanding among peoples.
4. RFE/RL provides a model for local media, assists in training to enhance media professionalism and independence, and develops partnerships with local media outlets.
5. RFE/RL fosters closer ties between the countries of the region and the world's established democracies.

Bringing news to people who need it
Radio Free Europe/Radio Liberty[78]

During the Cold War, the Soviet Union and other members of the Warsaw Pact regularly jammed RFE/RL's signals. In 1988, Soviet leader Mikhail Gorbachev ended jamming, allowing RFE/RL signals to reach a broader audience and allowing RFE/RL services to enter into a closer relationship with the people and journalists to whom they were broadcasting.

---

[78] "About RFE/RL: Bringing the News to People who Need It," Copyright © 2007. RFE/RL, Inc. Reprinted with the permission of Radio Free Europe/Radio Liberty, 1201 Connecticut Ave., NW, Washington DC 20036.

RFE/RL's contribution to the end of communism in this region was acknowledged by virtually everyone. Polish leader Lech Walesa said its role was comparable to the one the sun plays to the earth.

Former Estonian President Lennart Meri nominated RFE/RL for the Nobel Peace Prize and then-Russian President Boris Yeltsin personally intervened to help create an RFE/RL bureau in Moscow after the failed August 1991 coup.

Because of RFE/RL's role in fighting communism, many thought that the radios had fulfilled their mission and could be disbanded. But officials across the region stressed the continuing need for precisely the kind of broadcasts RFE/RL has brought to this region.

Former Czech President Václav Havel spoke for many when he said that "we need your professionalism and your ability to see events from a broad perspective."

Nonetheless, RFE/RL did cut back in some areas even as it expanded in others. It closed its Hungarian service in 1993, and the Polish Service in 1997, while its Czech Service was substantially reduced and joined with Czech Public Radio to establish a new public affairs radio program. The Broadcasting Board of Governors in Washington ended funding for broadcasting to the Czech Republic September 30, 2002.

In January 1994, RFE/RL began broadcasts to the countries of the former Yugoslavia. In October 1998, the Persian Language (Farsi) Service began broadcasting to Iran, and Radio Free Iraq began broadcasting in Arabic to Iraq. In March 1999, RFE/RL started broadcasting to Kosovo in Albanian and in 2001 the Latvian service launched a special bridge-building program in Russian for the Russian minority in Latvia. In September 2001, RFE/RL started broadcasting to Macedonia in both Macedonian and Albanian languages. Broadcasting in Dari and Pashto to Afghanistan began January 30, 2002. RFE/RL's newest language service, the North Caucasus, began broadcasting in Avar, Chechen, and Circassian on April 3, 2002.

Currently, RFE/RL's 18 services broadcast programs in the following 28 languages: Albanian, Arabic, Armenian, Avar, Azerbaijani, Bashkir, Belarusian, Bosnian, Chechen, Circassian, Crimean Tatar, Croatian, Dari, Georgian, Kazakh, Kyrgyz, Macedonian, Montenegrin, Pashto, Persian, Romanian, Russian, Serbian, Tajik, Tatar, Turkmen, Ukrainian, and Uzbek.

With all these changes, the future of RFE/RL seems assured. Its services will continue to bring news and information to people who need them throughout the 21st century.

VOA Journalistic Code
Voice of America (1995)

Preamble

Since 1942, the Voice of America has built a global reputation as a consistently reliable source of news and information. Accuracy, balance, comprehensiveness and objectivity are attributes audiences around the world have come to expect of VOA broadcasters and their product. These standards are legally mandated in the VOA Charter (Public Laws 94-350 and 103-415). Because of them, VOA has become an inspiration and information lifeline to nations and peoples around the world.

Summary

Adhering to the principles outlined in the Charter, VOA reporters and broadcasters must strive for accuracy and objectivity in all their work. They do not speak for the U.S. government. They accept no treatment or assistance from U.S. government officials and agencies that is more favorable or less favorable than that granted to staff of private sector news agencies. Furthermore, VOA professionals, careful to preserve the integrity of their organization, strive for excellence and avoid imbalance or bias in their broadcasts.

The Voice of America pursues its mission today in a world conflict-ridden and unstable in the post Cold War era. Broadcasting accurate, balanced and complete information to the people of the world, and particularly to those who are denied access to accurate news, serves the national interest and is a powerful source of inspiration and hope for all those who believe in freedom and democracy.

The Code

All staff who report, manage, edit and prepare programming at VOA in both central and language services therefore subscribe to these principles:

Sourcing

VOA news and programming must be rigorously sourced and verified. VOA normally requires a minimum of two independent (non-VOA) sources before any newswriter, background writer, political affairs writer, correspondent or stringer may broadcast information as fact in any language.

The only exceptions to the double-source requirement are facts directly confirmed by a VOA journalist or significant news drawn from an official announcement of a nation or an organization. In those rare instances when a secondary source offers exclusive news (e. g., a verified news agency exclusive interview with a chief of state or prominent newsmaker), this story is attributed to the originating agency by name.

Accuracy and Balance

Accuracy and balance are paramount, and together, they are VOA's highest priority. Accuracy always comes before speed in VOA central service and language programming. VOA has a legal obligation to present a comprehensive description of events, reporting an issue in a reliable and unbiased way. Though funded by the U.S. government, VOA airs all relevant facts and opinions on important news events and issues. VOA corrects errors or omissions in its own broadcasts at the earliest opportunity.

VOA is alert to, and rejects, efforts by special interest groups, foreign or domestic, to use its broadcasts as a platform for their own views. This applies to all programs and program segments, including opinion or press roundups, programs discussing letters, listener comments or call-in shows. In the case of call-ins, views of a single party must be challenged by the interviewer if alternative opinions are unrepresented. In interviews, points of possible discussion are submitted in advance if requested by an interviewee of stature (e. g., a chief of state).

VOA journalists (including correspondents, news and language stringers, political affairs writers and program hosts) avoid at all times the use of unattributed pejorative terms or labels to describe persons or organizations, except when the individuals and groups use those labels to describe themselves or their activities.

In news, features and current affairs programming, VOA broadcasters will meticulously avoid fabricating, distorting or dramatizing an event. If sound at an event illustrates the reporter's account of that event and is edited for time, the remaining sound effect reflects what occurred in an accurate and balanced way. If there is a risk of misleading the audience, no use will be made of sound effects not actually recorded at the event being described.

Context and Comprehensiveness

VOA presents a comprehensive account of America and the world, and puts events in context. That means constant vigilance to reflect America's and the world's political, geographical, cultural, ethnic, religious and social diversity. VOA programming represents the broadcast team's best effort to seek out and present a comprehensive account of the event or trend being reported.

VOA broadcasters will avoid using announcing or interviewing techniques that add political coloration or bias to their reportage or current affairs programming. Music will not be used to make editorial statements. VOA journalists and all those preparing news and feature programming avoid any action or statement that might convey the appearance of partisanship.

Procedures

When performing official duties, VOA broadcasters leave their personal political views behind. The accuracy, quality, and credibility of the Voice of America are its most important assets, and they rest on listeners' perception of VOA as an objective source of world, regional, and U.S. news and information. To that end, all VOA journalists will:

1: Always travel on regular, non-diplomatic passports, and rely no more and no less than private sector correspondents on U.S. missions abroad for support, as set out in the guidelines for VOA correspondents.

2: Assist managers whose duty is to ensure that no VOA employee, contract employee or stringer works for any other U.S. government agency, any official media of another state, or any international organization, without specific VOA authorization.

3: Adhere strictly to copyright laws and agency regulations and always credit the source when quoting, paraphrasing, or excerpting from other broadcasting organizations, books, periodicals or any print media.

In addition to these journalistic standards and principles, VOA employees recognize that their conduct both on and off the job can reflect on the work of the Voice of America community. They adhere to the highest standards of journalistic professionalism and integrity. They work to foster teamwork, goodwill and civil discourse in the workplace and with their colleagues everywhere in the world, all to enhance the credibility and effectiveness of the Voice of America.

An instrument of national security policy
Ronald Reagan, NSDD-45 (1982)[79]

This presidential policy document firmly re-established U.S.-sponsored international broadcasting as a national security instrument, subject not only to the guidance of the Secretary of State, but of the National Security Advisor to the President. In modernizing U.S. international broadcasting, National Security Decision Directive (NSDD) 45 re-oriented the Voice of America back to its originally intended purpose of serving as an official voice of the U.S. government, responsive to U.S. diplomatic concerns yet maintaining the editorial integrity of independent news organizations. This dual purpose is often difficult for broadcasters and policymakers alike to accept, but, as the NSDD shows, safeguards are built in.

While NSDD-45 has been superseded and the structures changed, the document is an effective exhibit of the national security importance of international broadcasting.

International broadcasting constitutes an important instrument of the national security policy of the United States. Improvement in the

---

[79] "United States International Broadcasting," National Security Decision Directive Number 45, July 15, 1982. Declassified secret document.

programming and technical quality of U.S. international broadcasting is a requirement of the highest priority. Allocation of budgetary and other resources required to implement the improvements authorized by this memorandum shall be accorded the same priority as in the case of other programs deemed vital to the national security.

The Voice of America (VOA) of the International Communication Agency will remain the official broadcasting voice of the U.S. Government, receiving policy guidance from the Secretary of State and the Director, ICA. VOA should take steps to strengthen existing mechanisms for relating program content to current U.S. foreign and national security policy objectives, while ensuring the integrity of news broadcasting and serving long-range U.S. broadcasting goals and interests in accordance with its legislative charter. Commentary and analysis should incorporate vigorous advocacy of current policy positions of the U.S. Government.

The Radio in the American Sector of Berlin (RIAS) will continue to broadcast to East Germany under the supervision of the Director, International Communication Agency. A review should be undertaken to ensure that appropriate policy guidance is available to RIAS.

Radio Free Europe/Radio Liberty (RFE/RL), a private corporation funded by the Congress and subject to oversight by the Board for International Broadcasting, will continue as an independent organization operating as a surrogate free radio for the Soviet Union and Eastern Europe. A new entity for broadcasting to Cuba, Radio Marti, is currently being established and will function in a manner analogous to RFE/RL. Both radios shall operate in a manner not inconsistent with the broad objectives of U.S. foreign and national security policy.

[Classified paragraph redacted]

Technical cooperation and joint planning between U.S. international broadcasters, including RFE/RL and Radio Marti, will be undertaken on a regular basis as a matter of policy. At the same time, care should be taken to maintain the autonomy and special character of the surrogate radios.

Guidance for determining language and broadcast hours for VOA and RFE/RL will continue to be the responsibility of the Secretary of State and the Assistant to the President for National Security Affairs, acting in consultation with the Director, International Communication Agency, and the Chairman of the Board for

International Broadcasting. The revised guidance prepared in conjunction with this directive is approved.

VOA and RFE/RL will undertake a major, long-term program of modernization and expansion over the period FY 84 to FY 89, affecting program-related as well as technical aspects of their operations. Funding for elements of this program that are subject to rapid implementation will be sought in FY 83. The technical criteria used for planning facility modernization shall be those specified in NSSM 245, until such time as further experience and research provide a better basis for measuring signal requirements. While short wave is and will remain for the foreseeable future the primary medium of U.S. international broadcasting, medium and long wave are preferable wherever technically and politically feasible.

Diplomatic requirements deriving from this modernization and expansion program shall be given high priority by the Department of State. Acquisition of new transmitting sites and facilities should be a priority matter on the political agenda of bilateral relations with appropriate countries. Attention should also be given to renewal of facility requirements which have lapsed, with permission for augmentation as necessary, and to negotiation for the use of out-of-band frequencies. Finally, planning for the upcoming high frequency World Administrative Radio Conference should be accelerated, and priority given to protecting and where possible expanding the frequencies available to the U.S. for international short wave broadcasting.

Particularly in view of the recent renewal of jamming of VOA by the Soviet Union, it is essential that the U.S. take all possible steps to overcome jamming of U.S. international broadcasts and to ameliorate its effects. Continuing interagency study needs to be given to political as well as technical aspects of jamming and possible countermeasures. A major, coordinated effort should be undertaken to press the jamming issue diplomatically in all appropriate international and bilateral fora.

Direct broadcasting by satellite (DBS), while unlikely to provide an alternative to ground-based international broadcasting for the foreseeable future, nevertheless offers a potentially important supplement to our existing broadcasting capabilities. Further study should be undertaken immediately of the technical parameters of a variety of plausible DBS systems for international broadcasting, with particular attention to the role of DBS in a jammed environment.

Study is also required on a priority basis of the role of U.S. international broadcasting facilities and operations in periods of crisis and war. The Departments of State and Defense as well as the International Communication Agency and the Board for International Broadcasting should review existing guidance in this area and make recommendations for closer integration of our international broadcasting effort into political and military contingency planning.

[signed] Ronald Reagan

A clear and continuing mission
Radio Free Europe/Radio Liberty[80]

After the Soviet collapse in 1991, many thought RFE/RL had outlived its usefulness. That turned out not to be the case. RFE/RL's post-Soviet roles are spelled out in a forward-looking mission statement that maintains the traditions of the successful past.

Radio Free Europe/Radio Liberty's mission today remains what it has been for nearly half a century: promoting democratic values and institutions by disseminating factual information and ideas.

From Central Asia to the Pacific, from the Baltic to the Black Sea, from Russia to Central Asia to the Persian Gulf, countries are struggling to overcome autocratic institutions, violations of human rights, ethnic and religious hostilities, and severely controlled media. RFE/RL exists to help the peoples of this enormous region overcome these problems by promoting the values of democracy and free-market economics in ways that also promote the stability essential to global peace.

Based on the conviction that the first requirement of democracy is a well-informed citizenry and building on a half century of surrogate broadcasting, Radio Free Europe/Radio Liberty has five goals:

> *First*, to provide objective news, analysis, and discussion of domestic and regional issues crucial to successful democratic and free-market transformations.

---

[80] "About RFE/RL: A Clear and Continuing Mission," Copyright © 2007 RFE/RL, Inc. Reprinted with the permission of Radio Free Europe/Radio Liberty, 1201 Connecticut Ave. NW, Washington DC 2036.

Second, to help to strengthen civil societies by projecting democratic values.

Third, to strive to combat ethnic and religious intolerance by promoting mutual understanding among all groups.

Fourth, to establish a model for local media, assist in training to enhance media professionalism and independence and, when possible, develops partnerships with local media outlets.

Fifth, to seek to foster closer ties between the countries of this region and the world's established democracies.

Each of its 18 services apply [sic] these principles according to local circumstances. In some RFE/RL broadcast countries, the station has an extremely good working relationship with local authorities and journalists. But in other cases, the station must deal with official antipathy and enforced isolation from local journalists. These differences are reflected in the programming of specific services. But amidst all this diversity, there remains the fundamental mission of RFE/RL: helping people create the conditions of freedom in which they can make decisions for themselves and for their countries.

Democracy and security in U.S. foreign policy:
The role of RFE/RL
Thomas A. Dine (2001)[81]

As the longest-serving president of RFE/RL, Thomas A. Dine oversaw the re-orientation of the radios during the failed attempt at pro-western and democratic rule in Russia, and the aftermath of the September 11, 2001 attacks. In the speech below, delivered prior to 9/11, Dine outlines the radios' role in American foreign policy execution, and their new utility in areas like the war-torn Balkans. Dine's comments also show how RFE/RL remained on the forefront of predicting major international political trends. Dine is one of the few senior American officials (the RFE/RL director is not a U.S. government official but is

---

[81] Thomas A. Dine was president of Radio Free Europe/Radio Liberty from 1997 to 2005. This item is from his speech, "Democracy and security in U.S. foreign policy: The role of RFE/RL," given at the Heritage Foundation, March 22, 2001. Copyright © 2007. RFE/RL, Inc. Reprinted with the permission of Radio Free Europe/Radio Liberty, 1201 Connecticut Ave. N.W., Washington DC 20036.

*appointed by the independent, bipartisan Broadcasting Board of
Governors which, in turn, is appointed by the President of the
United States) to note the dictatorial turn of Russian President
Vladimir Putin. In his comments, Dine was decidedly not on-
message with the presidential administration.*

*Following the pre-9/11 speech appears the text of a presentation
that Dine made in 2004. The second speech illustrates the radios'
role in combating Islamist extremism and political instability in
general, and shows how the radios can adapt to address changing
national security priorities.*

At the dawn of the American experience, Benjamin Franklin
presciently observed that "those who would sacrifice essential
liberties for a little temporary safety deserve neither liberty nor
safety."

Over the last 200 years, many people have invoked Franklin's
admonition, but all too often, they have failed to understand its
implications both domestically and internationally. Some have
presented his comment as an invocation to fight against efforts to
defend national security, while others have argued that his words
highlight the need to do just that in the pursuit of more distant but
more important goals.

Such misreadings of Franklin are especially unfortunate because in
fact this American founder was pointing to a link which has
informed American domestic and foreign policy for most of our
national history. We promote security at home and abroad precisely
by promoting essential liberties. And when, under the press of
events, we somehow forget that link, we almost always get into
trouble.

I am very pleased to have this opportunity to speak to you today
about this issue because it is at the core of what Radio Free
Europe/Radio Liberty is doing across an enormous part of the world.
Through our broadcasts of timely and accurate information and
thoughtful analysis, we are promoting democracy in countries which
have known little of it in the past and which are facing enormous
obstacles in moving toward it even now. And in so doing, we are
promoting American national security by helping to transform the
world in ways that will fulfill Franklin's injunction.

Today I would like to discuss three aspects of this problem with
you: first, the philosophical relationship between liberty and
security; second, the challenges RFE/RL has successfully overcome

in the past but still faces in the present; and third, what I see as frightening trends, both in the countries we broadcast to and in the West as well, that could threaten the development of democracy in countries with whose fate ours is inevitably tied.

Liberty and Security

Neither in the United States nor elsewhere do most discussions focus on the relationship between democratic liberties and national security. On the one hand, this is a reflection of just how embedded this notion is in the minds of national security theorists and actors. But on the other hand, it also reflects the way in which national security policy is made and especially the short time horizon of some who make it.

More than any other country, the United States has been involved in the promotion of democracy around the world. We are unique in that our first document as a country, the Declaration of Independence, begins not with a list of grievances or special claims by Americans but rather by the invocation of a universal principle that all peoples have the right to run their own affairs rather than to have others run them.

And even if sometimes Americans forget that, others around the world look to us more because of that than because of our weapons or our economic prosperity or our cultural leadership.

Since World War II, the United States, the first "new nation" to use Seymour Martin Lipset's classic formulation, has promoted the rise of new nations around the world, a process that has not been easy or without problems. In that period, the number of countries has increased by four times, and the percentage of those with some form of democratic governance has increased dramatically as well. In short, thanks to American efforts, democracy is no longer the exception; it is the rule, and even more, the expectation of all peoples around the world.

In that sense at least, Francis Fukuyama was right in arguing that the events of 1989 and 1991 involving the end of the Soviet external and internal empire did in fact represent the end of history, the final agreement about what is the only defensible form of government.

And that process of the spread of democratic institutions has contributed in major ways to the current unprecedented security and prosperity that the American people currently enjoy – even in these days of heightened nervousness about the stock market averages!

No policy maker in Washington would disagree that the spread of democratic liberties around the world has contributed to our security in this way. But because of the nature of the positions they occupy, most of them do not focus as much as they might on promoting democratic change. They are focused on narrower and more short-term issues, and consequently, they often do not reflect on such a long-term process.

That has been especially true over the last decade given the triumphalism many Americans felt in the wake of the collapse of communism in Europe, a collapse that lead many people to conclude that the United States had already made sufficient contributions to this process and that in the future we could focus on ourselves rather than on others.

This is not the first time Americans have reached that kind of a conclusion, and it is not the first time that such conclusions have proven to be misplaced.

The Role of RFE/RL in Transforming Societies

Radio Free Europe/Radio Liberty is one of the key expressions of the American understanding that promoting democracy promotes American national security. For 50 years – and this is our anniversary year – RFE/RL broadcasts have helped people living under authoritarian regimes or making the difficult transition from them to achieve their goals of liberty. And in achieving that liberty, they become better partners of the United States, and the world becomes a more secure place.

Throughout the Cold War, there was a national consensus in the United States about this, about the role of RFE/RL in promoting positive change. With the fall of the Berlin wall and with the collapse of the communist experiment in Europe and Eurasia, however, that consensus began to fray. Many people felt that RFE/RL had done its job, had completed its mission, and thus should pass from the scene.

But such views were misplaced for three reasons. First, they failed to understand the nature of RFE/RL. Second, they ignored the problems facing the post-communist countries. And third, they were overly optimistic about what kind of changes were possible.

RFE/RL was anti-communist because it represented a positive commitment to democracy and freedom. It was committed to democracy and freedom because it was anti-communist. Hence, our task has not been achieved because of the collapse of communism. We can only be said to have achieved our victory once challenges to freedom and democracy in these countries have been eliminated. That time is not yet, and I fear it will not be soon.

Indeed, in an image popularized by Steve Erlanger of the *New York Times*, the events of 1989 and 1991 were like the rise of a group of birds from a tree in reaction to a shotgun shell explosion. Now that the sound has dissipated, most of the birds have simply resettled back on the tree, many of them on the very same branches.

Across our broadcast region, most of the people in power would have been in power had the events of 1989 and 1991 never taken place. Not surprisingly, they are restoring not only the Soviet-era anthem but also Soviet-era practices like suppression of media freedom and hence the undermining of the foundations of democracy there and security for both them and us.

In Russia, in Ukraine, in so many places, journalists are being attacked, media outlets are being strangled, and leaders intolerant of any criticism are having their way. Indeed, in many cases, the only source of uncensored news most people have is from our broadcasts and those of other international broadcasters.

But before expanding on this and another threat to the promotion of liberty and security, I would like to call attention to another aspect of RFE/RL's contribution. As many of you know, we were never permitted to broadcast to the former Yugoslavia during the Cold War. The reasons for that lie in realpolitik. But unfortunately, we are now seeing some of the consequences of those decisions made many years ago.

Our broadcasts not only bring people accurate information but they help to build bridges across divides that various people have sought to exploit and inflame. Many conflicts that were predicted at the time of the demise of the Soviet Union have not happened or been as severe as might otherwise have been the case because we were able in our broadcasts to build bridges between them, between the Armenians and the Azerbaijanis, between the peoples of Central Asia. Our success in this was not total, but I am convinced that had we been broadcasting to Yugoslavia earlier, some of the bloodshed there might not have occurred, and that if we are given a role in Macedonia, we might yet be able to calm the situation, promote democracy, and hence advance our national security interests.

Two disturbing trends

Finally, I would like to point to two disturbing trends, one in the region we broadcast to and another here in the United States. As I have already suggested, the governments in our broadcast region are moving away from democracy rather than toward it in all too many cases. Russian President Putin is increasingly authoritarian and looks good only in comparison with the chaos of the immediate past or the even more authoritarian rulers elsewhere in the post-Soviet states. And in Iraq and Iran, our broadcasts are promoting precisely the kind of freedom that will have to come to the peoples of those two long-suffering countries if they and we are to have a secure future in that part of the world.

A decade ago, we were all optimists about what would be possible in these countries. Now, we increasingly are all pessimists. Many here believe that there is little prospect that any of these countries can move toward democracy any time soon and hence argue that we should simply adopt a strategy of waiting them out, an argument I would suggest that Franklin would find deeply troubling.

But this pessimism has compounded another trend here in Washington that I think we must resist as well. The end of the Cold War saw the dissolution of a consensus among three different groups, who like a troika worked together then but who increasingly are going their own ways. Among those who opposed communism were some who did so for purely geopolitical reasons, others who opposed communism as an economic system, and still a third group who worked against it because it was anti-democratic.

While the Soviet Union still existed, the different approaches of these three were seldom on public view. All of them could agree on the need to continue to oppose what President Ronald Reagan wisely called "the evil empire." But with the end of the Soviet Union, each of these three groups has tended to advance its agenda with less and less reference to the importance of the other two.

The geopoliticians call for a kind of neo-containment, arguing that this is the best or perhaps the least bad option. They often have written off any chance of democratic change and insist that national security considerations must trump issues of democratization. The advocates of capitalism often argue that as long as Russia and these other countries move toward a free market, the other freedoms will follow in due course. Their views often lead them to argue that accepting a little temporary authoritarianism is a price worth paying.

And that leaves the advocates of democracy, those who want to continue the struggle against regimes which deny or seek to deny their citizens basic democratic rights, somewhat isolated. Obviously, RFE/RL is part of this third group.

In short, my purpose today is not to suggest that anyone should ignore either geopolitical calculations or the importance of free markets. These are critical elements. My purpose is to argue, as Benjamin Franklin did two centuries ago, that we are most likely to achieve our national security goals when we promote democracy together with those other agendas. And equally, I want to insist, we will likely find our own security undermined if we ignore or downplay the importance of democracy and its essential liberties in pursuing our national security.

Communicating to the world's most volatile hotspots
Thomas A. Dine (2004) [82]

There's a Washington conversation that I have over and over again. Someone asks me what I do. I say, "I'm the head of Radio Free Europe/Radio Liberty." The person then says one of two things: "I didn't know Radio Free Europe still existed," or "But isn't Europe already free?" Today I want to address these misconceptions about RFE/RL: that Europe is free; that RFE/RL focuses solely on Europe; in short, that RFE/RL is a Cold War relic and not relevant to today's world.

To start, though, let me give you a brief overview of who we are. RFE/RL broadcasts to 19 countries in 28 languages, none of which is English. 19 of our 28 language services are directed at majority-Muslim populations. We have bureaus in every one of our countries but Iran and Turkmenistan.

We are a "surrogate broadcaster," which means that our mission, unlike that of Voice of America, is to broadcast news and information about the individual countries listening to us, not about the United States – unless the news from Washington involves one or more of our countries. In addition to radio, RFE/RL is very

---

[82] Thomas A. Dine, President, RFE/RL, speech to the Woodrow Wilson Center, May 6, 2004. Copyright © 2007. RFE/RL, Inc. Reprinted with the permission of Radio Free Europe/Radio Liberty, 1201 Connecticut Ave. NW, Washington DC 20036.

prominent on the Internet – nearly all of our broadcast services operate top-notch local-language websites, and our main website averages about 6 million page views a month. We are also on television in a handful of countries.

Let me now address the first question, "Isn't Europe already free?" People often forget that the eastern border of Europe is not Warsaw or Bucharest or even St. Petersburg – it's the Ural Mountains, two time zones east of Moscow. To put it another way – the geographic center of Europe isn't Germany or Austria. It's Ukraine. We can divide our European countries into two groups: the former Yugoslavia and the former Soviet Union.

It is a mistake to believe that the arrest of Milosevic marked the end of the turmoil in the former Yugoslavia. Most of it is politically and economically crippled; the odds of further ethnic bloodshed are high; corruption is pervasive; and the emergence of a free press has been stunted.

In Serbia, the euphoria that greeted the ouster of Milosevic has given way to a prevailing attitude that can best be described as a noxious brew of nationalism and self-pity. The strongest party is now the ultra-nationalistic Serbian Radical Party, and vestiges of Milosevic's criminal regime survive nearly intact – the assassination of Prime Minister Djindjic last year was merely the most tragic example of its continuing influence. Meanwhile, the economy is a shambles, and since foreign investors want little to do with Serbia, there is no improvement in sight.

Furthermore, Serbia's territorial integrity is anything but certain. In Montenegro, about half the people want to secede from the federation with Serbia, while the other half want to stay. And in Kosovo, the worst ethnic violence since NATO's military action erupted in March of this year. Analysts say that, far from being an isolated incident, this latest outbreak of hostilities was the tip of the iceberg. When you consider that unemployment in Kosovo is between 60% and 70%, and that a majority of the population lives in poverty, it's hard to be hopeful that tolerance will prevail. If ethnic violence does recur in Kosovo, it will certainly destabilize another of our broadcast countries – Macedonia – where 25% of the population is ethnic Albanian.

Finally, Bosnia and Herzegovina has also been unable to move beyond nationality-based infighting. Local government bodies are strictly loyal to members of their own nationality, and the nationalistic ruling parties resist market reforms because they fear they will lose their grip on power. For the politicians in power in Bosnia, the war is not over, but merely in remission.

The reason RFE/RL plays such a critical role in the Balkans is that it is the only local-language media outlet that speaks to, and for, all the ethnic groups; the rest of the media have come to serve as inflammatory voices of intolerance. The uniqueness of our programming is reflected in our outstanding ratings-our numbers in the former Yugoslavia are consistently among the highest in our broadcast portfolio.

The second group of our European countries is, as I mentioned, the former Soviet Union, and, if I haven't depressed you enough already, I have to tell you that the former Soviet Union makes the former Yugoslavia look like Switzerland. Everyone in this room remembers the sense of hope we felt when the U.S.S.R. collapsed. Fifteen nations had been freed from Moscow's control, and each of them would pursue its own path not only towards an independent national identity, but towards freedom and democracy. Alas, with the exception of the three Baltic republics, the freedom-and-democracy part hasn't proven true.

Let's begin with the three countries of the Caucasus, where our weekly listenership ratings are very high, close to 20%. When the Soviet Union collapsed, Armenia was certainly considered one of the republics likeliest to succeed. It was a Christian country with close ties to the West, a highly educated populace, and a cohesive, talented diaspora. But, after an initial period of reform, Armenia has regressed into a corrupt oligarchy. No wonder it has lost nearly a third of its population to emigration since 1992.

Azerbaijan, too, seemed promising, mainly because western investors were flocking there for its oil. However, it, too, has succumbed to oligarchy, and in fact last year, Azerbaijan earned the dubious distinction of becoming the first former Soviet republic in which power was transferred from father to son.

To complete the Caucasian triumvirate: Georgia experienced happy news at the end of last year, when a peaceful protest movement led to the collapse of Eduard Shevardnadze's corrupt government, and the election of a true democrat, Mikhail Saakashvili, to the presidency. Unfortunately, President Saakashvili has inherited a mess. Two provinces want to secede from Georgia and unite with Russia; a third region, Adjaria, has demanded more independence from Tbilisi; its infrastructure is decimated; and corruption is endemic among its workforce.

In the early hours of this morning, the Adjaria crisis came to an end when its warlord was persuaded by [Defense] Minister Ivanov of Russia to step down and seek asylum in Moscow. Our Georgian Service broadcast all last night and this morning, live.

The next country in RFE/RL's European portfolio, Moldova, is the poorest nation in Europe. In 2001, Moldova became the first former Soviet state to elect an unreformed Communist president; every year, President Voronin pays his respects at the monument to Lenin in the capital. To visit Moldova is to take a trip to a Twilight Zone in which there are lots of old people, lots of children, and almost no one in between-they've all left to go find work in other countries. Over the last our years, our Moldovan Service has doubled its listenership.

Further north, we have Belarus, Europe's most repressive nation. Belarus is run by a psychopath named Alexander Lukashenka, who openly admires Stalin and who did business with Saddam Hussein. Needless to say, Lukashenka isn't very fond of RFE/RL, which is probably why this year our Minsk bureau has been burglarized, threatened with eviction, and visited by the tax police.

Russia is one of the great underreported stories in the world today. Here we have a former superpower that, having experimented with democracy, has reverted to autocracy. My Moscow colleagues tell me that they have not felt such a climate of enforced orthodoxy since the 1970s. Putin is so powerful, and so feared, that no one in the Russian government arrives at work before noon, and no one leaves before 10 p.m. – because that is the schedule that Putin keeps. The last time the Kremlin observed this ominous practice was during the rule of Stalin.

Just this week, the Committee to Protect Journalists named Russia one of the ten worst places in the world to be a journalist, citing President Putin's use of sham lawsuits and corporate maneuvers to virtually eliminate independent media. Television and radio are now little more than an arm of the Kremlin. Meanwhile, Putin continues to go to great lengths to obstruct coverage of the war in Chechnya, something we at RFE/RL experienced in 2000, when our reporter Andrei Babitsky was kidnapped in Chechnya by Russian FSB [the re-named internal security apparat of the old KGB], disappeared for over 5 weeks, and finally dumped out of the trunk of a car in Mahashkala, Dagestan one cold February day.

We complete this survey of our European broadcast area with the biggest disappointment of all: Ukraine. With a well-educated population of 48 million, Ukraine had the potential to become one of the great nations of Europe. Instead, under the corrupt rule of President Leonid Kuchma, Ukraine has become an embarrassment. It has forged commercial relationships with Iran, Syria, Libya, and Iraq. The Kuchma administration has also aggressively subverted the democratic process, employing an array of dirty tricks and brutal tactics. It is no wonder that "Ukraine fatigue" has become a term of art in the State Department and at the EU.

Ukraine will elect a new president in October. But Kuchma is so determined to keep his cronies in power that he has unleashed a severe crackdown on independent media – and his main target is RFE/RL. In February, our most important affiliate network in Ukraine, after being taken over by supporters of Kuchma, kicked us off the air. In March, a Kyiv station that had begun to air RFE/RL programming two days earlier was raided and closed by the authorities. And on that very same day, the director of another station was killed in a car accident while on his way to a meeting with an RFE/RL representative. With an election just months away, Kuchma feels he cannot afford to have RFE/RL around.

I give you this tour of Eastern Europe not only to show that Europe is not free, but because something very important is at stake here. Right now, the United States is engaged in a massive effort to promote democracy in the Middle East. But I worry that by focusing on the Middle East, we are neglecting to finish the job much closer to home, in Eastern Europe. We suffer from a sort of "political attention deficit disorder"; we pay attention whenever missiles are launched, but once the bombs stop falling, we stop watching. Most Americans think that Europe has been taken care of, and we can now move on to the Middle East. But, as I have just described, a large part of Europe has not been taken care of.

Furthermore, experts agree that one of the pillars of Putin's political identity going forward will be an increasingly assertive foreign policy in places that used to report to Moscow. Since the former republics of the Soviet Union have such shoddy governments now, and are in such dire straits economically, I am very apprehensive about what Eastern Europe may look like in the near future. We cannot discount the possibility that not one but several dictatorships will be reborn in the heart of Europe.

To address the second widespread misconception about RFE/RL, that we are solely engaged with Europe: the facts are otherwise.

About half of the countries to which we broadcast are in Asia. And they, too, desperately need what RFE/RL offers.

Let's start with Iran, because this has been a depressing talk so far, and Iran is a country I have high hopes for. Iran may be run by religious fanatics, but its population is young, pro-West, and pro-democracy. 70% of the Iranian population is under the age of 30. The regime is doomed, as a simple matter of demographics.

Because of the extraordinarily youthful skew of Iran's population, we decided to try something a little different with Iran. In December of 2002, we launched a joint venture with our sister entity, Voice of America, called Radio Farda. Radio Farda is a 24-hours-a-day, 7-days-a-week station that combines, in a fast-paced format, eight hours of serious news coverage each day with a mix of Western and Iranian pop music.

The response has been extraordinary: over 20% of Iranians between the ages of 18 and 29 listen to Radio Farda at least once a week. Over 40,000 visitors a day use the Farda website to listen to the station over the Internet. Thousands of messages a week pour into Farda's telephone call-in service. And 76% of the Iranian people consider it a reliable source of news and information. So much for the Great Satan. The theocrats are obviously scared, and last year they started jamming Farda's broadcast signal, blocking access to its website, and incarcerating our correspondents.

Another Asian hotspot is Afghanistan. In the wake of the 9/11 terrorist attacks, members of the House of Representatives asked us to create a broadcast service to Afghanistan. Four months after the attacks, Radio Free Afghanistan was up and running, broadcasting 12 hours a day in Dari and Pashto to that beleaguered country.

Reminiscent of scenes in movies when someone who's been crawling through the desert for days finally finds water and gulps it down with tremendous intensity, the response to our broadcasts in Afghanistan has been overwhelming. This is because under the Taliban, the people weren't just denied objective news and information – they were denied radios. In Kabul now, 54% of Afghans listen to us weekly, and in the northern city of Mazar-e Sharif that figure climbs to 68%. Nothing in my job makes me happier than reading the messages we get from our listeners, male and female. Radio Free Afghanistan has made an immediate difference in the lives of the newly free Afghan people.

But recall the "political A.D.D." that I mentioned earlier. I am worried that the United States and its allies are not following through on their promise to rebuild the country. Afghanistan today does not have functioning institutions. Outside Kabul, security is worse than it was under the Taliban. Aid workers are being murdered at an alarming rate, and as a result relief organizations are drastically scaling back operations. The capital barely has contact with, let alone control over, the rest of the country, which is run by regional warlords. And our correspondents believe the Taliban is regrouping. Obviously, Afghanistan will remain one of our most important broadcast targets for years to come.

I'm going to skip over Iraq, where we broadcast in Arabic and Kurdish, for two reasons. First, I think it's safe to say that everyone in this room is well aware of what's going on there. Second, to my enormous regret, the Administration's FY05 budget calls for the termination of Radio Free Iraq at the end of this fiscal year. It is now up to Congress to decide whether to acquiesce or continue funding it to the tune of $2.2 million a year. Whatever the outcome, I am delighted with what RFI has accomplished in its five years; the latest research shows that a whopping 34.4% of Iraqis listen to us each week.

I'll conclude this tour of our Asian broadcast area with the five Central Asian former republics of the Soviet Union: Kazakhstan, Kyrgyzstan, Tajikistan, Turkmenistan, and Uzbekistan.

The most benign of the bunch are Kyrgyzstan and Tajikistan, where reporters do operate with relative autonomy, provided that they don't make any trouble for the people in power. Unfortunately, that's as good as it gets in Central Asia today. Each of the other three states has, since obtaining independence from Moscow, morphed into a post-Soviet version of The Sopranos, where one crime family rules through intimidation and violence.

In Kazakhstan, it's the Nazarbayev family, and they don't like it when journalists stick their noses in their business. In the last three years, newspapers have been burglarized, their employees beaten, and their offices burned to the ground. Three independent TV stations were shut down in 2002 alone. Journalists who dare investigate the corrupt business practices of the Nazarbayev family are sent to jail. Soon RFE/RL may be the only independent media outlet operating in Kazakhstan – the rest are all controlled by the President's daughter, Darigha.

Uzbekistan is run by the Karimov family, and conditions there are worse than they are in Kazakhstan. Journalists who report on the crime, corruption, and poverty plaguing Uzbekistan are routinely fired – and they're the lucky ones; many have been arrested, injured, and jailed. In many cases, it is publicity by RFE/RL that saves these brave journalists from lengthier prison sentences. I myself felt a surge of intense contempt for the Uzbek regime last year, when a group of 20 thugs, no doubt working for the government, surrounded one of our correspondents as he reported on an incident at Tashkent's central market, beat him, and stole his equipment.

The final Mafia state in Central Asia is Turkmenistan, and, though it may be hard to believe after the foregoing discussion, Turkmenistan is the worst of all of them. The dictator of Turkmenistan, Saparmurat Niyazov, has constructed a cult of personality there that would have made Romania's Ceausescu blush. Every newspaper lists Niyazov as its founder. All editors are personally appointed by Niyazov. Censorship is total. The most important news story, every day, is the magnificence of Niyazov.

We have correspondents in Turkmenistan, but they must work in secret, using pseudonyms. Unfortunately, they do not always succeed in remaining anonymous. In the past year alone, several of our reporters in Turkmenistan have been abducted, beaten, and jailed. And our stringer in Moscow was savagely beaten just last week. That these brave men and women are willing to risk their lives so that their compatriots can at least hear a little bit of truth every day never fails to move me. They are true heroes.

As you can see, Radio Free Europe/Radio Liberty has as much to do with Asia as it does with Europe. In fact, since we are funded by the government, our priorities as an organization largely track its priorities, and right now the biggest priority of the government is combating terrorism. That's why I always have to laugh when people claim that RFE/RL is a relic – especially since 19 of our 28 broadcast languages are directed at predominantly-Muslim populations.

In fact, as part of the War on Terror, RFE/RL hopes to redouble its radio, television, and Internet efforts to the five Central Asian states over the next 12 months. Although these former Soviet states may seem to have little to do with Islamist terrorism, we at RFE/RL believe that Central Asia could well be the next front in the global War on Terror. Already, at least two terrorist organizations are operating within these countries, seeking to establish Islamic theocracy. Most importantly, these Central Asian nations are exactly the kind of places that can become breeding grounds for terrorism. Remember that almost all of the terrorists of 9/11 came not from

Muslim countries whose governments professed hatred of the United States (Iran, Iraq, Afghanistan) but from Muslim countries whose governments are friendly with the United States: Saudi Arabia and Egypt. The same is true of these Central Asian states, where west-friendly autocrats rule over Muslim populations, and where the U.S. government has made alliances of necessity while pursuing the larger goal of toppling the Taliban and Saddam Hussein.

As the people living under these regimes become more and more bitter about the hopelessness of their lives, they are drawn to more radical belief systems. The best way to combat the growth of such radicalism is not to make society less free, as these Central Asian dictators have done, but to make it more free. RFE/RL looks forward to intensifying the fight to make Central Asia a freer, and therefore safer, place.

I hope that I have succeeded today in getting my message across. RFE/RL is not a Cold War relic, but a modern media organization communicating to the world's most unstable hotspots. Today we cannot know what the next Afghanistan will be – just as we can't know where the next Srebrenica massacre will occur, or where the next militant Islamic revolution will erupt. But the likelihood is that many people there are listening to RFE/RL, and they are grateful that we have not stopped fighting for our shared values: the free flow of information, human rights, freedom and democracy.

Mission, vision, priorities, strategic goals and objectives
Broadcasting Board of Governors (2007)[83]

After the reorganization of international broadcasting under the Broadcasting Board of Governors (BBG), the national security mission was publicly absent. Congress mandated the BBG to focus on the promotion of democracy.

The 9/11 attacks resulted in the restoration of the overt national security function; the BBG stated that its broadcasting would "provide accurate and objective news and information to priority areas in support of the war against terrorism." On the following pages is the executive summary of the Strategic Plan of the BBG, current as of 2007.

---

[83] Broadcasting Board of Governors, "Marrying the Mission to the Market: Strategic Plan 2002-2007," p. 4.

The BBG mission is:

To promote and sustain freedom and democracy by broadcasting accurate and objective news and information about the United States and the world to audiences overseas.

The long-term vision for the BBG is:

A flexible, multi-media, research-driven U.S. International Broadcasting System, incorporating regional networks and single-country operations, that reaches mass audiences by programming the distinct content of the Voice of America and the surrogate services through state-of-the art formats and the distribution channels – AM, FM, audio and video satellite, shortwave, and the Internet – that our audiences use and we control.

Focus

The BBG now supports 65 broadcast languages through over 90 language services (counting VOA and the surrogates separately) to more than 125 markets worldwide. Congress has highlighted the need for the BBG to concentrate on supporting democracy and cover issues related to the establishment of democratic institutions. The focus is clear: U.S. international broadcasting should prioritize those countries and regions that lack democracy or are still making the transition to democracy and are consequently still vulnerable.

Broadcast Language Priorities

In its broad support of U.S. foreign policy, the BBG sets three major priorities in the post-9/11/01 time frame of this strategic plan:

- to provide accurate and objective news and information to priority areas in support of the war against terrorism;
- to provide clear and accurate information to regions of the world where freedom of information is suppressed or denied, or to areas that lack freedom and democracy;
- to serve humanitarian efforts by assisting nations in crisis, or are suffering epidemics and illiteracy.

Key Factors

Two key factors influence the BBG in achieving its vision and continued success in accomplishing the mission – market challenges and internal challenges.

Market Challenges:
- Branding and Positioning – create a distinctive contemporary identity.
- Target Audiences – determine language service-by-language service target audiences.
- Formats and Programs – update outmoded formats and programs.
- Delivery and Placement – ensure broadcasts are easily seen and heard.
- Marketing and Promotion – improve awareness levels so that audiences know where and when to tune in and what type of information they will receive if they do.
- Technology – maximize use of new media.

Internal Challenges:
- Consolidate and rationalize – leverage all of our resources to maximize impact in our priority markets.
- Coordinate among BBG entities – increase coordination and cooperation among the many disparate broadcasting components, each of which has its own history and tradition.
- Resources – allocate resources in a fair and comprehensive manner.
- Market competitiveness – strengthen our multi-media profile by funding and conducting research, carrying out marketing and promotion, securing talented language-qualified journalists, broadcasters and technicians.
- Intergovernmental Relations – establish an overall relationship of mutual respect, trust, and cooperation within the U.S. government's foreign policy community, while safeguarding the BBG's journalistic independence.

Strategic Goals and Objectives

The over-arching aim of the Broadcasting Board of Governors is to achieve an increasingly effective international broadcasting system that reaches significant audiences where most needed in support of U.S. strategic interests. It is in the context of this broad purpose that the following goals and objectives should be considered.

Goal I – Design a Broadcasting Architecture for the 21st Century.
* *Create the Worldwide U.S. International Broadcasting System*
* *Realign the BBG Organizational Structure*

Goal II – Expand the U.S. International Broadcasting System through Regional Networks and Single-Country Priority Initiatives
* *Launch the Middle East Radio Network and Make It a Success*
* *Harmonize Radio Free Afghanistan and VOA in the Afghanistan Radio Network*
* *Pioneer Anti-terrorism Broadcasting*
* *Reach the Two Continental Giants: Russia and China*

Goal III – Employ Modern Communication Techniques and Technologies
* *Accelerate Multi-media Development, Infusing More TV and Internet into the Mix*
* *Adopt the Principles and Practices of Modern Radio "Formatics"*
* *Control the Distribution Channels that Audiences Use*
* *Go Local in Content and Presence*
* *Tailor Content to the Audience*
* *Drive Innovation and Performance with Research*

Goal IV – Preserve our Most Precious Commodity – Credibility – and Ensure Overall Programming Excellence
* *Maintain the Firewall*
* *Update and Enforce Journalism Standards*
* *Perform Periodic Program Reviews of All Broadcast Services*

Goal V – Revitalize "Telling America's Story" to the World
* *Be a Model of a Free Press and Democracy in Action*
* *Concentrate on Those Aspects of America that Research Tells Us Interest Individual Audiences*
* *Present Targeted Editorials that are Relevant to Local and Regional Concerns*

- *Use Formats, Presentation Techniques, and On-air Presence that Will Appeal to Audiences*
- *Maximize Interactive Use of the Internet as a Ready Reference Source for Presidential Speeches and Other Vital Documents*

Goal VI – Shore up Our Surge Capability
- *Upgrade Existing Shortwave Transmitter and Support Systems to Ensure Backbone of Our Surge Capability*
- *Develop a Rapid-response Capability – Low power, Portable AMs and FMs.*

Words and Language

Aphorisms about words

A gentle answer turns away wrath, but a harsh word stirs up anger.

— Proverbs 15:1

There's small Revenge in Words, but Words may be greatly revenged.

— Benjamin Franklin[84]

Abuse of words has been the great instrument of sophistry and chicanery, of party, faction, and division of society.

— John Adams[85]

The new circumstances in which we are placed call for new words, new phrases, and for the transfer of old words to new objects.

- Thomas Jefferson[86]

The difference between the almost right word and the right word is really a large matter — 'tis the difference between the lightning bug and the lightning.

— Mark Twain[87]

---

[84] "R. Saunders," pseudonym for Benjamin Franklin, in *Poor Richard's Almanac*, 1735 edition.

[85] John Adams, letter to J. H. Tiffany, March 31, 1819, in Charles Francis Adams, ed., *The Works of John Adams, With Life*, Vol. 10 (Little, Brown 1856).

[86] Thomas Jefferson, Letter to John Waldo, Monticello, August 6, 1813, cited by H. L. Mencken, *The American Language: An Inquiry Into the Development of English in the United States* (Alfred A. Knopf, 1921), Introduction.

When you shoot an arrow of truth, dip its point in honey.
– Arabian proverb[88]

The wound of words is worse than the wound of swords.
– Arabian proverb

Learn to call what is white, white and what is black, black; call evil what is evil, and good what is good.
– Pope John Paul II[89]

Distortion of language in wartime
Thucydides (5th century B.C.) [90]

Thucydides, in his history of the Peloponnesian Wars, noted how the combatants' distortion of language paralleled the upturning of society during the Corcyrean civil war of 427 B.C.:

To fit in with the change of events, words, too, had to change their usual meanings. What used to be described as a thoughtless act of aggression was now regarded as the courage one would expect to find in a party member; to think of the future and wait was merely another way of saying one was a coward; any idea of moderation was just an attempt to disguise one's unmanly character; ability to understand a question from all sides meant that one was totally unfitted for action. Fanatical enthusiasm was the mark of a real man....

---

[87] Mark Twain (Samuel L. Clemens), Letter to George Bainton, October 15, 1888, cited by George Bainton, *The Art of Authorship* (D. Appleton and Company, 1890), pp. 87-88.
[88] As cited by TalkIslam.com.
http://www.talkislam.com/iquotes/index.php?nCatId=108.
[89] Pope John Paul II, *Homily to University Students*, Rome, March 26, 1981.
[90] Thucydides, *History of the Peloponnesian War*, 3.82[.4], trans. Rex Warner (Penguin, 1954, 1972). Richard Crowley translates 3.82.4 as, "Words had to change their ordinary meaning and to take that which was now given them."

Thought corrupts language, and vice-versa
George Orwell (1946) [91]

The great enemy of clear language is insincerity. When there is a gap between one's real and one's declared aims, one turns as it were instinctively to long words and exhausted idioms, like a cuttlefish squirting out ink. . . . All issues are political issues, and politics itself is a mass of lies, evasions, folly, hatred and schizophrenia. When the general atmosphere is bad, language must suffer. . .

But if thought corrupts language, language can also corrupt thought. A bad usage can spread by tradition and imitation, even among people who should and do know better.

When a word is true and false
Václav Havel (1989) [92]

Alongside words that electrify society with their freedom and truthfulness, we have words that mesmerize, deceive, inflame, madden, beguile, words that are harmful – lethal even. . . . The same word can, at one moment, radiate great hope; at another, it can emit lethal rays. The same word can be true at one moment and false the next, at one moment illuminating, at another deceptive. . . . For forty years, an allergy to that beautiful word has been engendered in me, as it has in every one of my fellow citizens, because I know what the word has meant here for all those forty years: ever mightier armies ostensibly to defend peace. . . .

The same word can be humble at one moment and arrogant the next. And a humble word can be transformed easily and imperceptibly into an arrogant one, whereas it is a difficult and

---

[91] George Orwell, "Politics and the English Language," in Sonia Orwell and Ian Angus, eds., *George Orwell: In Front of Your Nose, 1946-1950*, Vol. 4 (Boston: Nonpareil Books, 2002), p. 137. Orwell was a British author, essayist and journalist.

[92] Václav Havel, "A Word About Words," *in absentia* speech, Frankfurt, Germany, October 15, 1989, trans. A. G. Brain, published in the *New York Review of Books*, January 18, 1990. Havel is a former dissident playwright who became the first post-communist president of Czechoslovakia and the Czech Republic. The text in English appears on Havel's Website at: www.vaclavhavel.cz.

protracted process to transform an arrogant word into one that is humble.

Carelessness in adopting the language of our opponents
Fred Charles Iklé, (1970s) [93]

Paradoxically, despite the fact that the State Department and other government agencies bestow so much care on the vast verbal output of Communist governments, we have been careless in adopting the language of our opponents and their definitions of conflict issues in many cases where this is clearly to our disadvantage.

Or perhaps this is not so paradoxical. It might be precisely because our officials spend so much time on the opponents' rhetoric that they eventually use his words – first in quotation marks, later without.

Semantic infiltration
Daniel Patrick Moynihan (1979) [94]

[Semantic infiltration] is the process whereby we come to adopt the language of our adversaries in describing political reality. The most brutal totalitarian regimes in the world call themselves 'liberation movements.' It is perfectly predictable that they should misuse words to conceal their real nature. But must we aid them in that effort by repeating those words? Worse, do we begin to influence our own perceptions by using them?

. . . Even though the State Department proclaimed its neutrality in the conflict there, its very choice of words – its use of the vocabulary of groups opposed to our values – undermined the legitimacy of the pro-Western political forces in the area. We pay for small concessions at the level of language with large setbacks at the level of practical politics. . . .

---

[93] Fred Charles Iklé, cited in Daniel Patrick Moynihan, "Further Thoughts on Words and Foreign Policy," *Policy Review*, Spring 1979. A defense strategist, Iklé was director of the U.S. Arms Control and Disarmament Agency in the 1970s and served as Under Secretary of Defense under President Reagan. Moynihan was U.S. Ambassador to the United Nations under President Ford and in 1976 was elected to the U.S. Senate, where he served four terms.

[94] Moynihan, Ibid., pp. 53, 58-59.

[That] totalitarians will seek to seize control of the language of politics is obvious; that our own foreign affairs establishment should remain blind to what is happening is dangerous. . . .

The costs of inattention seem to escape even those among us who pride ourselves on their 'hardheadedness' in matters of geopolitics and military strategy. This is not a phenomenon of one administration, but almost, I think, of our political culture.

Defense against distortions of language
Advisory Commission on Public Diplomacy (1984) [95]

The United States has no institutional defense against its own misinterpretations of true meanings, or against the conscious efforts of adversaries to induce or reinforce its own misunderstandings.

Concerned about the problem during the heated years of the Cold War, the U.S. Advisory Commission on Public Diplomacy, under the leadership of Edwin J. Feulner, Jr., made the following observation and recommendation. No enduring government action was taken.

We believe that the times require a conscious effort to improve the accuracy and political impact of words and terms used by our leaders in speaking to the world. By so doing, they can help disclose the hypocrisy and distortions of hostile propaganda. This is not a problem that will go away, and we must be prepared to deal with it on a systematic and continuing basis....

[The Commission recommends] that a task force be created, under the National Security Council and including representatives of the Departments of State and Defense and USIA [U.S. Information Agency], to assess the problem and propose an institutionalized means to respond to inaccurate or misleading terminology in international political discourse.

---

[95] Edwin J. Feulner, Jr., Chairman, United States Advisory Commission on Public Diplomacy, *The Role of USIA and Public Diplomacy*, January 1984.

Take back the language
Ronald Reagan (1983)[96]

[U.S. policy will be to] prevent the Soviet propaganda machine from seizing the semantic high-ground in the battle of ideas through the appropriation of such terms as "peace."

Know the traditional meanings of Islamic terms
Layla Sein (2002)[97]

Since the concept of *jihad* comes from the root word *jahada* (to strive or struggle for self-betterment from an ethical-moral perspective) and that of *hirabah* comes from the root word *hariba* (to fight, to go to war or become enraged or angry), an etymological and theological examination of these words provides a valid framework through which the religious legitimacy of suicide bombings in today's global community can be analyzed...

To delve into a comparative study of these Islamic concepts is to expose how hirabah is being paraded by terrorist groups as jihad. By defining hirabah as jihad, such terrorist groups as al Qaeda and others promote their terrorist agendas by misleading young, religiously motivated and impressionable Muslims to believe that killing unarmed and non-combatant civilians are activities of jihad, and hence a ticket to paradise...

If activities of fear and terror associated with hirabah are used to define the meaning of jihad in hopes of recruiting Muslim youth to undertake suicide bombings and other criminal activities, Muslim theologians need to define the nature of what is happening to stop the hijacking of Islam by terrorists.

---

[96] Ronald Reagan, "Management of Public Diplomacy Relative to National Security," National Security Decision Directive Number 77, January 14, 1983. Declassified secret document.
[97] Layla Sein is with the Association of Muslim Social Scientists.
Excerpted from "Editorial," Association of Muslim Social Scientists *AMSS Bulletin* 3, no. 4 (2002).

Reclaim the true meanings
Asma Afsaruddin (2002)[98]

The important battle of semantics is not about window-dressing but about reclaiming the true meaning of jihad – which refers to the noblest human 'struggle' or 'endeavor' to realize God's will for a just and merciful society on earth – from those who would willfully abuse it. The Qur'anic and classical notion of jihad signifies a continuing enterprise on the part of the religious to uphold what was good and resist what is evil: this enterprise, is, after all, at the root of every civilized society and thus ultimately conducive to true peace.

Qur'an and Muhammad made emphatic distinctions
Sayyid M. Sayyid (2003)[99]

The Qur'an and the sayings of the prophet emphatically distinguished the term jihad from hirabah, a destructive act of rebellion committed against God and mankind. Hirabah is an act of terrorism, a subversive act inflicted by an individual or a gang of individuals, breaking the established norms of peace, civic laws, treaties, agreements, moral and ethical codes... While as different forms of jihad are highly commendable acts of virtue, hirabah is respected as a despicable crime... *Individuals and groups indulging in hirabah are condemned as criminals, subjected to severe deterrent punishments under Islamic law and warned of far more punishment and humiliation in the life after life.* (Emphasis added)

---

[98] Asma Afsaruddin, is Associate Professor of Arabic and Islamic Studies at the University of Notre Dame. Excerpt from letter to Jim Guirard. The author acknowledges Guirard for providing many of the quotations used in this chapter. Guirard's website is www.truespeak.org.
[99] Sayyid M. Sayyid is Secretary General of the Islamic Society of North America (ISNA), a Saudi-funded entity that is the largest distributor of Wahhabi-sponsored religious propaganda in the United States. Excerpted from a letter to Jim Guirard, cited by Guirard, "Properly Condemning the al Qaeda Blasphemy," *The American Muslim*, April 21, 2003.

What we should be saying is, . . .
James Guirard (2001)[100]

[The *Washington Post*] should begin avoiding al Qaeda's patently false labels "holy war" and "jihad" and begin substituting for them the truthful and religiously appropriate terms. Here are several semantic tools that are urgently needed to condemn – in Islamic religious terminology – those we now call "terrorists":

1. *Hirabah* (hee-RAH-bah) – This antonym for jihad and the term for a treasonous and forbidden "war against society."
2. *Hirabah shaitaniyah* (hee-RAH-bah shay-THAN-ee-yah) – For emphasis, a forbidden "satanic war against society," involving the wanton killing of innocents and even of innocent fellow Muslims.
3. *Hartaka* (HAR-tah-kah) – The word for "heresy," as in bin Laden's heresy to Islam.
4. *Muy'tadoon* (moo-tah-DOON) – The Koran's word for murderous "transgressors," whose aggression can be resisted by all necessary means, including execution.
5. *Fasad mufsidoon* (fah-SAHD moof-see-DOON) – The Koran's term for ruthless "mischief makers" or, in today's parlance, evildoers (of the sort who would wage Hirabah shaitaniyah).
6. *Jahannam* (ja-HAHN-ahm) – The Koran's word for the "hellfire" to which Allah will condemn those evil-doers who refuse to cease and to repent their criminality.

While it will require time and effort to get such Arabic and Islamic words – even the English translations – into the language of the media and the body politic, the urgent need for truth-in-labeling demands it.

---

[100] Jim Guirard, "Tools for Anti-Terrorists," *Washington Post*, November 24, 2001. Reprinted with permission.

Islamic words, ideas and customs can be our best ally
J. Michael Waller (2007)[101]

Islamic words, ideas, laws and customs can be the United States' best ally in the war as long as they are properly understood, used in the proper cultural context, deployed by spokespersons with message authority, and relentlessly magnified and repeated. Mastery of the proper vocabulary is vital in U.S. message-making for several reasons. The proper vocabulary:

- will help break the extremists' domination of the ideas of jihad and martyrdom, the very ideas that bolster the will to murder;
- will help restore a non-violent way for people to manifest their fears and anxieties, hopes and aspirations;
- will sow doubt and division in the extremists' support bases, and increase collaboration with international counterterrorism authorities;
- may cause some extremists before, during and after recruitment to begin questioning their ideology and the consequences of their "martyrdom";
- will strengthen the traditional scholars and clergy, and the politicians and peoples who follow them;
- will help offer a Qur'anic justification for uniting in a war against the terrorists;
- will help break the spirit and will of the enemy; and
- will help to discredit and ultimately destroy the viability of the enemy's ideology and ideas.

Inaccurate or inappropriate use of language, or unwillingness to make full and proper use of languages and terms as rhetorical devices and weapons in their own right, serves the enemy. Recapturing and preserving the proper meanings of words can discredit and negate the power of the enemy's ideas, especially among the populations where the enemy recruits and operates. At the same time, the proper use of words provides positive, unifying themes that cater to local cultures and strengthen civil societies. Words can be the ultimate precision guided weapons in the war of ideas: they can

---

[101] Excerpted from J. Michael Waller, *Fighting the War of Ideas like a Real War* (The Institute of World Politics Press, 2007), pp. 74-75. Copyright © 2007.

be deployed to the targets immediately, require no bureaucratic reorganization, and cost nothing. The barriers to their proper use include ignorance, political correctness and the unwillingness of officials to make words work to help win the war.

Psychological Planning and Strategy

Any effort to influence mass audiences requires the skilled use of psychology. Psychological efforts must be carefully planned and incorporated in an overall strategy to influence perceptions, affections and actions of people abroad, and to influence the decisions of their leaders.

It can be difficult to coordinate and measure the psychological impact of U.S. diplomatic positions, statements, initiatives and aid programs in diverse countries and circumstances around the world. But as the struggle against communism showed, psychological planning and strategy were critical to bringing about a victory for the United States, its allies and its cause.

We begin with a State Department memorandum about the Psychological Strategy Board (PSB), which President Truman founded in 1951 as a senior planning and coordinating body.

Every policy can have a psychological dimension
Psychological Strategy Board (1952) [102]

. . . the title of the PSB [Psychological Strategy Board] itself suggested that there were particular psychological problems that required attention, and to illustrate my understanding of the term I distinguished between the policy of undertaking an aid program in the Middle East and, within such a program, deciding to carry out aid projects designed to elicit the desired response of some particular group.

[PSB Deputy Director Tracy Barnes] said that it seemed to him that if the PSB tried to work out projects calculated to secure the support of all the different groups in the Middle East, the net result would be consideration of the whole, broad question of an aid

---

[102] "Functions of the PSB," Department of State Memorandum of Conversation, March 26, 1952. Declassified confidential document courtesy of the National Security Archive, George Washington University.

program and he could not understand the distinction. He referred to the fact that the State Department and Defense, as well as [Secretary of State Averell] Harriman, all had to consider the question of foreign aid and decide what to do, and the FSB was a mechanism through which they could make the decision.

When I said that a great many considerations entered into the decision as to the size of the program, the desirability of military or economic aid, etc., and that I did not see how the whole problem could be properly considered to be within the scope of the PSB, Mr. Barnes said that the various agencies were represented and he thought the high officials on the Board should be able to express the views of their agencies and vote on the questions presented in a way that would stick.

I told him that many parts of the Department were involved in such a subject as the foreign aid program and that the interdepartmental panels of the PSB did not seem to me to provide a practicable way of preparing positions on all of the matters involved. I said there were a great variety of interdepartmental relationships through which general policies and progress of the Government were arrived at and I assumed he did not think of the PSB as superseding all of these other relationships.

Mr. Barnes admitted that many decisions, involving several agencies, were made about which the PSB knows nothing, but he said he did not see why general policy decisions could not be made by the PSB if the members desired. He emphasized the fact that the Board was not the Staff, but high representatives of several agencies and these officials should be able to speak with authority for their agencies.

I said that I had assumed that the NSC [White House National Security Council] was the agency through which the general policy decisions of the Government were most frequently made, and I asked Mr. Barnes to tell me how he viewed the respective roles for the NSC and the PSB. He said that it was difficult for him to see what the differences were and suggested that the PSB had a role as wide as that of the NSC. When I remarked that I did not believe the members of the PSB would want to use that mechanism for many of the decisions that came before the NSC, but instead would want to consider the psychological warfare aspects of various policies and programs, Mr. Barnes replied that it would be a waste of time for the members of the PSB to make decisions on the psychological desirability of a policy or program if such decisions were not binding on their respective agencies. I said that there were bound to be many other considerations to be taken into account, and I had thought the way the PSB could be most helpful was to take, for example, a particular objective set for th in an NSC paper and do some good, hard work on the best means of achieving that objective in psychological terms. In this way I felt the light that was needed in these matters could be intensified. Mr. Barnes felt that the FSB had been directed to broaden rather than narrow the focus.

[PSB official Edmund Taylor] referred to the draft NSC paper on the Arab States, Israel and Iran and said that paper was full of psychological implications. I said that we had to consider the psychological impact of nearly everything we did in the State Department. Mr. Taylor replied that the PSB had to deal with national policy in everything it did. . . .

Political and psychological offensives can outflank us militarily
Dwight D. Eisenhower (1958)[103]

When there is a truly unified public opinion there is a tremendous power generated by our free people. Further, when that public opinion is based upon knowledge and real understanding of the issues involved, then this tremendous power can produce and sustain constructive action, almost without limit.

But the prerequisite for such strength, I repeat, is knowledge and understanding. An important element is such an understanding that purely military defenses, no matter how powerful, can never insure any nation's security. Aggression that is political, psychological and economic can outflank military forces because of our failure to provide the necessary counter measures in those fields. The problem then is to create in the United States a true understanding of our proper relationship to the less developed countries, including the Mid East, as well as the measure necessary to keep those relationships healthy. . . .

Indeed, it is clear that there has not yet been created the determined, unified, aroused public opinion that would demand from the Congress the kind of support and action for these programs

---

[103] President Dwight D. Eisenhower, letter to Rev. Edward L. R. Elson, The National Presbyterian Church, Washington, D.C., July 31, 1958. Courtesy the National Security Archive, George Washington University.

which must be carried out effectively, imaginatively and honestly if we are to preserve the peace and lead the world to a better life.

Wisdom requires the long view
John F. Kennedy (1962)[104]

The leaders of the Communist world are not only confronted by acute internal problems in each Communist country – the failure of agriculture, the rising discontent of the youth and the intellectuals, the demands of technical and managerial groups for status and security. They are confronted in addition by profound divisions within the Communist world itself – divisions which have already shattered the image of communism as a universal system guaranteed to abolish all social and international conflicts, the most valuable asset which the Communists had for many years.

Wisdom requires the long view. And the long view shows us that the revolution of national independence is a fundamental fact of our era. This revolution cannot be stopped.

As new nations emerge from the oblivion of centuries, their first aspiration is to affirm their national identity. Their deepest hope is for a world where, within a framework of international cooperation, every country can solve its own problems according to its own traditions and ideals.

It is in the interests of the pursuit of knowledge – and it is in our own national interest – that this revolution of national independence succeed. For the Communists rest everything on the idea of a monolithic world – a world where all knowledge has a single pattern, all societies move toward a single model, all problems have a single solution, and all roads lead to a single destination.

The pursuit of knowledge, on the other hand, rests everything on the opposite idea – on the idea of a world based on diversity, self-determination and freedom. And that is the kind of world to which

---

[104] John F. Kennedy, "President Kennedy's Speech at University of California," March 23, 1962, *Public Papers of the Presidents*, Kennedy, 1962, p. 265.

we Americans, as a nation, are committed by the principles on which this republic was formed.

As men conduct the pursuit of knowledge, they create a world which freely unites national diversity and international partnership. This emerging world is incompatible with the Communist conception of world order.

It will irresistibly burst the bonds of Communist organization and Communist ideology. And diversity and independence, far from being opposed to the American conception of world order, represent the very essence of our vision of the future.

There used to be much talk a few years ago about the inevitable triumph of communism. We hear such talk much less now. No one who examines the modem world can doubt that the great currents of history are carrying the world away from the monolithic idea toward the pluralist idea – away from communism and toward national independence and freedom.

No one can doubt that the wave of the future is not the conquest of the world by a single dogmatic creed, but the liberation of the diverse energies of free nations and free men. No one can doubt that cooperation in the pursuit of knowledge must lead to freedom of the mind and of the soul.

The specter of thermonuclear war will hang over mankind; and we must heed the advice of Oliver Wendell Holmes of 'freedom leaning on her spear' until all nations are wise enough to disarm safely and effectively.

We must seize the vision of a free and diverse world – and shape our policies to speed progress toward a flexible world order.

This is the unifying spirit of our policies in the world. The purpose of our aid programs must be to help developing countries to move forward as rapidly as possible on the road to genuine national independence.

Our military policies must assist nations to protect the processes of democratic reform and development against disruption and intervention.

'Relatively low priority'
Foreign Affairs Committee, U.S. House of Representatives (1964)[105]

In the pursuit of its basic objectives in the world, the United States, unlike the Soviet Union, has assigned relatively low priority to the ideological and psychological area of foreign policy operations. The attention and the resources devoted to these operations do not begin to approach those expended on foreign military and economic activities.

There is a definite limit to the resources, both manpower and financial, which are available to the United States Government. Of necessity, priorities must be established in allocating these resources among different functions and programs. In the field of foreign policy, the military and the economic aspects of the crisis confronting the United States in the world scene have preempted the attention and overwhelmingly engaged the effort of our Government. Support for the ideological and psychological functions of foreign policy has been, until recently, wavering and marginal.

Virtually since the end of World War II, the conduct of our foreign policy has been dominated by the *military* aspects of the Communist threat. On a parallel level, the mammoth task of aiding the reconstruction of Western Europe and, subsequently, of helping to meet the aspirations for a better life in the developing countries, has also profoundly influenced both the thinking of our policymakers and the structure of governmental machinery through which our foreign policy flows. Between these two pressures, at times competing and at other times reinforcing each other, the ideological and psychological aspects of foreign policy have had a hard time coming to their own.

The emphasis on the military has introduced a degree of bias and produced certain malformations in governmental machinery devoted to the formulation and execution of United States foreign policy.

---

[105] *Ideological Operations and Foreign Policy*, Report No. 2 on *Winning the Cold War: The U.S. Ideological Offensive*, by the Subcommittee on International Organizations and Movements of the Committee on Foreign Affairs, U.S. House of Representatives, April 27, 1964, p. 7. Rep. Dante Fascell, Chairman.

Origins of U.S. psychological strategy
Stephen Tanous (2003)[106]

*Modern U.S. psychological strategy is rooted in the First World
War. In 2003, Col. Stephen Tanous USAF, was the Commandant's
Winner for Distinction in Research at the U.S. Army War College,
where he wrote the following essay as part of his Master's
program in strategic studies. As of this writing Tanous is
Commander of the 30th Space Wing at Vandenberg Air Force Base.*

*Tanous documents his essay extensively with footnotes and
illustrates it with pull quotes. As with other academic writings in
this book, this editor has removed the footnotes and pull quotes
for reprint clarity. The full text of the original document is
available at the Web address below.*

Information and the psychological element of national power were
first recognized by the United States as essential to the conduct of
war in World War I; until then, the U.S. had never conducted a
propaganda campaign. The government's first institutional attempt
was the formation of the Committee on Public Information,
established by executive order on 14 April 1917 and headed by
George Creel. He believed that the "fight for the minds of men" was
as important as the war on the ground. He claimed that "lies had the
force of divisions" and that the verdict of mankind would be held in
the jury of public opinion. His endeavors drove the organization
from its stand up in 1917 to its dissolution in November 1918 and
final report in mid-1919. The stated goals of the Committee were to
combat negative portrayal of the U.S. in foreign press, enhance
morale of the troops, engender support and belief in the United
States from the Allies, and convince the Central Powers of the
"ideals, determination, and invincibility" of this nation. Another part
of the Committee's efforts was to educate the world about America
as a nation, not merely engage in counter-propaganda.

The Committee's efforts employed all available media and
addressed both domestic and foreign audiences, including the
foreign language press. It had offices in every world capital.
Overseas, the U.S. controlled no media and was entirely dependent

---

[106] Excerpted from Col. Stephen Tanous USAF, "Building a Psychological
Strategy for the U.S.: Leveraging the Informational Element of National
Power," U.S. Army War College paper, April 2003. The complete text,
including footnotes, is at: http://handle.dtic.mil/100.2/ADA414554.

on the foreign press. Creel and the Committee made a special effort to ensure that the content of any statements forwarded by the Committee was truthful and unbiased, guarding against misstatements and correcting any false releases as soon as they were identified. Any censorship of U.S. film or print media was voluntary to avoid alienating the media outlets.

The Committee analyzed enemy propaganda to support counter-propaganda efforts. In addition, the Committee coordinated and controlled daily news related to military operations and acted on behalf of the Departments of State, War, Navy, Justice, and Labor, along with several war-related councils and boards. The Committee's products and initiatives directly addressed foreign-born Americans and Americans of foreign descent in their native languages to encourage support for the U.S. cause.

Creel understood the importance of accepting the contributions of non-English speaking American communities. He sought loyalty from inside these groups, not enforcing it from the outside. A Foreign Information Service touted the positive aspects of the U.S. to foreign language groups in the American press. The News Division of the Committee recognized the war was global and launched a 24-hour operation to support timely information dissemination.

The Committee focused on several key areas, including a World News Service, foreign mail, and films. Congressional enmity toward the Committee precluded establishment of a permanent public information activity, so it was abolished when the war ended. Creel pointed out that it was a "war organization only" and that a Committee for Public Information in peacetime would only cause on-going controversy, as it had from the moment it was created as a wartime measure.

The first major national effort that looked beyond the immediate requirements driven by a crisis or conflict was the establishment of a Psychological Strategy Board (PSB) by President Truman in June 1951. Truman's directive established the PSB under the National Security Council (NSC) to formulate and promulgate national-level psychological objectives, policies, and programs. The membership consisted of the Undersecretary of State, Deputy Secretary of Defense, Director of Central Intelligence, and the Chairman of the JCS, who served as military advisor for the integration of military psychological operations. Although an initial draft excluded overt economic warfare and restricted the PSB from conducting psychological operations, the final directive did not. Instead, it pointed out the integral relationship of economic activities in a psychological strategy as well as the need for centrally directed operations.

Eisenhower also recognized the importance of federal responsibility and direction for psychological warfare. He restructured the PSB as an Operations Coordinating Board and made it an equal player in the NSC. However, by 1955 certain efforts were delegated to the Planning Coordination Group (PCG), which included the President's National Security Advisor and Director of the U.S. Information Agency.

The PCG was chartered to lead interagency efforts and coordinate overall economic, psychological, and political activities and ensure interdepartmental planning. The PCG had no directive authority, but was tasked to wage psychological warfare against the Soviet bloc and act as a think tank to keep track of psychological dynamics. With a goal of concerted action, it was to develop "outline plans" that identified situations in each country, including agreed upon actions, responsibilities, measures of effectiveness, timing, and priorities. The PCG identified the need to analyze overseas impacts of public announcements and advanced a process by which the U.S. could take an official position and action on upcoming events. The PCG succeeded in coordinating several high level policies, including Open Skies, Atoms for Peace, and the U.S. position on political asylum. It ensured consistency among actions considered and taken on national security issues. For all it accomplished, the PCG suffered from several critical deficiencies, including the lack of a clear mission, interdepartmental infighting over equities, lack of organizational structure, resources, and budget, and, most importantly, lack of significant support from the President or his senior cabinet members. These shortcomings ultimately doomed the PCG.

President Kennedy abolished it and the OCB on 19 February 1961, subsuming its functions under existing agencies and activities, including the Oval Office, State Department, and USIA.

George Kennan's famous "X" article and its successor, NSC 68, laid the foundation for what is arguably the most successful U.S. psychological strategy. Kennan's "X" article describes the use of information to support U.S. actions and to create favorable impressions of the nation in the minds of foreign audiences. Kennan cited the need for coordination to avoid seams or conflicts between policy positions or actions. NSC 68 further declared that the information inherent in "practical demonstration" of the U.S. system can create situations which will induce accommodation, making use of force a last resort. The document also recognizes the need for covert political and economic warfare as well as overt and covert psychological warfare. Since U.S. policy sought to avoid the use of nuclear superiority to coerce or engage in "preventive" war, the policy of containment was described as a non-military effort to modify behavior, akin to calculated and gradual coercion. NSC 68 also lauded the psychological impact of military readiness as a deterrent – as part of an overall "political attitude."

The seeds planted by the "X" article and NSC 68 came to fruition under President Reagan. Three of his National Security Decision Directives – NSDD 130, 77, and 45 – defined U.S. policy for international information, management of public diplomacy relative to national security, and international broadcasting. NSDD 130, "U.S. International Information Policy," emphasized a global information strategy. It identified information, along with public diplomacy, as a strategic instrument and specified the need to coordinate other elements of national security policy and strategy as part of policy formulation.

NSDD 130 recognized that different programming was required for different countries, regions, elites, opinion centers, and general populations. It also noted that private and commercial information sources offered increased credibility over government dissemination. In addition, NSDD 130 directed DoD to develop overt peacetime PSYOP programs (OP3) and to coordinate OP3 activities as part of interagency plans for international information activities. As in earlier efforts, there was a recognized need for research on public opinion, media reaction, and cultural factors, as well as feedback mechanisms. Significantly, the document observed that "major national security policy studies and decision documents should include an impact of policy options or decisions on foreign opinion."

Reagan's policy on "Management of Public Diplomacy Relative to National Security," NSDD 77, focused on the organization, planning, and execution of public diplomacy. It defined U.S. public diplomacy efforts as "actions that generate support for U.S. national security objectives." NSDD 77 established a Special Planning Group (SPG) chaired by the Assistant to the President for National Security Affairs (APNSA), with membership consisting of the Secretary of State (SECSTATE), Secretary of Defense (SECDEF), Directors of the U.S. Information Agency (USIA) and Agency for International Development (USAID), and the Assistant to the President for Communications. The SPG was responsible for planning, directing, coordinating, and monitoring implementation of public diplomacy activities. It had four committees. The Public Affairs Committee planned and integrated major speeches and appearances with foreign and domestic dimensions. The International Information Committee directed actions in accord with information strategies; it also coordinated and monitored strategies in key functional or geographic areas. The International Political Committee planned and coordinated international political activities, ensured collaboration with related economic, diplomatic, and military efforts as well as with American society and business. Finally, an International Broadcasting Committee conducted diplomatic and technical planning for direct radio, TV, and other broadcasting.

The Reagan Administration considered international broadcasting so important that it promulgated NSDD 45, a separate document outlining its importance and role in national security policy. NSDD 45 focused on articulating U.S. policy and actions to foreign publics through the communications means available – Voice of America (VOA), Radio In East Berlin (RIAS), Radio Free Europe/Radio Liberty (RFE/RL), and Radio Marti – thereby ensuring availability of a surrogate free radio in target areas. The document also provided guidance to ensure the content of the programming supported U.S. policy objectives while "ensuring the integrity of news broadcasting" and maintaining "the autonomy and special character of the surrogate radios."

NSDD 45 further acknowledged the need for modern broadcasting facilities and an expanded transmission base, tasking VOA and RFE/RL to undertake long term expansion programs. It also tasked the Department of State to work the diplomatic and technical issues associated with acquiring new sites and facilities, going so far as to examine direct broadcast TV as a way to penetrate a jammed environment. Finally, NSDD 45 anticipated the need to use these assets in periods of crisis and war and tasked DoS and DoD to review efforts for integration of international broadcasting into political and military contingency planning, a hint of what was to come during the OPERATION ALLIED FORCE/NOBLE ANVIL campaign in 1999.

As mentioned previously, the most recent policy effort was the development of Presidential Decision Directive 68 (PDD 68), signed by President Clinton in April 1999. It sought to improve the "use of public information communicated to foreign audiences" with an explicit aim of developing an intentional internal public information strategy. *[Editor's note: PDD 68 is still classified and cannot be included in this Reader.]* Specifically, in addition to dealing with our global partners and allies on issues such as regional conflict and trade, the NSS calls for the effective use of "public diplomacy to promote the free flow of information and ideas to...those in societies ruled by the sponsors of global terrorism." PDD 68 specifically identified public affairs, public diplomacy, and international military information as elements of an international public information strategy designed to promote national interests and prevent and mitigate international crises.

The schedule of tasks assigned under the PDD was comprehensive, including the development a national IPI strategy to provide guidance on regional and transnational issues and a report on the status of implementation in key areas, such as training and human resources; engagement with international, non-governmental, and private voluntary organizations; overseas media; and funding. However, the initiatives directed by PDD 68 were not smoothly implemented. The Defense Science Board (DSB), in an October 2001 study, *Managed Information Dissemination*, identified numerous means at the disposal of the government, but highlighted a lack of "an immediate, responsive means to communicate with foreign audiences during heightened tensions or crises." Coordination efforts were further complicated when the US Information Agency was disbanded as the primary organization responsible for U.S. public diplomacy. This function now resides in DoS regional bureaus and the Office of International Information Programs. In addition, IPI efforts under PDD 68 have not received the sustained support required for its full implementation. Although President Bush revalidated PDD 68, the DSB report also noted that PDD 68 lacked sufficient implementing authorities and structure, failed to assign specific responsibilities to agencies, and never achieved strategic success. The tensions among public affairs, public diplomacy, and military operations present certain risks including U.S. public perception of coordinated information efforts, along with potential seams that an able adversary can exploit.

Psychological strategy defined

A discussion of psychological strategy must begin with a working definition. First, it must be understood that psychological strategy is a grand strategy that provides an overarching approach to the use of the diplomatic, economic, and military elements of national power. For the purposes of this study, a psychological strategy is defined as the comprehensive orchestration of the implied and explicit information associated with the use of the national elements of power (diplomatic, economic, and military) so that coherent, consistent messages, meanings and themes are conveyed in ways that shape and influence understanding of and support for U.S. beliefs, values, and national security policies. This definition borrows heavily from existing definitions of public diplomacy. But it goes further because public diplomacy is a process of dialogue and information-sharing. This definition includes "implied" information, because many economic and military actions have implied messages associated with their use (or non-use, as the case may be). The implied message associated with the use, or threatened use, of military force has been termed "coercive diplomacy." Combined with other peacetime military operations and public affairs, use or threatened use of force complements the stated aims of public diplomacy.

Elements of psychological strategy

A national psychological strategy must leverage the information inherent in the exercise of the national elements of power. This information presents itself through declarations of U.S. policy and its execution in the diplomatic, economic, and military arenas. The primary elements of a psychological strategy as defined above are public diplomacy, public affairs, international military information, and coercive diplomacy.

Public diplomacy

Public diplomacy is an essential element of a psychological strategy for two reasons. First, the rise in the quantity of information available to large publics everywhere directly affects public opinion and attitudes, which in turn influence the actions and decisions of governments. Second, perceptions are just as important as reality.

What appears to be true is assumed to be, more so in parts of the world that do not have access to a free press. The confluence of these two factors makes the job of U.S. public diplomacy – to inform, or to try to correct misinformed or disinformed publics – even more important.

Although there is no accepted definition, it is understood that the intent of public diplomacy (PD) is to communicate to foreign publics, through various means, a government's goals and policies as well as an understanding of its culture and values. Public diplomacy reached in its zenith during the Reagan Administration in the midst of the Cold War. It was a key element of NSDDs 77 and 130, since it offered the Eastern bloc countries an alternative to Soviet propaganda and helped hasten the collapse of communism. However, with the rise of global private media via the internet and satellites, the United States has relied on commercial media to broadcast America's message. As a result, the image of the United States abroad is one primarily based on the material aspects of American culture. Commercial media rarely elaborate on U.S. foreign policy or its impact in the international arena. Resources devoted to PD have decreased to the point where it now accounts for only eight percent of the State Department's budget.

Public diplomacy should be recognized as a strategic weapon and moved "from the sidelines to the core of diplomacy." The 2002 Report of the U.S. Advisory Commission on Public Diplomacy noted "U.S. foreign policy has been weakened by a failure to systematically include public diplomacy in the formulation and implementation of policy." As former USIA Director Edward R. Murrow put it, public diplomacy must be included in both the "takeoff" of policies, not just the "crash landings."

The Commission recommended that PD be recognized as a strategic component of American foreign policy. However, the U.S. must recognize that PD is not confined to long-term programs that communicate American beliefs and values, but must also be capable of clearly articulating U.S. policies to a global community who often views America positively as a culture but disagrees with the U.S. position on key issues. The U.S. approach must be tempered with the knowledge that it "should not be in the business of getting people to love us.... We should however, try to help the world understand us."

The issue of whether the United States is viewed with approval as the world's sole superpower is not as important as making sure the issue is addressed on the basis of complete and accurate reporting.

As we advance into the 21st century and continue to fight the war on terrorism, we must acknowledge this is a "total war" in the sense that all the elements of national power are in play. International discourse will take place not just with ruling parties and elites but more and more with the foreign publics themselves.

The need to communicate with publics uncovers a weakness that resulted from the integration of the USIA into the State Department. Specifically, the perception of the independence and utility of the USIA as an information activity was lost in the merger. In the CNN age of 24/7 news, there is a decided lack of agility on the part of the U.S. to respond to negative propaganda or inaccurate reporting. It may be time to "undo" this merger: As an independent activity, USIA would be better postured to act and react to this type of reporting as part of a comprehensive psychological strategy.

Currently, layers of State Department bureaucracy prevent real-time responses. Rapid response is invaluable in an era of instant reporting, where sound bites are played repetitively on CNN and sensationalized photographs are plastered on internet websites, often devoid of context. In addition, while many exchange programs have continued, they have been scaled back. As a result, media outlets such as VOA and RFE/RL do not serve as timely means of disseminating essential information, relying on programming more than real-time reporting. Although commercial media perform this function well, they do not, and should not be expected to, act as advocates for U.S. policies.

One way of dealing with this seeming incongruity is to create reportable "events" rather than programming and then allow the current media outlets to propagate the message. Another option is to develop a series of outlets designed specifically to support strategic communication. The drawback is that once they are recognized as "official" government outlets, they tend to be dismissed and become only marginally effective. ...

The function of public affairs (PA) is to provide timely and accurate information relating to government goals, policies and actions to domestic audiences. While all federal departments have public affairs offices, the primary departmental PA offices offering information on the conduct of foreign policy are the State Department's Bureau of Public Affairs within the office of the

Undersecretary for Public Diplomacy and Public Affairs, and the Assistant Secretary of Defense for Public Affairs. Both are charged with getting the message out to the American people on the rationale for U.S. foreign affairs policy. These offices facilitate the free flow of information to the media, the public and select internal audiences.

However, as technology has evolved, PD and PA have simply become two sides of the same coin. Communication technology is daily becoming more global – direct broadcast TV covers not just regions, but is broadcast to worldwide audiences. Further, the Internet is by design transnational and global. When the President of the United States addresses the U.N. as part of a public diplomacy initiative and requests a display of international solidarity against Iraqi intransigence on WMD programs, the audience is international. In a similar situation in January 2003, a news briefing by Defense Secretary Donald Rumsfeld and Chairman of the Joint Chiefs of Staff General Richard Myers to the Foreign Press Center at the Pentagon was broadcast to Baghdad by U.S. Air Force Commando Solo aircraft.

As the "firewall" between PA and PD continues to deteriorate, messages cannot be considered strictly foreign or domestic. The 1948 Smith-Mundt Act was written specifically to prevent domestic dissemination of any "information about the United States, its people, and its policies" prepared for foreign dissemination. The 1985 Zorinsky Amendment prohibits funds authorized for appropriation to the USIA to be used "to influence public opinion in the United States, and no program material prepared by the United States Information Agency shall be distributed within the United States." These laws should be amended to reflect the new reality of unrestricted real-time global communication, allow domestic dissemination of material intended for foreign audiences, and permit State Department (since USIA was disbanded) appropriated funds to influence domestic public opinion. In short, the laws are archaic and information policy should be based on current communications realities and capabilities.

As the means of global communication proliferate, it becomes more difficult to "de-link" U.S. domestic politics from foreign affairs and maintain two separate messages. The domestic agenda will reign supreme and force the hand of foreign policy. We run the risk of a disconnect between the domestic and foreign messages. In January 2003 such seams were apparent in efforts to gain foreign and domestic support for war with Iraq over ongoing efforts to eliminate Iraqi weapons of mass destruction. When France, Germany, and Russia withdrew support, there was a concurrent demand from the American public for the Bush Administration to make its case for war. The need to use the U.N. as a forum to garner support for U.S. policies clearly demonstrates the potential synergies and pitfalls of gaining support from both foreign and domestic audiences.

Developing a psychological strategy

A common complaint is that U.S. national leaders often fail to move beyond a reactive approach to information. The U.S. seems to lack an effective means to plan for and disseminate government-sponsored information or to leverage outside channels, or to anticipate reactions to its policies or activities. An overarching strategy will ensure the administration analyzes any potential action and anticipates consequences.

A three-pronged approach would work. The "proactive" approach focuses continuing actions supporting U.S. positions on key global issues. The "active" approach concentrates on interests rather than issues; it extends to the analysis of the impacts of short-term or opportunistic actions (typically, coercive diplomacy, use of force, economic sanctions, changes to diplomatic or trading status, etc) and the potential impacts to long-term objectives. Finally, the "reactive" approach anticipates the government's responses to unintended or unforeseen outcomes.

Failure to deal with short-term negative press can have long-term implications. Development of a comprehensive psychological strategy avoids the predominantly reactive approach taken to date during times of crisis or conflict. It helps U.S. policymakers avoid the appearance of conflict or inconsistency between positions on key global issues and actions as the world's sole superpower. These approaches can be woven into an effective foreign policy "blanket" only if the designers of a national psychological strategy understand the audience they are trying to reach, tailor the message accordingly, and communicate it effectively.

Understanding the "influence space"

As with any communication, there are three key considerations: the audience, the medium, and the message. An effective psychological strategy must account for these components – what the October 2001 DSB Study calls "a three-dimensional influence space describing publics, channels, and U.S. national interests for each country or sub-region." Failing to address any of the three could render the U.S. unable to attain the support and advocacy it desires for its foreign policy measures, both at home and overseas.

Foreign and Domestic "Publics"

The most important and perhaps most undervalued element in the exercise of U.S. national power is the need to understand the audience. Any effective exchange between two groups requires an understanding of both the individuals within the group, the psychology of the group, and sensitivity to cultural context. Accounting for the "operating environment" or "target culture" either in a domestic or international context is critical to achieving understanding and credibility. American foreign policy may well succeed or fail based on how well we understand the cultures, beliefs, and values of the target audience.

However, Americans tend to make two incorrect assumptions about communicating U.S. foreign policy: (1) that merely getting the message out is enough and (2) that the world sees events the way we do – that U.S. interests are common global concerns and that our notions of fair play and due process are universal. As Charlotte Beers, the Undersecretary for Public Diplomacy and Public Affairs, observed in her remarks to the Washington Institute for Near East Policy, "The inevitable bottom line of any communication is: 'Just because you say it doesn't mean I believe it – or even hear you.'"

Simply stated, conveying the message does not add up to influence, and conferring information does not guarantee understanding. While there are numerous public and private means of assessing U.S. public reaction to foreign policy initiatives, the same level of effort and resources are not dedicated to measuring the responses of foreign audiences. Although there are many means available to help the U.S. understand the various foreign publics and gauge reaction to U.S. policies and actions, the nation expends little effort to do this, considering the potentially huge return on investment. America must spend more on foreign public opinion polling, attitudinal research, and target marketing. Consider this: In 2001, the State Department spent $5 million on worldwide opinion polling, half of what Mike Bloomberg spent on polling for the New York City mayor's race.

A psychological strategy must specify short and long-term objectives in order to focus on the "right" populations. Once execution begins, the U.S. must remember who the target is, so the strategy can properly aim its "info bullets." Amorphous discussions about reaching out to the Arab or Muslim "street" diffuse effort. Subsets of populations that need to be targeted may include the middle class, business owners, and academics that are in a position to influence government. Focused polling and research efforts offer a means for identifying influential "soft" supporters of U.S. policies; they may become "hard" supporters who increase dialogue and understanding of U.S. initiatives. Providing these supporters with a context, "warts and all," for U.S. policy and actions could be vital to defusing sensitive issues related to the deployment and employment of U.S. forces overseas in support of coercive diplomacy during a crisis situation.

While this approach could lead to informed criticism of U.S. policies and efforts overseas, the improved dialogue also results in increased credibility. In addition, understanding the nuances of societies can help to avoid "target saturation" and apathy by informing us when certain issues lose support, when given approaches to informing audiences begin to fail, or for "inoculating" an audience before a new or modified U.S. foreign policy position or initiative is released. Finally, these groups and individuals, if properly informed, can become a significant "medium" for the message as well.

Channels

In the information age, the "crowded universe" of communications channels – newspapers, magazines, radio, TV, cell phones, e-mail, internet chat rooms and web sites, including exchanges and speakers – means the U.S. has a "smaller and smaller voice" in the global arena. Cultivating channels is essential to the success of a national psychological strategy. At least two considerations come to mind: the ubiquity of the message and the credibility of the transmission media. Ubiquity of the message facilitates sending an accurate, consistent message. Credibility is essential for the message to make an impact with the target audience.

Likewise, communications channels and media must maintain a perception of objectivity and independence. The U.S. currently has no independent ability to talk "directly" to foreign audiences through the media in a timely fashion. Merely disseminating information during a crisis does little to accomplish this end, particularly when the origin is known or suspected to be the U.S. military or is considered to be a U.S. "mouthpiece." In addition, the U.S. cannot count on international news media to advocate U.S. positions and policies for the same reason. Finally, restricted or denied access in regions or countries lacking a free press complicates information sharing. A lack of access magnifies the impact of "official" state-controlled media, making US public diplomatic efforts even more important. In these situations, the need for additional, impartial means of communicating with foreign publics in a consistent, coherent, and timely manner is all the greater. Establishing a number of reliable sources to provide information to foreign audiences will build needed credibility. Creating this set of circumstances will allow the U.S. to bridge what Edward R. Murrow once described as the most important stretch between speaker and listener, "the last three feet."

The key technical means available to the U.S. are the various activities overseen by the Broadcasting Board of Governors (BBG), which manages U.S. civilian diplomatic broadcast efforts such as the Voice of America, Radio Free Europe/Radio Liberty, Radio Free Asia, internet activities, etc. The U.S. has recently agreed to be more active in its outreach to foreign publics through avenues such as VOA, as well as increasing outlets by moving from a radio-based approach to direct broadcast TV and the Internet. In addition, changes to the U.S. approach to public affairs must be considered as technology advances and the "firewall" between PD and PA breaks down. Increased international TV markets and the Internet have made it virtually impossible to influence foreign publics without that information being available to and affecting domestic audiences. As noted earlier, changes in how the U.S. conducts business in this respect will require policy and legal changes.

Other available channels include those associated with regional U.S. military activity. A full integration of theater commanders' Theater Security Cooperation Plans (TSCPs), OP3 and PA efforts into a strategic framework will provide consistent themes and messages in peacetime by establishing a foundation that demonstrates U.S. military policy in action through advertised force movements, military-to-military contacts, joint exercises and training, port visits, etc. Leveraging these outlets during crisis and wartime can directly support coercive diplomacy.

International programs need to be "global with a regional cast" in order to facilitate understanding over the final three feet. The State Department's Fulbright and international visitor exchange programs – considered the "bread and butter" of public diplomacy – in addition to DoD's IMET, National Defense University International Fellows programs, and other international exchange programs are long-term assets with potential strategic value if properly supported. Communicating to foreign publics through foreign opinion leaders, our allies, and foreign journalists is important; these elites, if convinced of our policy position, bring credibility to the table. Finally, a change in State Department culture is necessary – one that empowers ambassadors, embassies, and Foreign Service Officers and other U.S. officials abroad to engage regional leaders and media groups. The diversity of this approach will lend authority to the message as well.

Building these channels will provide a credible means of disseminating the U.S. foreign policy message and ensuring the message and intent are clearly communicated to both foreign and domestic audiences. However, the follow-through is just as important as the wind up. As Edward R. Murrow noted, "no cash register rings when somebody changes his mind."

We need to seek feedback from the target audiences. The same media research that helps us understand the audience can be used to gauge the success of the communication, letting us know whether the message is being received as intended. Feedback helps determine the psychological impact of the message and its effect on foreign policy implementation. As noted in the October 2001 DSB Study, "effective communication is only possible if strategists commit time and resources to understand audiences before they disseminate information and evaluate its effectiveness after they disseminate it." Without the analysis and evaluation in place to determine the effectiveness of the attempted communication, it will be impossible to properly tailor the message or the means of dissemination.

Interests

Having discussed the audience and the means of communicating with them, it is necessary to return to the issue of the message.

Earlier, the need to address this issue from three perspectives was raised. The "proactive" perspective is an issue-based approach; it focuses on such subjects as multilateral trade, democracy and human rights, weapons of mass destruction, terrorism, drugs and global crime, refugees, migration, or disease and famine.

Recently, the Kyoto Treaty, the International Criminal Court, and the Comprehensive Test Ban treaty come to mind as examples of ongoing international issues. These activities often lead to policy statements, treaties, conventions, summit statements, or the like. The "active" approach is interest-based, more concerned with the actual exercise of national power on the international scene, such as the current deployment of force to the Middle East, the nuclear impasse with North Korea, U.S. support to Israel, conferring Most-Favored-Nation trading status and its potential impact on other international relationships and long-term objectives. Done correctly, the "active" approach lays the groundwork for the successful execution of coercive diplomacy.

In the "reactive" approach, the U.S. deals with "seams" in its policies and actions. Two recent examples were the unanticipated counter-propaganda to U.S. airdrops of food in Afghanistan shortly after the start of Operation Enduring Freedom, and the cry of "double standard" from North Korea in contrasting U.S. treatment of them after voluntary revelation of their nuclear program with U.S. treatment of Iraq, who claims to have no weapons of mass destruction. Both issues are examples of how failure to deal with short-term negative press can have long-term implications.

National issues and interests that are going to be played out in the forum of domestic and foreign public opinion must be decided up front. A common theme in current literature is the need to recognize that the US does not require universal adoration and that it "is better to be respected than loved."

The proponents of this position advise us to improve understanding of American values, goals, and policies. Charlotte Beers has emphasized the need to define "who America is" to foreign audiences. The extent of foreign understanding of American beliefs and values will influence the U.S. ability to clearly articulate policy on global and regional issues, such as global warming, the ICC, NATO expansion, etc. As policy is developed, part of the process should include an analysis of global and regional reactions. The State Department's Office of International Information Programs (IIP), responsible for the direction of strategic communication from the State Department, is routinely left out of this process.

Conversely, military peacetime PSYOP efforts are usually issue-oriented and unlike wartime PSYOP efforts, not always deconflicted with national messages and themes. The October 2001 DSB study noted that the "US Government routinely disseminates information without dedicating the resources to coordinate sophisticated communications strategies." This disconnect takes on considerable importance as we undertake military action in Iraq or elsewhere. It will determine how the various publics in the affected regions, as well as those of potential allies, respond to US actions.

The problem with State Department efforts is that they focus almost exclusively on promoting understanding of U.S. culture, values, and beliefs, primarily among foreign publics and elites. The missing link is to communicate U.S. policy, its execution, and its impact on relations in the international community. Even in the wake of September 11, surveys show increased anti-American feelings on a global basis, not just in the Middle East. However, these same surveys tell us that American cultures, values, and economic system are not the target of this animosity; this enmity focuses on U.S. policies. Another method of developing context is to move the discussion from American values to a dialogue on individual freedoms. This approach steers the discussion away from whether or not the U.S. has the "right" moral values or "universal" beliefs, taking it back to the local situation within the foreign body politic. This situation-specific tactic provides a more meaningful backdrop for questions about U.S. foreign policy than clashes over values or beliefs. Overall, interests and issues highlighted by American foreign policy suffer from unclear articulation, misunderstanding, or honest opposition. A national psychological strategy will enable us to develop prioritized themes and messages associated with U.S. positions on key international issues and interests. The strategy will ensure a consistent message, promote open dialogue, and establish a viable context for policy formulation, dissemination of information, interaction of officials in the field, as well as unilateral or coalition efforts involving military force or the other elements of power.

The bottom line is that the U.S. must recognize the importance of understanding the audience, the channel, and the message to successfully execute a psychological strategy. The . . . suspension of a TV campaign intended to win the hearts and minds of Muslim audiences overseas offers an excellent example of our lack of an effective approach to gain this understanding. The portrayal of the success of Muslim-American immigrants in one- and two-minute sound bites, instead of articulating the rationale for U.S. policy, is instead an example of the continued inability of U.S. public diplomacy to realize who the U.S. is trying to talk to and what America should be saying. The senders thought they were communicating a positive message about the tolerance and diversity of U.S. society. The Muslim audience received another message conveying U.S. superiority to their indigenous cultures.

Management of public diplomacy
Relative to national security
Ronald Reagan, NSDD-77 (1983) [107]

This National Security Decision Directive (NSDD) issued in early 1983 provides a nearly full-service management precedent for more effective public diplomacy efforts in which the White House takes charge and coordinates the often resistant bureaucracy. Though President Reagan signed the document, which is written in the first person, the principal author was Carnes Lord, now a professor at the Naval War College and author of Losing Hearts and Minds? Public Diplomacy and Strategic Influence in an Age of Terror *(Praeger, 2006).*

Readers will note the structure that Reagan was setting up: a means to empower the normally weak White House National Security Council staff to coordinate public diplomacy across government agencies, and to monitor and enforce coordination and follow-through.

I have determined that it is necessary to strengthen the organization, planning and coordination of the various aspects of public diplomacy of the United States Government relative to national security. Public diplomacy is comprised of those actions of the U.S. Government designed to generate support for our national security objectives.

---

[107] "Management of Public Diplomacy Relative to National Security," National Security Decision Directive Number 77, January 14, 1983. Declassified secret document.

A Special Planning Group (SPG) under the National Security Council will be established under the chairmanship of the Assistant to the President for National Security Affairs. Membership shall consist of the Secretary of State, Secretary of Defense, the Director of the United States Information Agency, the Director of the Agency for International Development, and the Assistant to the President for Communications or their designated alternate. Other senior White House officials will attend as appropriate. Senior representatives of other agencies may attend at the invitation of the chairman.

The SPG shall be responsible for the overall planning, direction, coordination and monitoring of implementation of public diplomacy activities. It shall ensure that a wide-ranging program of effective initiatives is developed and implemented to support national security policy, objectives and decisions. Public diplomacy activities involving the President or the White House will continue to coordinated with the Office of the White House Chief of Staff.

Four interagency standing committees will be established, and report regularly to the SPG. The SPG will ensure that guidance to these committees is provided, as required, so that they can carry out their responsibilities in the area of public diplomacy. The SPG will further periodically review the activities of the four permanent coordinating committees to insure that plans are being implemented and that resource commitments are commensurate with established priorities.

The NSC Staff, in consultation with the regular members of the SPG, will provide staff support to the SPG and facilitate effective planning, coordinating and implementing of plans and programs approved by the SPG. The NSC Staff will call periodic meetings of the four committee chairmen or their designees to ensure inter-committee coordination.

Public Affairs Committee: This coordinating committee will be co-chaired by the Assistant to the President for Communications and the Deputy Assistant to the President for National Security Affairs. This group will be responsible for the planning and coordinating on a regular basis of U.S. Government public affairs activities relative to national security. Specifically, it will be responsible for the planning and coordination of major speeches on national security subjects and other public appearances by senior officials, and for planning and coordinating with respect to public affairs matters concerning national security and foreign policy events and issues with foreign and domestic dimensions. This committee will coordinate public affairs efforts to explain and support major U.S. foreign policy initiatives.

International Information Committee: This committee will be established under the chairmanship of a senior representative of the Department of State. A senior representative of the United States Information Agency shall serve as vice chairman of the committee. This group will be responsible for planning, coordinating and implementing international political activities in support of United States policies and interests relative to national security. Included among such activities are aid, training and organizational support for foreign governments and private groups to encourage the growth of democratic political institutions and practices. This will require close collaboration with other foreign policy efforts – diplomatic, economic, military – as well as close relationship with those sectors of the American society – labor, business, universities, philanthropy, political parties, press – that are or could be more engaged in parallel efforts overseas. This group will undertake to build up the U.S. Government capability to promote democracy, as enunciated in the President's speech in London on June 8, 1982 [establishing the National Endowment for Democracy]. Furthermore, this committee will initiate plans, programs and strategies designed to counter totalitarian ideologies and aggressive political action moves undertaken by the Soviet Union or Soviet surrogates. This committee shall be empowered to make recommendations and, as appropriate, to direct the concerned departments and agencies to implement political action strategies in support of key policy objectives. Attention will be directed to generate policy initiatives keyed to coming events. Close coordination with the other committees will be essential.

International Broadcasting Committee: This committee will be chaired by a representative of the Assistant to the President for National Security Affairs. This committee will be responsible for the planning and coordination of international broadcasting activities sponsored by the U.S. Government consistent with existing statutory requirements and the guidance established by NSDD 45. Among its principal responsibilities will be the diplomatic and technical planning relative to modernization of U.S. international broadcasting capabilities, the development of anti-jamming strategies and techniques, planning relative to direct radio broadcast by satellite and longer term considerations of the potential for direct T.V. broadcasting.

Each designated committee is authorized to establish, as appropriate, working groups or ad hoc task forces to deal with specific issues or programs.

All agencies should ensure that the necessary resources are made available for the effective operation of the interagency groups here established.

Implementing procedures for these measures will be developed as necessary.

[Signed] Ronald Reagan

U.S. international information policy
Ronald Reagan, NSSD-130 (1984) [108]

In National Security Decision Directive Number 130, President Reagan issued a new international information strategy that seamlessly combined public diplomacy and broadcasting with psychological operations. The full text of NSDD-130 follows.

International information is an integral and vital part of U.S. national security policy and strategy in the broad sense. Together with the other components of public diplomacy, it is a key strategic instrument for shaping fundamental political and ideological trends around the globe on a long-term basis and ultimately affecting the behavior of government.

While improvements have been made in U.S. international information programs and activities over the last several years, there is a need for sustained commitment over time to improving the quality and effectiveness of U.S. international information efforts, the level of resources devoted to them, and their coordination with other elements of U.S. national security policy and strategy. The role of international information considerations in policy formulation needs to be enhanced, and wider understanding of the role of international information should be sought within the Executive Branch as well as with the Congress and the public.

The fundamental purpose of U.S. international information programs is to affect foreign audiences in ways favorable to U.S. national interests. Such programs can only be credible and effective

---

[108] "U.S. International Information Policy," National Security Decision Directive Number 130, March 6, 1984. Declassified secret document.

by respecting accuracy and objectivity. At the same time, the habits, interests, expectations and level of understanding of foreign audiences may differ significantly from those of the domestic American audience, and require different approaches and emphases in the selection and presentation of information. While U.S. international information activities must be sensitive to the concerns of foreign governments, our information programs should be understood to be a strategic instrument of U.S. national policy, not a tactical instrument of U.S. diplomacy. We cannot accept foreign control over program content.

International Information Strategy

Essential to a successful global information strategy is recognition of the diversity of the audiences the U.S. seeks to address. Beyond the obvious differences among Western, Communist country and Third World audiences, there are significant ideological and cultural differences within countries and regions between elites, key option sectors, and the general population. Programming must be more effectively differentiated to reach these audiences. The critical importance of elites in the formation of public opinion must be recognized. At the same time, intensified efforts must be made to address the general population in areas where government control of elite communications is strict. Specific information themes and strategies outlined in the study accompanying this directive should serve as the general basis for U.S. international information programming.

International Radio Broadcasting

International radio broadcasting is the U.S. Government's most effective means of communicating the truth directly to the peoples of the world. Improvement in the U.S. international broadcasting effort must continue to enjoy the highest priority. National Security Decision Directive 45 affirmed the essentials of existing U.S. policy relative to U.S. international broadcasting and, among other things, authorized a major, long-term program of modernization and expansion, approved revised guidance for determining languages and broadcast hours, and called for a major effort to overcome jamming of U.S. broadcasts and ameliorate its effects. A review of implementation of NSDD 45 should be undertaken to include recommendations concerning the possible initiation of new language services. It should also incorporate reports on programming policy and objectives relating to international audiences of the Radio in the American Sector of Berlin and our Armed Forces Radio and Television Service.

Other International Information Instruments

Several other instruments of international information merit special attention and long-term planning and development.

More systematic thought needs to be given to the opportunities offered by international television broadcasting. A conceptual study should be undertaken of technical and political options for U.S. international television broadcasting over the next several decades.

In the area of publications, steps should be taken to reconstitute as a major ongoing program support for publishing and disseminating abroad books and other publications. This includes strengthening a working partnership between the USG and the private sector to make available broad serious works on American or Western institutions and principles.

In addition to the traditional instruments of international information, new technologies (particularly in the area of audio and video tape cassettes) have created new instruments whose potential should be explored.

It is important to recognize that information disseminated by private and commercial organizations is likely to have special credibility with many audiences. A high priority should be placed on improving liaison and cooperation with, and support of, appropriate private sector information efforts.

An interagency study in support of U.S. objectives relative to the free flow of information and the potential of new communications technologies should be carried out under the auspices of the Senior Planning Group. Special attention shall be given as to how to overcome barriers to information flow and how to utilize communications technologies to penetrate closed societies.

Information and Communications Assistance

Strategically targeted information and communications assistance to other nations can contribute significantly to achieving U.S. objectives. It should be recognized as an integral part of U.S.

international information activities. A study should be undertaken by the Senior Interagency Group on International Communications and Information Policy to define the role and contributions of the various agencies involved and to develop long-term strategy in this area.

International Information Policy in Peace and War

In view of the importance of psychological factors in maintaining the confidence of allied governments and in deterring military action against U.S. national interests, and in order to be prepared for the immediate and effective use of psychological operations (PSYOP) in crisis and in wartime, it is vital that the Armed Forces maintain a strong and active information capability. Revitalization and full integration of PSYOP in military operations and planning should be a high priority of the Department of Defense. In order to employ PSYOP effectively and economically, a set of national guidelines and a funded program will be established and roles and relationships of the agencies that are involved will be defined. The Department of Defense is directed, with appropriate interagency coordination and in accordance with national law and policy, to participate in overt PSYOP programs in peacetime. The SPG should take the lead in developing coordinated interagency plans, including the utilization of DoD capabilities, for international information activities in support of national security objectives.

Crisis and wartime conditions impose special requirements on U.S. international information activities. In wartime or during crises (which may be defined as periods of acute tension involving a threat to the lives of American citizens, or the imminence of war between the U.S. and other nations), U.S. international information elements should be ready to initiate special procedures to ensure policy consistency, timely response and rapid feedback from the intended audience. Appropriate agencies should review and, as necessary, develop procedures for their operations during crises.

International Information: Functional Requirements

Research on public opinion, media reaction, and cultural factors needs to be substantially improved and more fully coordinated and applied to U.S. information activities. The proposed Foreign Opinion Research Advisory Group (FOR A) is hereby approved, and agencies should seek funding for it as required.

There is an urgent requirement for more extensive and sophisticated training of USG personnel in the international information environment, and in substantive and technical requirements of effective international and intercultural communication. Agencies should review their existing training programs and augment them as necessary. In the area of career development, a special effort should be made by all agencies to develop career tracks which encourage qualified individuals to remain in the field of international information.

The lack of adequate resources devoted to international information remains a problem of fundamental importance. All Executive departments with significant activities in the international or national security areas should comprehensively review their participation in and support of U.S. international information activities, with a view both to increasing resources devoted to this area within current allocations and establishing clear requirements for future budgetary submissions.

There is a need to enhance the role of international information considerations in the national security policy process. Wherever appropriate, major national security policy studies and decision documents should include an assessment of the impact of policy options or decisions on foreign opinion and on the international information environment generally.

In order to generate the public consensus that is essential to support a vigorous international information effort, agencies will review current mission statements and other existing policy declarations and revise them as necessary to reflect the guidance provided by this directive and the accompanying study. Other activities in support of this objective should be pursued by the involved agencies on a coordinated basis.

[Signed] Ronald Reagan

Restructuring public diplomacy
Bill Clinton (1998) [109]

Seeking a post-Cold War "peace dividend" and joining forces with Senate Foreign Relations Committee Chairman Jesse Helms, the Clinton administration abolished the U.S. Information Agency (USIA) and merged it into the State Department.

The following seven pages are excerpted from President Bill Clinton's request to Congress in the Foreign Affairs Reform and Restructuring Act of 1998.

III. The Public Diplomacy and Public Affairs Missions

We place very high priority on public diplomacy with foreign audiences, and are firmly committed to integrating public diplomacy more fully into foreign policy. Our goal is to strengthen public diplomacy through its integration into the policy process. Negotiations on such issues as NATO enlargement, Iraqi sanctions, and global climate change show the value of being proactive in informing and influencing foreign publics, NGOs, and others. These audiences are playing greater roles on international issues as communications improve and pluralism expands. When public diplomacy strategies are applied from the outset as policy is formulated, policy and its articulation will improve and be more persuasive to foreign publics and policy-makers.

What Will Happen to the U.S. Information Agency (USIA)

Current Responsibilities

Public diplomacy promotes U.S. national security and other interests by seeking to understand, inform, and influence foreign publics and policy-makers, and by broadening the dialogue between American citizens and institutions and their counterparts abroad. In comparison, public affairs is the provision of information to the

---

[109] Submitted by President Clinton to the Congress on December 30, 1998, Pursuant to Section 1601 of the Foreign Affairs Reform and Restructuring Act of 1998, as Contained in Public Law 105-277.

public, press, and others about the policies and activities of the U.S. government.

Different aspects of the public diplomacy mission roughly correspond to the role of each of the Agency's current major programmatic elements (current USIA broadcasting functions are enumerated in Chapter IV on International Broadcasting):

Bureau of Information (I), Area Offices, and USIS Posts Abroad – Inform and seek to influence foreign opinion-makers by presenting U.S. positions on policy issues through a variety of products, including the daily Washington File, expert speakers (in person and in digital video or telepress conferences), Information Resource Centers overseas, electronic journals and Web sites, and print publications. The I Bureau provides a rapid response to implement public diplomacy strategies for U.S. foreign policy and national security initiatives, including in crises, and to post requests for materials tailored to particular foreign audiences.

Bureau of Educational and Cultural Affairs (E), Area Offices, and USIS Posts Abroad – Broaden long-term dialogue with foreign publics through a variety of person-to-person exchanges, including the Fulbright Program for scholars, teachers, and students; the International Visitors program to bring foreign leaders to the U.S.; Citizen Exchanges efforts to develop international exchange programs through nonprofit American institutions; and programs to affiliate U.S. and foreign academic institutions, advise foreign students about American colleges and universities, foster the teaching abroad of U.S. studies and the English language, and strengthen educational institutions abroad.

Office of Research and Media Reaction (R) – Seeks to understand foreign publics through opinion polling abroad and, utilizing reporting from USIS posts abroad and other media, to analyze attitudes toward U.S. policies and activities in the foreign media.

Personnel

USIA has 6,714 full-time permanent positions, of which 2,689 are engaged in broadcasting activities. The remaining 4,025 consist of 655 Americans and 2,079 Foreign Service Nationals (FSN) overseas, and 1,291 positions in the U.S.

Key Issues Considered

Budget Structure – Funding for public diplomacy (excluding exchange and academic programs, which have and will continue to have their own appropriations) will be incorporated through increases to existing Congressional appropriations to State for Diplomatic and Consular Programs Abroad, the Security and Maintenance of Buildings Abroad, Representation Allowances, Emergencies in the Diplomatic and Consular Service, and the Capital Investment Fund. In the appropriation for Diplomatic and Consular Programs Abroad, State will separately plan for, identify, and account for public diplomacy resources for programs and products aimed at foreign audiences, and foreign national personnel and other programmatic expenses of public diplomacy sections of embassies and missions abroad and in appropriate offices in State.

Organizational Structures – We will promote maximum appropriate synergy of public diplomacy and public affairs activities under the oversight of the new Under Secretary for Public Diplomacy and Public Affairs. The Under Secretary will oversee State's Bureau of Public Affairs (PA), although State's spokesperson will continue to have daily contact with the Secretary and Deputy Secretary. The Under Secretary will also oversee the new Bureau of Information Programs and International Exchanges, which will be responsible for exchange and academic programs and will produce information programs and products tailored to influence foreign opinion-makers. The Assistant Secretary for Information Programs and International Exchanges will oversee three deputy assistant secretaries, who will be responsible for academic exchange programs, professional exchange programs, and international information programs, respectively.

Smith-Mundt and Zorinsky Amendments – In legislation over the years, Congress has restricted USIA's public diplomacy apparatus from being used to influence U.S. public opinion. The Foreign Relations Authorization Act of 1972 amended the Smith-Mundt Act to include a ban on disseminating within the United States any "information about the United States, its people, and its policies" prepared for dissemination abroad. The Zorinsky Amendment added a new prohibition: "no funds authorized to be appropriated to the United States Information Agency shall be used to influence public opinion in the United States, and no program material prepared by the United States Information Agency shall be distributed within the United States." The Foreign Affairs Reform and Restructuring Act of 1998 (the Act) addresses the application of these restrictions to State, giving it the flexibility to allocate personnel and other resources effectively and efficiently. In integrating USIA, State will observe all applicable legal restrictions.

Consistent with Congressional intent, public diplomacy information efforts will focus on programs and products for foreign audiences. Exchange programs will continue to engage American and foreign participants and organizations under the Mutual Educational and Cultural Exchange Act of 1961 (Fulbright-Hays).

The establishment of a public diplomacy organization reflects the high importance attached to public diplomacy and its distinctive aspects. As an example of the latter, public diplomacy officers engage foreign audiences with techniques, language skills, and area knowledge not duplicated in domestic public affairs activities. At the same time, much policy content is the same for foreign and domestic audiences, e.g., State's daily press briefings and fact sheets on policy issues. These messages are delivered both to domestic and foreign audiences by many of the same media, e.g., CNN, the World Wide Web, and international wire services. More than half of the journalists whom State serves on a daily basis work for foreign media, and State and USIA web pages can be accessed from anywhere.

Proposed Integration into State

The Under Secretary for Public Diplomacy and Public Affairs will advise the Secretary of State on public diplomacy and public affairs. The Under Secretary will provide policy oversight for two bureaus dealing with public diplomacy and public affairs, and coordinate such activities in State. State's Strategic Plan will encompass public diplomacy goals, and respective Bureau and Mission Performance Plans will reflect targets and projects for each region, country, and functional area. The office will have nine full-time permanent positions, all from USIA. The Under Secretary will chair the interagency international public information (IPI) Core Group, which will develop and coordinate U.S. public information strategies and activities to address regional and transnational threats and crises.

USIA's Office of Research and Media Reaction will be merged with its parallel State components. We will look to even more sophisticated ways to understand and evaluate trends in foreign opinion. Its public opinion research function (35 full-time permanent positions) and its media reaction division (six full-time permanent positions) will be incorporated into the Bureau of Intelligence and Research. Six of the Office of Strategic Communications and Program Coordination's full-time permanent positions will go to the Bureau of Information Programs and International Exchanges, as well as one nonreimbursable one. The seventh full-time permanent position will transfer to State's Policy Planning Staff.

The office of the new Assistant Secretary for Information Programs and International Exchanges will be formed from the staff of USIA's current offices of the Associate Director for Information and the Associate Director for Educational and Cultural Affairs. A staff of twelve full-time permanent positions, formerly in the USIA General Counsel's office, will report to the Assistant Secretary and be responsible for exchange visitor program designations; one additional full-time permanent position, responsible for film attestations under the Beirut Convention, will also transfer to the Assistant Secretary's office. The Assistant Secretary will be supported by the continuing efforts of the Cultural Property Advisory Committee and the Fulbright Scholarship Board (three full-time permanent positions).

International information activities will continue to emphasize rapid response, cross-functional teamwork, and field orientation. Thus, the achievements of USIA's innovative Bureau of Information, launched four years ago as a Reinvention Laboratory based on Vice President Gore's National Performance Review and the best practices of private industry, will be maintained and strengthened under the leadership of the Deputy Assistant Secretary for Information Programs. It will incorporate the Office of Strategic Communications (six full-time permanent positions and one nonreimbursable position). There will be a total of 215 full-time permanent American domestic positions plus 16 overseas American and one FSN.

These international information services will be available to all bureaus and overseas posts, to provide them with the assistance they need to advance U.S. interests abroad. Information programs will be prepared in response both to Washington initiatives and to post needs. Guided by country information, including polling data, and other available information, the assistance provided in these programmatic packages, will enable the field to aggressively promote our foreign policy goals through world-class information services.

Educational and cultural activities will be carried out in the Bureau of Information Programs and International Exchanges under the direction of the Deputy Assistant Secretary for Academic Exchanges and the Deputy Assistant Secretary for Professional Exchanges. It will have 273 full-time permanent American positions domestically, including nine positions involved in grants management that were originally in the USIA central contracts office, plus 11 overseas.

The Bureau of Information Programs and International Exchanges will be supported by an administrative office drawn from existing support positions, plus the transfer of 33 full-time permanent positions from USIA's current Management Bureau, which has been providing these services.

Similar State and USIA information-related support functions will be combined into existing State structures. USIA's print operations and associated support (22 American and 91 foreign national full-time permanent positions) will join State's. Domestic library activities will be combined (two full-time permanent positions.) Efforts to promote U.S. foreign policy on the Internet will be combined and coordinated and domestic libraries will be merged.

The three USIA foreign press center operations and its offices in Washington, New York, and Los Angeles (24 full-time permanent positions) will be transferred to the Bureau of Public Affairs.

Consistent with the Act, BBG personnel who carry out Worldnet TV interactives (12 full-time permanent positions) will be transferred to State's Bureau of Public Affairs. Additionally, the Foreign Broadcast Support Unit (eight full-time permanent positions) will be transferred to the Foreign Press Centers in the Bureau of Public Affairs.

USIA's area offices will integrate where practical and efficient into State's regional bureaus (103 full-time permanent positions), building on the successful European Bureau/Office of West European Affairs model. Units in regional bureaus will coordinate public diplomacy activities of their respective embassies and missions abroad. Overseas 447 full-time permanent American positions and 1,720 FSN positions will engage in public diplomacy work.

Public diplomacy personnel (initially 25 full-time permanent positions, drawn from USIA's staff, area, and support offices) will be added to State's functional bureaus. These units will advise on policies from a public diplomacy perspective, and help develop public diplomacy strategies on regional and thematic basis to promote such U.S. national goals in areas such as counter terrorism, narcotics, arms control, and nonproliferation.

One position from ACDA's Bureau of Public Affairs will transfer to State's Office of the Historian, located in PA [Public Affairs].

Positive Outcomes

The two bureau structure will bring together all elements charged with presenting and interpreting U.S. foreign policy to public audiences. It will give public diplomacy practitioners greater access to the foreign policy formulation process. The new structure will ensure that the policy content of State's domestic and international outreach programs is consistent and coordinated, yet tailored for specific target audiences. It will ensure that all applicable legal requirements are adhered to. And it will strengthen State's Bureau of Public Affairs by increasing its press expertise.

By placing public diplomacy staffs in State's regional and functional bureaus, the new structure will offer a better integrated mechanism for identifying and acting on priority public diplomacy issues, and coordinating Washington resources with the needs of the field. International broadcasting will preserve its editorial integrity while adding new services and maintaining close ties with State, complementing other U.S. public diplomacy efforts in support of U.S. foreign policy interests.

Useful reminder: Be there at takeoff, not just at crash landings
Edward R. Murrow (1961)[110]

Public diplomacy and international broadcasting leaders were kept in the dark before the invasion of Cuba at the Bay of Pigs in April, 1961. That was unacceptable to USIA Director Edward R. Murrow, who was livid that he had no prior knowledge so as to be able to inform the world when the exile invasion occurred.

---

[110] Alan L. Heil, Jr., *Voice of America: A History* (Columbia, 2003), p. 70. Murrow's reported demand to President Kennedy is often cited, but the editor could not find the primary source.

As is often the case, public diplomacy and international broadcasting would be relied on to help clean up the mess after the fact. When news of the failed invasion broke, Murrow made his famous dictum for foreign policy planners:

They expect us [USIA] to be in on the crash landings ... we had better be in on the takeoffs.

Other sources say that Murrow reportedly told President Kennedy the same thought, but in more quotable form:

If you want me in on the landings, I'd better be there for the takeoffs.

Public Diplomacy and Propaganda

Is public diplomacy a form of propaganda? Objectively speaking, the answer is yes: public diplomacy is a form of persuasive communication intended to modify the target audience's perceptions, attitudes and behavior. But propaganda is such a loaded word thanks to World Wars I and II, with such negative connotations, that most public diplomats avoid the term completely.

U.S. officials disagree on difference
USIA Alumni Association, publicdiplomacy.org[111]

. . . some U.S. Government officials and others contended that U.S. public diplomacy programs are not propaganda. Others still contend, however, that since propaganda can be based on fact, public diplomacy can be equated with propaganda i.e. ideas, information, or other material disseminated to win people over to a given doctrine. If based on falsehoods and untruths, while still propaganda, it is best described as "disinformation."

Propaganda agency
Edward R. Murrow (1963)[112]

I believe that no propaganda agency, which is what we are [USIA], should either anticipate or prejudice policy. I think we must at all times reflect with fidelity the national policy and purpose. It is, of course, impossible to make good propaganda out of bad policy.

---

[111] "Public diplomacy and propaganda," on website of U.S. Information Agency Alumni Association, 2002, www.publicdiplomacy.org/1.htm.
[112] "Statement of Hon. Edward R. Murrow, Director, U.S. Information Agency," in *Winning the Cold War: The U.S. Ideological Offensive*, Hearings before the Subcommittee on International Organizations and Movements of the Committee on Foreign Affairs, U.S. House of Representatives, 88th Congress, First Session, Part I, March 28, 1963, p. 6.

Call it what you want
Richard Holbrooke (2001)[113]

Call it public diplomacy, or public affairs, or psychological warfare, or – if you really want to be blunt – propaganda. But whatever it is called, defining what this war is really about in the minds of the one billion Muslims in the world will be of decisive and historic importance.

Books are weapons
Franklin D. Roosevelt (1942)[114]

President Franklin D. Roosevelt made himself clear about how he viewed books as wartime tools. He wrote the following letter to publisher W. W. Norton, Chairman of the Council on Books in Wartime, in 1942.

Dear Mr. Norton:

I take pleasure in sending this greeting to the Council on Books in Wartime for its December six meeting.

In our country's first year of war, we have seen the growing power of books as weapons. Through books we have appraised our enemies and discovered our allies. We have learned something of American valor in battle. We have, above all, come to understand better the kind of war we must fight and the kind of peace we must establish.

This is proper, for a war of ideas can no more be won without books than a naval war can be won without ships. Books, like ships, have the toughest armor, the longest cruising range, and mount the most powerful guns. I hope that all who write and publish and sell and administer books will, on the occasion of your meeting, rededicate themselves to the single task of arming the mind and spirit of the American people with the strongest and more enduring weapons.

---

[113] Richard Holbrooke was U.S. Ambassador to the United Nations under President Bill Clinton. Richard Holbrooke, "Get the Message Out," *Washington Post*, October 28, 2001.

[114] President Franklin D. Roosevelt, letter to W. W. Norton, December 1, 1942. Copy of letter in collection of this book's editor.

Propaganda battle: from VOA to bulletins to health campaigns
Edward W. Barrett (1951) [115]

*In this 1951 letter, a senior State Department official comments
on the "propaganda battle" in Iraq. USIE refers to the U.S.
Information and Educational Exchange, which was the precursor to
the U.S. Information Agency (USIA). USIS refers to the U.S.
Information Service, which was the USIE and USIA office in
American embassies abroad.*

. . . I was particularly interested in hearing your reactions to the
"propaganda battle."

The Department [of State] does recognize the tremendous power
of radio. We hope to increase the time on the air of the Arabic VOA;
also, we recognize the fact that we must present a stronger signal
than we have at the present. There are always budgetary limitations,
as you know.

. . . we must tell the world of our widespread commitments. We
are trying to do this in a number of ways, one of which is the Middle
East Bulletin. In Iraq, the Bulletin is distributed in English, Arabic,
and Kurdish. . . . The Kurdish situation is delicate since the Iraqi
officials quite naturally fear that we will arouse Kurdish nationalism,
whereas – as we tell them – our effort is merely to reach as wide an
audience as possible with our messages regarding the present world
ideological conflict.

Poverty and ill health care are indeed two great problems of the
people of the area. USIE has a medical library in each of its
information centers, medical films and film strips for distribution,
and also medical newsletters. Point IV will offer the people technical
know-how. Did you by any chance view any of the excellent USIE
Disney health films – simple, direct explanations in an attractive
form on a number of local diseases and how to avoid them? They are
often shown with a Kurdish language soundtrack. Did you also see
the effective anti-malaria poster produced by USIS Baghdad?

---

[115] Edward W. Barrett was Assistant Secretary of State for Public Affairs at
the time. Excerpt from a letter to Dr. George G. Cameron, Department of
Near Eastern Studies, University of Michigan, Ann Arbor, Michigan,
November 13, 1951. Courtesy of the National Security Archive, George
Washington University.

Public diplomacy, propaganda and rhetoric
Mark Blitz (1986) [116]

Public diplomacy . . . is seemingly a euphemism for *propaganda*, which is itself a variation of what the earliest political thinkers understood as *rhetoric*. Indeed, public diplomacy displays the art of euphemism and embellishment thought to be chief tool of its trade....

Although its promulgators do not believe propaganda is false (in fact, it is normally true), the term propaganda strikes us as somehow unsavory – a fancy species of lying, perhaps minor lying in the best of causes, but lying nonetheless. However much twentieth-century social scientists once expected it might be, propaganda has never been a value-free term.

A better term, normally used in place of propaganda, is information. We do not propagandize, but inform. Today, however, information suggests a mindless generating of passively accepted facts; it has lost the sense of shaping interest in its original meaning. It strikes the diplomatic ear as a bit too one-sided or imperialistic a term. Hence, we have the occasional use of communication as the euphemism for propaganda. Embracing almost any activity, however, communication is too vacuous a concept to have much meaning; it is especially vacuous when it shades into sharing, relating, and "being open" (its meaning when used synonymously with informing and persuading).

Public diplomacy is, therefore, a substitute for public information or public communication as the decent term for what would otherwise be called propaganda. Beyond this, if we consider the root sense of information and some of the senses of propaganda, we notice that public diplomacy is primarily the active shaping of public opinion by telling or displaying the truth – not merely the injection of undigested material into an opinion that has already been formed.

---

[116] Mark Blitz, "Public Diplomacy and the Private Sector," in Richard Staar, ed., *Public Diplomacy: USA versus USSR* (Hoover Institution Press, 1986), pp. 95-96. Reprinted from *Public Diplomacy: USA versus USSR*, edited by Richard F. Staar, with the permission of the publisher, Hoover Institution Press. Copyright © 1986 by the Board of Trustees of the Leland Stanford Junior University. Blitz is a former professional staff member of the Senate Foreign Relations Committee and was associate director of the U.S. Information Agency. He is the Fletcher Jones Professor of Political Philosophy at Claremont McKenna College.

The traditional term for this practice is civic (or public) persuasion, or better, civic education because persuasion carries too artful and sly a connotation. The publics in question, however, are foreign, so the term civic education fails to differentiate our subject clearly enough. Although it is altogether proper for citizens to give themselves and their children continuing civic education, to educate foreigners seems a bit meddlesome and may be interpreted as unwarranted interference in someone else's affairs. Therefore, public diplomacy is a useful and diplomatic way of conceptually differentiating the civic education of foreigners form the civic education of fellow citizens.

Public diplomacy also refers to the kind of civic education that occurs in public, not secretly or in private. Governments usually talk to other governments secretly or, at least, behind doors that initially are closed. Their persuasion can then exercise skills and use facts that cannot always be displayed publicly to advantage. In contrast, public diplomacy refers to the open education of foreigners, most of whom are private citizens and not government officials.

To summarize, public diplomacy is the open civic education of citizens of other countries using means that are not deliberately false. The point of public diplomacy is primary political (although it often uses nonpolitical methods), and there is nothing knowingly false in what it does (although which facts should be emphasized, when, and where is a matter of judgment).

Counterpropaganda:
Never Let the Other Side Control the Story

'Keep the enemy in the wrong'
Samuel Adams (1775)[117]

. . . it is a good Maxim in Politicks as well as War to put & keep the Enemy in the wrong.

Insulate the homefront against foreign intrigue
George Washington, Farewell Address (1796)[118]

In his last statement in public life, George Washington warned the nation that foreign governments and forces would exploit America's open society and its internal divisions. Even nations considered favored or friendly, the first president cautioned, would try to lure Americans into their own conflicts and create unnecessary antagonisms. To insulate the country from such outside pressures, Washington cautioned about what he called "the insidious wiles of foreign influence." The following is excerpted from his Farewell Address of September 19, 1796.

---

[117] Samuel Adams, letter to Richard Henry Lee, March 21, 1775, reprinted in W. V. Wells, *Life of Samuel Adams*, Vol. II (Boston, 1865), pp. 256, 257, 281. Samuel Adams was the main propagandist of the American independence movement and the American Revolution. He founded the Sons of Liberty in Boston and the Committees of Correspondence, and served as a member of the First and Second Continental Congresses, and signed the Declaration of Independence.

[118] George Washington, "Farewell Address," September 19, 1796. Text courtesy of the Avalon Project, Yale Law School and the Library of Congress. Curiously, the text of the address that appears on the State Department website as of July 2007, is redacted. Someone has omitted several passages including Washington's warning "to guard against the impostures of pretended patriotism." See the redacted text at: http://usinfo.state.gov/usa/infousa/facts/democrac/49.htm.

Antipathy in one nation against another, disposes each more readily to offer insult and injury, to lay hold of slight causes of umbrage, and to be haughty and intractable, when accidental or trifling occasions of dispute occur.

Hence frequent collision, obstinate, envenomed, and bloody contests. The nation, prompted by ill-will and resentment, sometimes impels to war the government, contrary to the best calculations of policy. The government sometimes participates in the national propensity, and adopts through passion what reason would reject; at other times, it makes the animosity of the nation subservient to projects of hostility instigated by pride, ambition and other sinister and pernicious motives. The peace often, and sometimes, perhaps, the liberty of nations, has been the victim.

So, likewise, a passionate attachment of one nation for another produces a variety of evils. Sympathy for the favorite nation facilitating the illusion of an imaginary common interest in cases where no real common interest exists, and infusing into one of the enmities of the other, betrays the former into a participation in the quarrels and wars of the latter, without adequate inducement or justification. It leads also to concessions to the favorite nation of privileges denied to others, which is apt doubly to injure the nation making the concessions; by unnecessarily parting with what ought to have been retained; and by exciting jealousy, ill-will, and a disposition to retaliate, in the parties from whom equal privileges are withheld; and it gives to ambitious, corrupted, or deluded citizens (who devote themselves to the favorite nation) facility to betray, or sacrifice the interests of their own country, without odium, sometimes even with popularity; gilding, with the appearances of a virtuous sense of obligation, a commendable deference for public opinion, or laudable zeal for public good, the base or foolish compliances of ambition, corruption, or infatuation.

As avenues to foreign influence, in innumerable ways, such attachments are particularly alarming to the truly enlightened and independent patriot. How many opportunities do they afford to tamper with domestic factions; to practise the arts of seduction; to mislead public opinion; to influence or awe the public councils! Such an attachment of a small or weak nation, toward a great and powerful one, dooms the former to be the satellite of the latter.

Against the insidious wiles of foreign influence (I conjure you to believe me, fellow-citizens), the jealousy of a free people ought to be constantly awake; since history and experience prove, that foreign influence is one of the most baneful foes of republican government. But that jealousy, to be useful, must be impartial; else it becomes the instrument of the very influence to be avoided, instead of a defence against it. Excessive partiality for one foreign nation, and excessive dislike of another, cause those whom they actuate, to see danger only on one side; and serve to veil and even second the arts of influence on the other. Real patriots, who may resist the intrigues of the favorite, are liable to become suspected and odious; while its tools and dupes usurp the applause and confidence of the people, to surrender their interests.

We need resources to combat covert propaganda
Philip Habib (1986) [119]

Veteran diplomat Philip Habib, at a 1986 Hoover Institution conference on public diplomacy, called for an adequately financed and staffed government institution for dealing with semi-covert "gray" and covert "black" operations by adversaries. Habib made his comments in the larger context of the public diplomacy reorganization under NSDD-75.

A possible additional element to the structural system in Washington might deal with the gray or black types of Soviet activity in the field of public diplomacy. This has not been adequately explored: We have sufficient means to deal with the overt aspects, but we need an instrument to contend with covert Soviet public diplomacy. We do not have a sufficiently institutionalized instrument for coping with that problem, in part because it is probably going to take more than people and thought to develop the necessary counteractions. One man, or a subcommittee of the NSC meeting, sporadically thinking about the problem is not the way we should deal with it.

---

[119] Philip Habib, "Concluding Remarks," in Richard F. Staar, ed., *Public Diplomacy: USA versus USSR* (Hoover Institution Press, 1986), p. 285. Reprinted from *Public Diplomacy: USA versus USSR*, edited by Richard F. Staar, with the permission of the publisher, Hoover Institution Press. Copyright © 1986 by the Board of Trustees of the Leland Stanford Junior University.

Counterpropaganda: An absolute essential
Herbert Romerstein (2006)[120]

A democratic society must understand the techniques of disinformation in order to develop effective counterpropaganda. However, a democratic society cannot use disinformation not only for moral reasons but for practical ones: in our open society the truth would soon come out. Although this appears to be a weakness, in fact it was a strength when we refuted Soviet disinformation. America's reputation as a truth teller and the Soviet reputation as a lie teller helped us refute their propaganda themes and discredit the Soviet Union for using them.

As early as the 1980s, but even more so in our present information age, when disinformation is spread to one audience it can be replayed to a more sophisticated audience to the detriment of the disinformer. The United States was able to show European audiences examples of Soviet disinformation targeting the Third World. The Europeans easily saw through the lies. That exposure helped damage the image of the Soviet Union at the time when Moscow desperately wanted to look good to the Western democracies. The exercise sensitized the West Europeans to Soviet disinformation and propaganda directed at them.

Nazi Germany entered World War II with intensive experience in propaganda and counterpropaganda. In 1939, the British tried every way they could to convince Hitler not to start the war. Nazi Propaganda Minister Joseph Goebbels authored Berlin's reply. He said, "Your English propaganda tricks are absurd. There was a time when we National Socialists possessed no power, and yet we were able to overcome our political opponents at home. That trained us in the work of propaganda."

The British responded with both overt (white) propaganda (signed by the British government) and unsigned (gray) propaganda. Later in the war, they dropped falsely attributed (black) propaganda over German lines. Black, white and gray are terms developed during World War II. They only refer to the attribution not the truth of the

---

[120] Herbert Romerstein was director of the Office to Counter Soviet Active Measures at the United States Information Agency, and is an adjunct professor at The Institute of World Politics. This passage is excerpted from *Strategic Influence: Public Diplomacy, Counterpropaganda and Political Warfare* (IWP Press, 2007). Copyright © 2007 by IWP Press.

data. For the most part, British propaganda to Germany was true regardless of the attribution. Two gray booklets were printed in England for distribution to publications in neutral countries. Although not officially attributed to the British government, they exposed specific Nazi propaganda claims as being false.

How to identify misinformation
U.S. Department of State (2005)

The State Department has a small, one-man office devoted full-time to countering international falsehoods about the United States and its allies. The department is forbidden by the Smith-Mundt Act of 1948 to share with the American public the facts and counter-arguments used to defeat anti-U.S. falsehoods.

State's counter-misinformation Web page, http://usinfo.state.gov/media/misinformation, does not appear on the State Department's www.state.gov search engine. A brief detection guide follows. Ellipses indicate excised portions containing hyperlinks to more detailed information about each subject.

How can a journalist or a news consumer tell if a story is true or false? There are no exact rules, but the following clues can help indicate if a story or allegation is true.

- Does the story fit the pattern of a conspiracy theory?
- Does the story fit the pattern of an "urban legend?"
- Does the story contain a shocking revelation about a highly controversial issue?
- Is the source trustworthy?
- What does further research tell you?

Does the story fit the pattern of a conspiracy theory?

Does the story claim that vast, powerful, evil forces are secretly manipulating events? If so, this fits the profile of a conspiracy theory. Conspiracy theories are rarely true, even though they have great appeal and are often widely believed. In reality, events usually have much less exciting explanations.

The U.S. military or intelligence community is a favorite villain in many conspiracy theories.

For example, the Soviet disinformation apparatus regularly blamed the U.S. military or intelligence community for a variety of natural disasters as well as political events. In March 1992, then-Russian foreign intelligence chief Yevgeni Primakov admitted that the disinformation service of the Soviet KGB intelligence service had concocted the false story that the AIDS virus had been created in a US military laboratory as a biological weapon. When AIDS was first discovered, no one knew how this horrifying new disease had arisen, although scientists have now used DNA analysis to determine that "all HIV-1 strains known to infect man" are closely related to a simian immunodeficiency virus found in a western equatorial African chimpanzee, *Pan troglodytes troglodytes*. But the Soviets used widespread suspicions about the U.S. military to blame it for AIDS. . . .

In his book *9/11: The Big Lie*, French author Thierry Meyssan falsely claimed that no plane hit the Pentagon on September 11, 2001. Instead, he claimed that the building had been struck by a cruise missile fired by elements within the U.S. government. No such vast conspiracy existed and many eyewitness accounts and evidence gathered on the scene confirmed that the hijacked airliner had struck the building. But, nevertheless, the book was a best-seller in France and has been translated into 19 languages, demonstrating the power that even the most groundless conspiracy theories can have. . . .

Does the story fit the pattern of an "urban legend?"

Is the story startlingly good, bad, amazing, horrifying, or otherwise seemingly "too good" or "too terrible" to be true? If so, it may be an "urban legend." Urban legends, which often circulate by word of mouth, e-mail, or the Internet, are false claims that are widely believed because they put a common fear, hope, suspicion, or other powerful emotion into story form.

For example, after the September 11 attacks, a story arose that someone had survived the World Trade Center collapse by "surfing" a piece of building debris from the 82nd floor to the ground. Of course, no one could survive such a fall, but many initially believed this story, out of desperate hope that some people trapped in the towers miraculously survived their collapse. . . .

Another September 11 urban legend is that an undamaged Bible was found in the midst of the crash site at the Pentagon. In reality, it was a dictionary. But, if a Bible had survived unscathed, that would have seemed much more significant, and been seen by many as a sign of divine intervention. . . .

Since 1987, the false story that Americans or others are kidnapping or adopting children in order to use them in organ transplants has been widely believed. There is absolutely no evidence that any such event has ever occurred, but such allegations have won the most prestigious journalism prizes in France in 1995 and Spain in 1996. . . .This urban legend is based on fears about both organ transplantation and international adoptions, both of which were relatively new practices in the 1980s. As advances in medical science made organ transplantation more widespread, unfounded fears began to spread that people would be murdered for their organs. At the same time, there were also unfounded fears about the fate of infants adopted by foreigners and taken far from their home countries. The so-called "baby parts" rumor combined both these fears in story form, which gave it great credibility even though there was absolutely no evidence for the allegation.

In late 2004, a reporter for Saudi Arabia's *Al Watan* newspaper repeated a version of the organ trafficking urban legend, falsely claiming that U.S. forces in Iraq were harvesting organs from dead or wounded Iraqis for sale in the United States. This shows how the details of urban legends can change, to fit different circumstances....

Highly controversial issues

AIDS, organ transplantation, international adoption, and the September 11 attacks are all new, frightening or, in some ways, discomforting topics. Such highly controversial issues are natural candidates for the rise of false rumors, unwarranted fears and suspicions. Another example of a highly controversial issue is depleted uranium, a relatively new armor-piercing substance that was used by the U.S. military for the first time during the 1991 Gulf War.

There are many exaggerated fears about depleted uranium because people associate it with weapons-grade uranium or fuel-grade uranium, which are much more dangerous substances. When most people hear the word uranium, a number of strongly held associations spring to mind, including the atomic bomb, Hiroshima, nuclear reactors, radiation illness, cancer, and birth defects.

Depleted uranium is what is left over when natural uranium is enriched to make weapons-grade or fuel-grade uranium. In the process, the uranium loses, or is depleted, of almost half its radioactivity, which is how depleted uranium gets its name. But facts like this are less important in peoples' minds than the deeply ingrained associations they have with the world "uranium." For this reason, most people believe that depleted uranium is much more dangerous than it actually is. . . .

Another highly controversial issue is that of forbidden weapons, such as chemical or biological weapons. The United States is regularly, and falsely, accused of using these weapons. . . .

In the same way, many other highly controversial issues are naturally prone to misunderstanding and false rumors. Any highly controversial issue or taboo behavior is ripe material for false rumors and urban legends.

Consider the source

Certain websites, publications, and individuals are known for spreading false stories, including:

- Aljazeera.com, a deceptive, look-alike website that has sought to fool people into thinking it is run by the Qatari satellite television station Al Jazeera
- Jihad Unspun, a website run by a Canadian woman who converted to Islam after the September 11 attacks when she became convinced that Osama bin Laden was right
- Islam Memo (Mafkarat-al-Islam), which spreads a great deal of disinformation about Iraq.

There are many conspiracy theory websites, which contain a great deal of unreliable information. Examples include:

- Rense.com
- Australian "private investigator" Joe Vialls, who died in 2005
- Conspiracy Planet

Extremist groups, such as splinter communist parties, often publish disinformation. This can be especially difficult to identify if the false allegations are published by front groups. Front groups purport to be independent, non-partisan organizations but actually controlled by political parties or groups. Some examples of front groups are:

- The International Action Center, which is a front group for a splinter communist party called the Workers World Party
- The Free Arab Voice, a website that serves as a front for Arab communist Muhammad Abu Nasr and his colleagues.

Research the allegations

The only way to determine whether an allegation is true or false is to research it as thoroughly as possible. Of course, this may not always be possible given publication deadlines and time pressures, but there is no substitute for thorough research, going back to the original sources. Using the Internet, many allegations can be fairly thoroughly researched in a matter of hours.

For example, in July 2005, the counter-misinformation team researched the allegation that U.S. soldiers in Iraq had killed innocent Iraqi boys playing football and then "planted" rocket-propelled grenades (RPGs) next to them, to make it appear that they were insurgents.

Using a variety of search terms in "Google," a researcher was able to find the article and photographs upon which the allegations were based. Because weapons did not appear in the initial photographs, but did appear in later photographs, some observers believed this was evidence that the weapons had been planted and that the boys who had been killed were not armed insurgents.

The researcher was also able to find weblog entries (numbered 100 and 333, on June 26 and July 15, 2005) from the commanding officer of the platoon that was involved in the incident and another member of his platoon. The weblog entries made it clear that:

- the teenaged Iraqi boys were armed insurgents;
- after the firefight between U.S. troops and the insurgents was over, the dead, wounded and captured insurgents were initially photographed separated from their weapons because the first priority was to make sure that it was impossible for any of the surviving insurgents to fire them again;
- following medical treatment for the wounded insurgents, they were photographed with the captured weapons displayed, in line with Iraqi government requirements;

- the insurgents were hiding in a dense palm grove, where visibility was limited to 20 meters, not a likely place for a football game, and they were seen carrying the RPGs on their shoulders.

Thus, an hour or two of research on the Internet was sufficient to establish that the suspicions of the bloggers that the weapons had been planted on innocent Iraqi boys playing football were unfounded.

Finally, if the counter-misinformation team can be of help, ask us. We can't respond to all requests for information, but if a request is reasonable and we have the time, we will do our best to provide accurate, authoritative information.

Definitions of misinformation and disinformation
U.S. Department of State (2005)[121]

The State Department's counter-misinformation page offers definitions of misinformation and disinformation, as compiled by the office's one-man staff over a 20-year period.

There are no universally agreed-upon definitions of misinformation and disinformation, but this is how the terms are used on this Web site:

Disinformation refers to false or misleading information that is deliberately spread by a government, organized political group, an individual or other entity. The issue of intent is key; if the intent is to spread false or misleading information, it is disinformation

Misinformation refers to false or misleading information that is spread unintentionally. If one unwittingly spreads false or misleading information, that is misinformation. Of course, many times it is impossible to ascertain intentions, so it may not be clear whether false information represents disinformation or misinformation.

Misinformation can be further subdivided into:

Media Mistakes which happen frequently given the pressure of deadlines and imperfect knowledge.

---

[121] Accessed May 15, 2007 on the State Department's counter-misinformation page: http://usinfo.state.gov/media/misinformation.

Urban Legends – Untrue stories that are widely believed because they speak to a widespread fear, hope, or other emotion.

Conspiracy Theories – Belief that powerful, evil hidden forces are secretly manipulating the course of world events and history.

Some examples may make the definitions clearer.

Disinformation: The USSR's disinformation campaign on AIDS is the classic example. The Soviet intelligence and security service, the KGB, had a special service, Service A, for spreading false information. For example, soon after AIDS was recognized as a new disease, Service A concocted the story that the AIDS virus had been developed as a biological weapon by the Pentagon at Fort Detrick, Maryland, and was used in experiments on prisoners, which was allegedly why it initially appeared in New York, described as the largest big city near Fort Detrick. Several major U.S. cities are actually much closer to Fort Detrick than New York, including Washington, DC, Baltimore, and Philadelphia, but few non-Americans realize that.

On March 17, 1992, Yevgeniy Primakov, who was then head of the Russian Foreign Intelligence Service, a successor of the KGB, admitted that "the articles exposing U.S. scientists 'crafty' plot against mankind [in allegedly manufacturing AIDS] were fabricated in KGB offices," as reported in the March 19, 1992 issue of the Russian newspaper *Izvestiya*. The Soviets knew the allegations were false, but spread them as part of their policy of spreading vicious lies about the United States. This is disinformation.

Media Mistakes: On December 6, 2001, the leading French newspaper Le Monde published an article stating that Hamid Karzai, who later became the head of Afghanistan's provisional government and then president of Afghanistan, had "acted, for while, as a consultant for the American oil company Unocal, at the time it was considering building a pipeline in Afghanistan." This statement is not true. Unocal spokesman Barry Lane stated that an exhaustive search of all the company's records made it clear that Mr. Kazrzai was "never a consultant, never an employee" of Unocal. This initial mistake by Le Monde has been repeated numerous times by other publications and websites, spreading the misinformation.

Urban Legends: One classic urban legend is the so-called "baby parts" myth. The false allegation is that Americans or others are kidnapping or adopting children from Latin America or other regions to use in organ transplants. This totally untrue story started as a word-of-mouth rumor, broke into the media in 1987 in

Guatemala, and has circulated widely ever since. Media accounts giving credence to this false allegation won the most prestigious journalism prizes in France in 1995 and in Spain in 1996. The origins of this rumor and its spread in the world media are examined in the United States Information Agency report, The Child Organ Trafficking Rumor: a Modern "Urban Legend," which was submitted to the United Nations Special Rapporteur on the Sale of Children, Child Prostitution and Child Pornography in December 1994.

The "baby parts" myth was spurned by advances in organ transplantation that made organ theft seem more plausible to some. Other advances in technology have led to similar urban legends. When microwave ovens were first introduced, apprehensions about possible health effects of this new technology gave rise to the story about the person who tried to dry their wet cat or dog in the microwave, only to have it explode. Urban legends give a narrative, story form to widespread hopes and fears, which is why they are widely believed. For example, in the wake of the September 11 attacks, an urban legend arose that someone had survived the World Trade Center collapse by "surfing" a piece of concrete down from the 80th floor to the ground. No such event occurred, but this false report circulated, reflecting the hope that some of the people trapped high in the towers could have miraculously survived their collapse.

Conspiracy Theories: Conspiracy theories are similar to urban legends, but center around the idea that powerful, evil hidden forces are secretly manipulating the course of world events and history and that nothing is as it seems. The book 9/11: The big lie by French author Thierry Meyssan (published as *L'Effroyable Imposture* ("The Horrifying Fraud") in French) is an example of conspiracy thinking. Meyssan suggests that no plane hit the Pentagon on September 11 and that, instead, a cabal of conspirators within the U.S. government attacked the Pentagon with a cruise missile with a depleted uranium warhead in order to manufacture an excuse for greater defense spending and war against the Taliban. Meyysan did not interview or credit the eyewitnesses to the September 11 events, who reported seeing a plane strike the Pentagon, and he offers no explanation for what happened to American Airlines flight #77 and its 64 passengers and crew, but inconvenient facts such as these are regularly ignored or dismissed by conspiracy theories in favor of extraordinarily complex and convoluted conspiracies, for which there is no evidence, merely uninformed speculation. Nevertheless, by blaming powerful alleged villains, conspiracy theories find a wide audience for whom suspicions are much more powerful in forming beliefs than logic, reason, or facts.

The Interagency Active Measures Working Group:
An eyewitness account of U.S. counterpropaganda strategy
Herbert Romerstein (2006)[122]

How can the national security and foreign policy communities work to counter adversary or enemy propaganda against the U.S. and its allies?

The U.S. allowed decades of Soviet propaganda to go practically unchallenged until the early 1980s. Herbert Romerstein was a senior congressional intelligence committee staff member at the time. He worked with lawmakers of both parties and with the White House to establish the need for the systematic collection and analysis of Soviet propaganda and a means of actively combating Soviet disinformation.

Among the key elements: active intelligence and counter-intelligence collection, extensive use of defectors, and a coordinated interagency mechanism under White House authority. In the following section, Romerstein describes the successful effort that has many applications in today's conflicts. One can easily liken those acting on behalf of the Soviets in the 1970s and '80s with American-based groups and individuals working on behalf of the Islamist extremists today.

The United States government did not regularly combat Soviet disinformation and active measures until 1982, after congressional committees forced the issue into the public. U.S. leaders then recognized the importance of combating Soviet propaganda directly and at a high level. The Reagan administration established an ad hoc body, the Interagency Active Measures Working Group, coordinated from the White House to implement a strategic response.

Disinformation had been a Soviet technique since shortly after the Russian Revolution. In the early days of the Cold War, the CIA tracked Soviet disinformation and forgeries and periodically

---

[122] Herbert Romerstein, "The Interagency Active Measures Working Group: An Eyewitness account of the U.S. government's confrontation of Soviet disinformation," in Waller, ed., *Strategic Influence*, op. cit., ch. 8.

attempted to expose them. During the mid-1970s the CIA, severely damaged by the Senate (Church Committee) and House (Pike Committee) Intelligence Committees, turned inward. The Agency did little to respond to anti-American disinformation.

On April 20, 1978 the CIA director, Stansfield Turner, testified before the House Intelligence Committee. He reported new regulations to prevent the CIA from using American media. Congressman John Ashbrook (R-OH) asked him "Do the Soviet bloc intelligence services use newsmen from non-Communist countries as sources, witting or unwitting, agents of information, disinformation, or agents of influence?" Turner answered: "We certainly suspect that highly. I am not sure that I have concrete evidence." Congressman Ashbrook asked that CIA prepare an unclassified report on this subject.

The report was prepared by CIA and published as an appendix to the hearing on *The CIA and the Media*. Congressman Ashbrook kept pressing the CIA to take a more pro-active role in exposing KGB anti-American disinformation. In October 1979 the CIA had a stroke of luck. Stanislav Levchenko made contact with American officials and asked for political asylum in the United States. Major Levchenko was the head of the Active Measures Line of the KGB station or *rezidentura* in Tokyo. Each KGB station was divided into units called Lines. Active Measures was a Soviet term for influence operations that included disinformation, forgeries and agents of influence.

Levchenko explained to the CIA the workings of the Soviet apparatus and how it was carried out, under his direction, in Japan. Based on his information, and that of Ladislav Bittman who had been the deputy head of the Czechoslovakian Intelligence Service's Disinformation Department, the CIA understood many of the operations that were being carried out against the United States and reported to policy makers and Congress on these activities.

In February 1980 the House Intelligence Committee published a hearing on Soviet *Covert Action (The Forgery Offensive)*. It contained a lengthy CIA report and the testimony of John McMahon, the CIA's Deputy Director, accompanied by four undercover CIA officers. The CIA cleared the testimony for public release. Two weeks later the Committee heard the testimony of Ladislav Bittman. The published hearing record provided a lengthy unclassified insight into the KGB activities in this area.

On September 17, 1980 the press spokesman for the Carter White House, Jody Powell, called a press conference to denounce a forged Presidential Review Memorandum on Africa that suggested a racist policy on the part of the United States. Congressman Ashbrook instructed me to investigate the forgery. It first appeared in an African-American newspaper in San Francisco called the *Sun Reporter* in its edition dated September 18, 1980, but distributed a few days earlier. The *Sun Reporter's* political editor, Edith Austin, claimed in that issue of the paper to have received the document from the "African official on her recent visit on the continent." Edith Austin had been affiliated with the *Sun Reporter* for many years, and has a long record of radical activities in the San Francisco area. The publisher of the *Sun Reporter* was Dr. Carlton Goodlett. Dr. Goodlett was a long-time supporter of communist causes. At that time, Goodlett served as a member of the Presidential Committee of the World Peace Council, which had been exposed in the 1978 report as the major international Soviet front organization. As we studied Soviet forgeries, we found that a number of them were surfaced through the international Soviet fronts particularly the World Peace Council.

During the 1980 hearing, Congressman Ashbrook responded to the CIA testimony that the Soviet Union was subsidizing the foreign Communist Parties. He asked, "How much of that do you trace back to the United States?" Deputy CIA Director McMahon responded that there was no CIA interest in the Communist Party of the United States "since the Communist Party functions openly in the United States...I am sure it can receive funds from anybody as long as they duly report it, by law." Ashbrook answered, "I hope that you do not accept the idea that the Communist Party is a legitimate party." McMahon responded that "talking to the Bureau [FBI] on this point is the proper place to direct that question. We just cannot respond to it."

The House Intelligence Committee at the request of Congressman Ashbrook asked for an FBI briefing on Soviet active measures. The FBI agreed but insisted that only limited staff could attend the briefing and that no transcript be taken. Some Senate staffers asked to attend but the FBI refused their request. The briefing was an eye-opening account of Soviet operations in the United States, but not until almost two years later would the FBI make this information available to the American people.

When the Reagan Administration came into office, the atmosphere changed. Now, the United States would directly challenge Soviet disinformation and active measures. In 1981 an Interagency Active Measures Working Group was established at the State Department. Deputy Assistant Secretary of State Dennis Kux, a career Foreign Service Officer, was the chairman. Representatives of the CIA, the FBI, Department of Defense, and the United States Information Agency were among the government agencies that served in the group. Kux was not only the chairman but developed some of the ways to raise the cost to the Soviets for their anti-American disinformation activities. CIA and FBI provided information on a regular basis.

In 1981, while a Professional Staff member of the House Intelligence Committee, I was brought in to brief the Working Group on the subject. In 1983, I left the House Intelligence Committee and went to the United States Information Agency where I was head of the new Office to Counter Soviet Disinformation. In that capacity I became a member of the Interagency Working Group. I was soon joined by USIA staffer Pete Copp, an experienced journalist. After Copp's retirement, Todd Leventhal, who had come to USIA from Voice of America, joined me at the Working Group.

Under Dennis Kux' leadership the Working Group organized briefing trips to various countries. We briefed not only the governments but the press and academics. It was Kux' idea to collect Soviet disinformation that had been used in Third World countries and provided to audiences in Western Europe. Our theme was "These Soviet stories are obviously lies – so how can you believe what the Soviets tell you." This created problems for the Soviet propagandists in Europe who were sometimes careful to use "gentle" themes in trying to appeal to the public.

My previous experience as a Professional Staff member of the House Intelligence Committee came in handy when we would get questions such as "Doesn't everybody do this?" or "Doesn't the CIA do disinformation?" My answer was "No." I pointed out that during my six years doing oversight on CIA covert actions, there was not a single time that they used political propaganda forgeries. I would say "I have seen forgeries signed President Reagan, President Carter and other U.S. government officials. I have never seen a forgery signed Brezhnev, Andropov, Gorbachev, or any other Soviet official."

In July 1982 both the CIA and FBI agreed to participate in a hearing on "Soviet Active Measures" before the House Intelligence

Committee. This was the first time that the FBI agreed to allow public use of its information on this subject. The CIA's Deputy Director, John McMahon was again a witness. Edward J. O'Malley, Assistant Director for Intelligence of the Federal Bureau of Investigation, testified on the following day.

The Committee also heard the testimony of Stanislav Levchenko. The release by the Committee of the testimony was the first public appearance of the former KGB major. On the instructions of the Committee I then organized two press conferences for Levchenko, one with the American press and one with the foreign press. I also organized a meeting for Levchenko with a delegation of members of the Japanese Diet. This meeting, hosted by Congressmen C. W. "Bill" Young (R-FL), was in response to a request of the Japanese lawmkers to hear from Levchenko a detailed account of his operations in Japan as head of the KGB Active Measures Line.

After I became a member of the Interagency Working Group, I frequently had the opportunity to consult with Levchenko. He explained Soviet operations and on a few occasions briefed journalists and academics with me. On October 20, 1986, the USIA held a press conference at its Foreign Press Center. The occasion was the surfacing of a KGB forgery signed with my name. We immediately exposed the forgery and an article appeared in the *Washington Post* describing Soviet forgeries rather than one attacking the United States as the KGB intended.

The Interagency Working Group was able to combine the information from USIA posts around the world, CIA reporting, and FBI investigations. USIA was an important part of the information gathering process. With USIA posts, called USIS abroad, reporting to headquarters on disinformation and forgeries, they were a front line unit for American defense. As with all government agencies, the USIA's Public Affairs Officers (PAO) were a mixed bag. There were many that were hardworking valuable government officials. This was particularly true in India and in some African countries, where the PAOs used local employees to carefully read the press, watching for anti-American disinformation and forgeries. A few PAOs were of little use to us, interested only in distributing press releases and the daily "Wireless File" which reprinted articles from the American press.

The hardworking PAOs were inspired by the leadership of USIA Director, Charles Z. Wick, who periodically sent them "Z-grams" urging them to pay attention to Soviet anti-American disinformation.

It was clear from our experience with the Active Measures Working Group that bureaucrats needed high level encouragement to carry out the sometimes-difficult assignments. Not all of them appreciated the guidance. The Working Group itself was encouraged by the interest of William Casey, Director of the CIA, high level State Department support, and the input of John Lenczowski who represented the National Security Council and actually attended some of the meetings. High-level State Department support was shown, for example, when Lawrence S. Eagleburger, Under Secretary of State for Political Affairs, wrote an article for *NATO Review* in April 1983, titled "Unacceptable Intervention, Soviet Active Measures." The article showed a picture of Levchenko briefing on Soviet disinformation.

The Working Group issued a series of State Department Foreign Affairs Notes that USIA distributed to journalists, academics, and other interested persons abroad by the United States Information Agency. One of the publications distributed by the Working Group was the House Intelligence Committee hearing on Soviet Active Measures. It was important to show foreign audiences that there was congressional support for exposing Soviet disinformation.

In June 1985 the State Department and CIA cosponsored a conference on "Contemporary Soviet Propaganda and Disinformation." The members of the Active Measurers Working Group, including CIA, State Department and USIA officers took part in the conference. Among the active participants were Stan Levchenko, Ladislav Bittman, Peter Deriabin and Ilya Dzhirkvelov, two former KGB officers. Michael Voslensky, a distinguished scholar who had left the Soviet Union also participated, as did John Lenczowski, representing the National Security Council. The proceedings were published by the Government Printing Office and distributed abroad by USIA.

In 1985 the Congress passed a law requiring that the Interagency Working Group publish a series of reports on Soviet active measures. In response to this, the State Department published three reports in 1986, 1987 and 1989. Significantly, the FBI provided reports printed in these publications on Soviet active measures in the United States. This was particularly useful when we briefed foreign governments to encourage them to share with us examples of Soviet operations in their countries.

In 1987 the House Appropriations Committee instructed USIA to prepare reports on Soviet active measures in the era of glasnost. In

March 1988, Charles Wick presented the first of such reports to the Congress. He said, "In 1987, the House Appropriations Committee requested that the USIA prepare a report on Soviet active measures in the era of glasnost. Soviet active measures, which include forgeries and disinformation, have been a significant problem in U.S.-Soviet relations. I presented the report to the House committee on March 8, 1988. It was prepared by USIA's Office to Counter Soviet Active Measures, which is headed by Herbert Romerstein. Todd Leventhal, the Policy Officer on Soviet Disinformation and Active Measures, works in that office and had the major responsibility of compiling the report." In 1992 Leventhal wrote the last of the reports required by the House Committee on Appropriations. The USIA distributed these reports through its posts around the world.

The 1989 State Department report explained what the U.S. government was doing to counter Soviet disinformation particularly the Soviet lie that AIDS was deliberately created in U.S. government laboratories. According to the State Department, "U.S. policy has been to respond vigorously to Soviet disinformation, on both diplomatic and public levels. The State Department's Bureau of European and Canadian Affairs and Bureau of Public Affairs, the USIA, American Embassies and U.S. Information Service centers abroad, and the VOA have been actively engaged in unmasking and combating the Moscow product at home and around the world. Via the VOA in particular, millions of Soviet listeners during the past year learned that their government was still vigorously practicing information deception abroad – a policy that could hardly bode well for hopes of real *glasnost* at home.

"Along with these coordinated information efforts, the United States made clear at several government-to-government levels that there could be no cooperation with the Soviet Union on the cure and treatment of AIDS while the Soviets continued to disseminate the lie that U.S. scientists had deliberately created and spread the disease. At an April 1987 session of the U.S.-USSR Joint Health Committee, Health and Human Services (HHS) Assistant Secretary Robert Windom and Surgeon General C. Everett Koop directly expressed to Soviet opposite numbers their 'strong displeasure' at Moscow's attempts to 'use a grave international public health problem for base propaganda purposes.'"

The Soviets stopped using the AIDS disinformation story. It became clear, as Dennis Kux had predicted, that they would back off when the cost of their lies became too much for them.

During a Reagan-Gorbachev summit meeting, USIA Director Charles Wick confronted Gorbachev personally about Soviet disinformation. Gorbachev responded "no more lies, no more disinformation." This became grist for our mill. As new disinformation stories appeared, we pressured the Soviets on their failure to carry out Gorbachev's promise.

In 1987 and 1988, the USIA director had a series of meetings with Valentin Falin, then head of Novosti Press Agency and later the head of the International Department of the Central Committee of the Communist Party of the Soviet Union. The International Department was the coordinating body for Soviet disinformation and active measures. The black (covert) disinformation was carried out by KGB. The white (overt) disinformation was carried out by the Central Committee Propaganda Department. The International Department, not only coordinated the other two, but carried out gray (not very well concealed) disinformation and propaganda through the foreign Communist Parties and the international Soviet fronts.

When Wick met with Falin, he knew he was dealing with a major Soviet propagandist. He pressed Falin on the issue of Soviet disinformation. We later learned more about Falin's role. In September 1991, the Moscow publication *Kuranty* carried a story saying, "the head of the American information service, USIA, lodged a personal protest to then APN (Novosti) Chairman V. Falin. The addressee was selected extremely well. Shortly before the sensational 'discovery,' a special group of staff and not only staff, 'undercover' APN employees was created by Falin's personal order under the direction of Colonel M., newly invited to join the agency. It is said that Falin had met the disinformation professional while serving as an ambassador to [then] West Germany." According to the article, the Colonel's unit was disbanded due to "forceful pressure" from the U.S.

In September 1988, the USIA sent a delegation to the Soviet Union to meet with Falin and his associates. Wick again pressed the issue of disinformation. Early in the discussion, Wick emphasized that Soviet disinformation continued to be a major problem impeding better relations between the United States and the Soviet Union. I then raised the question about the AIDS disinformation story and pointed out that Novosti had distributed it around the world. One aspect of the story was a false quotation from the late Congressman Ted Weiss (D-NY) who was supposed to have said that AIDS was created in U.S. government laboratories. I said that the quotation came not from the U.S. "mass media" which Falin had claimed but from a monthly homosexual newspaper with a circulation so small that USIA had difficulty even locating a copy. What we did however was have a letter addressed to me by Congressman Weiss denying that he had made such a statement. I presented the letter to Falin.

Falin suggested that it would be useful to have regular meetings between Americans and Soviets on the issue of disinformation. I responded that this would be good to do on a working level. Falin agreed and he and I met separately to organize the meetings. As a result, Todd Leventhal and I met regularly with officials of the Soviet embassy where we had the opportunity to answer the disinformation stories.   We reported on these meetings to the Interagency Active Measures Working Group. The inability of our Soviet counterparts to authenticate the disinformation stories was valuable to the Working Group as we worked out ways of pressuring them.

A counterinsurgency approach to counterpropaganda
Andrew Garfield (2006)[123]

The defeat of the insurgency and terrorism in Iraq requires an approach that does not focus on the eradication of such threats through force of arms alone. Instead, a much more holistic approach is required that addresses the underlying causes of the insurgency and the perceptions of those who have embraced extremist ideas, or who have provided the insurgents with safe havens, recruits and resources. To defeat these adversaries we must therefore adopt our

---

[123] Excerpted from Andrew Garfield, "Recovering the lost art of counterpropaganda: An assessment of the war in Iraq," in *Strategic Influence: Public Diplomacy, Counterpropaganda and Political Warfare* (IWP Press, 2007), Chapter 7. Garfield is a former British military and civilian intelligence officer who served on the U.K. Ministry of Defence Planning Staff. He addresses information operations in Iraq in his book, *Succeeding in Phase IV: British Perspectives on the U.S. Effort to Stabilize and Reconstruct Iraq* (Foreign Policy Research Institute/Global Security Media, 2007).

own asymmetric approach that seeks to influence the Iraqi population. The approach must persuade Iraqis to reject extremism and violence through a combination of dialogue, inducements and the proportionate use of force. The main characteristic that distinguishes campaigns of insurgency from other forms of war is that they are *primarily* concerned with the struggle for men's minds.

Success in Iraq therefore requires effective engagement and dialogue with key segments of the Iraqi population, achieved in part through a comprehensive information campaign. This type of campaign has variously been described as information operations, propaganda, strategic communications, influence operations, psychological operations and perception management. While the terminology may vary, the intent is the same: to influence the hearts and minds of key target audiences through the effective use of information. This dialogue must extol the virtues of the Iraqi government and of the Coalition, while repeatedly highlighting the vices of the insurgency. It must also effectively challenge the propaganda of the insurgency, an enemy that has been far more effective than the authorities at engaging a local population.

The overall aim of this information campaign is to win support for our actions or at least the acquiescence of the affected population. The campaign should bolster morale, which has been severely stressed by the shock effect of the years following the 2003 invasion; by unwelcome or unfamiliar change; and because of deprivation, loss, and intimidation. This campaign must also challenge the personal appeal, ideology and propaganda of the insurgents, who seek to promote their own agenda to encourage supporters or coerce the uncommitted and who attempt to portray every Iraqi government and Coalition action negatively or steal the credit for our rare successes – for example, by portraying political or economic improvements or a redress of grievances as resulting only from their violent campaigns.

The keys to a successful information campaign are to develop lines of persuasion and messages that will actually resonate with the target audiences, use culturally sensitive and relevant narratives, and exploit *all possible avenues* to reach hearts and minds. The counterinsurgents' information campaign must be timely, quickly exploiting all successes and rapidly challenging enemy propaganda before opportunities are lost and the lies and deceits of the insurgents gain credibility. In an asymmetric conflict, we simply cannot allow an information vacuum to develop because it will be filled with gossip and with the lies of the insurgents and extremists. This type of campaign will fail by simply extolling a government ideology and vague abstractions such as the benefits of democracy or a free-market economy. Instead it must focus on what really matters to people – local and personal issues such safety, jobs and representation.

To achieve these objectives requires the coordination of a broad range of capabilities and expertise, little of which is found in sufficient numbers or quality within either the Iraqi government or the Coalition. These include the types of skills and experience found in the advertising, marketing, public relations, lobbying and political campaign industries, and within the broadcast, print and new media. And of course, this all has to be done in a foreign language to an audience that is culturally alien to the Coalition.   The Coalition therefore faces a number of significant challenges in Iraq that it must overcome in order to win the war of ideas with the insurgents and extremists.

The current situation: Losing the war of ideas

From firsthand experience in Iraq, I can only conclude that we are losing not simply the physical battle but perhaps even more importantly the psychological conflict. So far the Coalition has failed to systematically counter enemy propaganda either by responding rapidly with effective counter messaging or more proactively by directly challenging the messages, methods and ideology that the insurgents and extremists promote and exploit. The Coalition's mostly uncoordinated and largely ineffectual strategic communications efforts to date have failed to gain any significant traction with key segments of the Iraqi population.

In contrast, the insurgents have secured the initiative in the struggle for the hearts and minds of contested populations. Although the Coalition has achieved some sustained success at the tactical level, most often by psychological operations (PSYOP) units, it has been too little to late to counter the words and deeds of our asymmetric adversaries – adversaries who clearly understand that they are engaged in a psychological rather than physical conflict. *The enemy's psychological conflict strategy is designed not to lead to the military defeat of the Coalition, but instead to the collapse of local Iraqi support for their government and the support of Coalition publics and political leaders at home for the war itself.*

Against both targets, one can only conclude that the insurgents currently have the upper hand.

In the face of what can only be described as propaganda onslaught, we have demonstrated ourselves to be little more than dedicated amateurs in the war of Ideas in Iraq, while our adversaries have shown themselves to be remarkably effective propagandists. This is nothing new for the western democracies in fighting insurgencies. More than four decades ago David Galula, a French army officer who served in China, Greece, Southeast Asia and Algeria, pointed out in his seminal work on counterinsurgency, "If there is a field in which we were definitely and infinitely more stupid than our opponents it was propaganda."

In Iraq, the insurgents, extremists, and militia groups have shown themselves to be highly adept at releasing timely and effective messages that undermine support for the Iraqi government and Coalition and which bolster their own reputation and perceived potency. They are quick to exploit Coalition failures and excesses; they respond rapidly to defend their own actions, often by shifting blame to the authorities; and they are able to hijack Coalition successes and present them as proof that change only occurs as a result of their own violent campaign. They clearly have taken a leaf out of the insurgent playbook written by the Brazilian anarchist Carlos Marighela. He wrote in his doctrine for urban guerrilla warfare the following advice:

It would be necessary to turn political crises into armed conflicts by performing violent actions that will force those in power to transform a political situation into a military situation. That will alienate the mass who, from then on, will revolt against the army and police and thus blame them for the state of things.

Adversary capabilities

How have our adversaries established their dominance in the information space? The answer is simple: Through the effective use of words and deeds. Like numerous other asymmetric opponents before them, the insurgents and terrorists in Iraq have expertly utilized violence as the most effective of their propaganda tools. This is certainly not a new strategy. For example, the 19th Century revolutionary Johannes Most advocated the systematic use of terror by small groups of activists utilising the most modern technology

available in pursuit of what he termed the "propaganda of the deed."
Our opponents have exploited the propaganda of numerous violent
deeds to intimidate the uncommitted, to undermine confidence in the
authorities, to bolster and expand their own support base, to
demonstrate their potency, to provoke a disproportionate military
response from the Iraqi authorities and the Coalition, and to initially
sow the seeds and then fan the flames of sectarian conflict.

Recognizing that the use of violence is intended primarily to
achieve psychological effects, the insurgents in Iraq have adopted
both an attritional and maneuverist approach to its application. They
have conducted an effective attritional psychological campaign
using improvised explosive devices (IED), small scale attacks,
snipers, mortars and rockets to inflict a steady stream of casualties.
These attacks, which have had no significant impact on Coalition
combat effectiveness, have sapped the morale of Coalition publics
and politicians.   The insurgents have also demonstrated their
maneuverist tendencies by orchestrating attacks to coincide with key
events such as U.S. elections in order to achieve a desired political
impact in Washington.

To support their violent campaign and also as a line of operation in
its own right, our adversaries in Iraq have utilized numerous
multimedia channels to convey sophisticated messages to multiple
audiences. They have manipulated journalists and media outlets to
ensure that their messages and actions are conveyed to the widest
possible audience. They have produced countless CDs and DVDs
which are distributed widely within contested communities. They
have exploited the mosques in order to convey their messages to the
faithful enhanced with an apparent divine by extremist Imams. They
have encouraged the spread of extremist graffiti which provides
communities with a constant and intrusive reminder of the presence
and potency of these groups and serves as a defiant gesture towards
the authorities.   They have posted flyers, distributed leaflets,
published newspapers and authored articles and editorials.

They have used SMS text messaging and Iraq's telephone system
to reach vulnerable individuals and even to target members of the
Coalition. They have exploited the arts including paintings, poetry
and songwriting.   The insurgents are also expertly exploiting
information technology and the Internet to great effect, thereby
increasing their ability to reach mass audiences and to respond
quickly and effectively to Iraqi government and Coalition messaging
with their own counterarguments.   By contrast the Coalition is

largely precluded from cyberspace for fear of blowback to the domestic audiences at home – an ill informed, knee jerk decision that has all but handed key terrain in the war of ideas to our adversaries.

Most worryingly of all, the insurgents both Shia and Sunni are using violence to silence their critics thereby creating an information vacuum that they then fill. They generally do all of this far faster than the Coalition – deploying messages that really do resonate with the local populace and in real or near real time. Until the Coalition is able to counter this sustained, coordinated and effective enemy propaganda effort and seize the influence initiative, these adversaries will continue to be in the ascendancy in the war of ideas in Iraq.

Integration of Intelligence, Public Diplomacy
and Public Affairs

A model white paper
U.S. Department of State (1981)[124]

*The item in this section is an ideal public diplomacy document that
integrates intelligence collection and analysis with public
diplomacy for foreign audiences and public affairs for the people at
home.*

*In late 1980 and early 1981, Soviet-backed forces made a push to
help Communist guerrillas to topple the government of El
Salvador. The Reagan administration was in office for only a
month, and had to move quickly to prevent the Sandinista
revolution from spreading beyond Nicaragua. Reagan drew the line
in El Salvador.*

*Under White House direction, the State Department issued a
remarkable "white paper" during the administration's fifth week in
office. The paper combined battlefield and documentary
intelligence from the ground in El Salvador with human
intelligence, electronic intelligence and open-source information to
prove that the Soviet bloc was behind the Salvadoran insurgency.
A global Soviet "active measures" campaign lent formidable
propaganda support to the guerrillas.*

*Illustrated with maps, charts, weapons tables, photos of captured
weapons and other factual material, the white paper marked a
crucial early turning point against the guerrillas. The document
smashed the guerrillas' image of being a home-grown insurgency
of agrarian reformers and student leaders seeking a different type
of democracy; their international propaganda was decidedly non-
communist and they and their supporters took lengths to conceal*

---

[124] "Communist Interference in El Salvador," Special Report No. 80,
United States Department of State, Bureau of Public Affairs, February 23,
1981.

Soviet bloc support (by providing NATO weapons instead of standard Soviet-made equipment).

In a bid to discredit the white paper, FMLN supporters circulated a purported internal State Department document called a "dissent paper." The State Department pronounced the document a forgery, and the FBI attributed the forgery to the KGB, which had circulated the paper in Latin America several months earlier. Philip Agee, a former CIA officer who defected to Cuba, was involved with the forgery. In the aftermath of the white paper's release, two New York Times columnists quoted from the KGB forgery as if it was genuine. When alerted about the document, only one, Flora Lewis, issued a correction. (The unrepentant columnist was Anthony Lewis, who attacked the FBI for pursuing FMLN operatives inside the United States.)[125]

Despite bids to discredit the real State Department document, all the information in the white paper was proven true over the years as intelligence services, news organizations and guerrilla defectors independently corroborated everything.[126] "Communist Interference in El Salvador" is an ideal wartime public diplomacy document worthy of emulation. Its text is reprinted in full, though tables, sidebars and captions have been deleted.

Summary

This special report presents definitive evidence of the clandestine military support given by the Soviet Union, Cuba, and their Communist allies to Marxist-Leninist guerrillas now fighting to overthrow the established Government of El Salvador. The evidence, drawn from captured guerrilla documents and war materiel and corroborated by intelligence reports, underscores the central role played by Cuba and other Communist countries beginning in 1979 in the political unification, military direction, and arming of insurgent forces in El Salvador.

From the documents it is possible to reconstruct chronologically the key stages of the growth of the Communist involvement:

---

[125] See J. Michael Waller, *The Third Current of Revolution: Inside the North American Front of El Salvador's Guerrilla War* (University Press of America, 1991), pp. 38-39.

[126] See, for example, Christopher Andrew and Vasili Mitrokhin, *The World Was Going our Way: The KGB and the Battle for the Third World* (Basic Books, 2005), Chapter 6, "Revolution in Central America," pp. 115-138.

- The direct tutelary role played by Fidel Castro and the Cuban Government in late 1979 and early 1980 in bringing the diverse Salvadoran guerrilla factions into a unified front;
- The assistance and advice given the guerrillas in planning their military operations;
- The series of contacts between Salvadoran Communist leaders and key officials of several Communist states that resulted in commitments to supply the insurgents nearly 800 tons of the most modern weapons and equipment;
- The covert delivery to El Salvador of nearly 200 tons of those arms, mostly through Cuba and Nicaragua, in preparation for the guerrillas' failed "general offensive" of January 1981;
- The major Communist effort to "cover" their involvement by providing mostly arms of Western manufacture.

It is clear that over the past year the insurgency in El Salvador has been progressively transformed into another case of indirect armed aggression against a small Third World country by Communist powers acting through Cuba.

The United States considers it of great importance that the American people and the world community be aware of the gravity of the actions of Cuba, the Soviet Union, and other Communist states who are carrying out what is clearly shown to be a well-coordinated, covert effort to bring about the overthrow of El Salvador's established government and to impose in its place a Communist regime with no popular support.

I. A Case of Communist Military Involvement in the Third World

The situation in El Salvador presents a strikingly similar case of Soviet, Cuban, and other Communist military involvement in a politically troubled Third World country. By providing arms, training, and direction to a local insurgency and by supporting it with a global propaganda campaign, the Communists have intensified and widened the conflict, greatly increased the suffering of the Salvadoran people, and deceived much of the world about the true nature of the revolution. Their objective in El Salvador as elsewhere is to bring about – at little cost to themselves – the overthrow of the established government and the imposition of a Communist regime in defiance of the will of the Salvadoran people.

The Guerrillas: Their Tactics and Propaganda. El Salvador's extreme left, which includes the long-established Communist Party of El Salvador (PCES) and several armed groups of more recent origin, has become increasingly committed since 1976 to a military solution. A campaign of terrorism – bombings, assassinations, kidnappings, and seizures of embassies – has disrupted national life and claimed the lives of many innocent people.

During 1980, previously fragmented factions of the extreme left agreed to coordinate their actions in support of a joint military battle plan developed with Cuban assistance. As a precondition for large-scale Cuban aid, Salvadoran guerrilla leaders, meeting in Havana in May, formed the first Unified Revolutionary Directorate (DRU) as their central executive arm for political and military planning and, in late 1980, the Farabundo Marti People's Liberation Front (FMLN), as the coordinating body of the guerrilla organizations. A front organization, the Revolutionary Democratic Front (FDR), was also created to disseminate propaganda abroad. For appearances sake, three small non-Marxist-Leninist political parties were brought into the front, though they have no representation in the DRU.

The Salvadoran guerrillas, speaking through the FDR, have managed to deceive many about what is happening in El Salvador. They have been aided by Nicaragua and by the worldwide propaganda networks of Cuba, the Soviet Union, and other Communist countries.

The guerrillas' propaganda aims at legitimizing their violence and concealing the Communist aid that makes it possible. Other key aims are to discredit the Salvadoran Government, to misrepresent U.S. policies and actions, and to foster the impression of overwhelming popular support for the revolutionary movement.

Examples of the more extreme claims of their propaganda apparatus – echoed by Cuban, Soviet and Nicaraguan media – are:

- That the United States has military bases and several hundred troops in El Salvador (in fact, the United States has no bases and fewer than 50 military personnel there);
- That the government's security forces were responsible for most of the 10,000 killings that occurred in 1980 (in their own reports in 1980, the guerrillas themselves claimed the killings of nearly 6,000 persons, including noncombatant "informers" as well as government authorities and military).

In addition to media propaganda, Cuba and the Soviet Union promote the insurgent cause at international forums, with individual governments, and among foreign opinion leaders. Cuba has an efficient network for introducing and promoting representatives of the Salvadoran left all over the world. Havana and Moscow also bring indirect pressure on some governments to support the Salvadoran revolutionaries by mobilizing local Communist groups.

II. Communist Military Intervention: A Chronology

Before September 1980 the diverse guerrilla groups in El Salvador were ill-coordinated and ill-equipped, armed with pistols and a varied assortment of hunting rifles and shotguns. At the time the insurgents acquired weapons predominantly through purchases on the international market and from dealers who participated in the supply of arms to the Sandinistas in Nicaragua.

By January 1981 when the guerrillas launched their "final offensive," they had acquired an impressive array of modern weapons and supporting equipment never before used in El Salvador by either the insurgents or the military. Belgian FAL rifles, German G-3 rifles, U.S. M-1, M-16 and AR-15 semiautomatic and automatic rifles, and the Israeli Uzi submachinegun and Galil assault rifle have all been confirmed in the guerrilla inventory. In addition, they are known to possess .30 to .50 caliber machineguns, the U.S. M-60 machinegun, U.S. and Russian hand grenades, the U.S. M-79 and Chinese RPG grenade launchers, and the U.S. M-72 light antitank weapon and 81mm mortars. Captured ammunition indicates the guerrillas probably possess 60mm and 82mm mortars and 57mm and 75mm recoilless rifles.

Recently acquired evidence has enabled us to reconstruct the central role played by Cuba, other Communist countries, and several radical states in the political unification and military direction of insurgent forces in El Salvador and in equipping them in less than 6 months with a panoply of modern weapons that enabled the guerrillas to launch a well-armed offensive.

This information, which we consider incontrovertible, has been acquired over the past year. Many key details, however, have fallen into place as the result of the guerrillas' own records. Two particularly important caches were recovered from the Communist Party of El Salvador in November 1980 and from the Peoples' Revolutionary Army (ERP) in January 1981. This mass of captured documents includes battle plans, letters, and reports of meetings and travels, some written in cryptic language and using code words.

When deciphered and verified against evidence from other intelligence sources, the documents bring to light the chain of events leading to the guerrillas' January 1981 offensive. What emerges is a highly disturbing pattern of parallel and coordinated action by a number of Communist and some radical countries bent on imposing a military solution.

The Cuban and Communist role in preparing for and helping to organize the abortive "general offensive" early this year is spelled out in the following chronology based on the contents of captured documents and other sources.

Initial steps. The chronology of external support begins at the end of 1979. With salutations of "brotherly and revolutionary greetings" on December 16, 1979, members of the Communist Party of El Salvador (PCES), National Resistance (FARN), and Popular Liberation Forces (FPL) thank Fidel Castro in a letter for his help and the help of your party comrades . . . by signing an agreement which establishes very solid bases upon which we begin building coordination and unity of our organizations." The letter, written in Havana, was signed by the leaders of these three revolutionary organizations.

At an April 1980 meeting at the Hungarian Embassy in Mexico City, guerrilla leaders made certain "requests" (possibly for arms). Present at this meeting were representatives of the German Democratic Republic, Bulgaria, Poland, Vietnam, Hungary, Cuba, and the Soviet Union.

In notes taken during an April 18, 1980 meeting of the Salvadoran Communist Party, party leader Shafik Handal mentions the need to "speed up reorganization and put the Party on a war footing." He added, "I'm in agreement with taking advantage of the possibilities of assistance from the socialist camp. I think that their attitude is magnificent. We are not yet taking advantage of it." In reference to a unification of the armed movement, he asserts that "the idea of involving everyone in the area has already been suggested to Fidel himself." Handal alludes to the concept of unification and notes, "Fidel thought well of the idea."

Guerrilla Contacts in Havana. From May 5 to June 8, 1980, Salvadoran guerrilla leaders report on meetings in Honduras,

Guatemala, Costa Rica, and Nicaragua. They proceed to Havana and meet several times with Fidel Castro; the documents also note an interview with the German Democratic Republic (GDR) Chairman Erich Honecker in Havana. During the Havana portion of their travels, the Salvadoran guerrilla leadership meets twice with the Cuban Directorate of Special Operations (DOE, the clandestine operations/special forces unit of the Cuban Ministry of Interior) to discuss guerrilla military plans. In addition, they meet with the Cuban "Chief of Communications."

During this period (late May 1980), the Popular Revolutionary Army (ERP) is admitted into the guerrilla coalition after negotiations in Havana. The coalition then assumes the name of the Unified Revolutionary Directorate (DRU) and meets with Fidel Castro on three occasions.

After the Havana meetings, Shafik Handal leaves Havana on May 30, 1980 for Moscow. The other Salvadoran guerrilla leaders in Havana leave for Managua. During the visit of early June, the DRU leaders meet with Nicaraguan revolutionary leaders (Sandinistas) and discuss: (1) a headquarters with "all measures of security"; (2) an "international field of operations, which they (Sandinistas) control"; and (3) the willingness of the Sandinistas to "contribute in material terms" and to adopt "the cause of El Salvador as its own." The meeting culminated with "dinner at Humberto's house" (presumably Sandinista leader [defense minister] Humberto Ortega).

Salvadoran Communist Party Leader's Travels in the East. From June 2 to July 22, 1980, Shafik Handal visits the USSR, Vietnam, the German Democratic Republic, Czechoslovakia, Bulgaria, Hungary and Ethiopia to procure arms and seek support for the movement.

On June 2, 1980, Handal meets in Moscow with Mikhail Kudachkin, Deputy Chief of the Latin American Section of the Foreign Relations Department of the CPSU [Communist Party of the Soviet Union] Central Committee. Kudachkin suggests that Handal travel to Vietnam to seek arms and offers to pay for Handal's trip.

Continuing his travels between June 9 and 15, Handal visits Vietnam where he is received by Le Duan, Secretary General of the Vietnamese Communist Party; Xuan Thuy, member of the Communist Party Central Committee Secretariat; and Vice Minister of National Defense Tran Van Quang. The Vietnamese, as a "first contribution," agree to provide 60 tons of arms. Handal adds that "the comrade requested air transport from the USSR."

From June 19 to 24, 1980, Handal visits the German Democratic Republic (GDR), where he is received by Hermann Axen, member of the GDR Politburo. Axen states that the GDR has already sent 1.9 tons of supplies to Managua. On July 21, GDR leader Honecker writes the GDR Embassy in Moscow that additional supplies will be sent and that the German Democratic Republic will provide military training, particularly clandestine operations. The GDR telegram adds that although Berlin possesses no Western-manufactured weapons – which the Salvadoran guerrillas are seeking – efforts will be undertaken to find a "solution to this problem." (NOTE: The emphasis on Western arms reflects the desire to maintain plausible denial.)

From June 24-27, 1980, Handal visits Czechoslovakia where he is received by Vasil Bilak, Second Secretary of the Czech Communist Party. Bilak says that some Czech arms circulating in the world market will be provided so that these arms will not be traced to Czechoslovakia as the donor country. Transportation will be coordinated with the German Democratic Republic.

Handal proceeds to Bulgaria from June 27 to June 30, 1980. He is received by Dimitir Stanichev, member of the Central Committee Secretariat. The Bulgarians agree to supply German-origin weapons and other supplies, again in an apparent effort to conceal their sources.

In Hungary, from June 30 to July 3, 1980, Handal is received by Communist Party General Secretary Janos Kadar and "Guesel" (probably Central Committee Secretary for Foreign Affairs Andras Gyenes). The latter offers radios and other supplies and indicates Hungarian willingness to trade arms with Ethiopia or Angola in order to obtain Western-origin arms for the Salvadoran guerrillas. "Guesel" promises to resolve the trade with the Ethiopians and Angolans himself, "since we want to be a part of providing this aid." Additionally, Handal secures the promise of 10,000 uniforms to be made by the Hungarians according to Handal's specifications.

Handal then travels to Ethiopia, July 3 to July 6. He meets Chairman Mengistu and receives "a warm reception." Mengistu offers "several thousand weapons," including: 150 Thompson submachienguns with 300 cartridge clips, 1,500 M-1 rifles, 1,000 M-14 rifles, and ammunition for these weapons. In addition, the Ethiopians agree to supply all necessary spare parts for these arms.

Handal returns to Moscow on July 22, 1980 and is received again by Mikhail Kudachkin. The Soviet official asks if 30 Communist youth currently studying in the USSR could take part in the war in El Salvador. Before leaving Moscow, Handal receives assurances that the Soviets agree in principle to transport the Vietnamese arms.

Further Contacts in Nicaragua. On July 13, representatives of the DRU arrive in Managua amidst preparations for the first anniversary celebration of Somoza's overthrow. The DRU leaders wait until July 23 to meet with "Comrade Bayardo" (presumably Bayardo Arce, member of the Sandinista directorate). They complain that the Sandinistas appear to be restricting their access to visiting world dignitaries and demanding that all contacts be cleared through them. During the meeting, Arce promises ammunition to the guerrillas and arranges a meeting for them with the Sandinista "Military Commission." Arce indicates that, since the guerrillas will receive some arms manufactured by the Communist countries, the Sandinista Army (EPS) will consider absorbing some of these weapons and providing to the Salvadorans Western-manufactured arms held by the EPS in exchange. (In January 1981 the Popular Sandinista Army indeed switched from using U.S.-made weapons to those of Soviet and East European origin.)

The DRU representatives also met with visiting Palestine Liberation Organization (PLO) leader Yasir Arafat in Managua on July 22, 1980. Arafat promises military equipment, including arms and aircraft. (A Salvadoran guerrilla leader met with FATAH leaders in Beirut in August and November, and the PLO has trained selected Salvadorans in the Near East and in Nicaragua.)

On July 27, the guerrilla General Staff delegation departs from Managua for Havana, where Cuban "specialists" add final touches to the military plans formulated during the May meetings in Havana.

Arms Deliveries Begin. In mid-August 1980, Shafik Handal's arms-shopping expedition begins to bear fruit. On August 15, 1980, Ethiopian arms depart for Cuba. Three weeks later the 60 tons of captured U.S. arms sent from Vietnam are scheduled to arrive in Cuba.

As a result of a Salvadoran delegation's trip to Iraq earlier in the year, the guerrillas receive a $500,000 logistics donation. The funds are distributed to the Sandinistas in Nicaragua and within El Salvador.

By mid-September, substantial quantities of the arms promised to Handal are well on the way to Cuba and Nicaragua. The guerrilla logistics coordinator in Nicaragua informs his Joint General Staff on September 26 that 130 tons of arms and other military material supplied by the Communist countries have arrived in Nicaragua for shipment to El Salvador. According to the captured documents, this represents one-sixth of the commitments to the guerrillas by the Communist countries. (NOTE: To get an idea of the magnitude of this commitment, the Vietnamese offer of only 60 tons included 2 million rifle and machinegun bullets, 14,500 mortar shells, 1,620 rifles, 210 machineguns, 48 mortars, 12 rocket launchers, and 192 pistols.)

In September and October, the number of flights to Nicaragua from Cuba increased sharply. These flights had the capacity to transport several hundred tons of cargo.

At the end of September, despite appeals from the guerrillas, the Sandinistas suspend their weapons deliveries to El Salvador for 1 month, after the U.S. Government lodges a protest to Nicaragua on the arms trafficking.

When the shipments resume in October, as much as 120 tons of weapons and materiel are still in Nicaragua and some 300-400 tons are in Cuba. Because of the difficulty of moving such large quantities overland, Nicaragua – with Cuban support – begins airlifting arms from Nicaragua into El Salvador. In November, about 2.5 tons of arms are delivered by air before accidents force a brief halt in the aircraft.

In December, the Salvadoran guerrillas, encouraged by Cuba, begin plans for a general offensive in early 1981. To provide the increased support necessary, the Sandinistas revive the airlift into El Salvador. Salvadoran insurgents protest that they cannot absorb the increased flow of arms, but guerrilla liaison members in Managua urge them to increase their efforts as several East European nations are providing unprecedented assistance.

A revolutionary radio station – *Radio Liberacion* – operating in Nicaragua begins broadcasting to El Salvador on December 15, 1980. It exhorts the populace to mount a massive insurrection against the government. (References to the Sandinistas sharing the expense of a revolutionary radio station appear in the captured documents.)

On January 24, 1981, a Cessna from Nicaragua crashes on takeoff in El Salvador after unloading passengers and possibly weapons. A second plane is strafed by the Salvadoran Air Force, and the pilot and numerous weapons are captured. The pilot admits to being an employee of the Nicaraguan national airline and concedes that the flight originated from Sandino International Airport in Managua. He further admits to flying two earlier arms deliveries.

Air supply is playing a key role, but infiltration by land and sea also continues. Small launches operating out of several Nicaraguan Pacific ports traverse the Gulf of Fonseca at night, carrying arms, ammunition, and personnel. During the general offensive on January 13, several dozen well-armed guerrillas landed on El Salvador's southeastern coast on the Gulf of Fonseca, adjacent to Nicaragua.

Overland arms shipments also continue through Honduras from Nicaragua and Costa Rica. In late January, Honduran security forces uncover an arms infiltration operation run by Salvadorans working through Nicaragua and directed by Cubans. In this operation, a trailer truck is discovered carrying weapons and ammunition destined for Salvadoran guerrillas. Weapons include 100 U.S. M-16 rifles and 81mm mortar ammunition. These arms are a portion of the Vietnamese shipment: A trace of the M-16s reveals that several of them were shipped to U.S. units in Vietnam where they were captured or left behind. Using this network, perhaps five truckloads of arms may have reached the Salvadoran guerrillas.

The availability of weapons and materiel significantly increases the military capabilities of the Salvadoran insurgents. While attacks raged throughout the country during the "general offensive" that began on January 10, it soon became clear that the DRU could not sustain the level of violence without suffering costly losses in personnel. By the end of January, DRU leaders apparently decided to avoid direct confrontation with government forces and reverted to sporadic guerrilla terrorist tactics that would reduce the possibility of suffering heavy casualties.

III. The Government: The Search for Order and Democracy

Central America's smallest and most densely populated country is El Salvador. Since its independence in 1821, the country has experienced chronic political instability and repression, widespread poverty, and concentration of wealth and power in the hands of a few families. Although considerable economic progress took place in the 1960s, the political system remained in the hands of a traditional economic elite backed by the military. During the 1970s, both the legitimate grievances of the poor and landless and the growing aspirations of the expanding middle classes met increasingly with repression. El Salvador has long been a violent country with political, economic, and personal disputes often resulting in murders.

The Present Government. Aware of the need for change and alarmed by the prospect of Nicaragua-like chaos, progressive Salvadoran military officers and civilians overthrew the authoritarian regime of General Carlos Humberto Romero in October 1979 and ousted nearly 100 conservative senior officers.

After an initial period of instability, the new government stabilized around a coalition that includes military participants in the October 1979 coup, the Christian Democratic Party, and independent civilians. Since March 1980, this coalition has begun broad social changes: conversion of large estates into peasant cooperatives, distribution of land to tenant farmers, and nationalization of foreign trade and banking.

Four Marxist-Leninist guerrilla groups are using violence and terrorism against the Salvadoran Government and its reforms. Three small non-Marxist-Leninist political parties – including a Social Democratic Party – work with guerrilla organizations through the Democratic Revolutionary Front (FDR), most of whose activities take place outside El Salvador.

The Government of El Salvador – headed since last year by Jose Napoleon Duarte, the respected Christian Democrat denied office by the military in the Presidential elections of 1972 – faces armed opposition from the extreme right as well as from the left. Exploiting their traditional ties to the security forces and the tendency of some members of the security forces to abuse their authority, some wealthy Salvadorans affected by the Duarte government's reforms have sponsored terrorist activities against supporters of the agrarian and banking reforms and against the government itself.

A symbiotic relationship has developed between the terrorism practiced by extremists of both left and right. Thousands have died without regard to class, creed, nationality, or politics. Brutal and still unexplained murders in December of four American churchwomen – and in January of two American trade unionists – added U.S. citizens to the toll of this tragic violence. The United States has made clear its interest in a complete investigation of these killings and the punishment of those responsible.

Despite bitter resistance from right and left, the Duarte government has stuck to its reform programs and has adopted emergency measures to ease the lot of the poor through public works, housing projects, and aid to marginal communities. On the political front, it has offered amnesty to its opponents, scheduled elections for a constituent assembly in 1982, and pledged to hand power over to a popularly elected government no later than mid-1983.

The government's pursuit of progress with order has been further hampered by the virtual breakdown of the law enforcement and judicial system and by lack of an effective civil service.

The introduction of these reforms – some of which are now clearly irreversible – has reduced popular support for those who argue that change can only come about through violence. Few Salvadorans participate in antigovernment demonstrations. Repeated calls by the guerrillas for general strikes in mid- and late-1980 went unheeded. The Duarte government, moreover, has made clear its willingness to negotiate the terms of future political processes with democratic members of all opposition forces – most notably, by accepting the offer of El Salvador's Council of Bishops to mediate between the government and the Democratic Revolutionary Front.

In sum, the Duarte government is working hard and with some success to deal with the serious political, social, and economic problems that most concern the people of El Salvador.

U.S. Support. In its commitment to reform and democracy, the Government of El Salvador has had the political support of the United States ever since the October 1979 revolution. Because we give primary emphasis to helping the people of El Salvador, most of our assistance has been economic. In 1980, the United States provided nearly $56 million in aid, aimed at easing the conditions that underlie unrest and extremism. This assistance has helped create jobs, feed the hungry, improve health and housing and education, and support the reforms that are opening and modernizing El Salvador's economy. The United States will continue to work with the Salvadoran Government toward economic betterment, social justice, and peace.

Because the solution in El Salvador should be of the Salvadorans' own making and nonviolent, the United States has carefully limited its military support. In January, mounting evidence of Communist involvement compelled President Carter to authorize a resupply of weapons and ammunition to El Salvador – the first provision of lethal items since 1977.

IV. Some Conclusions

The foregoing record leaves little doubt that the Salvadoran insurgency has become the object of a large-scale commitment by Communist states outside Latin America.

- *The political direction, organization, and arming of the insurgency is coordinated and heavily influenced by Cuba – with active support from the Soviet Union, East Germany, Vietnam, and other Communist states.*
- *The massing and delivery of arms to the Salvadoran guerrillas by those states must be judged against the fact that from 1977 until January 1981 the United States provided no weapons or ammunition to the Salvadoran Armed Forces.*
- *A major effort has been made to provide "cover" for this operation by supplying arms of Western manufacture and by supporting a front organization known as the Democratic Revolutionary Front to seek non-Communist political support through propaganda.*
- *Although some non-Communist states have also provided material support, the organization and delivery of this assistance, like the overwhelming mass of arms, are in the hands of Communist-controlled networks.*

In short, over the past year, the insurgency in El Salvador has been progressively transformed into a textbook case of indirect aggression by Communist powers through Cuba.

Public Diplomacy After 9/11

New target: networks
George W. Bush (2003)[127]

The struggle against international terrorism is different from any other war in our history. We will not triumph solely or even primarily through military might. We must fight terrorist networks, and all those who support their efforts to spread fear around the world, using every instrument of national power – diplomatic, economic, law enforcement, financial, information, intelligence, and military. Progress will come through the persistent accumulation of successes – some seen, some unseen. And we will always remain vigilant against new terrorist threats. Our goal will be reached when Americans and other civilized people around the world can lead their lives free from fear of terrorist attack.

A three-dimensional strategy
National Commission on Terrorist Attacks Upon the United States (2004) [128]

Informally known as the "9/11 Commission," the bipartisan panel proposes a strategy to attack terrorists and their organizations, prevent further growth of Islamist terrorism, and protect against and prepare for further terrorist attacks. Public diplomacy is not explicit in the following passage, but the section outlines the basic approach that public diplomacy efforts should take.

The enemy is not just "terrorism." It is the threat posed specifically by Islamist terrorism, by Bin Laden and others who

---

[127] *National Strategy for Combating Terrorism* (The White House, February 2003), p. 2.
[128] National Commission on Terrorist Attacks Upon the United States, *The 9/11 Commission Report, Final Report* (Government Printing Office, 2004), pp. 16-18.

draw on a long tradition of extreme intolerance within a minority strain of Islam that does not distinguish politics from religion, and distorts both.

The enemy is not Islam, the great world faith, but a perversion of Islam. The enemy goes beyond al Qaeda to include the radical ideological movement, inspired in part by al Qaeda, that has spawned other terrorist groups and violence. Thus our strategy must match our means to two ends: dismantling the al Qaeda network and, in the long term, prevailing over the ideology that contributes to Islamist terrorism.

The first phase of our post-9/11 efforts rightly included military action to topple the Taliban and pursue al Qaeda. This work continues. But long-term success demands the use of all elements of national power: diplomacy, intelligence, covert action, law enforcement, economic policy, foreign aid, public diplomacy, and homeland defense. If we favor one tool while neglecting others, we leave ourselves vulnerable and weaken our national effort.

What should Americans expect from their government? The goal seems unlimited: Defeat terrorism anywhere in the world. But Americans have also been told to expect the worst: An attack is probably coming; it may be more devastating still.

Vague goals match an amorphous picture of the enemy. Al Qaeda and other groups are popularly described as being all over the world, adaptable, resilient, needing little higher-level organization, and capable of anything. It is an image of an omnipotent hydra of destruction. That image lowers expectations of government effectiveness.

It lowers them too far. Our report shows a determined and capable group of plotters. Yet the group was fragile and occasionally left vulnerable by the marginal, unstable people often attracted to such causes. The enemy made mistakes. The U.S. government was not able to capitalize on them.

No president can promise that a catastrophic attack like that of 9/11 will not happen again. But the American people are entitled to expect that officials will have realistic objectives, clear guidance, and effective organization. They are entitled to see standards for performance so they can judge, with the help of their elected representatives, whether the objectives are being met.

We propose a strategy with three dimensions: (1) attack terrorists and their organizations, (2) prevent the continued growth of Islamist terrorism, and (3) protect against and prepare for terrorist attacks.

Attack Terrorists and Their Organizations

- Root out sanctuaries. The U.S. government should identify and prioritize actual or potential terrorist sanctuaries and have realistic country or regional strategies for each, utilizing every element of national power and reaching out to countries that can help us.
- Strengthen long-term U.S. and international commitments to the future of Pakistan and Afghanistan.
- Confront problems with Saudi Arabia in the open and build a relationship beyond oil, a relationship that both sides can defend to their citizens and includes a shared commitment to reform.

Prevent the Continued Growth of Islamist Terrorism

In October 2003, Secretary of Defense Donald Rumsfeld asked if enough was being done "to fashion a broad integrated plan to stop the next generation of terrorists." As part of such a plan, the U.S. government should

- Define the message and stand as an example of moral leadership in the world. To Muslim parents, terrorists like Bin Ladin have nothing to offer their children but visions of violence and death. America and its friends have the advantage-our vision can offer a better future.
- Where Muslim governments, even those who are friends, do not offer opportunity, respect the rule of law, or tolerate differences, then the United States needs to stand for a better future.
- Communicate and defend American ideals in the Islamic world, through much stronger public diplomacy to reach more people, including students and leaders outside of government. Our efforts here should be as strong as they were in combating closed societies during the Cold War.
- Offer an agenda of opportunity that includes support for public education and economic openness.
- Develop a comprehensive coalition strategy against Islamist terrorism, using a flexible contact group of leading coalition governments and fashioning a common coalition approach on issues like the treatment of captured terrorists.
- Devote a maximum effort to the parallel task of countering the proliferation of weapons of mass destruction.

- Expect less from trying to dry up terrorist money and more from following the money for intelligence, as a tool to hunt terrorists, understand their networks, and disrupt their operations.

A new strategy: 'Beyond elites to strategic communities'
Patricia S. Harrison (2004)[129]

. . . the findings and recommendations of the 9/11 Commission's Report present challenges for all of us. In the realm of public diplomacy, the report calls on us to define our message and ourselves, to stand for a better future, to defend our ideals and values, and to offer opportunity to youth.

We know that our greatest strength lies in our values. Whether as a new nation struggling for independence more than two centuries ago or now, when we have all the privileges and burdens of a global power — the heart of the American message to the world is one of values. We also understand that if we do not define ourselves, others will do it for us.

Following September 11, 2001, in discussions with the Administration and Congress, and in conjunction with our embassies, the Broadcasting Board of Governors and others, we began to move forward with a strategy for America's public diplomacy. The foundation of our public diplomacy strategy is to engage, inform and influence foreign publics in order to increase understanding for American values, policies and initiatives. Through traditional programs and all the tools of technology, involving both the public and private sectors, we are communicating the principles and values that underpin our policies and define us as a nation. At the same time, we are working to increase mutual understanding and respect between the people of the United States and those of other countries.

After 9/11, we redirected funds to enable us to move quickly and reach beyond elites to strategic communities comprising young

---

[129] Patricia S. Harrison, Assistant Secretary of State for Educational and Cultural Affairs, Statement Before the House Committee on Government Reform: Subcommittee on National Security, Emerging Threats, and International Relations, Washington, D.C., August 23, 2004. Harrison was acting under secretary for public diplomacy and public affairs in 2004 and 2005.

people, religious leaders, as well as the universe of people responsible for the education and development of young people — "youth influencers" from education ministers to classroom teachers to clerics, coaches and parents. We developed programs to reach people of good will, moderate groups working for the development of tolerant civil societies, journalists, women's groups, local leaders, clerics, community activists and more.

We have communicated our policy message through daily press briefings and public outreach by our missions around the world, as well as through our expanded web presence, speakers and publications. And, we communicate America's message through more than statements and speeches. In fact, one of the most powerful components of our public diplomacy programs are the 80,000 Americans who are reaching out to host our more than 30,000 academic, cultural and professional exchanges annually. We are working with 1,500 public-private organizations to improve lives in communities throughout the world. We know that one of our great assets in public diplomacy is the American people themselves, as they really are, not as they are caricatured. Programs that bring Americans and foreign citizens in direct contact can and do have tremendous positive impact.

We have formed partnerships with local institutions overseas, media and NGO's and others to extend our reach. We are funding English language programs, the language of opportunity for young people worldwide and, in the process, conveying information about U.S. society and values.

We continue to seek new ways to maintain important connections at a global grassroots level. For example, at a time when security concerns can constrain our ability to engage, one of our programs, American Corners provides a unique opportunity to maintain our involvement.

Media in all of its forms, from the Internet to print and broadcast, is an important component of public diplomacy. Our investment in training for journalists and cooperative television provides influential professionals with an entree to American society, where they can see for themselves how media in a free society works and observe for themselves that America is a free country with citizens of many faiths worshiping in their own way and coexisting equally. In other words, they can see how a civil society enhances the lives of all its citizens.

The vast majority of people around the world, including people in the Arab and Muslim world, share our values of freedom, human rights, opportunity and optimism, but many do not recognize America as champion of those values. We must compete to get our message across in an increasingly crowded and difficult competitive information environment, and Mr. Chairman, we do compete. We are working with the U.S. Agency for International Development to ensure recipients of our assistance recognize that assistance does come from the American people. The new Policy Coordinating Committee (PCC) on Muslim Outreach will strengthen coordination with the Department of Defense and other agencies. Our websites in Arabic and other critical languages communicate values as well as policy. Our partners in broadcasting, the Broadcasting Board of Governors, are dedicated to this objective.

Mr. Chairman, I believe our public diplomacy efforts are working in the right direction but there is a need to do more.

The Commission recommends that we work with moderate Arabs and Muslims to develop an "Agenda of Opportunity" built around education and economic development, a critical component of public diplomacy outreach. The report also advised that we must "rebuild the scholarship, exchange, and library programs that reach out to young people and offer them knowledge and hope." It is only through education and true communication that, as the 9/11 Commission Report puts it, "a moderate consensus can be found." We began to address this challenge, immediately following September 11, 2001, but this is not the work of weeks or months. It is the work of years and generations.

As a government, we must commit to a long-term and sustainable investment, engaging with people of good will at all levels of society, and especially to youth and those who influence youth. We must commit to increasing the numbers of people who can experience America beyond the headlines and misconceptions, through a visit to the U.S., interactions with Americans in their own country, through American Centers and through print and broadcast media and the Internet. We must demonstrate our many positive values as a society – such as rule of law, civil society, women's rights, religious tolerance and freedom of the media – to as many foreign individuals as possible, so that they can be advocates within their own countries for a civil and sustainable future.

We welcomed the 9/11 Commission Report as it has affirmed the many important steps we have taken since 9/11, including refocused funding to priority regions, especially the Middle East and South Asia, which now account for 25 percent of all Department funding for exchanges. Through our International Visitor and other public diplomacy programs, we have prioritized themes such as religious tolerance, ethnic diversity, the value of an independent media, NGO management, civil society and governance, elections and educational reform in the Muslim world. We have also increased our foreign journalist tours and television cooperative productions in these regions. The primary audiences are young student and political leaders, women and journalists.

We launched CultureConnect, the cornerstone of our cultural diplomacy, a program that selects American men and women who have achieved prominence in literature, the performing arts, sports, and other areas and serve as Cultural Ambassadors overseas with a focus on non-elite youth. We have also launched Citizen Diplomats, another new initiative, that allows everyday Americans the opportunity to share their skills and expertise with people in other countries. We are also sending 900 American speakers to foreign posts each year; and have held over 450 digital video conferences.

Public Diplomacy Officers from our South Asia and Near Eastern Affairs Bureaus were on the ground immediately following the military campaigns in both Afghanistan and Iraq. Our 30 public diplomacy officers in Iraq constitute the largest public diplomacy operation in the world. By the end of FY 2004, the International Visitor Program will have developed a range of programs for Iraqi mayors, educators, spokespeople, NGO representatives and women. Throughout the world, and especially in those countries with significant Muslim populations, our public diplomacy staffs are focused and working to reach those communities with an American message of hope and opportunity.

In the wake of 9/11, we began to produce a stream of print and electronic materials describing for foreign audiences, in their own languages, the events of 9/11 and the need to fight against those who have committed or wish to commit terrorist acts, as well as the achievements made in that struggle, particularly in Afghanistan and Iraq. More than 3,000 articles on terrorism have been published in the daily Washington File since 9/11. In the year following 9/11, the increase was 250 percent.

The Bureau of International Information Programs' (IIP's) print materials in Arabic are used by our embassies who share the material daily with press, academic, political and economic contacts either directly or indirectly through targeted mailing lists. The materials are available to foreign publics directly on the Internet on our IIP sites, which receive over 3,100 page views per day. Also, over 1,200 Arabic users have signed up independently to receive our material each day on the Arabic listserv. Use is monitored and reported through our embassies in weekly reports citing placement of Arabic material from IIP's Washington File.

We have established Arabic websites: Our USINFO Middle East web page, http://usinfo.state.gov, is linked to 470 other Arabic sites. Since 9/11, we have quadrupled the number of pages that we have been producing in Arabic. Before 9/11, we translated 3,000 to 4,000 words per day; now we translate between 12,000 and 15,000 per day. Our policy focus on the region, the President's vision for Middle East peace, policy emphasis on the proposed Middle East Free Trade Area and Middle East Partnership Initiative provide new material for daily Arabic translation. Critical audiences identified by our Missions abroad include government officials, scholars, university professors, researchers, media representatives, and self-selected listserv recipients. Our statistical reporting on Arabic language web sites indicates that 85% of our web users are based overseas with more than 50% from the Middle East, notably Saudi Arabia, Egypt, UAE, Kuwait and Syria as leading users.

Since 9/11, we have also increased by one-third our Arabic translation staff and opened a Persian language capacity. In May of 2003, we opened a Persian language website, engaging Iranian youth and youth influencers. Working with the Coalition Provisional Authority and the new Embassy in Baghdad, we introduced Arabic papers on the "Principles of Democracy" to inform Iraqis as their new government is shaped.

One of our most visible and effective public diplomacy tools is American Corners. A visitor to an American Corner, which can be housed in a university or an office building, finds computers, books, magazines, and information about life in the United States, our government and our culture. More than 140 American Corners are now in operation around the world, and our goal is to establish another 60 this year, with an emphasis on the Muslim world. In South Asia and other regions, our missions continue to operate American Centers – significant community institutions that serve as platforms for public outreach and as models of shared commitments to models of educational excellence.

Under the Bureau of Public Affairs (PA), both the Foreign Press Centers for print and radio and Office of Broadcast Services for television have increased substantially the number of journalist tours to our country, and 50 percent are with journalists from Arab and Muslim-majority countries. Since 9/11, the Foreign Press Center has included in its programming a set of special briefings specifically designed for Arab and Muslim media, including briefings by senior-level officials like Secretaries Powell, Rumsfeld and Ridge, as well as Dr. Rice. During this time, there has been unprecedented access by the foreign media to U.S. Government officials.

After 9/11, we created the Media Outreach Center in London, which is actively reaching out to Arab media in London, many of which have wide exposure throughout the Middle East.

Television and video products continue to be powerful strategic tools for bringing America's foreign policy message to worldwide audiences. PA has engaged international audiences with television pieces and documentary productions through television Co-Ops – filmed domestically by foreign broadcasters – and reverse Co-ops in host countries. We are helping Arab and Muslim journalists produce balanced reports and documentaries on topics from policy to culture. We continue to produce "good news" stories on reconstruction in Iraq and Afghanistan that American and foreign news editors have incorporated in their programs, and we are distributing Department-oriented videos to foreign media outlets worldwide. We have purchased the re-broadcast and educational rights to over 100 commercial documentaries showing America's government, society and values for broadcast on the American Embassy Television Network. The most popular series has been the American history program, "Freedom: A History of the U.S." The other most requested titles include "American Cinema", "Searching for the Roots of 9/11 with Thomas Friedman" and "Frontline: Muslims."

Nearly every post in every region of the world has requested tapes and reported on the exceptional results. For example, two Indonesian stations broadcast the 26-part series "Framework for Democracy," a documentary series about the reality of how a democratic government works. A Chinese audience viewed "Hollywood and the Muslim World," raising the confidence that peaceful resolutions could be achieved between the Muslim world and the U.S.

To measure the effectiveness of our video products, we have partnered with *NewsMarket*, an Internet-based worldwide video distribution service, which markets and distributes our products to more than 2,000 broadcasters and news agencies worldwide and provides routine monitoring and placement reports.

Our public diplomacy bureaus, in partnership with our regional bureaus around the world, have worked together to allay fears about domestic security and to educate foreign travelers about the revamped U.S. visa process through the "Secure Borders, Open Doors" campaign, an interagency effort involving the Department of Homeland Security and others as well as State. Features of this initiative include a special website – www.unitedstatesvisas.gov – promotional materials and speaking points. Other materials on changes in our visa policy have been developed and promoted, with an educational video to be released in six languages this fall.

The Middle East Partnership Initiative, funded at almost $250 million, fosters reforms to expand political participation and increase the economic and educational opportunities available to the people of the Middle East and North Africa, with an emphasis on opportunities for women and youth.

Within our broad programs in the Arab and Muslim world, we have as a strategic priority a focus on younger audiences within these regions. Following September 11, 2001, the Bureau of Educational and Cultural Affairs (ECA) launched Partnerships for Learning (P4L), which directs ECA exchanges towards youth and youth influencers in the Arab and Muslim world to build long-term sustainable relationships. P4L is based on the premise that if terror is the common enemy, education is the common value. The ultimate goal of P4L is the establishment of close and sustained partnerships with other nations that help provide young people with quality education and opportunities in life that will deter them from despair and hate.

Since FY 2002, ECA has dedicated over $40 million dollars to this new initiative. In FY 2005, ECA has requested an additional $25 million for P4L, which would increase funding for the P4L initiative to over $65 million. All of this will go to the Arab and Muslim world.

With this funding, we have initiated our country's first-ever government-sponsored high school program with the Arab and Muslim world. Last year, we had 170 students living with American families and attending U.S. high schools. This year, we will have 480, including students from Iraq and Afghanistan. By the 06-07 school year, we plan to have 1,000 high school students from the Arab and Muslim world studying side-by-side with our youth. This program was made possible through the volunteerism of hundreds of Muslim-American host families.

We have also created a new, undergraduate program specifically targeted at the non-elite, gifted young men and women from the Arab world who would otherwise have no opportunity for foreign study and first-hand exposure to the United States.

Under P4L, we also resumed the long-suspended Fulbright programs in Afghanistan and Iraq. We have directed $3.1 million to fund a microscholarship initiative for English language instruction to more than 3,400 youth from disadvantaged backgrounds in the Muslim world. In July 2003, we also initiated a monthly Arabic youth magazine, "Hi", which now is available throughout the Arab world and has led to an interactive "web-zine" that last month attracted 30,000 visitors and well over 700,000 page views. What we are actively doing dovetails exactly with the recommendation from the 9/11 commission that our scholarship and exchange programs "reach out to young people and offer them knowledge and hope."

There is much more that needs to be done, and we are working now to put in place initiatives that I believe will strengthen public diplomacy for the years ahead.

The need to improve oversight and coordination of public diplomacy was identified in the report from the Public Diplomacy Advisory Group for the Arab and Muslim World, the "Djerejian Group." A specific recommendation in this and other reports was the establishment of an Office of Policy, Planning and Resources for Public Diplomacy and Public Affairs within the Office of the Under Secretary. We have identified people and resources necessary to create this office, which will assist the Under Secretary in developing a wide-ranging strategic vision for public diplomacy, oversight for resource allocation, and performance evaluation capacities that previously did not exist. I know public diplomacy performance measurement has been a concern, and though many public diplomacy activities are difficult to measure, I am pleased that this new office will be taking on this important task. Subject to a congressional notification letter, we hope to have the office up and running by September.

Another recommendation of the Djerejian Report was to reinvigorate an interagency Policy Coordinating Committee (PCC). We have done that, concentrating initially on Muslim outreach. I am now co-chairing this PCC, with the NSC, and we are examining ways to engage and support potential allies, opinion leaders, NGO's and youth influencers such as religious leaders, teachers and journalists in countries worldwide with significant Muslim populations. Our challenge is to move beyond quick-fix solutions to improve America's image, to create long-term sustainable relationships among people of good will at every level, especially in emerging and strategic communities.

Working with the Department's regional bureaus, the PCC has requested and received reports from our embassies on their specific strategies for Muslim outreach, the programs they are implementing which are working and those programs not yet in place they believe would be effective. Embassies are already heavily involved in Muslim outreach. The PCC will help us to take a broader view of the challenges and develop strategic approaches that can be applied to specific countries and regions.

Another priority endeavor is our engagement of the private sector in public diplomacy. Secretary Powell, an advocate of public-private partnerships, has asked the Office of the Under Secretary to take the lead in engaging with the private sector in support of a wide-range of programs and initiatives. We launched the first Sister Cities International Partners for Peace Initiative between Iraq and the U.S., an initiative announced by the First Lady at the G-8 Summit. We worked with private sector partners to support the performance of the Iraqi National Symphony at Kennedy Center, and we are working with the Wheelchair Foundation to establish a new Middle East initiative to donate thousands of wheelchairs to Iraq, Morocco, Jordan, Oman and other areas in the Arab world.

Our outreach to the business community taps into America's strength: volunteerism. To enhance the scope of current programming and deliver our country's strategic public diplomacy and public affairs messages, we are working with the Bureau of Economic and Business Affairs and the U.S. Department of Commerce and have reached out to U.S. corporations and associations such as the U.S. Chamber of Commerce Center for Corporate Citizenship, the Business Roundtable, National Foreign Trade Council, Business for Diplomatic Action, Council on Competitiveness and the Young Entrepreneur Organization. We are evaluating corporate stewardship and corporate social responsibility trends demonstrated by U.S. companies throughout the Arab and Muslim world and working to expand our outreach to complement and highlight America's generous private sector contributions.

Interagency coordination is active, as described earlier with regard to the PCC, in addition to other interagency working groups. I would also like to note that the Department continues its close working relationship with the Broadcasting Board of Governors. Secretary Powell is a board member, and I represent him at the board meetings in my role as the acting Under Secretary. The 9/11 Commission's report commends the BBG for its new initiatives to reach out to the Arab and Muslim world. Radio Sawa and Radio Farda, along with the Middle East Television station Alhurra, and the new Urdu and Indonesian VOA services are reaching broader audiences with innovative and unbiased programming. Because of these initiatives, our country is now being presented in a much more honest context in regions where our media presence is vital.

In conclusion, Mr. Chairman, September 11, 2001 was a wake-up call for public diplomacy as for all of America. In the almost three years since that horrendous day, we have channeled much of our public diplomacy program toward the Arab and Muslim world. We are developing new programs and refining our strategy, and I believe we are making progress. Recent steps, including our new Office of Policy, Planning and Resources as well as the new Policy Coordinating Committee, will contribute substantially to our ability to carry out our mission and meet the recommendations of the 9/11 Commission and others. We are undertaking a new, comprehensive process of measurement to determine that our strategy and programs are effective. . . .

Strategy still needed
Advisory Commission on Public Diplomacy (2004) [130]

The information revolution has meant that more power is in the hands of individuals: the power to communicate globally, the power to engage in international dialogue and the power to influence their leaders. As a result, international public opinion and understanding are key to the success of American foreign policy. The pervasive 24-hour global communications environment requires responsiveness, but not hastiness; messages and strategies must be carefully crafted

---

[130] Barbara Barrett, et al., *2004 Report of the United States Advisory Commission on Public Diplomacy*, "Conclusion."

and coordinated, with regard to content and presentation, before they are communicated to audiences worldwide.

As noted throughout this report, significant progress has been made in many areas, but there is still much that can be accomplished. Three themes in this report illustrate what can be done: structure, responsiveness and measurement. The agents and structures of public diplomacy need to be properly coordinated to achieve maximum efficiency. Public diplomacy messaging must become more strategic and responsive, and at the same time must properly reflect the values and attitudes of target audiences. Anecdotal evidence is important and in some cases is the only way to determine whether programs are working; yet, at the same time, public diplomacy requires objective measurement through data collection, opinion polling and surveys to ensure that desired effects are being achieved.

As numerous reports, organizations and officials have attested, public diplomacy should be a national security priority. This Commission believes this need is now widely recognized in government. However, as international public opinion continues to influence the success of American foreign policy objectives, an aggressive strategy and increased allocation of resources are necessary to fulfill the recommendations of this report. This Commission looks forward to working with the administration and Congress to achieve a better understanding of and dialogue with the world.

Nothing at the top
National Security Council (2005)[131]

Inadvertently illustrating the lack of political direction and interagency coordination of public diplomacy and strategic communication, a National Security Council staff member passed the buck in a message to an outside public diplomacy practitioner in 2005:

We do not do public diplomacy here.

---

[131] National Security Council staff member, name redacted, in email dated April 6, 2005.

'Lack of clarity' in Saudi Arabia – five years later
Office of the Inspector General, U.S. Department of State (2006)[132]

Few countries are as important to the United States as Saudi Arabia, whose influence throughout the Muslim world and whose role as the world's largest oil exporter have long made it a crucial policy partner. New issues now crowd the bilateral agenda. Key U.S. objectives in the relationship are rooting out terrorist cells in Saudi Arabia, controlling the flow of money to extremist groups abroad, and support for political, economic, and social reforms.

The Office of Inspector General (OIG) found that the Ambassador and deputy chief of mission effectively manage these issues and the mission's personnel. They do so in an environment shaped by continuing security concerns, including managing the trauma of the December 2004 armed attack on Consulate General Jeddah. OIG found that there is an inherent and unacknowledged conflict between the U.S. government's desire to expand this policy agenda and the current staffing mix and level. Because of continued security concerns, nonemergency employees and dependents were ordered to leave in April 2004. However, the Department's decision to assign staff to one-year, unaccompanied tours of duty imperils good management. There are long staffing gaps in key positions, inexperienced first- and second-tour officers in middle-grade positions, and only a handful of seasoned officers available to supervise and coordinate. Coordination between the section chiefs at Embassy Riyadh and the inexperienced officers at the constituent posts has been irregular and inconsistent.

The staffs of the consular sections and of the Department of Homeland Security operations in Riyadh and Jeddah coordinate well to fulfill their mandated visa-issuance requirements. Nonetheless, they are increasingly unable to meet on a timely basis the rising Saudi interest in travel to the United States for business and study. OIG endorses the mission's plans to reinstitute nonimmigrant visa issuance in Dhahran, once a permanent staff is in place and the necessary construction is completed.

---

[132] United States Department of State and the Broadcasting Board of Governors, Office of the Inspector General, "Inspection of Embassy Riyadh, Saudi Arabia, and Constituent Posts," OIG Report ISP-I-06-14A, February 9, 2006.

The mission's public diplomacy strategy suffers from a lack of clarity. Embassy Riyadh and the two consulates general need to discuss in a more coordinated and continuing fashion their goals for media contact and public diplomacy. Although key reporting areas were left uncovered, Embassy Riyadh and the consulates general have produced a large amount of informative and influential reporting, despite staffing limitations that particularly affect the mission's reporting elements. The United States is losing upwards of $5 billion a year in sales because many U.S. companies have removed representatives from Saudi Arabia in part to the Department's travel advisory.

All three posts provide good administrative services and generally satisfactory management controls. The three information management sections are well managed and proactive about improving their operations. Morale is generally good among Americans and locally employed staff. In a climate of revolving-door management by Americans, the locally employed staff has performed extremely well

'Transformational public diplomacy'
Karen P. Hughes (2006)[133]

Expectations were high for presidential confidante Karen Hughes, the television journalist and campaign official who became Under Secretary of State for Public Diplomacy and Public Affairs in 2005. Echoing military rhetoric from the Pentagon's "defense transformation," she describes a "transformational public diplomacy" in a Texas policy speech in early 2006.

Last September, at my swearing-in ceremony as Under Secretary for Public Diplomacy and Public Affairs, President Bush said: "Spreading the message of freedom requires an aggressive effort to share and communicate America's fundamental values." He said that the war against terrorism "will not be won by force of arms alone," but that "we must also defeat them in the battle of ideas." President Bush instructed the Secretary of State and me to "marshal all the resources of the federal government to this critical mission." And

---

[133] Karen P. Hughes, Under Secretary of State for Public Diplomacy and Public Affairs, "Remarks at the Shell Distinguished Lecture Series," Baker Institute for Public Policy, Houston, Texas, March 29, 2006.

added: "Public diplomacy is the job of every member of my administration."

Now those were pretty clear marching orders – so for the past seven months my team and I have been hard at work to put in place a long-term foundation for what I call "waging peace" –and I use the word waging very intentionally because I believe that we must be very focused and clear about the commitment and years of effort that success will require. I truly believe that there is no more urgent challenge for America's national security and for the future of all the world's children than this task of reaching out to the rest of the world to foster common interests and values and confront common threats together. Our mission is further defined in the new National Security Strategy, which the White House released early this month.

"The United States is in the early years of a long struggle," it states, "similar to what our country faced in the early years of the Cold War…A new totalitarian ideology now threatens." It goes on to say this is not a battle of religions, as our opponents would like to make it – instead: "The transnational terrorists confronting us today exploit the proud religion of Islam to serve a violent political vision: the establishment, by terrorism and subversion, of a totalitarian empire that denies all political and religious freedom."

At a time of threat and so much turmoil in the world, America's public diplomacy is absolutely vital to our national security. As I prepared to begin this job, I was asked to come to the President's ranch in Crawford to outline a strategy. Now all you students here, I want you to think about this – my first day on the job was August 15th. I was asked to come to Crawford on August 11th to brief the president, vice president, secretaries of state and defense and our nation's military leaders on our strategy – before my first day on the job. Fortunately, I had spent the previous months during my preparation for confirmation hearings reading reports like the one developed by Ambassador Djerejian's group, reaching out to public diplomacy experts, former ambassadors, professionals at the State Department. I found there was actually a great deal of consensus about what needed to be done – it just needed someone to come in, re-energize a public diplomacy team that had had a difficult six years since the merger of the former United States Information Agency into the State Department – and start getting it done.

We began by outlining three strategic imperatives of our public diplomacy strategy:

First, we must offer people throughout the world a positive vision of hope that is rooted in America's belief in freedom, justice, opportunity and respect for all. I saw an interview of a young man in Morocco recently, who said: "For me, America represents hope of a better life." We represent that hope for people everywhere – and must always do so. America must continue to be that shining city on a hill that President Reagan spoke of – that's why we speak out for democracy, and against human rights offenders, for free press and against those who stifle religious freedom, for equal treatment for women and minorities and against the sex trafficking that threatens the lives of so many, especially young girls in the world today. People around the world should know that America proudly stands for not only our own rights but also for human rights and human freedom everywhere.

Our second strategic imperative is to isolate and marginalize the violent extremists, confront their ideology of tyranny and hate. We must undermine their efforts to portray the West as in conflict with Islam by empowering mainstream voices and demonstrating respect for Muslim cultures and contributions. That's why I've spent so much time reaching out to Muslim Americans – I believe they are an important bridge to Muslim communities across our world. One of our ambassadors, Tom Korologos, recently hosted a small conference in which he invited Muslim Americans to meet with European Muslims in an informal and constructive setting. It was an interesting model we're encouraging others to emulate. We're also encouraging interfaith dialogue. Last week in Washington, I spoke at the first international conference on faith and service, which brought together people of different faiths to encourage dialogue – and importantly brought together young people of different faiths who will go out and engage in service projects together – to help bridge divisions and bring about a better world. I also communicated with all our ambassadors encouraging them to support similar interfaith outreach programs in countries across the world. I recently talked with a Turkish woman in Berlin and asked whether I might visit her neighborhood. Not really, she told me quite honestly, many Muslims in Germany feel isolated from their own government and not interested in meeting with ours. Could I send a group of American Muslims to talk about how they live and work and worship in our country? Absolutely, that would be great, she told me.

Our third strategic imperative is to foster a sense of common interests/common values between Americans and people of different countries, cultures and faiths throughout the world. One of these ideas came from a meeting I had with Ambassador Wisner. While in a time of war and terrorism, we tend to focus on common threats, we must also focus on our common interests and common values. It is important to note that two of these three objectives are not just focused on the war on terror or Islamic communities, even though the press frequently refers to this job in the context of Muslim outreach – our public diplomacy actually involves the entire world. I recently returned from a 5-country trip to Latin America, because President Bush told me it should be one of my priorities. Our relationships with our neighbors in this hemisphere are incredibly important. Public diplomacy works as well to nurture and strengthen our transatlantic partnership with Europe, to build on our strengthening and strategic relationships with India and Pakistan, to reach out to people across an emerging China – and we also try to provide reliable information and establish relationships with people even when we don't have relations with their governments in countries such as Cuba and Iran.

We have many current and potential allies in this effort, because the values we are promoting do not belong to America – they are universal, meant for people everywhere and we seek to promote them with other nations and peoples in a spirit of partnership and respect. I love to cite an old Afghan proverb: "It takes two hands to clap." Public diplomacy is a conversation – a dialogue not a monologue – and that is why I began this job with a listening tour designed to show our friends and partners around the world that America wants to listen to their views, their concerns, their hopes. And I've continued to travel – next week, I'll go to Africa – to reach out to people across our world and talk about the things we have in common. People the world over want to be free to speak their minds and live in secure homes and neighborhoods. They want their governments to be fair and just and not corrupt. They want a quality education for their children. They want an opportunity to earn a good living and have their hard work provide greater prosperity and opportunity. They value science and technology and want to explore new frontiers together. Most of us want to live in societies that are free and just, not in those that subject people to tyranny, intimidation and thought control.

To promote this worldwide conversation and these universal values, we're relying on a set of tactics I call the four "E's" – some of you students may have seen them. As a communicator, I believe in boiling things down to basics and experience has taught me that just about the time people get sick of talking about something is about when it begins to sink in. So we have four E's: engage, exchange, educate and empower – and we've added a fifth, evaluation, mindful we need to measure results as best we can.

We need to engage more vigorously, explaining and advocating our policies in ways that are fast, accurate and authoritative. We are expanding exchanges – our single most successful public diplomacy tool over the last 50 years–and we are making them more strategic to engage young people and those who influence them including clerics, journalists, women and teachers. We have a wide array of study and exchange programs and opportunities to host exchange students. I urge you to visit our website – exchanges.state.gov and find out how you can be a part – we need you to be a part. As the president said, everyone has a public diplomacy role to play.

We have to do a better job of educating ourselves and others. I encourage America's young people to study abroad, learn more about other countries and cultures, and study the critical languages of the future so we can better communicate with the world. And we want young people to come study in America. As I travel the world, I meet many leaders who went to school or participated in exchange programs with the United States and I want the same thing to be true twenty and thirty years from now. We are increasing funding for English language training because it's something young people want – it expands their opportunities while at the same time opening an information door that helps them learn more about our values. Recognizing that successful public diplomacy will require the efforts of all of us, not just a few of us, we are working to empower our fellow Americans, the private sector, education leaders, Muslim Americans. In the struggle against violent extremists, for example, the voices of government officials are not always the most credible or powerful – Muslim Americans have far more credibility to debate issues of their faith than I do as a Christian.

Finally, we have created a new evaluation unit to improve our ability to measure success or failure. Even though Edward R. Murrow once famously said "no cash register rings when a mind is changed", it's important that we try to measure and understand the impact of our programs so we can direct funds where they are most effective. Earlier this year, we suspended publication of a magazine designed to reach out to Arab youth when an initial evaluation showed it wasn't having an impact on its target market. We are currently reviewing a number of other programs – we want to direct our resources to what works.

Our transformational public diplomacy is fundamentally changing the way we do business to become more effective in six key areas:

[First,] we are increasing funding for programs we know work and making them more effective. At a time of many competing budget demands, from disaster relief to the war against terror, we increased funding for exchanges in 2006 by 70 million dollars and President Bush has proposed an additional 48 million dollar increase in exchanges for 2007, because we know they work. People who come here see America, make up their own minds about us and almost always go home with a different and much more positive view of our country. We are reaching out to journalists, clerics, women leaders, teachers and bringing them on exchanges because they have a wide circle of influence. We are also inviting journalists to travel with exchange participants and report on their activities as we did with a recent sports diplomacy program with Venezuelan and Nicaraguan baseball players, so a wider audience of television viewers and newspaper readers can also participate in the exchange experience. We shifted resources to provide 9,000 high school students in 39 countries with significant Muslim populations up to two years of English language instruction exchange programs because we know it is successful.

[Second,] we are improving the way government communicates. This is a challenge because of how much communications has changed – rumors go around the world in an instant. We are working to get our government on the same page–quite literally. You may have heard NPR's coverage of our new rapid response center at the State Department. We put that in place to monitor media around the world, with a special emphasis on pan-Arab media – Ambassador Djerejian's group strongly recommended this and it was our honor recently to give him a tour – this center puts out a daily early morning summary of stories driving news around the world, and sums up America's message in response – it's now sent to all Cabinet Secretaries, Ambassadors, public information officers and military leaders around the world – and many have told me it is providing them with information that helps them advocate more effectively on behalf of our country and our policies. We are in the process of setting up regional hubs, to position spokesmen in key media centers like Dubai – their full time job will be to get on television and media and advocate our values and policies. We've dramatically increased our presence on Arab media – State Department personnel made 148 appearances on Arab and regional media in January and February alone – a good number of them in Arabic.

And we are unleashing our people – we have changed the rules which used to require pre-clearance from Washington before media interviews. Now ambassadors and Foreign Service officers are not only free but expected to give interviews on all established policies with no advance approval at all. We want our embassy personnel to be not only a presence, but the face and voice of America on media in countries across our world. This is a huge change in culture – and to make it effective, we're working to improve our training and provide tools and information to help ambassadors speak out more forcefully and effectively – and we have changed the promotion precepts so public diplomacy skills and work are now part of the criteria for promotion for all in the Foreign Service.

A third major change: public diplomacy is helping shape policy. Members of my senior staff and I now attend the Secretary's senior policy meetings at the State Department, and we've institutionalized a higher level and more vigorous presence for public diplomacy in the regional bureaus where much of policy is originally developed. A new deputy assistant secretary for public diplomacy now works in each bureau, reporting to the assistant secretary and to me – literally knitting together policy and public diplomacy. After my travels, I regularly meet with the President, Secretary Rice, the National Security Advisor and others to report on what I've learned and what we can do better. For example, I recently traveled to Latin America with Secretary Rice for the inaugural of Chile's first woman president, a great occasion – we met with many Latin American leaders and a group of our ambassadors and I went on from there and traveled to four other countries. As I reported to the President, we heard the same things almost everywhere – that while both the American government and individual Americans themselves are doing a great deal to improve the lives of people in Latin America – not very many people know about it. President Bush has doubled development assistance to Latin America during his tenure – and many of the leaders I met with didn't realize that – and said we often didn't shape our programs in ways that made their benefits clear to average people. President Bush views Latin America as a priority – and he's now instructed us to look at ways to make our programs more effective, to set clearer goals, focus our programs and partner with the private sector to get maximum results – then make sure we communicate what we are doing – a perfect example of the intersection of public diplomacy and policy.

Fourth, we are forging new partnerships. Earlier today, I met with officials Houston Intercontinental – one of pilot airports where we are working with the travel industry, with Department of Homeland Security and with local officials to make arrival points our country more welcoming. I've been telling people that you never get a second chance to make a first impression. We brought together university presidents for their first ever summit in Washington and are working with them and the Commerce Department to better market American higher education to students around the world. We started the Fortune Women's Entrepreneurship Initiative, which brings women business leaders from around the world to America to work with women at Fortune 500 companies. Microsoft and the International Institute for Education are training 1,000 women in the United Arab Emirates in information technology. Major corporations including Pfizer, Citicorp, Xerox, GE, UPS, Pepsico, John Deere, American Electric Power, and Asset Management Advisors raised more than $100 million to help victims of Pakistan's earthquake and flooding in Central America. The Aspen Institute has partnered with us on journalism schools to bring international journalists here for work-study programs. All of these partnerships are critically important to creating good will for our country.

A fifth major change is we are enhancing our use of technology. Building on the president's State of the Union, where he said "for people everywhere, America is a partner for a better life," we've launched a new website to tell the real-people stories of how America is partnering around the world to help people have better lives. We've launched a new web-based interactive program, "democracy dialogues" to foster discussion about different aspects of democracy, and added podcasts, web-chats and digital video conferences to share American messages in more places and more languages. I've got a working group looking at ways we might use MP3 players, DVDs and other current technologies to better tell America's story especially to young people. I'm meeting with technology leaders from Oracle, Dell, the Gates Foundation, to discuss ideas of how we might partner with them in ways that enhance access to technology and thus information on opportunity for more people around the world.

Finally, we are working to de-legitimize terrorism. At speeches around the world, I've been making the case that people of values, people of all faiths, people of conscience need to work together to do for terrorism what was done to slavery – it went from being internationally accepted to being an international pariah – largely because people made moral arguments against it based on people's fundamental rights of equality. All the world's great religions teach that life is precious, taking of innocent life is wrong. We've challenged our ambassadors to bring together leaders of different faiths in countries throughout the world to deliver that message clearly and consistently.

We are also seeking to more effectively engage with mainstream leaders in the many diverse Muslim communities across our world. The fact is that the majority of those killed by terrorists since the September 11 attacks have been Muslims.

Many Islamic clerics, as well as other secular and religious defenders of freedom, are standing up to push back against terrorist violence.

We have seen gatherings of senior clerics in Jordan and elsewhere issue statements that debunk terrorists' claims to be acting in accordance with the scriptures of the Koran. Many Muslim scholars have publicly condemned terrorism, citing Chapter 5, Verse 32 of the Koran, which states that killing an innocent human being is akin to killing all of humanity.

Last summer we saw a group of Iraqi women come together to create a campaign, called Pledge for Iraq, to call for human rights and equality before the law. This group lobbied political parties and candidates and generated support from more than 250 political and civil society leaders.

After the despicable bombing of one of Islam's holiest shrines, the Mosque in Samarra, Iraq's leading Shi'a cleric, Grand Ayatollah Sistani, condemned the bombing on the ground that its purpose was to foment sectarian conflict.

More recently we saw ordinary people in Iraqi cities and towns protesting against those who continue to kill hundreds and thousands of people with their car bombs, videotaped beheadings, and other atrocities.

We also saw popular demonstrations in Morocco and Jordan against suicide bombers and against the murder in Iraq of Arab diplomats.

More and more, people are standing up against these tactics of terror and it is up to all of us to speak up loud and clear and say as President Bush has stated so powerfully – that difference is never a license to kill.

To advance the President's democracy agenda and open up repressive regimes, we are working to make "political space" for courageous dissidents and journalists whose voices are too often stifled. When we put a spotlight on what is happening, it makes it harder for leaders to repress the voices of freedom. Yesterday's Washington Post had an article quoting the editor of a new paper in Egypt – among the first to publish criticism of the regime – who said Egyptians have discovered dissent and that the space for press freedom opened only because of America. "U.S. pressure on the Mubarak regime has been the catalyst for most of the change we have seen," said the editor.

As I hope you can tell, we have a lot underway – and there is much, much more to do. This is the work of decades – as the President said when he gave me my marching orders, we are in a time that requires the same type of commitment that enabled us to prevail in an earlier era, when communists denied freedom to millions of the world's citizens. In that era we encouraged Americans to study Russian language and history and culture so we could better understand the aspirations of the Russian people and the psychology of those who oppressed them.

Today the struggle for freedom has shifted to new regions of the world. We need a similar all-out effort because this engagement will determine the kind of world our children live in.

I want to close with two stories that sum up America's diplomacy at work in the world.

Last fall I stood in Aceh and looked out at the ocean where the tsunami, a 30-foot high black wall of water came crashing in at 60 miles an hour. Residents there who somehow survived, showed me hundreds of patches of cement – all that was left of homes that had once stood there and so many lives that ended there. I witnessed those who survived coming together, agreeing on property divisions and neighborhood maps – beginning the process of rebuilding. And I met the future – a group of Fulbright students who will be studying in Texas and Arkansas as a result of the American fundraising drive led by former Presidents Bush and Clinton. I met a young man whose goal is to get a master's degree in English so he can return to Aceh and take the place of the English teacher who had taught him but who was killed in the tsunami. That investment in the lives of individual people sums up public diplomacy – it's people driven and as that young man illustrates, our investment in his education has the potential to make a difference in so many other lives and so many other futures.

A couple of years ago, after the fall of the Taliban, I toured a reading program in Afghanistan, where young girls who previously had been banned from going to school were learning to read. I met a young woman who said she wanted to be a writer, and she hoped one day to write a book. I told her I was at the time working on a book of my own and said I would like to say something on her behalf in my book until she was able to write hers.

Her answer through the translator was quick and unequivocal. She said, "Women should be able to go to school and work and choose our own husbands." She was 13 years-old.

As I was leaving, the translator grabbed my arm and stopped me, and said, "She wants to tell you something else: Please don't forget them. Please help them live in freedom."

And I have to tell you, the eyes of that little girl followed me all the way home ever since. It is both our privilege and our duty to help that young girl and others like her live in freedom. The people of each nation must walk their own path to the future, but America can come alongside in a spirit of respect and partnership and help light the way.

2006 audit: "Strategic approach still lacking"
Government Accountability Office (2006)[134]

Nearly five years after the 9/11 attacks, the State Department had yet to devise a government-wide public diplomacy strategy or implement its own strategy within the Foreign Service.

No government entity has been as persistent about demanding a public diplomacy strategy as the Government Accountability Office

---

[134] Jess T. Ford, Director of International Affairs and Trade, U.S. Government Accountability Office, Testimony before the Subcommittee on Science, the Departments of State, Justice and Commerce, and Related Agencies, House Committee on Appropriations, "U.S. Public Diplomacy: State Department Efforts Lack Certain Communication Elements and Face Persistent Challenges," May 3, 2006, GAO-06-707T.

(GAO), the independent investigative arm of Congress. A 2006 GAO report found that while the State Department had expanded and focused its public diplomacy efforts, progress was slow and lacking an integrated, strategic approach.

The audit, as with those of other years, sheds light on State Department public diplomacy operations in general: insufficiently trained staff, overworked staff, a bunker mentality at key diplomatic posts that limits programming and public access, slow decision-making, poor implementation, and a lack of a sense of urgency.

While the language of the audit, as with most GAO products, is understated and diplomatic, the report is clear about how the office viewed the condition of American public diplomacy. State has followed most of GAO's policy prescriptions.

Summary

Since the terrorist attacks of September 11, 2001, State has expanded its public diplomacy efforts globally, focusing particularly on countries in the Muslim world considered to be of strategic importance in the war on terrorism. Since 2001, State has increased its public diplomacy resources, particularly in regions with significant Muslim populations. From 2004 to 2006, funding in two regions with significant Muslim populations – the Near East and South Asia – increased 25 and 39 percent, respectively. However, public diplomacy staffing levels have remained largely the same during that period.

Since 2003, we have reported that the government lacked an interagency public diplomacy strategy to guide the activities of disparate agencies, and it continues to lack this strategy. We also noted that State did not have a strategy to integrate its diverse public diplomacy activities and that efforts to effectively engage the private sector had met with mixed success. State has begun to address these shortcomings. In 2005, State developed a strategic framework to focus its public diplomacy efforts and related tactics to achieve its goals, including marginalizing extremists and promoting understanding of shared values. However, the department has not issued guidance to its posts abroad on how to implement these strategies and tactics. In addition, our report released today reveals that posts' public diplomacy efforts generally lack important strategic communication elements found in the private sector, which we and others have suggested adopting as a means to better communicate with target audiences. These elements include having core messages, segmented target audiences, in-depth research and analysis to monitor and evaluate results, and an integrated communication plan to bring all these elements together. State officials indicated that the department has begun an effort to develop communication plans for 15 pilot posts, but it remains to be seen whether these communication plans will contain all of these strategic elements.

State faces multiple challenges in implementing its public diplomacy programs, especially at the field level. These challenges include concerns related to staff numbers, time available for public diplomacy activities, staff language capabilities, and the need to balance security with public outreach. According to State data, roughly 15 percent of its public diplomacy positions overseas were vacant in 2005. Several embassy officials indicated that insufficient numbers of staff and lack of staff time for public diplomacy activities hinder outreach efforts. We also identified this problem in our 2003 report, where a survey of Public Affairs officers in the field showed that more than 50 percent said that the number of public diplomacy officers was inadequate and more than 40 percent said the amount of time available for public diplomacy activities was insufficient. The Secretary of State recently announced plans to reposition some staff, including plans to shift 28 public diplomacy officers from posts in Europe and Washington, D.C., to China, India, and Latin America, as well as to the Muslim world. Additionally, our report notes that 30 percent of officers in language-designated public diplomacy positions in the Muslim world have not attained the level of language proficiency required for their positions, hampering their ability to engage with foreign publics. In addition to these staffing challenges, security concerns limit public diplomacy activities, especially in the Muslim world. Security, along with budgetary concerns, has forced embassies to close publicly accessible facilities and curtail certain public outreach efforts, sending the unintended message that the United States is unapproachable. The department has attempted to compensate for the lack of public presence through a variety of means, including the use of small-scale external facilities, and expanded embassy speaker programs.

We have made several recommendations since 2003 to the Secretary of State to address strategic planning issues, private sector engagement, and staffing challenges related to public diplomacy. For example, in 2003, we recommended that the Secretary develop a strategy that integrates private sector techniques into its public diplomacy efforts and that the Secretary strengthen efforts to train Foreign Service officers in foreign languages and public diplomacy. Today's report recommends that the Secretary develop written guidance detailing how the department intends to implement its public diplomacy goals as they apply to the Muslim world and strengthen existing systems of sharing best practices to more systematically transfer knowledge among embassies around the world. The primary purpose of these proposed actions is to help officers in the field strategically plan and implement public diplomacy programs in line with the Under Secretary's articulated goals. State has consistently concurred with our findings and recommendations for improving public diplomacy and indicated that the department, in several cases, is taking appropriate actions, such as developing a broad public diplomacy strategy and strengthening strategic planning at the post level. However, the department has not established a timetable for many of these actions, including the issuance of an interagency public diplomacy strategy and the creation of the Office of Private Sector Outreach....

Strategy, planning, and coordination efforts are inadequate

Since 2003, we have reported on the lack of strategic elements to guide U.S. public diplomacy efforts. Despite several attempts, the United States still lacks an interagency public diplomacy strategy. While State has recently developed a strategic framework for its public diplomacy efforts, it has not issued guidance on how this framework is to be implemented in the field. In addition, posts generally lack a strategic approach to public diplomacy.

Government lacks an interagency public diplomacy strategy

In 2003, we reported that the United States lacked a governmentwide, interagency public diplomacy strategy, defining the messages and means for communication efforts abroad. We reported that the administration had made a number of aborted attempts to develop a strategy, but to date no public diplomacy strategy has been developed. The lack of such a strategy complicates the task of conveying consistent messages, which increases the risk of making damaging communication mistakes. State officials said that the lack of such a strategy diminishes the efficiency and effectiveness of governmentwide public diplomacy efforts, while several reports concluded that a strategy is needed to synchronize agencies' target audience assessments, messages, and capabilities.

On April 8, 2006, the President established a new Policy Coordination Committee on Public Diplomacy and Strategic Communications. This committee, to be led by the Under Secretary for Public Diplomacy and Public Affairs is intended to coordinate interagency activities to ensure that:

- all agencies work together to disseminate the President's themes and messages;
- all public diplomacy and strategic communications resources, programs, and activities are effectively coordinated to support those messages; and
- every agency gives public diplomacy and strategic communications the same level of priority that the President does.

According to department officials, one of the committee's tasks will be to issue a formal interagency public diplomacy strategy. It is not clear when this strategy will be developed.

State has developed public diplomacy strategic framework but lacks implementing guidance

In 2005, the Under Secretary established a strategic framework for U.S. public diplomacy efforts, which includes three priority goals: (1) support the President's Freedom Agenda with a positive image of hope; (2) isolate and marginalize extremists; and (3) promote understanding regarding shared values and common interests between Americans and peoples of different countries, cultures, and faiths. The Under Secretary noted that she intends to achieve these goals using five tactics – engagement, exchanges, education, empowerment, and evaluation – and by using various public diplomacy programs and other means. This framework partially responds to our 2003 recommendation that the department develop and disseminate a strategy to integrate all State's public diplomacy efforts and direct them toward achieving common objectives. However, the department has not yet developed written guidance that provides details on how the Under Secretary's new strategic framework should be implemented in the field.

In 2005, we noted that State's efforts to engage the private sector in pursuit of common public diplomacy objectives had met with mixed success and recommended that the Secretary develop a strategy to guide these efforts. State is currently establishing an office of private sector outreach and is partnering with individuals and the private sector on various projects. The Under Secretary plans to institutionalize this function within the department surrounding key public diplomacy objectives, but it is unclear when this office will be established and whether it will develop a comprehensive strategy to engage the private sector.

Posts lack a strategic approach to public diplomacy

GAO and others have suggested that State adopt a strategic approach to public diplomacy by modeling and adapting private sector communication practices to suit its purposes. . . . However, based on our review of mission performance plans and on fieldwork in Nigeria, Pakistan, and Egypt, we found that the posts' public diplomacy programming generally lacked these important elements of strategic communications planning. In particular, posts lacked a clear theme or message and did not identify specific target audiences. According to a senior embassy official in Pakistan, the United States has too many competing messages, and the post needs to do a better job of defining and clarifying its message. Posts also failed to develop detailed strategies and tactics to direct available public diplomacy programs and tools toward clear, measurable objectives in the most efficient manner possible. Finally, posts lack detailed, country-level communication plans to coordinate their various activities. . . .

Recently, State has begun to help posts improve their strategic communications planning. For example, the department has issued guidance on preparing fiscal year 2008 mission performance plans that calls for more strategic thinking and planning than was required in the past, including identification of specific target audiences, key themes and messages, detailed strategies and tactics, and measurable performance outcomes that can clearly demonstrate the ultimate impact of U.S. public diplomacy efforts. If fully implemented, this guidance should begin to address the shortcomings we found in mission performance plans; however, it will not be implemented for another 2 years, raising significant concerns about what the department intends to do now to address strategic planning shortfalls. Moreover, it is unclear whether this guidance will include all the strategic elements from private sector communication practices.

In addition to this guidance, the department is currently developing a sample country-level communication plan and has asked 15 pilot posts to develop specific plans for their host countries. These plans are intended to better focus U.S. efforts to counter ideological support for terrorism, according to State. Part of this process will include the development of a key influencers analysis to help identify target audiences in each country. State officials said that they expect to have plans for these countries by fall or winter 2006.

Staffing challenges and security concerns limit U.S. public diplomacy activities

Public diplomacy efforts in the field face several other challenges, many of which are heightened in the Muslim world. Officials at posts we visited said they lacked sufficient staff and time to conduct public diplomacy tasks, and we found that many public diplomacy positions are filled by officers without the requisite language skills. Furthermore, public diplomacy officers struggle to balance security with public access and outreach to local populations

Insufficient staff and lack of staff time hinder public diplomacy activities

While several recent reports on public diplomacy have recommended an increase in spending on U.S. public diplomacy programs, several embassy officials stated that, with current staffing levels, they do not have the capacity to effectively utilize increased funds. According to State data, the department had established 834 public diplomacy positions overseas in 2005, but 124, or roughly 15 percent, were vacant. Compounding this challenge is the loss of public diplomacy officers to temporary duty in Iraq, which, according to one State official, has drawn down field officers even further. Staffing shortages may also limit the amount of training public diplomacy officers receive. According to the U.S. Advisory Commission on Public Diplomacy, "the need to fill a post quickly often prevents public diplomacy officers from receiving their full training." In addition, public diplomacy officers at post are burdened with administrative tasks and thus have less time to conduct public diplomacy outreach activities than previously. One senior State official said that administrative duties, such as budget, personnel, and internal reporting, compete with officers' public diplomacy responsibilities. Another official in Egypt told us that there was rarely enough time to strategize, plan, or evaluate her programs. These statements echo comments we heard during overseas fieldwork and in a survey for our 2003 report. Surveyed officers told us that, while they manage to attend functions within their host country capitals, it was particularly difficult to find time to travel outside the capitals to interact with other communities. This challenge is compounded at posts with short tours of duty, which include many in the Muslim world. According to data provided by State, the average tour length at posts in the Muslim world is about 22 percent shorter than tour lengths elsewhere. Noting the prevalence of one-year tours in the Muslim world, a senior official at State told us that Public Affairs officers who have shorter tours tend to produce less effective work than officers with longer tours.

To address these challenges, we recommended in 2003 that the Secretary of State designate more administrative positions to overseas public affairs sections to reduce the administrative burden. Officials at State said that the Management bureau is currently considering options for reducing the administrative burden on posts, including the development of centralized administrative capabilities offshore. State is also repositioning several public diplomacy officers as part of its transformational diplomacy initiative; however, this represents a shift of existing public diplomacy officers and does not increase the overall number of officers in the department.

Language deficiencies pronounced, especially in the Muslim world

In 2005, 24 percent of language-designated public diplomacy positions were filled by officers without the requisite language proficiency, similar to our findings in 2003. At posts in the Muslim world, this shortfall is even greater, with 30 percent of public diplomacy positions filled by officers without sufficient language skills. This figure is primarily composed of languages that are considered difficult to master, such as Arabic and Persian, but also includes languages considered easier to learn, such as French.

Embassies must balance security and public outreach

Security concerns have limited embassy outreach efforts and public access, forcing public diplomacy officers to strike a balance between safety and mission. Shortly after the terrorist attacks of September 11, 2001, then-Secretary of State Colin Powell stated, "Safety is one of our top priorities... but it can't be at the expense of the mission." While posts around the world have faced increased threats, security concerns are particularly acute in countries with significant Muslim populations, where the threat level for terrorism is rated as "critical" or "high" in 80 percent of posts. . . .

Security and budgetary concerns have led to the closure of publicly accessible facilities around the world, such as American Centers and Libraries. In Pakistan, for example, all of the American Centers have closed for security reasons; the last facility, in Islamabad, closed in February 2005. These same concerns have prevented the establishment of a U.S. presence elsewhere. As a result, embassies have had to find other venues for public diplomacy programs, and some activities have been moved onto embassy compounds, where precautions designed to improve security have had the ancillary effect of sending the message that the United States is unapproachable and distrustful, according to State officials. Concrete barriers and armed escorts contribute to this perception, as do requirements restricting visitors' use of cell phones and pagers within the embassy. According to one official in Pakistan, visitors to the embassy's reference library have fallen to as few as one per day because many visitors feel humiliated by the embassy's rigorous security procedures.

Other public diplomacy programs have had to limit their publicity to reduce the risk of becoming a target. A recent joint USAID-State report concluded that "security concerns often require a 'low profile' approach during events, programs or other situations, which, in happier times, would have been able to generate considerable good will for the United States."

This constraint is particularly acute in Pakistan, where the embassy has had to reduce certain speaker and exchange programs. State has responded to security concerns and the loss of publicly accessible facilities through a variety of initiatives, including

American Corners, which are centers that provide information about
the United States, hosted in local institutions and staffed by local
employees.

According to State data, there are currently approximately 300
American Corners throughout the world, including more than 90 in
the Muslim world, with another 75 planned (more than 40 of which
will be in the Muslim world). However, two of the posts we visited
in October 2005 were having difficulty finding hosts for American
Corners, as local institutions fear becoming terrorist targets.

'Guided by our tactics' - Major public diplomacy accomplishments for 2005-2006
U.S. Department of State (2006)[135]

*The following text is an official State Department summary of its
public diplomacy strategy by the end of 2006. The self-
congratulatory summary features initiatives that are important in
themselves, but that do not fit together well strategically or make
significant contributions to the war efforts.*

*Symptomatic of State's scattershot approach, the many small
initiatives do not add up to the sum of their parts, and they leave
many areas unaddressed. The text of the entire eight-page
document is reprinted here in full, with the exception of pull-
quotes, captions and pictures, including five photos of the Under
Secretary of State for Public Diplomacy and Public Affairs.*

STRATEGIC DIRECTION: *Since the fall of 2005, a
reinvigorated public diplomacy team has been implementing a
comprehensive strategy based on three strategic objectives:*

- Offer people throughout the world a positive vision of hope and
  opportunity that is rooted in America's belief in freedom,
  justice, opportunity and respect for all.
- Isolate and marginalize the violent extremists; confront their
  ideology of tyranny and hate. Undermine their efforts to portray
  the west as in conflict with Islam by empowering mainstream

---

[135] "Major Public Diplomacy Accomplishments 2005-2006," Office of
Public Diplomacy and Public Affairs, U.S. Department of State, December,
2006.

voices and demonstrating respect for Muslim cultures and contributions.

• Foster a sense of common interests and values between Americans and people of different countries, cultures and faiths throughout the world.

Guided by our tactics of **Engage,** **Exchange,** **Educate,** *and* **Empower,** *we have launched an array of new initiatives and strengthened existing programs by making them more strategic.*

ENGAGE: *We are engaging more vigorously, explaining our policies in ways that are fast, authoritative, accurate.*

Rapid Response Unit (RRU): Under Secretary Hughes established new unit within the Bureau of Public Affairs to monitor and translate major world media real-time, produce a daily report on stories driving news around the world and give the U.S. position on these issues. Distributed daily to U.S. cabinet and sub-cabinet officials, U.S. ambassadors, public affairs officers, regional combatant commanders, and elsewhere.

"Echo Chamber" Messages: We have created a new product to provide U.S. ambassadors and others clear, common-sense guidance so they are better able to advocate U.S. policy on major news stories and policy issues. Provided to Voice of America policy office for use in crafting editorials reflecting the views of the U.S. Government.

Regional Public Diplomacy Hubs: We have created hubs in key media markets where spokesmen's full time job will be to advocate U.S. policies on regional media, especially television. Our first three hubs opened during the summer of 2006 in London, Brussels, and Dubai.

Greetings from America: This series of radio programs, now broadcast in Indonesia and Pakistan, presents American society and culture through the eyes of foreign exchange students studying in the United States. The programs highlight America's welcoming environment for Muslims and those of other faiths, as well as American popular culture and our educational system. *Greetings from America* (GFA) segments featuring Indonesian students currently reach 24 million 15-25 year-old radio listeners in Islamabad/Rawalpindi, Karachi and Lahore. The five-minute segments air 12 times a week in each country.

"Strategic Speakers" Program: Launched a more focused program, sending 88 U.S. speakers to selected countries to engage media, individuals and groups on issues dealing with: 1) building democracy, 2) increasing international security (particularly against terrorism) and 3) emphasizing the importance of trade and development. In some of the most successful programs, American Muslims engaged counterparts in critical regions on Muslim life in America. These programs are crafted to ensure maximum impact in advancing policy goals on these issues.

Engage Foreign Audiences: Modeled public diplomacy outreach for other government officials through an extensive program of international travel, foreign media interviews and listening events. The Under Secretary traveled to the Middle East, Europe, Africa, South and East Asia, and South and Central America, both to listen and to determine how we can more effectively communicate and partner with the voices of toleration and peace.

Reaching out to the People of Iran: Quadrupled policy and feature publishing on the State Department's Persian web site, including profiles of successful Iranian-Americans. Monthly visits now exceed 142,000, with more than 62% of visitors coming from inside Iran. In August, Ambassador Greg Schulte, the U.S. permanent representative to the IAEA and the U.N. Mission in Vienna, Austria, began a Persian language Q&A program on non-proliferation issues, to talk to Iranians about the advantages of joining the global community and the downside to pursuing nuclear weapons. Iranians joining the "Schulte blog" range from 14 year-old students to octogenarians, and have moved the discussion beyond nuclear issues to include human rights and visas for Iranian citizens. We are developing additional web publications and electronic and speaker programs to engage Iranian expatriates in Dubai and other regional centers on topics of mutual interest, including human rights, economic freedom, U.S. policy toward Iran and its neighbors and peaceful uses of nuclear energy.

Expanded Presence on Arab Media: Department officials quadrupled our appearances on Arab and regional media over the past year, a large number of these in Arabic. We now have the capacity in Washington to respond immediately to breaking news and are working on having this in the field by summer.

Broadcasting Board of Governors (BBG): As the Secretary's representative to the Broadcasting Board of Governors, Under

Secretary Hughes regularly attends board meetings and provides strategic policy guidance.

EXCHANGE: *We are increasing key programs and making them more strategic to reach young people and those who influence them – such as clerics, journalist, teachers, and women.*

Fortune/State Department International Women Mentoring Program: Assistant Secretary Dina Habib Powell announced this unique mentoring program at the 2005 Fortune's Most Powerful Women Summit. Emerging women in business around the world partner with Fortune's Most Powerful Women to develop management and business skills while gaining experience in the cutting-edge U.S. business environment. Women from Bangladesh, Bolivia, the Czech Republic, Guatemala, Indonesia, Kenya, Pakistan, Polan [sic], Russia, and South Africa, among many others, joined women from partner companies such as Microsoft, Avon, and Time Inc.

Edward R. Murrow Journalism Program: Journalists representing television, radio, and print media from over 100 countries had the opportunity to examine journalistic practices in the United States through visits to media outlets and government and academic institutions across the country. In partnership with leading schools of journalism, including the University of Southern California's Center on Public Diplomacy at the Annenberg School for Communication, the Edward Murrow program featured intensive academic seminars on journalistic principles. Academic sessions were enhanced by "job shadowing" and opportunities for the journalists to observe the U.S. press in action. The program concluded in Washington, DC with an international symposium for journalists, arranged in cooperation with the Aspen Institute, which highlighted trends and contemporary challenges facing the media in the U.S. and around the world. Other partners for the pilot program included: University of Oklahoma, Gaylord School of Journalism, University of Kentucky School of Journalism and Telecommunications, University of North Carolina at Chapel Hill, School of Journalism and Mass Communication, University of Texas at Austin School of Journalism; Missouri School of Journalism, University of Missouri at Columbia [punctuation as in original].

Iraqi Young Leaders Exchange Program: President George W. Bush, in a joint press conference with Iraqi Prime Minister Nuri al-Maliki, announced a new program for the rising generation of young Iraqis, who represent the future leadership of the developing democratic nation. The program will serve two hundred male and female students from all regions and sectors of Iraqi society. Beginning summer 2007, the initiative will bring high school and university students to the United States for two innovative programs designed to promote mutual understanding, leadership development, educational transformation, and democratic ideals.

Exchanges with Iran: The Bureau of Educational and Cultural Affairs has devised a comprehensive plan to re-engage the Iranian people. Through exchanges such as the International Visitor Leadership Program, Sports Initiatives, Fulbright Seminars, Foreign Language Teaching Assistance, and a Study in the U.S. Advising Center based in Dubai, it will engage the Iranian people to promote greater understanding, and provide further exposure to U.S. society, institutions, and values.

Global Cultural Initiative: Announced by Mrs. Laura Bush and Under Secretary of State Karen Hughes in September 2006, the Global Cultural Initiative is designed to deepen our friendships with people of all countries. Through the Global Cultural Initiative, and with the support of the State Department, private arts institutions will join our country's federal cultural agencies in renewing our commitment to cultural diplomacy and to the role that the arts and artists can play in promoting international understanding and building bridges between people and societies.

World Cup Kids Exchange Program June 2006: In conjunction with the 2006 World Cup in Germany, the Bureau of Educational and Cultural Affairs sponsored a delegation of 30 youth soccer players to participate in the World Cup Sports Initiative in Washington, DC, New York City, and Germany. The young athletes, boys and girls ages 13-18, represented 13 countries, including Afghanistan, Bahrain, Bolivia, China, Indonesia, Lebanon, Malaysia, Morocco, Nigeria, Pakistan, South Africa, Uganda and Uzbekistan. The initiative, a partnership with the U.S. Soccer family, reflected the theme of this year's World Cup in Germany, "a time to make friends," with an emphasis on building international understanding and respect between young people around the world.

International Fulbright Science Award for Outstanding Foreign Students in Science and Technology: The Bureau of

Educational and Cultural Affairs created new Fulbright Science Scholarships to be awarded in worldwide competition to attract the world's best science students to the United States for training.

EDUCATE: *We are expanding our most effective and eagerly sought programs, English language teaching, and* [sic; end of text in original]

U.S. University Presidents Summit: The U.S. University Presidents Summit on International Education engaged leaders of U.S. higher education in a renewed partnership to strengthen international educational [sic] and emphasize its importance to our national interests. Secretaries Rice and Spellings called this summit in January 2006 to initiate dialogue between the U.S. government and the private sector and to foster collaborative efforts to strengthen on [sic] the future of U.S. higher education in a global arena. A highlight of the summit was the renewed emphasis on the National Security Language Initiative which seeks to increase the numbers of Americans mastering critical needs languages. Also announced at the summit was an initiative which aims to bring students from six countries around the world to study at U.S. community colleges. Towards that end, Assistant Secretary of State Dina Habib Powell just recently announced the creation of a new Community College Exchange Initiative which will bring over 1000 Egyptian students to U.S. community colleges for one year of vocational and professional study in fields critical to Egypt's economic growth and development. Building on the goals of the summit, Secretary Spellings and Assistant Secretary Powell led a historic delegation of university presidents on a three-country Asian tour to promote the U.S. as a premier destination for higher education opportunities, highlight the special measures to expedite student visas, and deliver the message that the U.S. welcomes foreign students.

English ACCESS Microscholarship Program: Recognizing the relevance and reach of our English language teaching programs, we shifted FY2005 resources and additional support from Congress in FY 2006 to provide 9,000 high school students in 44 countries with significant Muslim populations up to two years of English language instruction in their own communities and schools. This gives young people a valuable tool to help them obtain better education and jobs, and opens the door to greater understanding about America.

EMPOWER: *We recognize that the voices of government officials are not always the most credible or powerful in countering the ideology of violent extremists so we are working to empower other mainstream voices in America and around the world.*

Citizen Dialogue Program: The Citizen Dialogue Program empowers American Muslim citizens to tell their personal stories to key overseas audiences, underscoring that Islam is a vibrant part of American society. The program sends small, diverse groups of American Muslims to share their experiences with students, young professionals, community and government leaders, religious scholars, and journalists in strategically important countries. They serve as credible messengers with their fellow Muslims overseas, many of whom are not aware of the strength and diversity of Muslim life in America. There have been two pilot trips in the Citizen Dialogue program during 2006. The first trip took three participants – Mehdi Alhassami, a recent George Washington University graduate, Dr. Yahya Basha, President of Basha Diagnostics,[136] and Dr. Talal Eid, an Iam and Muslim Chaplain – to Berlin, The Hague and Copenhagen. In addition to town halls in Muslim communities, they visited schools, mosques, and other community centers to meet with young people and community leaders. The participants, all of whom are fluent in Arabic, engaged with the local media through roundtables and television and radio interviews. The participants were Noorain Khan, a Rhodes scholar recipient who is fluent in Urdu, Kareema Daoud, a Georgetown University PhD candidate and State Department student-trainee, and Dr. Ikram Khan, a general surgeon from Las Vegas, NV. They met with students and professors at universities, visited a madrassa, engaged with community leaders, and were interviewed on popular television and radio programs.

American Muslim Communities: Initiated a comprehensive effort to link Muslim Americans into public diplomacy efforts,

---

[136] Editor's comment: Yahya Basha was President of the American Muslim Council in 2001, a group founded and run by Abdurahman Alamoudi. Alamoudi. Alamoudi also founded the Muslim chaplain program in the United States military, was convicted of terrorist-related crimes relating to an assassination plot against the crown prince of Saudi Arabia and is serving a federal prison sentence in the United States.

successfully planned and led overseas speaking tours for Muslim American citizens, and brought on new staff member focused specifically on women's empowerment, especially in the Islamic world. Undertook numerous outreach activities with Muslim American communities, working to amplify their voices and foster debate with Muslim communities worldwide against terror and violence.

Empowering Women Around the World: With the leadership of Secretary Rice, the Department is committee to creating greater political, economic, and educational opportunities to support women worldwide in their desire to live their lives with freedom, respect, and dignity. Under Secretary Hughes has attended a number of major women's conferences to highlight the important role women play in the world as agents of change, advocates for education and health, and arbiters of peace and reconciliation.

Business Women Leaders Summit: The Women Business Leaders Summit in Jordan is a public-private sector outreach to facilitate connections between American, Jordanian, and broader Middle Eastern business communities. Fifty women executives and business owners whose endeavors span all business sectors in Bahrain, Egypt, Jordan, Kuwait, Lebanon, Morocco, the Palestinian territories, Saudi Arabia, Syria, and the United Arab Emirates will join 50 highly successful women business leaders from the United States in late February 2007. The Arab businesswomen will travel to the United States in the spring of 2007 to visit their American partners' companies and exchange views on management styles and business skills. Participants in the Summit will share best practices and hear from some of the most accomplished business women.

"We are laying a foundation for public diplomacy to be successful today and over time."

- Under Secretary of State Karen P. Hughes

TRANSFORMATIONAL PUBLIC DIPLOMACY: *A New Architecture for Public Diplomacy at the State Department*

We are transforming the way we do business at the State Department and working to institutionalize reforms and make public diplomacy more effective.

Encouraging Speaking on the Record: Streamlined clearance process to eliminate requirement that ambassadors obtain pre-clearance from Washington before conducting media interviews; ambassadors and other senior USG officials are now encouraged to speak out using common sense and policy guidance provided from Washington.

Integrating Public Diplomacy into Policy: Elevated public diplomacy presence to the regional bureaus; a new Deputy Assistant Secretary for Public Diplomacy in each regional bureau dual-reports to the regional Assistant Secretary and the Under Secretary for Public Diplomacy; this provides what has been a missing link between Washington headquarters and field officers.

Strengthening Public Diplomacy Specialty: Revamping training, career development, assignments, and other issues to ensure that public diplomacy Foreign Service officers have meaningful assignments, adequate training, effective evaluation and promotion opportunities. Offering enhanced media training to ensure senior officials and public diplomacy officers engage with the media more aggressively.

Secretary's Global Repositioning Initiative: One-third of the Foreign Service positions being redeployed this year to critical regions are public diplomacy officers.

Revised Promotion Precepts: To include public diplomacy skills and work criteria for promotion for all in the Foreign Service.

New Evaluation Unit: Created a combined evaluation unit to help develop the "culture of evaluation" across the public diplomacy bureaus. Began evaluation of several key programs, including the American Corners program, the ACCESS English Language training program and others. As a result of initial evaluation data, have suspended publication of *Hi* magazine fending further review of how best to reach our target audience.

Public-Private Partnerships

We are actively engaging the private sector to harness the combined resources and talent to achieve our strategic objectives and to make America more welcoming to people from around the world.

Office of Public/Private Sector Partnership: The Office of Private Sector Outreach was created to develop innovative ways for the State Department to engage and work with U.S. businesses, universities, foundations, and the American people on our public diplomacy initiatives. The global presence, creativity and efficiency of these organizations make them invaluable resources and natural allies in our efforts to share America's story and ideals with each other. We are working to engage private sector leaders in dynamic initiatives to reach youth, women in business, entrepreneurs, teachers, journalists, and other key influencers around the world.

U.S.-Middle East Breast Cancer Awareness and Research Partnership: The U.S.-Middle East Partnership for Breast Cancer Awareness and Research unites critical American medical research institutions – such as the Susan G. Komen Foundation, MD Anderson Cancer Center, and Johns Hopkins Medicine – for the purpose of developing breast cancer awareness campaigns; increasing research, training and community-outreach efforts; and helping women in countries throughout the Middle East build the knowledge and confidence they need to be in charge of their own health. This partnership, in conjunction with the individual efforts that are being made by Middle Eastern countries to raise awareness and to provide better screening and treatment for breast cancer, represents the first collaborative effort to assist the region in eradicating the disease. The partnership was announced by First Lady Laura Bush at the Susan G. Komen Foundation's Mission Conference on Monday, June 12, 2006. In November 2006, Under Secretary Karen Hughes traveled to the United Arab Emirates to participate in medical roundtables and training workshops on awareness-building and community outreach. Efforts are already underway to expand the partnership to Saudi Arabia, Jordon [sic] and Morocco next year in order to further the goal of saving the lives of Arab women by sharing expertise and lessons learned, working with the women of the region and drawing on their own unique experiences and cultural perspectives to help defeat breast cancer.

South Asia Earthquake Relief Effort: In October last year, a devastating earthquake rocked the mountainous region of South Asia and more than 74,000 people were killed. The needs for the victims of this tragedy were so great that President George W. Bush asked five private sector leaders to launch a nationwide effort to encourage private and corporate donations: Jeff Immelt, Chairman and CEO, General Electric; Jim Kelly, former Chairman and CEO, United Parcel Service; Hank McKinnell Jr., Chairman and CEO, Pfizer; Anne Mulcahy, Chairman and CEO, Xerox; and Sanford Weill,

Chairman, Citigroup. This public-private partnership has raised more than $120 million in cash and in-kind contributions for earthquake relief and reconstruction.

Lebanon Partnership and The U.S.-Lebanon Fund: In response to the devastation from the recent conflict between Hezbollah and Israel, President Bush announced a delegation of American business leaders who have joined forces to help rebuild Lebanon: Cisco President and CEO John Chambers, Dr. Craig Barrett, chairman, Intel Corporation; Yousif Ghafari, chairman, GHAFARI, Inc.; and Dr. Ray Irani, Chairman, CEO, and President of Occidental Petroleum Corporation. With a spirit of compassion and partnership, this group announced a new economic and development fundraising effort to provide assistance to the people of Lebanon as they rebuild their country. Cisco President and CEO John Chambers who launched the initiative and other business representatives at the White House on Monday morning (9/25) [sic]. Chambers is joined in this effort by Dr. Craig Barrett, chairman, Intel Corporation, Yousif Ghafari, chairman, GHAFARI, Inc.; and Dr. Ray Irani, Chairman, CEO, and President of Occidental Petroleum Corporation [sic]. Assistant Secretary of State Dina Powell led the delegation's most recent visit to Lebanon on September 21-24, 2006.

Rice-Chertoff Initiative "Secure Borders, Open Doors": Part of the Rice-Chertoff Initiative announced in early 2006 is the "Model Points of Entry" Program. We are looking at two of our busiest international airports – Dulles in Washington and Inter-Continental in Houston – to find ways to make them more welcoming to visitors from other countries. We're enlisting America's private sector – such as Disney, Hilton and others – to draw upon their expertise in many things including world-class hospitality practices and line management and apply these practices to our international points of entry for the benefit and comfort of international citizens and guests. For example, the Houston airport has airport staff that speak 30 languages and greet international visitors when they arrive to help them through the customs process. We plan to develop and share the best practices from these airports with the rest of our international airports around the country.

De-legitimizing Terror

We must come together as a global community to say that no cause, no complaint, no grievance – no matter how legitimate – can ever justify the wanton killing of innocent life.

Convened High-level Inter-agency Group of Policy and Communications Professionals: To work on messages and plans to de-legitimize violent extremism and undermine ideological support for terrorists. Working sub-groups are looking at different aspects of the ideological struggle, including: terrorists use of the Internet, television programming, publishing, and alternative technologies. These working groups will make recommendations to the high-level group for incorporation into an inter-agency plan to undermine ideological support for terrorism.

Initiated a Strategic Focus on Pilot Countries: To more intensely concentrate our efforts and resources through interagency-coordinated and country-specific strategic plans that take advantage of all elements of national power. Through this effort we are developing strategic and country-specific public diplomacy plans for each pilot country which will facilitate greater lessons learned and best practices to be applied more broadly by our public diplomacy.

Developing Core Themes: To provide all U.S. Government officials with a uniform and effective message to counter the extremists' narrative.

Enhanced Technology Initiatives

We are expanding our use of communications technologies so that our message can compete in today's highly competitive information environment.

Public Affairs and International Information Programs Internet Outreach: Added pod casts [sic], web chats, and other web-based programs to share U.S. foreign policy messages with audiences around the world. Additional capacity to broadcast events, such as the President's State of the Union address, live in more languages worldwide.

Democracy Dialogues: Launched a new inter-active, web-based discussion of the principles of democracy. Every two months, a different theme will be featured.

"Partnership for a Better Life:" Launched a new website to provide visual gateway to stories of individuals and institutions benefiting from U.S. foreign aid, building on President Bush's State of the Union message that: "For people everywhere, America is a partner for a better life." Urging our ambassadors to highlight ways the American government and people are improving the lives of people in their host countries.

An urgent appeal
Eleven former VOA Directors (2007)[137]

We former directors of the Voice of America urgently appeal for a reversal by Congress of planned reductions in VOA that could silence the nation's largest publicly-funded overseas broadcast network in much of the world. Taken together, the cuts would seriously jeopardize our national security and public diplomacy. Further, they would deprive millions of people of access to a fully free and open media, a core value of what our nation is all about.

The Bush administration has proposed to eliminate VOA English in every continent except Africa, abolish services in Cantonese, Croatian, Georgian, Greek, Thai and Uzbek, cease radio broadcasts in Russian, Ukrainian, Serbian, Albanian, Bosnian, Macedonian, and Hindi (to India), and significantly scale back programming in Tibetan and Portuguese to Africa.

In view of:

- decisions by China, Russia, Iran, France and Al Jazeera TV to broadcast around the clock or increase airtime in our own language, English, spoken or understood by at least 1.6 billion people worldwide;
- a 23 percent increase in Russia's military budget as Vladimir Putin muzzles his own as well as foreign news and information outlets;
- new media restrictions and arrests or jailing of journalists in China, Tibet and Uzbekistan along with just declared martial law and an upsurge of extremist Muslim activity in Thailand;
- the volatile situation in the Balkans as Kosovo moves toward independence, and

---

[137] Courtesy of the USIA Alumni Association.

• VOA's proven cost effectiveness (more than 115 million listeners and viewers a week)

We urgently appeal for an increase of the proposed $178 million VOA budget to $204 million for fiscal year 2008 beginning October 1. This would be mandated to cover programming and transmission of services listed above, 3.9 percent of the entire U.S overseas broadcasting budget. This is a tiny but essential investment. Surveys show anti-American opinion abroad to be at an all-time high. At this critical moment in the post 9/11 era, the United States simply cannot, for its own long term strategic safety and security, unilaterally disarm in the global contest of ideas.

Mary G. F. Bitterman, Robert E. Button, Richard W. Carlson, Geoffrey Cowan, John Hughes, David Jackson, Henry Loomis, E. Eugene Pell, Robert Reilly, R. Peter Straus, Sanford J. Ungar

2007 Audit: Still no visible strategy
Government Accountability Office (2007)[138]

In its 2007 audit, the GAO found that even with reported improvements since 2005, the U.S. government still had no discernable public diplomacy strategy. The GAO used understated language to issue a scathing indictment.

"Beginning in 2003, we reported that the government lacked an interagency communications strategy. Four years later, a strategy still has not been released," according to the report, and the State Department had only "begun to consider techniques for communicating with broader foreign audiences."

Key problems identified in our prior reports include a general lack of strategic planning, inadequate coordination among agency efforts,

---

[138] Jess T. Ford, Director, International Affairs and Trade, Government Accountability Office, "U.S. Public Diplomacy: Strategic Planning Efforts Have Improved, But Agencies Face Significant Implementation Challenges," Testimony before the Subcommittee on International Organizations, Human Rights and Oversight, House Committee on Foreign Affairs, April 26, 2007. GAO Report GAO-07-795T. Tables, exhibits, footnotes and other materials are not included in this reprint. The editor has broken up large paragraphs in the original GAO text for ease in reading.

and problems with measuring performance and results. Beginning in 2003, we reported that the government lacked an interagency communications strategy. Four years later, a strategy still has not been released, although State officials told us that this will happen soon. Last month [March 2007], we also reported on challenges in marking and publicizing U.S. foreign assistance that may result in missed opportunities to increase public awareness of U.S. foreign aid activities. Accordingly, we recommended that State develop strategies and establish interagency agreements to better coordinate and assess the impact of U.S. marking and publicity programs.

We also reported that State did not have a strategy to integrate its diverse public diplomacy activities. State began to address this shortcoming in 2005 when the current Under Secretary for Public Diplomacy and Public Affairs developed a strategic framework to focus State's efforts on three priority goals: offer foreign publics a vision of hope and opportunity rooted in basic U.S. values, isolate and marginalize violent extremists, and nurture common interests and values.

However, State has not issued guidance on how its assorted public diplomacy activities will be coordinated to achieve these goals. In addition, posts' public diplomacy efforts generally lack important strategic communication elements found in the private sector, which GAO recommended that State adopt as a means to better communicate with target audiences. Key steps in this approach include defining core messages, identifying target audiences, developing detailed communication strategies and tactics, and using research and evaluation to inform and re-direct efforts as needed.

Finally, we and others have recommended that State develop more rigorous measures of effectiveness to better document the impact of its public diplomacy efforts. State has taken several steps towards this goal, including establishing a centralized office to better coordinate and direct the collection of performance data.

Regarding the BBG, we have noted that the Board launched a new strategic approach in 2001 that included a focus on supporting the U.S. war on terror. The BBG made this support tangible through several key initiatives, including the creation of Radio Sawa in 2002 and the Alhurra TV network in 2004, which are run by the Middle East Broadcasting Networks (MBN). While these are noteworthy attempts to help turn the tide of negative opinion in the Muslim world toward the United States, our August 2006 report on MBN recommended that several steps be taken to correct methodological concerns which could impact the accuracy of its audience research data. MBN continues to evaluate possible solutions to these concerns.

We also have reported that State and the BBG face multiple challenges in managing and implementing their public diplomacy programs. Several embassy officials indicated that insufficient numbers of staff and the lack of staff time for public diplomacy activities hinder outreach efforts.

To help address these concerns, the Secretary of State has repositioned some staff to posts with the greatest perceived shortages; however, significant shortfalls remain. In May 2006, we reported that approximately 15 percent of State's worldwide public diplomacy positions were vacant. Updated information provided by State shows that this problem has worsened and approximately 22 percent of such positions are now vacant. We reported that the State Department continues to experience significant shortfalls in foreign language proficiency in countries around the world. In our May 2006 report, we noted that this problem is particularly acute in the Muslim world, where 30 percent of language-designated public diplomacy positions are filled by officers without the level of language proficiency required for their positions, thus hampering their ability to engage with foreign publics.

State has taken steps to address language deficiencies by bolstering its language training activities. In addition, security concerns have forced embassies to close publicly accessible facilities and curtail certain public outreach efforts, sending the unintended message that the United States is unapproachable. The department has attempted to compensate for the lack of public presence in high threat posts through a variety of means, including the use of small-scale external facilities. The BBG faces the primary challenge of managing a disparate collection of multiple discrete broadcast entities. In addition, MBN faces several managerial challenges involving program review and evaluation, editorial oversight, internal control issues, and staff training.

Strategic Planning, Coordination, and Performance Measurement Remain Areas of Concern

Over the past 4 years, we have identified and made recommendations to State and the BBG on a number of issues related to a general lack of strategic planning, inadequate coordination of agency efforts, and problems with measuring performance and results.

Among other things, we have recommended that (1) communication strategies be developed to coordinate and focus the efforts of key government agencies and the private sector, (2) the State Department develop a strategic plan to integrate its diverse efforts, (3) posts adopt strategic communication best practices, and (4) meaningful performance goals and indicators be established by both State and the BBG.

Currently, the U.S. government lacks an interagency public diplomacy strategy; however, such a plan has been drafted and will be released shortly. While the department has articulated a strategic framework to direct its efforts, comprehensive guidance on how to implement this strategic framework has not yet been developed. In addition, posts generally do not pursue a campaign-style approach to communications that incorporates best practices endorsed by GAO and others. State has begun to take credible steps towards instituting more systematic performance measurement practices, consistent with recommendations GAO and others have made. Finally, although the BBG has added audience size as a key performance measure within its strategic plan, our latest review of MBN's operations call into question the potential value of this measure due to various methodological concerns.

Government Lacks an Interagency Public Diplomacy Strategy

In 2003, we reported that the United States lacked a governmentwide, interagency public diplomacy strategy, defining the messages and means for communication efforts abroad. We reported since then that the administration has made a number of unsuccessful attempts to develop such a strategy. The lack of such a strategy complicates the task of conveying consistent messages and therefore increases the risk of making damaging communication mistakes. State officials have said that it also diminishes the efficiency and effectiveness of governmentwide public diplomacy efforts, while several reports have concluded that a strategy is needed to synchronize agencies' target audience assessments, messages, and capabilities.

On April 8, 2006, the President established a new Policy Coordination Committee on Public Diplomacy and Strategic Communications. This committee, led by the Under Secretary for

Public Diplomacy and Public Affairs, intends to better coordinate interagency activities, including the development of an interagency public diplomacy strategy. We have been told this strategy is still under development and will be issued soon.

The U.S. government also lacks a governmentwide strategy and meaningful methods to ensure that recipients of U.S. foreign assistance are consistently aware that the aid comes from the United States. In March 2007, we reported that most agencies involved in foreign assistance activities had established some marking and publicity requirements in their policies, regulations, and guidelines, and used various methods to mark and publicize their activities.

However, we identified some challenges to marking and publicizing U.S. foreign assistance, including the lack of a strategy for assessing the impact of marking and publicity efforts on public awareness and the lack of governmentwide guidance for marking and publicizing U.S. foreign aid. To better ensure that recipients of U.S. foreign assistance are aware that the aid is provided by the United States and its taxpayers, we recommended that State, in consultation with other U.S. government agencies, (1) develop a strategy to better assess the impact of marking and publicity programs on public awareness and (2) establish interagency agreements for marking and publicizing all U.S. foreign assistance. State indicated that the interagency public diplomacy strategy will address assessment of marking and publicity programs and will include governmentwide marking and publicity guidance.

Private Sector Engagement Strategy Not Yet Developed

In 2005, we noted that State's efforts to engage the private sector in pursuit of common public diplomacy objectives had met with mixed success and recommended that the Secretary develop a strategy to guide these efforts. Since then, State has established an Office of Private Sector Outreach, is partnering with individuals and the private sector on various projects, and hosted a Private Sector Summit on Public Diplomacy in January 2007. However, State has not yet developed a comprehensive strategy to guide the Department's efforts to engage the private sector.

State Has Established a Public Diplomacy Strategic Framework but Lacks Implementing Guidance

In 2005, the Under Secretary established a strategic framework for U.S. public diplomacy efforts, which includes three priority goals: (1) offer foreign publics a vision of hope and opportunity rooted in the U.S.'s most basic values; (2) isolate and marginalize extremists; and (3) promote understanding regarding shared values and common interests between Americans and peoples of different countries, cultures, and faiths. The Under Secretary noted that she intends to achieve these goals using five tactics – engagement, exchanges, education, empowerment, and evaluation – and by using various public diplomacy programs and other means, including coordinating outreach efforts with the private sector. This framework partially responds to our 2003 recommendation that State should develop and disseminate a strategy to integrate its public diplomacy efforts and direct them toward achieving common objectives. State has not yet developed written guidance that provides details on how these five tactics will be used to implement the Under Secretary's priority goals. However, it should be noted that the Under Secretary has issued limited guidance regarding the goal of countering extremism to 18 posts selected to participate in a pilot initiative focusing on this objective.

Posts Lack a Campaign-Style Approach to Communications

We have recommended that State, where appropriate, adopt strategic communication best practices (which we refer to as the "campaign-style approach") and develop country-specific communication plans that incorporate the key steps embodied in this approach. As shown in figure 2 [deleted], these steps include defining the core message, identifying and segmenting target audiences, developing detailed communication strategies and tactics, and using research and evaluation to inform and re-direct efforts as needed. As noted in our May 2006 report, our review of public diplomacy operations in Nigeria, Pakistan, and Egypt in 2006 found that this approach and corresponding communication plans were absent. Rather, post public diplomacy efforts constituted an ad hoc collection of activities designed to support such broad goals as promoting mutual understanding.

In a recent development, 18 posts participating in the department's pilot countries initiative have developed country-level plans focusing on the countering extremism goal. These plans were developed on the basis of a template issued by the Under Secretary that requires each post to provide a list of supporting objectives, a description of the media environment, identification of key target audiences, and a list of supporting programs and activities. We reviewed most of the plans submitted in response to this guidance. Although useful as a high-level planning exercise, these plans do not adhere to the campaign-style approach, which requires a level of rigor and detail that normally exceeds the three-to four-page plans produced by posts in pilot countries. The plans omit basic elements, such as specific core messages and themes or any substantive evidence that proposed communication programs were driven by detailed audience research – one of the key principles embodied in the campaign-style approach. In the absence of such research, programs may lack important information about appropriate target audiences and credible messages and messengers.

State Is Making a Concerted Effort to Better Measure Program Performance and Impact

Based on prior reports by GAO and others, the department has begun to institute a more concerted effort to measure the impact of its programs and activities. The department created (1) the Office of Policy, Planning, and Resources within the office of the Under Secretary; (2) the Public Diplomacy Evaluation Council to share best practices; and (3) a unified Public Diplomacy Evaluation Office. The Department established an expanded evaluation schedule that is designed to cover all major public diplomacy programs. The department also has called on program managers to analyze and define their key inputs, activities, outputs, outcomes, and impact to help identify meaningful performance goals and indicators. Finally, the department recently launched a pilot public diplomacy performance measurement data collection project that is designed to collect, document, and quantify reliable annual and long-term outcome performance measures to support government reporting requirements.

BBG Has Strategy for International Broadcasting, but Audience Data May be Misleading

In 2001, the BBG introduced a market-based approach to international broadcasting that sought to "marry the mission to the market." This approach was designed to generate large listening audiences in priority markets that the BBG believes it must reach to effectively meet its mission. Implementing this strategy has focused on markets relevant to the war on terrorism, in particular in the Middle East through such key initiatives as Radio Sawa and the Alhurra TV network. The Board's vision is to create a flexible, multimedia, research-driven U.S. international broadcasting system.

We found that the BBG's strategic plan to implement its new approach did not include a single goal or related program objective designed to gauge progress toward increasing audience size, even though its strategy focuses on the need to reach large audiences in priority markets. The BBG subsequently created a single strategic goal to focus on the key objective of maximizing impact in priority areas of interest to the United States and made audience size a key performance measure.

However, in our August 2006 review of the Middle East Broadcasting Networks, we found that methodological concerns call into question the potential accuracy of this key performance measure with regard to Radio Sawa's listening rates and Alhurra's viewing rates. Specifically, we found that weaknesses in the BBG's audience surveys create uncertainty over whether some of Radio Sawa's or Alhurra's performance targets for audience size have been met. We recommended that the BBG improve its audience research methods, including identifying significant methodological limitations. The BBG accepted our recommendation and has informed us that it is currently considering how it will do so.

A Number of Internal and External Challenges Hamper U.S. Public Diplomacy Activities

Public diplomacy efforts in the field face several other challenges. Beginning with our September 2003 report on State's public diplomacy efforts, post officials have consistently cited several key challenges, including a general lack of staff, insufficient administrative support, and inadequate language training. Furthermore, public diplomacy officers struggle to balance security with public access and outreach to local populations. Finally, the BBG's disparate organizational structure has been viewed as a key management challenge that significantly complicates its efforts to focus and direct U.S. international broadcasting efforts.

Insufficient Staff and Lack of Staff Time Hinders Public Diplomacy Activities

Although several recent reports on public diplomacy have recommended an increase in U.S. public diplomacy program spending, several embassy officials stated that, with current staffing levels, they do not have the capacity to effectively utilize increased funds. According to State, the Department had 887 established public diplomacy positions (overseas and domestic) as of March 31, 2007, but 199, or roughly 22 percent, were vacant. Compounding this challenge is the loss of public diplomacy officers to temporary duty in Iraq, which, according to one State official, has drawn down field officers even further. Staffing shortages may also limit the amount of training public diplomacy officers receive. State is repositioning several public diplomacy officers as part of its transformational diplomacy initiative. However, this effort represents shifting existing public diplomacy officers and does not increase the overall number of officers, which we have noted were generally the same in fiscal years 2004 and 2006.

In addition, public diplomacy officers at posts are burdened with administrative tasks, and thus have less time to conduct public diplomacy outreach activities than they did previously. One senior State official said that administrative duties, such as budget, personnel, and internal reporting, compete with officers' public diplomacy responsibilities. Another official in Egypt stated that she rarely had enough time to strategize, plan, or evaluate her programs.

These statements echo comments we heard during overseas fieldwork and in a survey for our 2003 report. In that survey, officers stated that, although they manage to attend public outreach and other functions within their host country capitals, it was particularly difficult to find time to travel outside the capitals to interact with other communities. This challenge is compounded at posts with short tours of duty, including many tours in the Muslim world, as officials stated that it is difficult to establish the type of close working relationships essential to effective public diplomacy work when they are in country for only a short time. In our May

2006 report, we reported that the average length of tour at posts in the Muslim world is about 22 percent shorter than tour lengths elsewhere. Noting the prevalence of 1-year tours in the Muslim world, a senior official at State said that public affairs officers who have shorter tours tend to produce less effective work than officers with longer tours.

To address these challenges, we recommended in 2003 that the Secretary of State designate more administrative positions to overseas public affairs sections to reduce the administrative burden. Officials at State said that the Management bureau is currently considering options for reducing the administrative burden on posts, including the development of centralized administrative capabilities offshore.

Language Deficiencies Continue, Especially in the Muslim World

In August 2006, GAO reported that the State Department continued to experience significant foreign language proficiency shortfalls in countries around the world. Our May 2006 report noted this problem was particularly acute at posts in the Muslim world where Arabic – classified as a "superhard" language by State – predominates. In countries with significant Muslim populations, we reported that 30 percent of language-designated public diplomacy positions were filled by officers without the requisite proficiency in those languages, compared with 24 percent elsewhere. In Arabic language posts, about 36 percent of language-designated public diplomacy positions were filled by staff unable to speak Arabic at the designated level. In addition, State officials said that there are even fewer officers who are willing or able to speak on television or engage in public debate in Arabic. The information officer in Cairo stated that his office does not have enough Arabic speakers to engage the Egyptian media effectively. . . .

A strategy emerges
U.S. Department of State (2007)[139]

After the 2007 GAO report was released, the Office of the Under Secretary for Public Diplomacy and Public Affairs posted a long-awaited national strategy on the State Department's intranet.

The unclassified document, titled "U.S. National Strategy for Public Diplomacy and Strategic Communication," was not intended for public release at the time. The editor of this Reader was the first to publish the strategy, in his politicalwarfare.org blog.

The strategy is not a product for external propaganda purposes, but a roadmap reflective of official wartime thinking in the State Department and Bush Administration. The full text of the strategy is reprinted on the following pages.

"We will lead the cause of freedom, justice, and hope, because both our values and our interests demand it. We believe in the timeless truth: To whom much is given, much is required. We also know that nations with free, healthy, prosperous people will be sources of stability, not breeding grounds for extremists and hate and terror. By making the world more hopeful, we make the world more peaceful – and by helping others, the American people must understand we help ourselves."

President Bush at the White House Summit on Malaria, December 14, 2006

Mission and Priorities

The strength, success and security of the United States of America rest on our commitment to certain fundamental values and principles. These values gave birth to our nation, and govern our actions in the world. We believe all individuals, men and women, are equal and entitled to basic human rights, including freedom of speech, worship and political participation. While the forms of government will vary, we believe all people deserve to live in just societies that protect individual and common rights, fight corruption and are governed by the rule of law. Across the world, America seeks to work with other governments and nations in a spirit of

---

[139] "U.S. National Strategy for Public Diplomacy and Strategic Communication," Strategic Communication and Public Diplomacy Policy Coordinating Committee, U.S. Department of State, May 31, 2007.

partnership that supports human dignity and fosters peace and progress.

The National Security Strategy of the United States establishes eight national security objectives:

- To champion human dignity;
- To strengthen alliances against terrorism;
- To defuse regional conflicts;
- To prevent threats from weapons of mass destruction;
- To expand the circle of development;
- To cooperate with other centers of global power; and
- To transform America's national security institutions to meet the challenges and opportunities of the twenty-first century.

Public diplomacy and strategic communication should always strive to support our nation's fundamental values and national security objectives.   All communication and public diplomacy activities should:

- Underscore our commitment to freedom, human rights and the dignity and equality of every human being;
- Reach out to those who share our ideals;
- Support those who struggle for freedom and democracy; and
- Counter those who espouse ideologies of hate and oppression.

STRATEGIC OBJECTIVES

The United States Government seeks to partner with nations and peoples across the world in ways that result in a better life for all of the world's citizens.   As a multicultural nation founded by immigrants, America respects people of different cultures, backgrounds and faiths.   We seek to be a partner for progress, prosperity and peace around the world.

We have established three strategic objectives to govern America's public diplomacy and strategic communication with foreign audiences:

I. America must offer a positive vision of hope and opportunity that is rooted in our most basic values.

These values include our deep belief in freedom, and the dignity and equality of every person. We believe all people deserve to live in just societies that are governed by the rule of law and free from corruption or intimidation. We believe people should be able to speak their minds, protest peacefully, worship freely and participate in choosing their government. We want all people, boys and girls, to be educated, because we know education expands opportunity and we believe those who are educated are more likely to be responsible citizens, tolerant and respectful of each other's differences. We want to expand the circle of prosperity so that people throughout the world can earn a living and provide for their families. America has long been a beacon of hope and opportunity for people across the world and we must continue to be that beacon of hope for a better life.

II. With our partners, we seek to isolate and marginalize violent extremists who threaten the freedom and peace sought by civilized people of every nation, culture and faith.

We can achieve this goal by:

- Promoting democratization and good governance as a path to a positive future, in secure and pluralistic societies;
- Actively engaging Muslim communities and amplifying mainstream Muslim voices;
- Isolating and discrediting terrorist leaders, facilitators, and organizations;
- De-legitimizing terror as an acceptable tactic to achieve political ends; and
- Demonstrating that the West is open to all religions and is not in conflict with any faith.

III. America must work to nurture common interests and values between Americans and peoples of different countries, cultures and faiths across the world.

Far more unites us as human beings than divides us. Especially at a time of war and common threats, America must actively nurture common interests and values. We have shared interests in expanding economic opportunity, promoting peaceful resolution of conflicts, enhancing scientific collaboration, fighting diseases that respect no border, and protecting our common environment. A cornerstone of American policy and public diplomacy must be to identify, highlight and nurture common interests and values.

STRATEGIC AUDIENCES

Successful public diplomacy and strategic communication must address both mass audiences and specific target audiences. Certain media such as television, radio and the internet, as well as press and public affairs operations, reach a broad public. But public diplomacy efforts are also directed at narrower, more discrete groups, especially those that because of their expertise, stature, or leadership roles influence the decisions and opinions of others. Opinion leaders in foreign societies can be effective partners in advancing our broader public diplomacy goals. We need to tailor our public diplomacy and communication programs to specific audiences, using the most appropriate and effective media available. Those specific audiences include:

I. Key Influencers

"Key Influencers" are those whose views can have a ripple effect throughout society. They include clerics, educators, journalists, women leaders, business and labor leaders, political leaders, scientists and military personnel. Our public diplomacy programs and efforts should engage these key influencers, and especially encourage and empower them to speak out against the forces of violent extremism and in favor of peaceful resolution of disputes, tolerance and freedom.

II. Vulnerable Populations

Our public diplomacy and strategic communication must take into account demographic characteristics of different societies, and focus especially on those groups most vulnerable to extremist ideology:

Youth – A top public diplomacy priority should be reaching out to young people – the voters, entrepreneurs, and leaders of tomorrow. Many of our traditional public diplomacy programs, however, have not directly reached this demographic group, which makes up more than 50% of populations in the Middle East and elsewhere. We need to employ education and exchange programs as well as Internet and other forms of communication to reach this audience.

Women and Girls – Numerous studies have shown that when women are educated and empowered, they become the most effective agents of social change, progress and prosperity. Improving the educational and economic opportunities of women can have a profound impact on overall social stability, economic development and human rights. Educating women in developing countries helps improve overall family health, reduce illiteracy and stabilize communities. Of the 70 million people who are illiterate in the broader Middle East, more than two-thirds are women. Promoting education for women and girls in these societies is critical to their long-term success and to the advancement of liberty and opportunity.

Minorities – We need to reach out to marginalized groups such as indigenous populations, as well as racial and religious minorities who often do not have equal educational or economic opportunities. America also has great expertise and experience in helping develop opportunities for persons with disabilities; this should be shared more widely with countries across the world.

III. Mass Audiences

With increasing numbers of people across the world getting their news and information primarily from television, America must expand its presence on international broadcasts. USG broadcasting entities of the Broadcasting Board of Governors provide direct channels to mass audiences worldwide through television, radio and VOA's web site. We are rapidly developing improved capabilities to employ the power of Internet and other new technologies. USG officials in Washington and abroad are engaging more actively than ever with foreign media, including television and radio as well as print. Outreach through foreign media should be considered a basic work requirement for USG officials to the greatest extent possible. With mass audiences worldwide now receiving much of their news via television, all USG officials should make appearances on television news and information shows a special priority.

PUBLIC DIPLOMACY PRIORITIES

To achieve our mission, we have established the following priorities for public diplomacy programs and activities:

Expand education and exchange programs

The U.S. government should continue its recent trend of increasing funding for critical exchange programs, perhaps the single most effective public diplomacy tool of the last fifty years. Exchange programs should emphasize students (future leaders of society) and key influencers in society (clerics, women, journalists, business, scientists, government, military and political leaders) whose exchange experience can impact wider segments of society. The impact of exchanges should also be amplified through use of technology and media; both USG and private broadcasting should be invited and encouraged to produce documentaries and news coverage of exchange programs.

English language teaching is a priority program and should be expanded. Learning English provides a skill that helps young people improve their lives and job prospects, and helps counter extremism by opening a window to a wider world of knowledge. English language programs are among the most effective ways to reach young people before they are old enough to participate in exchange programs, and are particularly effective at expanding the horizons of young people from disadvantaged neighborhoods.

Agencies should also actively partner with the private sector to increase exchange and education opportunities through internships, mentoring and education programs in countries where they operate. Finally, agencies and embassies should partner with those who have a mutual interest in encouraging travel to the United States including the higher education community, travel and tourism industry, and business, scientific and technology communities.

Modernize communications

In an era when mass media, especially television, reaches mass audiences in an unprecedented way, United States government officials must significantly expand their presence and appearances on foreign media. United States Ambassadors should be the "voice" of America as well as its official representative and should make regular appearances on major foreign media, explaining U.S. policies, values and views.   The new State Department regional "hub" operations, designed to provide language trained spokesmen and more aggressive booking of American officials on regional media, should be continued and expanded beyond current locations in London, Brussels and Dubai.   High ranking officials, subject experts and employees with foreign language capabilities should be identified, encouraged and rewarded for making appearances on international media.   Interviews and appearances on foreign media should be a priority, not an afterthought, as part of international travel by high ranking government officials.   All agencies and embassies must also increase use of new technologies, including creative use of the internet, web chats, blogs and video story-telling opportunities on the Internet to highlight American policies and programs. The United States government should continue to expand the National Security Language Initiative to encourage more young Americans to learn critical foreign languages.

Promote the "diplomacy of deeds"

America's deeds – providing health care, education, economic opportunity, food and shelter, training for political participation, help after disasters – can communicate our values and beliefs far more effectively than all of our words.   Yet too few people (including those in our own country) know the tremendous impact Americans are making on lives around the world every day, through government programs, private and charitable programs, and the contributions of individual Americans.   These programs should be continued and expanded, especially in the areas people across the world care most about: health, education and economic opportunity. Health and science diplomacy (HIV/AIDS, malaria, avian influenza, military clinics, hospital ships, cancer detection and awareness, natural disaster prevention and scientific discoveries) have particular resonance and should be a priority for all embassies and agencies with health and science programs.   All agencies and embassies should make a major commitment to more aggressively tell the story of how these programs are helping people improve their lives and opportunities. Partnerships with the private sector, foundations, and religious and charitable organizations should also be encouraged through events like the White House Summit on Malaria to increase coordination and expand effectiveness and visibility.   America should also demonstrate respect for local culture, art and history across the world through expanded arts and cultural partnerships and support for the Ambassador's Fund for Cultural Preservation.

INTERAGENCY COORDINATION

The Policy Coordinating Committee (PCC) on Public Diplomacy and Strategic Communication led by the Under Secretary for Public Diplomacy and Public Affairs is the overall mechanism by which we coordinate our public diplomacy across the interagency community. To help accomplish our mission, the PCC will establish the following structures:

I. Counterterrorism Communications Center headquartered at the Department of State, with the core mission of developing messages and strategies to discredit terrorists and their ideology.

II. Interagency Crisis Communication Team

The National Security Council will initiate an interagency conference call immediately upon major breaking news that might have an impact on our efforts against violent extremism to coordinate message points. Call participants should include, at a minimum:

- White House Communications Office
- NSC Senior Communications Director/Spokesman
- White House Press Secretary
- State Department Public Diplomacy and Public Affairs
- Defense Department Public Affairs

Following the response decision, a conference call will be conducted with public affairs and communication representatives from relevant agencies to refine and coordinate unified messaging. The resulting message from the Counterterrorism Communications Center and appropriate official statements will be relayed to Cabinet secretaries, ambassadors and the military chain of command through the Rapid Response Unit at the State Department.

III. Regular Monitoring of Implementation

The Public Diplomacy and Strategic Communication PCC will meet regularly to review progress in implementing this communication strategy.

INITIAL COMMUNICATION ACTIVITIES

All segments of the USG have a role in public diplomacy and global communication. To ensure that we maximize the overall effectiveness of the USG to communicate around the world, each agency and embassy should:

I. Develop an agency-specific plan to implement the public diplomacy/strategic communication objectives in this document.

Agency plans should:

- Identify two or three programs/policies which the agency will highlight to support the overall public diplomacy/strategic communication goals
- Identify target audiences
- Assign responsibility and outline specific plans for communicating key programs and policies to the target audience through speeches, foreign travel, media interviews, etc.
- Identify:
  - o NGO and private sector partners with whom the agency works
  - o Subject matter experts who can explain and advocate U.S. policy
  - o Workers who speak foreign languages and could translate/participate in interviews
- Recommend envoys to advance public diplomacy efforts
- Outline current activities and programs that can be linked to support global public diplomacy
- Develop criteria to evaluate effectiveness

II. Basic Information Sharing

The State Department has created a new "Public Diplomacy Briefing Book" that is available via internal internet to update all USG officials on regional and country-specific policies, official statements and key messages. The briefing book should be a part of briefing and preparation for all USG officials prior to foreign travel so our messages are clear and consistent. All agencies should also assist in collecting and transmitting timely material to be featured on appropriate websites:

- Compelling stories (including pictures and videotape if possible) of how American programs are impacting people's lives. Interviews of those receiving health care, collaborating on scientific research and innovation, or participating in English language and exchange programs should be provided and featured on the State Department's "Partnership for a Better Life" website.
- A database of digital images and videos should be developed in conjunction with search engine technology.
- Material should include quotes in print and on video that represent mainstream Muslim views and rejection of terrorists/extremism.
- Best practices should be identified and shared through agency websites.

Audience Analysis: Understanding foreign public opinion is vital to successful communication. The USG should create a central repository of information and analysis of public opinion in different countries so we can better understand how citizens of other countries view us and what values and interests we have in common. Such information is currently collected by a number of different agencies (BBG, State Department INR, DOD, USAID, some individual embassies) as well as private sector organizations such as Gallup and PEW. Accurate, up-to-date information should be housed in one central location for interagency submissions and access. Information from this central repository should be available to all senior government communicators, and to the new Counterterrorism Communications Center, to help develop and monitor the effectiveness of messages.

III. Proactive Media Booking

The State Department's new regional media hubs in London, Brussels and Dubai are equipped to support messaging and booking of senior USG officials abroad to project American viewpoints.

NEEDED RESOURCES

Funding

The U.S. is engaged in an international struggle of ideas and ideologies, which requires a more extensive, sophisticated use of communications and public diplomacy programs to gain support for U.S. policies abroad. To effectively wage this struggle, public diplomacy must be treated – along with defense, homeland security and intelligence – as a national security priority in terms of resources. We must continue to significantly increase funding for all public diplomacy and strategic communication programs, but, specifically, we need urgent funding for priority programs such as people-to-people exchanges, English language summer and after-school programs for young people in strategic areas, science outreach projects, and new media outreach to keep up with evolving audiences and technology. Increased support for Public Diplomacy programming is vitally important to confront today's global challenges and the threat that terrorism poses to free peoples everywhere.

Congressional approval of FY2007 supplemental funding of $50 million for public diplomacy is an important first step towards providing the resources required for this effort. This supplemental funding will support priority programs in key countries in the effort to counter violent extremism, including a major new summer program offering English language teaching for young people ages 8-14 and increased digital outreach in critical languages.

CONCLUSION

Public diplomacy is, at its core, about making America's diplomacy public and communicating America's views, values and policies in effective ways to audiences across the world. Public diplomacy promotes linkages between the American people and the rest of the world by reminding diverse populations of our common interests and values. Some of America's most effective public diplomacy is communicated not through words but through our deeds, as we invest in people through education, health care and the opportunity for greater economic and political participation. Public diplomacy also seeks to isolate and marginalize extremists and their ideology. In all these ways, public diplomacy is "waging peace," working to bring about conditions that lead to a better life for people across the world and make it more difficult for extremism to take root.

ATTACHMENT A

ACTION PLAN FOR STRATEGIC OBJECTIVES

I. REINFORCE A POSITIVE VISION OF HOPE AND OPPORTUNITY

A. Seek opportunities to link programs and policies with America's values.

Examples

1. America sponsors scholarships for girls because we believe all children, boys and girls, are equal and equally deserving of the right to an education to improve their prospects in life.
2. America sponsors workshops on workers' rights because we believe all human beings are entitled to basic rights and fair treatment by their employers.
3. America provides development and disaster assistance to respond to human needs and suffering, regardless of culture, beliefs or nationality.
4. America issues reports on human rights, religious freedom and trafficking in persons because we believe all people everywhere should be able to worship as they wish and no person anywhere should be sold into slavery.
5. America is advocating greater freedom of expression and political participation in the Middle East because we believe those are the rights of all people, everywhere.
6. America is partnering with countries across the world to fight terrorism because it threatens the right of all people everywhere to live in security and peace.
7. America collaborates with scientists worldwide because shared knowledge and innovation can benefit all mankind.

B. Emphasize the diplomacy of deeds in all of America's development and disaster assistance.

Across the world, America feeds the poor, educates the illiterate, cares for the sick and responds to disasters. Yet often, the USG engages in so many different development projects that we get minimal recognition for any of them. Public affairs staff should identify the one or two development programs with the most impact and resonance in each specific country and work to drive home the message.

Example

Eradicating malaria is a top priority in a number of African countries. While we participate in many other programs, we should make sure every high-profile visitor, every ambassadorial event, every communication from American officials in these countries includes an update on our activities to wipe out malaria. New approaches should be developed to highlight progress: a chart at the front door of the embassy or consular office posts the growing number of lives saved; a regular radio update calls attention to milestones, the ambassador devotes the first paragraph of every speech to a progress report on fighting malaria. The USG needs to communicate in all we say and do that America is committed to partnering with people of each country to wipe out malaria.

1.   Spotlight ways in which American assistance is helping real people achieve better lives; collect and share success stories.

Example

Public affairs staff should videotape compelling stories from participants in USG programs (women in a literacy class who can now help their children with homework, farmers who make more money because of the improved quality of their crops, girls who are attending school for the first time, science students interacting with U.S. scientists to push the envelope of knowledge) and post them to appropriate web sites. A series of vignettes could be collected on CD or shared in a podcast so they can be made available to local teachers, the media, and others.

Highlight and suggest ways for media to "cover" exchange programs – perhaps by partnering with a local radio or television station who interview participants regularly or produce a documentary or news report. U.S. government broadcasting should likewise be encouraged to cover America's development assistance, education and exchange programs with feature programs and interviews with recipients.

2. Use Personal Examples in Communication.

- Speechwriters should incorporate appropriate personal anecdotes to demonstrate America's core values in remarks given by officials.
- Encourage journalists to report stories of how United States' programs, education and trade have benefited citizens and their families.

3. Establish plans for high-profile assistance in cases of major disaster that include strategic communication and public diplomacy.

USAID and military response to major disasters should be immediate and highly visible. Special priority should be placed on allowing press from the affected country and international media access to cover that assistance. When events are catastrophic (2005 tsunami, Pakistan earthquake, Lebanon destruction post-Israeli/Hezbollah war), highly visible presidential-level, private-sector teams should be recruited to raise private money and highlight the American's people's generosity and support for those affected.

4. Facilitate contributions (coordinated by USG through state.gov website) from the American people for specific disaster relief opportunities.

C. Broaden the reach of strategic communication by including all USG officials, high-profile Americans, the business sector and the education sector.

1. All senior USG officials should add at least one public diplomacy event in every country they visit when traveling on official USG business.

All Cabinet Secretaries should also participate in media interviews with foreign media (not merely foreign-based U.S. correspondents, but foreign television, radio and newspapers), and those media interviews should be strategically scheduled at the front end of the travel schedule to have the maximum impact, not as an afterthought.

Examples

- Appear on a highly rated television news or interview show
- Participate in a school program
- Visit a cultural site with local relevance
- Visit a health, science or education project the USG is sponsoring and highlight ways it is improving local lives

2. Designate and commission "Special American Envoys" to help promote American values.

These high-level representatives would reflect the diversity of America, should represent different fields (sports, health, science, music, acting) and could attract substantial news coverage/interest overseas.

3. Engage more private sector partners.

Agencies and embassies should identify and reach out to institutions, industries, foundations and private sector entities, especially those with a shared interest in attracting people to America and improving America's relations with people in specific countries.

Examples

- Travel and Tourism Industry
- Higher Education Community
- American Business and Labor Communities
- Provide government funding to develop public-private partnerships to advertise America as a higher education and tourism destination.

- Build coalitions of private sector disaster response partners similar to those assembled in Lebanon, Guatemala and Pakistan.
- Embassies should encourage American companies with operations in their countries to provide internships, education programs and exchange opportunities to help develop their work force and introduce more people to America; companies should be encouraged to partner with the embassy in sponsoring cultural and sports programs that foster interaction and respect between cultures.

4. Encourage Americans themselves to be citizen diplomats.

Examples

- Better links/information should be placed on U.S. Government web sites to help citizens understand cultural differences and show respect for other cultures
- American youth should be encouraged to learn critical languages
- Students should be encouraged to study world geography/history/culture
- Encourage Americans to become host families for exchange students and foreign visitors
- Encourage Americans to donate to global relief efforts that reinforce U.S. assistance programs.
- Evaluate and expand Department of Education partnerships in foreign countries.

II. ISOLATE AND UNDERMINE VIOLENT EXTREMISTS

The U.S. government needs to communicate more effectively, clearly and consistently to rebut terrorists' propaganda and undermine extremist ideology. To improve this effort, the State Department is in the process of establishing an interagency "Counterterrorism Communications Center" working with the Department's Rapid Response Unit to develop and deliver a proactive, coordinated USG message. This command center will have as its core function developing messages to undermine and marginalize extremist ideology and propaganda. The Counterterrorism Communications Center will also aggressively rebut and efficiently respond to actions and statements by terrorist groups and leaders across the world. It will actively seek opportunities to respond to breaking news, rebut negative messages and counter erroneous reporting. Appropriate agencies will detail experts to help support the work of the center. The center will be led by a Senior Foreign Service communication professional reporting directly to the Under Secretary for Public Diplomacy and Public Affairs; the deputy director will be a senior military officer from the Department of Defense. Working sub-groups are currently examining different aspects of the ideological struggle, including: terrorists' use of the Internet, television programming, publishing and alternative technologies. These working groups will make ongoing recommendations to the Policy Coordinating Committee for action.

A. Place strategic focus on critical countries in the ideological war against terror.

"Pilot Counties" have been designated to more intensely concentrate our public diplomacy efforts and resources in the ideological war through interagency-coordinated and country-specific plans that take advantage of all elements of national power. Each pilot country has written a plan outlining strategic goals, target audiences, and the programs/means to reach those audiences to undermine support for terrorism. Pilot countries have proposed additional programs and activities that will be implemented as funding becomes available. Pilot country projects are expected to facilitate best practices that can be applied more broadly to public diplomacy in other areas.

B. Identify and engage key influencers whose views have a ripple effect throughout society.

Such influencers include clerics, educators, journalists, physicians, women leaders, business leaders, scientists, and military personnel. Every appropriate diplomatic tool available should be used to nurture engagement, foster common values and interests with these influential individuals and encourage them to speak out against the extremists.

Examples

- Specialized exchange programs
- Academic and professional conferences
- Journalist workshops
- Embassy cultural events
- Military-to-military training and exchanges

1. Religious Leaders – The unique role of religion in the current war on terror requires that greater efforts be made to engage in dialogue with the leaders of faith-based communities. Moral and religious leaders such as clerics, imams, rabbis, monks and priests can foster tolerance and mutual respect among religions and their followers.

USG officials should seek opportunities to participate in events that resonate with local populations, including visits to important religious and cultural sites and hosting events such as Iftar dinners to demonstrate respect for different faiths.

Special efforts should be made by USG officials to highlight mainstream Muslim voices that condemn extremist violence.

Examples

- Quote mainstream voices in speeches or interviews
- Suggest individuals who condemn violence for media appearances
- Feature them in editorials/opinion pieces
- Feature them on USG broadcasting programs
- Sponsor interfaith programs and conferences featuring a diversity of mainstream voices.
- Encourage television programming on "faith matters" featuring guests who offer mainstream views of Islam, Christianity, Judaism and other faiths.
- Encourage foundations/think tanks/NGOs/universities to include mainstream views on Islam when sponsoring conferences and publishing academic articles.

2. Youth Audience – Because they are a sustainable force and will play a role for many years to come, more resources should be devoted to and specific outreach plans developed for specific segments of the youth audience, including early, middle, high school, university and young professionals.

Examples

- Sports diplomacy
- After school and summer youth enrichment programs
- Youth ambassador programs
- English language teaching programs
- Pre-college counseling and exam prep
- High school/college exchanges
- Cultural performances and collaboration
- Broadcasts tailored to young people with a mix of music and news
- Greater use of emerging media such as podcasts, webzines, etc.

3. Women and Girls – Educating and empowering women and girls should be a priority and programs should be significantly expanded.

Examples

- Establish women's centers that include computer training and democracy education
- Provide micro-finance grants and loans so women can start small in-home businesses
- Offer literacy programs that include information on nutrition and health
- Sponsor business mentoring conferences and exchanges
- Increase efforts against trafficking in persons
- Build networks of women scientists

4. Minority Groups – Special outreach should be directed to members of minority groups and indigenous people who often do not have full access to education and capital.

Example

- Martin Luther King scholarships are awarded in Colombia to African-Colombian students to promote the pursuit of higher education.

C. Undermine violent extremism by fostering a climate of openness and respect for religious diversity.

1.   Support Muslim-Americans' efforts to be a "bridge" between American and Muslim communities worldwide.

Examples

- Send teams of Muslim-Americans to Muslim communities abroad to engage in citizen dialogue.
- Sponsor "town hall meetings" between Muslim-American communities and Muslim audiences worldwide, suggest regular programs on USG broadcasting.
- Encourage the development of documentaries, reality shows, soap operas and other television shows that feature American families living in the Middle East and Middle Eastern families living in America.
- Engage the Muslim-American scientific community

D.   Foster grassroots worldwide condemnation against terror; make suicide bombing a matter of shame, not honor.

1. Encourage world leaders, especially leaders of diverse faith communities, to state clearly that no cause, no complaint and no grievance can ever justify the murder of innocents.

2. Cultivate partnerships with allied governments who are proactively engaged in the war on terror. Strengthen efforts, share appropriate information and reinforce themes to cooperatively and comprehensively respond.   Host and attend workshops, conferences and events to promote best practices and share ideas.

3. Highlight the human cost of terror.   Where culturally appropriate, foster awareness of the victims of terror and highlight

the human loss inflicted on the families and communities of victims.

Examples

- Encourage leaders of all faiths to speak out against suicide bombings; explain it violates the tenets of all faiths, including Christianity, Islam and Judaism.
- Encourage members of religious congregations to begin grassroots movements against terror.
- Remind audiences that violent extremism is rejected by the vast majority of Muslims around the world.
- Remind audiences that the victims of terror are often innocent children and women; they have come from more than 90 nations and many of them are Muslims.

E. Focus on the type of ideology and society the extremists want to impose on others throughout the world, especially Islamic nations.

The extremists have stated on numerous occasions that their goal is to create and impose a unified, dictatorial state on the proud and currently sovereign nations of the diverse Islamic world. The majority of civilized people do not want to live in the type of society the violent extremists seek. The best example is the society that was imposed by the Taliban in Afghanistan. Books were burned, music was banned; cultural icons were destroyed; girls were not allowed to go to school or learn to read; and women were not allowed to work – even if their husbands had been killed and they had no means of support. Freedom of expression and worship were not allowed; in fact, faith practices were so strictly proscribed that men could be punished if their beards were not the exact, appropriate length.

F. Confront Hate Speech.

Aggressively confront speech that encourages hate or incites violence and inflames misunderstandings around the world.

Examples

- Encourage tolerance in textbooks.

- Work with UNESCO and other international organizations to condemn hate speech and eliminate it from textbooks.

III. NURTURE AND PROJECT COMMON INTERESTS AND VALUES

Americans and people of different countries, cultures and faiths across the world share many common values and interests. America believes in the dignity and value of every human being in the world. We respect the historical and cultural roots of other political and social systems, even as we uphold the inalienable and fundamental human rights of every human being. Emphasizing these common interests and values must be an integral part of all USG communications.

A. Each agency should identify and build on areas in which their expertise/mandate corresponds with a common interest of the world.

Example

America has a shared interest with the people of the world in protecting and improving our environment/confronting climate change. Through participation in international conferences, interviews, and outreach programs, communicate America's common interest in improving our environment. Make sure all our officials frame their message by stating that we want to partner with other countries in ways that advance our common interest in improving the world's environment.

B. Develop active, agency-specific alumni networks of current and former official guests, speakers, professional exchanges and study programs as resources for outreach.

Examples

- Cultivate long-term relationships with participants and encourage collaboration on proposed initiatives to strengthen relationships.
- Encourage professional networking among individuals and share networks with agencies engaged in parallel programs.

C. Greater focus should be placed on three major areas that human beings across the world care most about: health, education and economic opportunity.

1. Health

Further commit America to working in partnership with other nations to eradicate preventable diseases. Convene conferences to focus/track progress and publicize major initiatives and encourage greater collaboration between government agencies (including DOD, HHS, USAID, VA) and foundations, NGOs, health care organizations (doctors/nurses/hospitals/pharmaceuticals) and religious congregations.

American health programs that reinforce this goal include:

- President's Emergency Plan for AIDS Relief
- Avian Flu response
- Malaria programs and summit
- Health diplomacy and training of medical professionals in the Americas
- Increased emphasis on material/infant mortality and immunization programs
- Efforts to improve water quality and supplies
- Military hospital ships, which are highly visible and should be deployed strategically to support public diplomacy
- Middle East breast cancer initiative

Further partnerships should be developed, and medical and science diplomacy envoys recruited to help champion America's commitment to better health for the people of the world.

2. Education

Every effort should be made throughout the USG to expand educational programs across the board, ranging from English teaching, teacher training, student exchanges, medical and science education exchanges, literacy training of all types, establishment of virtual science libraries (e.g. Iraq). Recent efforts such as the creation of major new after-school and summer English language training programs should be significantly expanded.

Example

English language teaching offers youth a job-related skill and improves their economic prospects, while opening a window to our shared values and the wider world of information. By hosting summer and after-school programs, we can reach young people in their own countries, before they are old enough to travel to America on exchange programs.

3. Economic Opportunity

America's support for micro-loans, job training, literacy and trade should be highlighted as examples of America's desire to improve prosperity for people across the world.

D. Expand private sector linkages.

Encourage international professional exchanges, ask companies to sponsor internship opportunities and joint professional projects.

E. Sharing the best of American culture mitigates negative images and misunderstanding.

Foster private sector partnerships to significantly expand cultural, sports, musical and artistic and scientific exchanges. Sports activities forge a common bond and teach teamwork, discipline, respect for others and abiding by rules. Art and culture are a shared language that taps into the range of human emotions and reminds us of our common humanity. Shared arts and cultural appreciation can help bridge political and policy differences. U.S. science and technology are widely respected in the Muslim world, and offer a promising entry point for engaging citizens and society.

Examples

- Global Cultural Initiative – USG will work with private sector partners to enhance exchanges of art, film, dance and music and share expertise in arts management.
- Islamic World Science Partnerships – USG will help build public-private partnerships in science collaboration, focusing on education, youth and women.

ATTACHMENT B

GENERAL COMMUNICATION GUIDELINES

Demonstrate respect. The most comprehensive survey we have conducted shows the number one thing the United States can do to improve public perception of our country is to demonstrate respect for other countries' culture and contributions; this is especially true in many Islamic countries. United States officials can demonstrate respect by: visiting important historic and cultural sites during foreign travel; actively scheduling "listening" events and opportunities to interact with foreign publics and listen to their point of view; planning events that demonstrate respect for different cultural and faith traditions; inviting respected local authors, historians, poets, musicians, etc to appear at USG sponsored events; and attending important cultural and historical events in other countries.

Use humility. The history of our own country is one of constantly striving and many times failing to live up to our own noble values. Our society is not perfect, and we should not be afraid to admit that we face many challenges and struggle to live up to our own ideals.

Use caution when dealing with faith issues in the public square. Government officials should be extremely cautious and if possible, avoid using religious language, because it can mean different things and is easily misconstrued. The extremists are murderers who pervert religion, members of a cult that promotes death and destruction rather than legitimate practitioners of any faith. When it is necessary to make a point that involves Islam, for instance, quote Muslim voices themselves. Also, avoid characterizing people of any faith as "moderate" – this is a political word which, when extended to the world of faith, can imply these individuals are less than devout and faithful. The terms "mainstream" or "majority" are preferable. Finally, avoid phrases such as the "Muslim community" that imply it is monolithic; Muslim communities, like other faith communities, are diverse.

Create platforms where divergent ideas are encouraged and freely and openly debated. Support conferences sponsored by think tanks and foundations and intellectual publications that foster debates. Seek to empower/highlight Muslim voices that speak out against terror and violence, even when they do not agree with every aspect of U.S. foreign policy.

Use good pictures and images.   Well-choreographed pictures and images convey emotion and/or action as well as a convincing story.

Suggestions:

- Before any event, think through a desired picture that would best capture and tell the story of the event.
- Where should the photo be taken – what is the background? The background should help convey where you are – the country, the city, the building, the environment. Should there be a flag in the background? Is there a banner behind or in front of the podium? Is a recognizable part of the building visible? What part of the building is recognizable? E.g., capture I.M. Pei's Pyramid as your background for an event at the Louvre rather than an unrecognizable column inside.
- Who should be in the picture? The principal along with those who are the focus of the event should be in the picture to help convey the story. Musicians? Youth? Government officials? E.g., if the Ambassador and State Minister for Education are speaking at a Fulbright event, make sure to get shots not just of the officials speaking but with Fulbright grantees in the photo.
- What is the action or the emotion? Are they dancing? Talking? Listening? Learning? Enthusiastic? Include props if that helps convey the story. E.g., if the Ambassador is meeting with 4th graders to give out books, the photo should include students holding the books, youth reading, pointing to a picture in the book, etc.
- The photographer should think through the location for the photo with all of the technical considerations in mind – not shooting into the sun, not in front of reflective glass or a mirror, not in shade or shadows, etc. The key people who need to be included in the shot should be identified.
- Look for the action or emotion. For action shots, get a tight shot rather than wide. A tight shot will convey more emotion in addition to the story. E.g., for a U.S. military big band in town with swing dancers, rather than capturing the whole

crowd, pick out one couple in full enthusiastic swing dancing in front of a large U.S. flag and banner of the event so the country and occasion are conveyed.

Develop a communication strategy to support public diplomacy events and policy developments. Carefully consider the target audience, desired goals and objectives, and the key messages to effectively reach target audiences, as well as how results will be measured. The "ABCDE" communication process model that follows is an example of a planning tool that can be used to think through the message and the best way to deliver it to a target audience.

ATTACHMENT C

CORE MESSAGES – GENERAL

- As a diverse, multi-cultural nation founded by immigrants, America includes and respects people of different nations, cultures and faiths.

- America seeks to be a partner for progress, prosperity and peace.

- The American government wants to work in partnership with nations and peoples across the world in ways that result in a better life for all the world's citizens.

- Because we believe all people are equal and equally valuable, we believe people everywhere should be free to speak their mind, to participate in their government, to worship as their conscience dictates, to assemble freely and to pursue opportunity, economic, political and creative.

- While we do not expect every country to shape its government like that of the United States, we believe that citizens should be able to participate in choosing their governments and that those governments should be accountable to their citizens. We believe all people want to live in societies that are just, governed by the rule of law, and not corrupt.

- We believe in universal education, with equal opportunity to learn for girls as well as boys.

- We believe in open markets and free trade to foster economic opportunity so all people have the ability to have productive jobs and provide for their families.

- As a nation where people are free to worship as their conscience dictates, we respect all faiths. Many Muslims live, work and worship freely in America and are an important part of American society.

CORE MESSAGES – SPECIFIC TO THE WAR ON TERROR

- All major world faiths, including Islam, Christianity, Judaism, Hinduism and Buddhism, teach that life is precious and that the taking of innocent life is wrong.

- The violent extremists we face in the war against terror do not represent, but instead pervert, Islam by advocating the mass murder of innocents – and most of their victims have been fellow Muslims.

- No grievance and no cause – no matter how legitimate they are – can ever justify acts of terror.

- Violent extremism is rejected by the majority of civilized people of all faiths.

- The majority of people of all faiths do not want to live in the type of society the violent extremists seek.

- The struggle against violent extremism should unite the nations and citizens of the world because terrorism threatens all the communities of the world. Acts of terror have brought tragedy, destruction, death and terrible grief to innocent people from Indonesia to Morocco, Spain to Jordan, England to India and Egypt. The victims of September 11th were citizens of more than 90 different countries and adherents of many faiths, including Christianity, Judaism and Islam.

- Terrorist attacks began long before the U.S. acted to remove the Taliban regime that was harboring al Qaeda in Afghanistan, or to remove Saddam Hussein's brutal regime from power in Iraq. The violent extremists, such as those who were responsible for the mass murder plot targeting airplanes in London in 2006, have long targeted innocent people. Their agenda is to impose a Taliban-like regime on the many proud and sovereign nations of the Islamic world, and they have nothing but intolerance for all those who do not share their extremist beliefs – including fellow Muslims.

- Through their indiscriminate killing of innocent people, the violent extremists have repeatedly shown their contempt for human life, regardless of race, ethnicity or religion.

- We saw the type of society the extremists seek in the Taliban rule of Afghanistan. Books were burned, music was banned, cultural icons were destroyed. Little girls were not allowed to go to school or learn to read, and women were not allowed to work to support themselves even if they were widowed and had no other means of support.

- The difference between democratic values and the type of society that the violent extremists want is stark:

  - Freedom vs tyranny
  - Tolerance and respect for differences vs. intolerance for any diversity
  - Religious freedom vs. state-imposed requirements of worship
  - Freedom of speech vs. imprisonment for differing views
  - Freedom to associate vs. restrictions on leaving your home
  - Education for all vs. no education for girls, limited education for boys
  - Accountable governments with citizen participation vs. un-elected, self-declared leaders.

- The violent extremists have killed thousands of Muslims, as well as innocent women, children and the elderly over the past several decades. The bombings of a wedding celebration in Jordan, bus passengers in London, and day laborers in Baghdad who were trying to earn money to support their families, are examples of cruelly calculated terrorist murders.

- The fight against terrorism is a concerted fight for values and principles that are universal. Much more unites us as citizens of the world than divides us. Across all borders, we share a common humanity. While the color of our skin, the language we speak, or the way we worship may be different, people everywhere aspire to speak their minds, participate in their society, worship freely, live in security, and pursue education, jobs and greater opportunities for their families.

- The ideology of the violent extremists uses a perverted religiosity to attempt to justify murder, terror, and violence. Yet such actions are always abhorrent and always wrong, and the international community, the interfaith community and decent men and women everywhere must speak out against those who advocate hate, violence and terrorism. We call on leaders of all faiths to work for mutual respect and understanding and to send a clear message: that killing oneself and murdering innocent people is always wrong.

- As an international community, we must foster debate, encourage education and provide information, to help people learn and make decisions for themselves, because we believe most people everywhere, of every faith, will choose freedom over tyranny and tolerance over intolerance.

- Despite al Qaeda's repeated attempts to characterize the world as being in the midst of a clash of civilizations, the simple fact is that the international community – east and west, north and south – has come together in unprecedented ways to confront common threats and ease human suffering. America is doing its part, working in partnership with countries throughout the Islamic world to improve the lives of Muslims. America is the largest bilateral donor of food and health aid to the Palestinian people. Americans were the largest providers of help to Muslims affected by the tsunami in Indonesia and the earthquake in Pakistan. We provide funds for Muslim girls and boys to go to school, for Muslim women to learn English, and for Muslim young people to get training for jobs. And in Afghanistan and Iraq, we are working in partnership with democratically elected Muslim leaders to provide freedom and security for Muslim populations that were brutally repressed under the Taliban and Saddam Hussein.

• As we look forward, we seek to work in a spirit of partnership with people and nations across the world to confront this ideology of hate and foster a climate of hope and opportunity. The U.S. is far from perfect, yet we believe the noble ideals of freedom and justice that guide us are right and true for human beings everywhere. We want to work in partnership with nations throughout the world in ways that will result in a more peaceful and prosperous world, and a better life for all people.

ATTACHMENT D

ADDITIONAL COMMUNICATION VEHICLES

USG Broadcasting

Consistent with the BBG's statutory mandate to operate in accordance with the highest standards of professional journalism and to safeguard the editorial integrity and independence of its broadcast organizations, as well as the BBG Strategic Plan for 2008-2013, the Broadcasting Board of Governors shall:

• Review existing strategies and resources in order to focus BBG efforts on the critical priority countries for U.S. foreign policy. Means of signal delivery (television, FM radio, internet, etc.) should vary according to audience demographics, media habits, trends, etc. Decisions should be made on the basis of thorough audience research and U.S. national priorities.

• Build upon BBG's reach and impact within the Islamic World, including augmentation of news gathering, reporting and programming for Alhurra TV and Radio Sawa, Radio Farda, etc.

• BBG's various programs should broaden and deepen overall coverage of Islam and foster interfaith dialogue, including discussion of Islam and modernity and Islam and democracy, ensuring the participation of mainstream Muslim voices.

• Help audiences in authoritarian countries understand the principles and practices of democratic, free and just societies.

• Engage the world in a conversation about America, including the presentation of accurate and comprehensive information to counter misinformation and disinformation about the United States, its policies, and culture, as well as the use of interactive dialogues with key audiences, such as youth.

• Broaden cooperation with U.S. public diplomacy, including playing an active role in the interagency strategic planning; facilitating the exchange of relevant data, including survey results and polling data, with other government agencies; and developing partnerships with like-minded institutes and foundations outside the government. BBG should consider covering newsworthy events sponsored by government agencies, such as exchange programs, health care, scientific collaboration, and education initiatives.

Non-BBG Activities:

Narrowcasting: In response to changing user habits and the dramatically different media landscape, new web-based approaches must be developed and expanded by all agencies. The interagency community should collaborate with technology professionals to identify recommendations on current trends and the most effective ways of reaching youth audiences.

Examples

- **Internet Outreach:** Pod casts, web chats, SMS text messaging, blogs, and other web-based programs are being developed and expanded to share U.S. foreign policy messages with audiences around the world. Additional capacity has been added to broadcast live events, such as the President's State of the Union address, in more languages worldwide.
- **Digital Outreach Team:** A new unit at the State Department engages on blogs and web chats in Arabic to correct misrepresentations of U.S. policy.
- **Democracy Dialogues**: A new interactive, web-based discussion of the principles of democracy has been launched. Every two months, a different theme is featured.
- **"Partnership for a Better Life:"** A website to provide a visual gateway to stories of individuals and institutions benefiting from

U.S. foreign aid has been established, building on President Bush's State of the Union message that: "For people everywhere, America is a partner for a better life." Our ambassadors are strongly encouraged to highlight ways the American government and people are improving the lives of people in their host countries.

ATTACHMENT E

EVALUATION AND ACCOUNTABILITY

As Edward R. Murrow once observed, no cash register ever rings when a mind is changed. The impact of information and education programs that touch the emotions, beliefs, intellects and allegiances of diverse audiences around the world is often difficult to gauge, especially when many public diplomacy activities may only produce long-term, rather than immediate, impact.

Nevertheless, all United States government agencies must build evaluation and measurement into strategic communication and public diplomacy program design. They must examine the effectiveness and impact of their efforts. While we cannot prove that additional USG appearances on television will change minds, we can track the growing number of interviews, the time allotted to representing America's point of view, and whether our key messages were in fact conveyed. Participants in our exchange and education programs can and should be interviewed to find out what aspects were most effective; speakers should be evaluated for quality and effectiveness in presenting American values and beliefs.

Evaluation should measure progress toward the achievement of goals, allowing managers to adjust methods and means, and make informed decisions about resources. Performance measurement and evaluation ensure accountability and transparency so that stakeholders, including the American public, can justify program expenditures as a prudent use of taxpayer funds.

The Policy Coordinating Committee should implement its evaluation and measurement strategy as follows:

• **Establish a culture of measurement:** The PCC will communicate to all departments and agencies the importance and value of evaluations and performance measurement using common standards and comparable data that support the three strategic imperatives. Increased commitment to data collection and reporting will help improve communication and public diplomacy programming and more effectively demonstrate the impact of our collective efforts.

• **Establish common core performance indicators:** The PCC will analyze the performance indicators submitted by departments and agencies with a view to approve a uniform set of relevant core indicators for use in all agencies. Individual agencies will then create sub-indictors to comprehensively evaluate supporting internal efforts. This will provide greater focus and coherence across agencies and bureaus, standardize and streamline processes for the field, and ensure data collection supports both processes.

• **Establish mechanisms for data collection:** Each individual agency and department shall allocate resources, establish indicators, and deploy mechanisms to gather relevant data. This evaluation process will be used to establish baselines and track the impact of public diplomacy programs and activities.

• **The PCC will conduct periodic agency-specific reviews** of public diplomacy and strategic communication efforts to validate successful programs, recommend the continuation of activities, and direct resources.

Technology's Challenges and Opportunities

They jammed our satellite. Now what?
Broadcasting Board of Governors (2003)

In July, 2003, the Broadcasting Board of Governors, a bipartisan, presidentially-appointed body in charge of civilian government broadcasting abroad, launched a news program series into Iran in an effort to help democratic forces fight and win national elections. As soon as the program began, the transponders on the Telstar-12 satellite above the Atlantic Ocean that beamed the signals from the United States to Iran, stopped operating. The U.S. discovered that the transponder was being jammed from coordinates in Bejucal, Cuba. Bejucal is the site of an electronic intelligence facility built by the Soviets but now run by the Chinese.

In the following news release, the BBG announces the jamming and the steps it took to stop it. It is clear from the announcement that the U.S. government was unable to stop the electronic attack on the American satellite in the decisivel first days and weeks of a critical broadcast operation.

Washington, D.C., July 15, 2003 - The Broadcasting Board of Governors (BBG) today condemned Cuba's jamming of U.S. international broadcasts to Iran, calling the action a "deliberate and malicious" effort to block Iranian audiences from gaining access to truthful news and information.

The BBG, the federal agency which oversees all U.S. non-military international broadcasting, also urged providers such as Intelsat and Eutelsat to stop giving service to countries that have jammed satellite transmissions to Iran, where pro-democracy advocates have staged repeated demonstrations against the ruling Islamic government.

"The BBG calls upon the international community to censure the states that have caused the interference," the nine-member board said in a unanimous resolution. "The BBG strongly condemns the

467

deliberate and malicious interference with its legitimate efforts to impart truthful, objective, and balanced news to its Iranian audience."

"Cuba's jamming of satellite transmissions is illegal and interferes with the free and open flow of international communications," said Kenneth Y. Tomlinson, the BBG's chairman. "This action is illegal, represents a major threat to satellite communication and must be stopped."

The jamming was first detected on July 6, the day the BBG's Voice of America (VOA) launched a daily, 30-minute, Persian-language television news and analysis program, *News and Views*, aimed at providing information to the millions of people who have access to satellite TV in Iran. The program, broadcast from 9:30 p.m.-10:00 p.m. in Iran, features original, in-depth news reporting from Iran, world news round-ups, analyses of issues and events and special interest and cultural features. Two other weekly VOA Persian-language television programs, *Next Chapter* and *Roundtable with You*, are also jammed.

The BBG said service providers have said the source of jamming is located near Havana, Cuba, which is about 90 miles from the coast of the United States.

The resolution urged the State Department and the Federal Communications Commission to "lodge an appropriate formal protest against the government of Cuba for this unwarranted and wrongful interference."

VOA's Persian-language television complements other BBG broadcasting to Iran, including Radio Farda, a 24-hour, seven-day-a-week, youth-oriented radio program that is a joint project of VOA and Radio Free Europe/Radio Liberty (RFE/RL), and VOA Persian radio service.

Resolution of the BBG

Whereas the Broadcasting Board of Governors' direct-to-home satellite broadcasts of daily, televised news programs to the Iranian people have been jammed since the approximate time of their inauguration on Sunday July 6th, 2003;

Whereas Iranian citizens have told BBG officials that they were being prevented from receiving intelligible reception of the Voice of America's televised news programs;

Whereas this interference constitutes a direct and effective violation of the United Nations' Universal Declaration of Human Rights' Article 19 that guarantees individuals the right "to seek, receive and impart information and ideas through any media and regardless of frontiers."

Whereas this interference constitutes a deliberate effort to block the public's access to satellite telecommunications, and as such represents a major threat to international satellite communications;

And whereas the best information of the service provider for transmission of televised news programming is that the source of jamming is located near Havana, Cuba;

Now therefore, be it resolved:

That the Broadcasting Board of Governors vigorously affirms the human rights of the Iranian people to seek and receive information and ideas;

That the Broadcasting Board of Governors strongly condemns the deliberate and malicious interference with its legitimate effort to impart truthful, objective, and balanced news to its Iranian audience;

That the Board of Broadcasting Governors calls upon the international community to censure the states that have caused this interference;

That the Board of Broadcasting Governors urges such service providers as Intelsat and Eutelsat to cease providing services to those states that have deliberately restricted the Iranian people's access to international broadcasting until and unless this illegal interference with the free and open flow of international communications ends.

That the Board of Broadcasting Governors urges the Department of State, the Federal Communications Commission and all appropriate elements of the U.S. government to lodge an appropriate formal protest against the government of Cuba for this unwarranted and wrongful interference.

Adopted this 15th Day of July, 2003 by the Broadcasting Board of Governors.

Uncle Sam's blog
Hampton Stephens (2005)[140]

. . . as the bureaucracy belatedly gears up to spread the message of liberty as an alternative to extremism and tyranny, there is evidence to suggest that independent, grassroots efforts to nurture democratic ideas in some of the world's most repressed societies are gaining momentum and could make old-style public diplomacy irrelevant. While the latest U.S.-sponsored public diplomacy efforts, such as the new Arabic television station Alhurra, rely on decidedly old-media formats, the Internet appears to be the medium through which future international political opinion will be influenced most significantly.

In most foreign countries, traditional media like Al Jazeera – against which Alhurra, established in February 2004, is designed to compete – is the place most citizens get their political information. However, the particular characteristics of the Internet and Web logs make them fertile ground for alternative political cultures to take root, especially in countries where the state attempts to control access to information. With their use of the Internet for organization and for communicating their ideology to new believers, terrorist groups like Al Qaeda have already demonstrated the power of networks to spread political movements. Less publicized so far is the growing use of the Internet by democrats to foster liberal culture in repressive countries.

In Iran, for example, there are more than 75,000 active Web logs [blogs] written in Persian, Iran expatriate Hossein Derakhshan, who now lives in Toronto and is a central figure in the Iranian blogosphere, told an audience at Harvard University's Internet and Society conference in December [2004]. Derakhshan says Web logs are the most trusted information medium among Iran's citizens, of which 70 percent are under the age of 30. He believes it is only a matter of time before blogs become a major political force.

Iran's ruling mullahs are clearly worried. The regime arrested a number of bloggers last year as part of a crackdown on journalists. The BBC reported Feb. 23 that Arash Sigarchi, who was arrested in

---

[140] Hampton Stephens, an Institute of World Politics alumnus, is editor-in-chief of WorldPoliticsReview.com. Excerpted from "Uncle Sam's Blog," *Boston Globe*, March 14, 2005. Copyright © 2005 by Hampton Stephens. Reprinted with permission.

January after criticizing the Iranian government on his own Web log, was recently sentenced to 14 years in prison. Another Iranian blogger, Mujtaba Saminejad, is awaiting trial in an Iranian jail.

Although the international blogging phenomenon is in its infancy, Internet trends spread fast, so U.S. foreign policy makers would do well to take notice soon. A chief aim of public diplomacy has always been to foster liberal political culture where authoritarian states are attempting to snuff it out. President Bush clearly believes America's interests are served by the spread of freedom and democracy. To that end, U.S. policy makers should recognize blogging as a perfect tool to promote the proliferation of independent democratic voices.

There is some indication that the U.S. foreign policy establishment is beginning to understand the Internet's potential in this area. The 2004 annual report of the Advisory Commission on Public Diplomacy recommended that the State Department "actively look for ways to use emerging software developments to expand its broadcasting reach over the Internet."

[A] professor of international communication at The Institute of World Politics, says, "While some in the State Department recognize the power of the Internet for public diplomacy, they are years behind the technology and show little sign of advancing soon." He proposes that the Broadcasting Board of Governors, which runs U.S.-sponsored broadcasting, "quickly integrate its radio and TV programming with Internet media to facilitate global, interactive networks of independent bloggers in English, Arabic, Farsi, Urdu, and other languages, united against Islamist extremism."

To accomplish this, the radio and television stations could feature "the best and most interesting bloggers" on their programs. . . . "The bloggers, in turn, would find it in their interests to draw listeners and viewers to U.S.-sponsored media."

That approach could do much to popularize political blogging in places where it already exists. At the same time, programs to expand blogging in countries where it has not yet taken root are needed. One organization's effort to expand blogging in the Arab world could provide a model for future government programs.

Spirit of America, a nonprofit group started by a California businessman to fund nation-building efforts in Afghanistan and Iraq, is developing a blogging tool to give Arabic speakers the same ability to create blogs as users of English software like Google's Blogger. The group says hosting each blog will cost just $12 a year. To make sure the tool is used to promote democratic ideals rather than, say, jihad against the West, each blog created with the tool will display banner ads promoting "groups, individuals, and news that, in the big picture, advance freedom, democracy, and peace in the region," according to Spirit of America.

It is easy to imagine the dramatic effect an influx of funding from the State Department could have on such a low-cost project. Though the youth of Iran are already largely pro-American, the creation of pro-democracy blogospheres in places like Syria could do much to encourage reform movements. Eventually, such movements would significantly increase the pressure for change on authoritarian regimes like that of Bashar Assad, giving the US government more options in its statecraft.

Although creating a community of bloggers depends on improving lagging access to the Web in non-democratic states, the availability of the Internet in even the poorest and most closed countries is growing rapidly. The number of Internet users in the Middle East increased 219 percent between 2000 and 2004, according to the advisory commission's report.

If the U.S. government is to harness the Internet to spread liberty, State Department officials will have to rethink their whole approach to public diplomacy. Whereas the Internet is, by its very architecture, decentralized, messy, and chaotic, the government's initial attempts to revamp public diplomacy after Sept. 11, 2001, drew on the slick, prepackaged ethos of Madison Avenue. . . . the Madison Avenue approach to public diplomacy appears to have fallen out of favor in the State Department. However, if U.S. officials have conceived of an approach that can overcome foreign skepticism about American "propaganda" while still aggressively fighting the battle of ideas that is critical to creating a freer, more open world, they have not publicized it.

The advantage of a public diplomacy that seeks to build indigenous communities of reform-minded bloggers is that no American bureaucrat needs to develop the correct tone for communicating American ideals. Instead, the message of liberty and democracy can be encouraged to spread from the very communities that public diplomacy campaigns are designed to reach in the first place.

Enhanced technology initiatives
U.S. Department of State (2006)[141]

The State Department's public reports on its online progress were vague through 2006, suggesting little initiative or accomplishment in embracing new media. In a report on its "Major Public Diplomacy Accomplishments" for 2005 and 2006, the office of the Under Secretary for Public Diplomacy and Public Affairs announced that it "added" small and inexpensive features such as podcasts to its international online presence, and implied that it provided "additional capacity" to broadcast live events in "more languages."

In a single sentence the public diplomacy office announced an online discussion of democratic principles that is updated every two months – an eternity by Internet standards and evidence that, as of December, 2006, State still did not understand the medium.

We are expanding our use of communications technologies so that our message can compete in today's highly competitive information environment.

Public Affairs and International Information Programs Internet Outreach: Added pod casts [sic], web chats, and other web-based programs to share U.S. foreign policy messages with audiences around the world. Additional capacity to broadcast events, such as the President's State of the Union address, live in more languages worldwide.

Democracy Dialogues: Launched a new inter-active, web-based discussion of the principles of democracy. Every two months, a different theme will be featured.

"Partnership for a Better Life:" Launched a new website to provide visual gateway to stories of individuals and institutions benefiting from U.S. foreign aid, building on President Bush's State of the Union message that: "For people everywhere, America is a partner for a better life." Urging our ambassadors to highlight ways the American government and people are improving the lives of people in their host countries.

---

[141] "Major Public Diplomacy Accomplishments 2005-2006," Office of Public Diplomacy and Public Affairs, U.S. Department of State, December, 2006.

Perhaps the State Department should try the Internet. . .
Hampton Stephens (2006)[142]

Until five years after the September 11, 2001 attacks, an Internet strategy was disturbingly absent from U.S. public diplomacy programs. The United States launched two Arabic broadcasting services, Radio Sawa and Alhurra television, but government broadcasters have seemed to ignore the promise of the Internet as a tool of public diplomacy. Comparing the Internet presences of Al Jazeera, the most popular television network in the Muslim world, and Alhurra, the American-funded network designed to compete with it, illustrates this point. Al Jazeera built an attractive, dynamic, interesting, interactive and personalized Web site comparable or even superior in quality to MSNBC's excellent news site. In 2002, in only its second year of operation, Al Jazeera's Web site received more than 161 million visits, according to the network.

But Alhurra broadcasters have not taken advantage of the synergy of the Internet and television. The State Department and the Broadcasting Board of Governors (BBG), the quasi-independent entity that runs U.S. government broadcasting which runs the outlets, showed no understanding of how the Internet works. The Voice of America (VOA), with a content-rich site in English and some other languages, eliminated its Arabic-language Website, and with it, shut off Arab editors who had been pulling the well-written stories from the Web and printing them in their own newspapers. For 18 months after the network's founding in February 2004, Alhurra's Web site was not merely less sophisticated than Al Jazeera's site; it could scarcely be called a Web site at all. It was an embarrassment: alhurra.com consisted of a single, static white page containing the station's logo, a basic schedule for the network's television programming, directions for tuning into its broadcast signal and a few words describing the network's mission. The site contained no outside links. While Al Jazeera delivered its online content directly to people's computers, cell phones and PDAs, Alhurra and the BBG did nothing.

---

[142] Hampton Stephens is editor of WorldPoliticsReview.com. This is an excerpt from his chapter in *Strategic Influence: Public Diplomacy, Counterpropaganda and Political Warfare* (IWP Press, 2007). Reprinted with permission.

Alhurra's new Web site, launched in August 2005, was a significant improvement, featuring text news stories as well as streaming audio and video feeds of Alhurra programs. Though the site looked more like that of a real news organization, qualitatively it still lagged behind its competitor. Its quality has been uneven and unprofessional. At the time this book went to print in mid-2007, Alhurra's homepage consisted of fresh, clean graphics and a broadcast schedule, but contained little visible content. It hosted almost nothing to interest anyone to come and visit, absorb information and take part in discussions.

Radio Sawa, the Arabic-language popular music and news station, has a Web site containing short print articles and audio clips of Sawa programming, and provides live audio streaming, but it is not nearly as comprehensive as Al Jazeera's site or, for that matter, as good as the Web sites of the vast majority of comparable professional news operations. Radio Sawa's Farsi-language cousin, Radio Farda, is better; it runs a Web site with lively and dynamic written news and graphics, and live audio streaming.

Secretary of State Condoleezza Rice and Under Secretary of State for Public Diplomacy Karen Hughes both vowed soon after taking office to expand the role of technology in U.S. public diplomacy. In September 2005, in one of her first speeches to State Department employees, Hughes announced a technology initiative to use the Internet, web chats, digital video and text messaging to communicate American ideals to foreign publics. Following this lead, the BBG said it planned to expand the scope of audio and video streaming across all its Web sites and make better use of new Internet technologies like Real Simple Syndication. The board has made the Web site of Radio Sawa the focal point of their Arabic-language Internet news operations. The speed and frequency with which the site's news stories are updated now compares more favorably with the sophisticated Voice of America News Web sites, and is the only significant U.S.-sponsored Arabic-language site on the Internet. The BBG is also continually working on ways to get around access restrictions that governments like China and Iran put on its Web sites.

The State Department's Bureau of International Information Programs has also made some initial efforts to use the Internet to communicate and spread American ideals. The most prominent example, a program called Democracy Dialogues, was launched in January 2006. Democracy Dialogues is a multilingual Web site that aims to educate people outside the United States about democratic principles. The site translates important democratic documents like the Declaration of Independence, the U.S. Constitution and the Emancipation Proclamation into Spanish, French, Russian, Chinese, Arabic and Persian. International democratic treatises, from the Magna Carta to the Helsinki Final Act, are also featured. For those Muslims who believe Islam is incompatible with liberalism, the sites publish the 1990 Cairo Declaration on Human Rights in Islam. Every two months, the site highlights a new democratic principle. So far, freedom of speech and women's rights have been featured topics, with "independent courts, free and fair elections, freedom of worship, and minority rights" planned for the future. Periodic Web chats with experts, discussion boards, and educational materials for foreign schools support each theme.

Is it working? In April 2006, State Department officials said the site received about 40,000 visitors in the first four months after its launch. That is not many. Nearly five years after 9/11 and three years after the invasion of Iraq, State said it had yet to market the site aggressively. State Department officials said in early 2006 that the Chinese and Arabic sites were proving to be most popular and that the most foreign visitors were coming from China, Egypt and Iran. But more popular than what? Forty thousand visitors in four months is only an average of 333 a day, out of a global population of 6.4 billion.

These first steps might show promise, but there are significant obstacles that must be overcome if the United States government is ever to compete with its enemies in using technology for propaganda. One problem is resources. The State Department has yet to make technology-driven public diplomacy a priority. Of the $591 million the BBG spent on international broadcasting in fiscal year 2005, just $6.9 million, or about 1 percent, went toward Internet services. As of May 2006, just two State Department employees were devoting "a majority of their time" to Democracy Dialogues. Meanwhile, the Pentagon has forged ahead with a huge online information presence through defenselink.mil and scores of other sites.

But resources could be the least of the problems. As the terrorists show, one can do much with little or no money. The real obstacles are lack of vision and will from the political leadership and trepidation from the bureaucracy where innovation is seldom rewarded. Few in the government are able to use the Internet as it must be used: a 24/7 battlespace of words and images, where a committed and persistent few, with the barest of resources, can have a disproportionately large influence on news and information.

Virtual Diplomacy Initiative
United States Institute of Peace (1997 -)[143]

The Initiative's mission is to explore the role of information and communications technologies (ICTs) in the conduct of diplomacy, particularly their effect upon international conflict management and resolution. The practical objective is to extract lessons and insights for future training of international affairs specialists, whether in government, international organizations, or the private sector. USIP [U.S. Institute of Peace] will accomplish this by:

- Analyzing how the information revolution is transforming international relations and conflict and impacting the institutional structures and operational effectiveness of groups engaged in crisis and conflict management;
- Identifying ways that ICTs can aid in preventing, managing, and resolving international conflict; and
- Fostering cooperation among crisis management groups using ICTs; encouraging partnerships and resource sharing; and attracting support for collaborative enterprises from business, industry, and philanthropic circles.

Themes

The Virtual Diplomacy Initiative encompasses five thematic tracks:

1. The "Revolution in Diplomatic Affairs" (RDA) track considers the effects and implications of an increasingly interdependent environment, influenced by the worldwide diffusion of revolutionary information and communications technologies, on the content, structure, and practice of diplomacy.

---

[143] "About the Virtual Diplomacy Initiative," United States Institute of Peace, www.usip.org/virtualdiplomacy/about.html

2. The "Netpolitik" track examines the emergence, reconfiguration, and redistribution of political influence on the basis of global connectivity, as information mobilizers compete and cooperate in pursuit of their interests.

3. The "Media and Conflict" track focuses on global "mediazation" – including the ascent of global and real-time media vehicles and formats, the competition for attention from both local and global audiences, and issues of accuracy, credibility, and transparency during periods leading up to, during, and after a crisis or conflict.

4. The "Good Practices Project" explores the role of information sharing within the humanitarian community and between it and military entities during complex emergencies.

5. The "Open Eyes" track encompasses the uses of remote-sensing technologies and geographic information systems in international conflict prevention, management, and resolution.

Origins

Lessons from the Institute's 10th anniversary conference, "Managing Chaos" guided the establishment of the Virtual Diplomacy initiative. Conference participants recognized the pivotal role of non-governmental organizations (NGOs) as new conflict managers in international conflict resolution and the need for improved coordination of effort, both within the NGO community and with government and international agencies, in providing services in the field. They pointed to the support for cooperation promised by emerging information technologies and the challenges faced by groups actively involved in conflict resolution in employing these tools effectively.

The Institute conceived the Virtual Diplomacy Initiative to help practitioners and scholars to understand and apply such technologies in preventing, managing, and resolving international conflict, and to explore the long-term impact of ICTs on the character of international relations.

In 1997, the Institute's Board of Directors added the Virtual Diplomacy Initiative to its mission, in recognition of the strategic importance of emerging technologies in shaping the nature of international conflict and diplomacy. Responding to the information age requirements for an organization working on international conflict prevention, management, and resolution, the Institute has integrated ICTs to meet the challenge of fulfilling its mission in the changing international landscape.

What Is Virtual Diplomacy

At its broadest, the term "virtual diplomacy" signifies the altered diplomacy associated with the emergence of a networked globe. At its narrowest, the term encompasses the decision-making, coordination, communication, and practice of international relations as they are conducted with the aid of information and communications technologies. Above all, the Virtual Diplomacy Initiative encourages the critical examination of an expanded and amplified diplomatic practice that includes anyone anywhere affected or plugged into any and all information and communications media.

Audience

The Institute seeks the views of civilian and military government agencies, international governmental bodies, non-governmental organizations, researchers and analysts, and the news media to assess the challenges and opportunities posed by ICTs to policy formation and implementation, coordination and collaboration, and information exchange and resource sharing. The Institute solicits the participation of business and R&D communities to understand, develop, and apply ICTs; and invites funders to provide guidance on the availability and acquisition of resources to enhance global interaction.

Citizen Public Diplomats

Private citizens play an increasing role in public diplomacy, both through traditional means such as education and exchanges, and through networked organizations and communication technology. Businesses, concerned by the United States' decline in prestige around the world, are also becoming more involved. Some of these efforts are coordinated with the State Department, but most are completely independent of the government.

Increased academic study and professional advocacy of public diplomacy is also evident, with centers such as the Public Diplomacy Institute at the George Washington University, the University of Southern California Center on Public Diplomacy, The Institute of World Politics, and the USIA Alumni Association. This section examines the activity of citizen public diplomats.

Ten things Americans can do to support public diplomacy
U.S. Department of State (2007)[144]

1. Host a youth exchange student in your home. (www.exchanges.state.gov/education/citizens/students)
2. Urge your local school board to include foreign languages from grade school through high school – and encourage your children to study a foreign language, world history and international news. (www.future.state.gov)
3. Encourage your children to correspond with an electronic pen pal overseas (such as www.epals.com) and to participate in study abroad programs. (www.exchanges.state.gov)
4. Get actively involved with organizations that have international programs, such as a local World Affairs Council (www.worldaffairscouncils.org) or non-profit service organizations with global outreach.

---

[144] "10 Things Americans Can Do to Support Public Diplomacy," information sheet, U.S. Department of State, undated, 2007.

5. Welcome foreign visitors by supporting international visitor programs (www.exchanges.state.gov/education/ivp)
6. Support international disaster relief programs and organizations that provide international medical assistance. (such as www.Interaction.org)
7. Encourage people-to-people dialogue with other faiths through personal outreach or through your own church, synagogue, mosque or other faith-based institution.
8. Volunteer to serve on short-term assignments overseas with the USA Freedom Corps' Volunteers for Prosperity program (www.USAFreedomCorps.gov) or with the U.S. Peace Corps. (www.peacecorps.gov)
9. Support cultural exchanges for artists, musicians and writers through your local arts institutions and international cultural programs. (www.exchanges.state.gov/education/citizens/culture; or others such as www.meridian.org)
10. Encourage your business or corporation to reach out in the countries where it has a presence, providing internships or supporting local schools and charities. (To learn more about private sector outreach around the world or discuss potential partnerships email publicdiplomacy@state.gov)

World citizen's guide: Practical advice for Americans traveling abroad
Business for Diplomatic Action (2006)[145]

Every American traveler abroad, for better or for worse, is a representative of the United States. Business for Diplomatic Action prepared a "World Citizen's Guide" consisting of 25 brief points that every American should remember and practice when visiting other countries. Reasonable people will differ with some of the points here and there, but in general the guide is a useful overview for the conscientious citizen-diplomat.

Business for Diplomatic Action also produced a 60-page booklet for students and an executive brochure of "16 tips for business travelers." The full documents are available at

---

[145] Business for Diplomatic Action, a nonprofit group, is devoted to bridging public diplomacy between the government and private sector, and to combating anti-Americanism abroad. Their homepage is www.businessfordiplomaticaction.org.

worldcitizensguide.org. Excerpts from the "World Citizen's Guide"
follow.

If your travels take you outside the United States, this primer on 'world citizenship' may be helpful.

For years, many people in the world have had a great fondness for America. They have admired our culture, our products and our cheerful, fun-loving nature. In recent years, however, there has been a significant shift in those feelings. Research studies show that, for a number of reasons, "favorability" ratings for America are declining around the world.

While it is true that the rise in negative feelings toward us may result from perceptions more than reality, it is also true that perceptions are powerful opinion makers. You, and the 55-60 million other Americans who travel abroad each year, have a unique opportunity to change at least some impressions of us from negative to positive. By following the few simple suggestions in this guide, you can have a better travel experience while showing America's best face to those you visit.

25 simple suggestions

Look. Listen. Learn. New places mean new cultures and new experiences. Don't just shop. See the sights, hear the sounds and try to understand the lives people live.

Smile. Genuinely. It's a universal equalizer.

Think big. Act small. Be humble. In many countries, boasting is considered very rude. It's easy to resent big, powerful people. Assume resentment as a default and play down your wealth, power and status. When Americans meet each other for the first time, our job (and implied status) is a key part of "who" we are, and how we introduce ourselves. This is less important elsewhere, and can be perceived as braggadocio.

Live, eat and play local. Once you get to know other Americans, don't start ignoring locals you knew before. Most people believe that Americans have the most fun when they are in their own company. Prove them wrong. The world is full of interesting and exciting things, people and places that you might never have heard of. Take some of it in.

Be patient. We talk fast. Eat fast. Move fast. Live fast. Many cultures do not. In fact, time is understood very differently around the world. In the short term, speed and instant satisfaction are less important than enjoying new culture.

Celebrate our diversity. We are a giant patchwork of many cultures, and not the singular people others envision. Find a way to share that.

Become a student again. Everybody abroad may not be aware of occurrences that are obvious for you (movies, music, baseball, Super Bowl winners, etc.). Try to find a few topics that are most important in the local popular culture.

Try the language. Try to speak some of the language even if the only thing you can say is "Hello." And "Thank you." It's okay to sound like a child. Making the effort is more endearing than off putting.

Refrain from lecturing. Whether on pollution, energy usage or the environment, it's not a polite stance. Nobody likes a know-it-all, and nobody likes a whole nation of them. Rightly or wrongly the U.S. is seen as appointing itself as policeman, judge and jury to the world. Be aware of this perception and try to understand other viewpoints.

Dialogue instead of monologue. When you're talking about the U.S. and your life there, ask people you're visiting how what you've said compares to what they do and how they live in their country.

Use your hands. Watch your feet. Gestures are a powerful language in any culture. Gestures are easier to learn than a language. Study up on them. Combine a basic knowledge of gestures with some very basic language to help you communicate better and more quickly.

Leave the clichés at home. Our clichés often don't mean much or maybe anything to people of other cultures and they are difficult to translate.

Be proud, not arrogant. People around the world are fascinated by the U.S. and the lives we Americans live. They admire our openness, our optimism, our creativity and our "can-do" spirit. But that doesn't mean they feel less proud of their country and culture. Be proud of being an American, but resist any temptation to present our way as the best way or the only way.

Keep religion private. Globally speaking, religion is not something you wear on your sleeve. Often it is considered deeply personal – not public. Some may have no knowledge of the Bible, nor is it appropriate to tell them about it unless you are a professional missionary identified as such.

Be quiet. Less is more. In conversation match your voice level to the environment and speakers. A loud voice is often perceived as a bragging voice. Casual profanity is almost always considered unacceptable.

Check the atlas. You may not believe anyone could confuse "Australia" with "Austria," but it happens. Everyone's home is important to them [sic]. It's helpful if you familiarize yourself with local geography.

Agree to disagree respectfully. Surely, there are people who object to actions or activities of our government, our industries and our culture. Not every objection is the same. Listen politely. Then respond appropriately.

Talk about something besides politics. Make yourself aware of the political environment of the region but don't offer a view if you don't have to. If pushed, ask the people with whom you're dealing a conversation what their thoughts are. Listen first. Then speak. And leave politics alone if you can. Speak of culture, art, food or family if you need another topic.

Be safety conscious, not fearful. If you went to certain parts of any city in the U.S., you'd better watch your wallet and make sure you had your wits about you. So why should it be any different anywhere else?

Dress for respect. Americans are fundamentally a casual people. Jeans, T-shirts and sneakers work for many of us much of the time, but there are people in other countries that [sic] believe such casualness is a sign of disrespect to them and their beliefs. Check out what is expected and bring scarves, headwear or whatever might be required.

Know some global sports trivia. Many countries don't play or watch American sports. So avoid filling your conversations with U.S. sporting allusions. There's a good chance people will not understand.

Keep your word. If you say that you will e-mail, find that book or baseball cap and send it, then make sure that you keep your promises.

Show your best side. Americans are a kind and generous people. You can help dispel the stereotype of the Ugly American; impress people with your kindness, curiosity and fair nature.

Be a traveler, not a tourist. Before you touch down in another country, learn as much as you can about it. Go beyond the guidebooks and pick up some of the music and the literature of the land. If you can, rent some movies from that country. Go online and search for information about the places you want to visit. You can get a great start through the resources we've put together at the World Citizens Guide website. Worldcitizensguide.org

Public diplomacy advocacy
Public Diplomacy Council (2007)

Citizen support of public diplomacy depends on the advocacy work of retired professionals in the field who devote their lives to awareness, academic study, and policy work. The Public Diplomacy Council is one of the leading organizations in Washington. Its mission statement follows.

The Public Diplomacy Council is a non-profit organization committed to the academic study, professional practice, and responsible advocacy of public diplomacy. Its members believe that understanding and influencing foreign publics, and dialogue between Americans and the citizens of other countries, are vital to the national interest and the conduct of 21st century diplomacy.

The Public Diplomacy Council was founded in 1988 as the Public Diplomacy Foundation. Dedicated to fostering greater public recognition of public diplomacy in the conduct of foreign affairs, the Foundation evolved to serve also as a resource and advocate for the teaching, training, and development of public diplomacy as an academic discipline.

In 2001, the Foundation joined The George Washington University's School of Media and Public Affairs and Elliott School of International Affairs to establish the Public Diplomacy Institute. The Foundation changed its name to the Public Diplomacy Council and became a membership organization with an elected board of directors. The Council maintains close ties with the USIA Alumni Association whose president is an ex-officio member of the Council's board of directors.

Objectives

The Public Diplomacy Council is committed to fostering awareness of the public, social, educational and cultural dimensions of world affairs. In recent years the Council and the Public Diplomacy Institute have become a primary source of information on the academic study of public diplomacy and on legislative and executive branch efforts to strengthen its use as an essential element of statecraft.

Assumptions

- Publics and their opinions matter increasingly in a globalizing world.
- U.S. statecraft should rely on careful analysis of the public dimension of issues.
- Informed judgments about global trends depend on an understanding of social and cultural dynamics and public opinion here and abroad.
- Civil society, the arts and educational communities are crucial intermediaries with counterparts in other nations.
- Public diplomacy budgets, training, and recruitment do not reflect the growing importance of public diplomacy.
- 21st century diplomacy will rely increasingly on mastery of modern telecommunications, yet the growth in mass communication creates a more urgent need for interpersonal communication.

Purposes

- Increase understanding of the public dimension of world affairs and of public diplomacy as an essential instrument of statecraft.
- Encourage teaching, research and writing about public diplomacy.
- Develop and promote high standards in the professional practice of public diplomacy.
- Encourage cooperative relations between the U.S. government and civil society, communications, arts, and educational and cultural institutions.
- Foster dialogue between the government and non-governmental sector about the changing role of publics in a

globalizing world and the impact on publics of new communications technologies.

• Build the bases for understanding public diplomacy and public perceptions by supporting the preservation of archival materials.

What the Law Says

Founding law: The Smith-Mundt Act and amendments
Public Law 402 (1948)

The Smith-Mundt Act of 1948 provided the legislative foundation for modern public diplomacy. The act, as amended, is still in force.

A small but controversial section of the law bars the State Department and U.S. Information Agency from disseminating information within the United States. Over the years, government lawyers, public affairs officers and others extended the Smith-Mundt provision well beyond what the law intended.

The text of the law shows that the Smith-Mundt Act specifically applies to the State Department and its affiliated agencies such as the former USIA. Yet since 2001, public affairs officers at the Pentagon and in the armed forces have repeatedly invoked Smith-Mundt as reason to veto critical information operations in support of the troops in Afghanistan and Iraq. This is an erroneous invocation. A reading of Smith-Mundt and its amendments shows that the law does not apply to the Department of Defense.

The original intent of the State Department restriction was not to prevent the U.S. government from waging domestic propaganda campaigns. Then-Senator Carl Mundt singled out the State Department because he believed at the time, the dawn of the Cold War, that the State Department was soft on the Soviet Union. By issuing foreign-oriented messages to the domestic public, Mundt reasoned, the State Department would undermine the presidency at home.

Other agencies and departments, including the Departments of Agriculture, Commerce, Health and Human Services, Labor, Transportation and Treasury, as well as the Department of Defense, have run domestic propaganda campaigns free of Smith-

Mundt constraints. Those campaigns – concerning smoking and other health issues, recycling, paying taxes, driving safely, and so forth – are designed to inform and influence the public, and to modify public attitudes and personal behavior.

With advances in information technology, many argue that the ban on State Department dissemination in the U.S. is obsolete; some say that the ban prevents American policymakers from exercising oversight of international broadcasts and programs.

As of this writing, federal lawmakers were complaining that they could not audit U.S. broadcasting to the Middle East due to lack of oversight, and that issue undercut confidence in U.S. message-making in the region. The operative text of the Smith-Mundt Act, as amended in the 1972 Foreign Relations Authorization Act, appears below, followed by the Zorinsky Amendment of 1985 and the Foreign Affairs Reform and Restructuring Act of 1998.

Title 22 USC, Chapter 18, Subchapter V – Dissemination Abroad of Information About the United States.

§ 1461. General authorization

This section is part of the 1972 Foreign Relations Authorization Act

(a) Dissemination of information abroad

The Secretary is authorized, when he finds it appropriate, to provide for the preparation, and dissemination abroad, of information about the United States, its people, and its policies, through press, publications, radio, motion pictures, and other information media, and through information centers and instructors abroad. Subject to subsection (b) of this section, any such information (other than "Problems of Communism" and the "English Teaching Forum" which may be sold by the Government Printing Office) shall not be disseminated within the United States, its territories, or possessions, but, on request, shall be available in the English language at the Department of State, at all reasonable times following its release as information abroad, for examination only by representatives of United States press associations, newspapers, magazines, radio systems, and stations, and by research students and scholars, and, on request, shall be made available for examination only to Members of Congress.

(b) Dissemination of information within United States

(1) The Director of the United States Information Agency shall make available to the Archivist of the United States, for domestic distribution, motion pictures, films, videotapes, and other material prepared for dissemination abroad 12 years after the initial dissemination of the material abroad or, in the case of such material not disseminated abroad, 12 years after the preparation of the material.

(2) The Director of the United States Information Agency shall be reimbursed for any attendant expenses. Any reimbursement to the Director pursuant to this subsection shall be credited to the applicable appropriation of the United States Information Agency.

(3) The Archivist shall be the official custodian of the material and shall issue necessary regulations to ensure that persons seeking its release in the United States have secured and paid for necessary United States rights and licenses and that all costs associated with the provision of the material by the Archivist shall be paid by the persons seeking its release. The Archivist may charge fees to recover such costs, in accordance with section 2116 (c) of title 44. Such fees shall be paid into, administered, and expended as part of the National Archives Trust Fund.

§ 1461–1. Mission of United States Information Agency

The mission of the United States Information Agency shall be to further the national interest by improving United States relations with other countries and peoples through the broadest possible sharing of ideas, information, and educational and cultural activities. In carrying out this mission, the United States Information Agency shall, among other activities –

(1) conduct Government-sponsored information, educational, and cultural activities designed –

(A) to provide other peoples with a better understanding of the policies, values, institutions, and culture of the United States; and

(B) within the statutory limits governing domestic activities of the Agency, to enhance understanding on the part of the Government and people of the United States of the history, culture, attitudes, perceptions, and aspirations of others;

(2) encourage private institutions in the United States to develop their own exchange activities, and provide assistance for those exchange activities which are in the broadest national interest;

(3) coordinate international informational, educational, or cultural activities conducted or planned by departments and agencies of the United States Government;

(4) assist in the development of a comprehensive national policy on international communications; and

(5) promote United States participation in international events relevant to the mission of the Agency.

Ban on domestic USIA activities
Zorinsky Amendment (1985)

§ 1461–1a. Ban on domestic activities by United States Information Agency

Except as provided in section 1461 of this title and this section, no funds authorized to be appropriated to the United States Information Agency shall be used to influence public opinion in the United States, and no program material prepared by the United States Information Agency shall be distributed within the United States. This section shall not apply to programs carried out pursuant to the Mutual Educational and Cultural Exchange Act of 1961 (22 U.S.C. 2451 et seq.). The provisions of this section shall not prohibit the United States Information Agency from responding to inquiries from members of the public about its operations, policies, or programs.

The Foreign Affairs Reform and Restructuring Act
U.S. House of Representatives, Report 105-432 (March 1998)

Smith-Mundt Sections

Section 333 addresses the complex question of how to apply restrictions in current law on USIA to influence public opinion in the United States once USIA is integrated into the Department of State. The Department has a responsibility to communicate with the American people on U.S. foreign policy, for example, to explain the importance of continuing U.S. involvement in international affairs. Subsection (a) makes clear that none of the restrictions applicable to USIA shall become applicable to public affairs and other information dissemination functions of the Secretary of State as carried out prior to any transfer of functions pursuant to this division. Subsection (b) provides that existing restrictions will, however, continue to apply to USIA public diplomacy programs (which are carried out abroad) once they are integrated into the State Department. This subsection preserves the exceptions in current law. Under this approach, public diplomacy programs that are unique to USIA, including the program material produced by them, shall continue to be subject to the restrictions of the Zorinsky Amendment and in the Smith-Mundt Act, as relevant. At the same time, the Department of State will be able to integrate the activities that it already performs, such as public outreach, direct public affairs contact with domestic and foreign press, and administrative activities, with such activities of the other foreign affairs agencies without these restrictions being applicable.

In addition, subsection (c) provides that funds that are specifically authorized in statute for such public diplomacy programs at the Department in the future shall not be used to influence public opinion in the United States, and that no program material prepared using such funds shall be distributed or disseminated in the United States. This provision makes clear that if an amount is specifically authorized in an authorization bill for such public diplomacy programs, such amount will be subject to these restrictions.

Subsections (d) and (e) create greater planning and budget transparency for how public diplomacy functions are integrated into the Department.

International Broadcasting Act of 1994
Public Law 103-236 (1994)

Section 303. Standards and Principles.

(a) ***Broadcasting Standards.*** United States international broadcasting shall:

(1)   be consistent with the broad foreign policy objectives of the United States;

(2)   be consistent with the international telecommunications policies and treaty obligations of the United States;

(3)   not duplicate the activities of private United States broadcasters;

(4)   not duplicate the activities of government supported broadcasting entities of other democratic nations;

(5)   be conducted in accordance with the highest professional standards of broadcast journalism;

(6)   be based on reliable information about its potential audience; and

(7)   be designed so as to effectively reach a significant audience.

(b) ***Broadcasting Principles.*** United States international broadcasting shall include:

(1)   news which is consistently reliable and authoritative, accurate, objective and comprehensive;

(2)   a balanced and comprehensive projection of United States thought and institutions, reflecting the diversity of United States culture and society;

(3)   clear and effective presentation of the policies of the United States Government and responsible discussion and opinion on those policies;

(4)   programming to meet the needs which remain unserved by the totality of media voices available to the people of certain nations;

(5)   information about developments in each significant region of the world;

(6)   a variety of opinions and voices from within particular nations and regions prevented by censorship or repression from speaking to their fellow countrymen;

(7)   reliable research capacity to meet criteria under this section;

(8)   adequate transmitter and relay capacity to support the activities described in this section; and

(9)   training and technical support for independent indigenous media through government agencies or private United States entities.

Section 305. Authorities of the Board [the Broadcasting Board of Governors, BBG]:

(c) ***Implementation***. The Director of the United States Information Agency and the Board, in carrying out their functions, shall respect the professional independence and integrity of the International Broadcasting Bureau, its broadcasting services, and grantees.

Foreign Affairs Reform and Restructuring Act of 1998
Public Law 105-277 (1998)

A reorganization plan and report of the Department of State following adoption of Public Law 105-277 states:

Under the Foreign Affairs Reform and Restructuring Act of 1998, the Broadcasting Board of Governors will become an independent federal entity by October 1, 1999. Consistent with the Act, international broadcasting will remain an essential instrument of U.S. foreign policy. The Board (including the Secretary of State who will be a statutory member of the Board) and State will respect the professional independence and integrity of U. S. international broadcasting.   (Note: under this law, the Secretary of State or his/her designee replaced the Director of the United States Information Agency. The Agency was abolished in the Act).

Pursuant to the Act, the BBG will become an independent Federal entity. This provides a "firewall" between State and the broadcasters to ensure the integrity of journalism. The Act thus ensures that the credibility and journalistic integrity of broadcasting will be preserved and enhanced. The Act also provides "deniability" for State when foreign governments complain about specific broadcasts.

Post 9/11 public diplomacy: What Congress passed into law

In the Intelligence Reform and Terrorism Prevention Act of 2004 (Public Law 108-468), Congress established parameters and priorities for an ideological campaign against what it called

"Islamist terrorism." Sections 7109 through 7118 of the law pertain directly to public diplomacy and international broadcasting.

Most of the operative sections are sense of the Congress resolutions and not legal mandates; consequently, some in the bureaucracy who disagree with the idea of battling Islamist ideology, or officials who fear innovation or controversy, have sought to avoid reference to the law.

While public affairs officers and others often work to restrict or even ban ideological message-making aimed at discrediting Islamist extremism, the 2004 law shows that Congress specifically called for such ideological campaigns within the national and global debate on the nature and future of Islam.

Federal law calls for public diplomacy offensive in Saudi Arabia
Public Law 108-468, Title VII § 7105 (2004)

"The Relationship Between the United States and Saudi Arabia"

(a) *Findings*. – Consistent with the report of the National Commission on Terrorist Attacks Upon the United States, Congress makes the following findings:

(1) Despite a long history of friendly relations with the United States, there have been problems in cooperation between the United States and Saudi Arabia.
(2) The Government of Saudi Arabia has not always responded promptly or fully to United States requests for assistance in the global war on Islamist terrorism.
(3) The Government of Saudi Arabia has not done all it can to prevent financial or other support from being provided to, or reaching, extremist organizations in Saudi Arabia or other countries.
(4) Counterterrorism cooperation between the Governments of the United States and Saudi Arabia has improved significantly since the terrorist bombing attacks in Riyadh, Saudi Arabia, on May 12, 2003, and the Government of Saudi Arabia is now pursuing al Qaeda and other terror groups operating inside Saudi Arabia.
(5) The United States must enhance its cooperation and strong relationship with Saudi Arabia based upon a shared and public commitment to political and economic reform, greater tolerance

and respect for religious and cultural diversity and joint efforts to prevent funding for and support of extremist organizations in Saudi Arabia and elsewhere.

(b) *Sense of Congress*. – It is the sense of Congress that there should be a more robust dialogue between the people and Government of the United States and the people and Government of Saudi Arabia in order to improve the relationship between the United States and Saudi Arabia.

Federal law calls for ideological campaign in Muslim world
Public Law 108-468, Title VII § 7106 (2004)

"Efforts to Combat Islamist Terrorism"

(a) *Findings*. – Consistent with the report of the National Commission on Terrorist Attacks Upon the United States, Congress makes the following findings:

(1) While support for the United States has plummeted in the Islamic world, many negative views are uninformed, at best, and, at worst, are informed by coarse stereotypes and caricatures.
(2) Local newspapers in countries with predominantly Muslim populations and influential broadcasters who reach Muslim audiences through satellite television often reinforce the idea that the people and Government of the United States are anti-Muslim.

(b) *Sense of Congress*. – It is the sense of Congress that –

(1) the Government of the United States should offer an example of moral leadership in the world that includes a commitment to treat all people humanely, abide by the rule of law, and be generous to the people and governments of other countries;
(2) the United States should cooperate with governments of countries with predominantly Muslim populations to foster agreement on respect for human dignity and opportunity, and to offer a vision of a better future that includes stressing life over death, individual educational and economic opportunity, widespread political participation, contempt for violence, respect

for the rule of law, openness in discussing differences, and tolerance for opposing points of view;
(3) the United States should encourage reform, freedom, democracy, and opportunity for Muslims; and
(4) the United States should work to defeat extremism in all its form, especially in nations with predominantly Muslim populations by providing assistance to governments, non-governmental organizations, and individuals who promote modernization.

Federal law calls for political action against Islamic dictatorships
Public Law 108-468, Title VII § 7107 (2004)

"United States Policy Toward Dictatorships"

(a) **Finding**. - Consistent with the report of the National Commission on Terrorist Attacks Upon the United States, Congress finds that short-term gains enjoyed by the United States through cooperation with repressive dictatorships have often been outweighed by long-term setbacks for the stature and interests of the United States.

(b) **Sense of Congress**. – It is the sense of Congress that –

(1) United States foreign policy should promote the importance of individual educational and economic opportunity, encourage widespread political participation, condemn violence, and promote respect for the rule of law, openness in discussing differences among people, and tolerance for opposing points of view; and
(2) the United States Government must encourage the governments of all countries with predominantly Muslim populations, including those that are friends and allies of the United States, to promote the value of life and the importance of individual education and economic opportunity, encourage widespread political participation, condemn violence and promote the rule of law, openness in discussing differences among people, and tolerance for opposing points of view.

Federal law calls for Muslim broadcast programming
Public Law 108-468, Title VII § 7108 (2004)

"Promotion of Free Media and Other American Values"

(a) Promotion of United States Values Through Broadcast Media. –

(1) *Findings*. – Consistent with the report of the National Commission on Terrorist Attacks Upon the United States, Congress makes the following findings:

(A) Although the United States has demonstrated and promoted its values in defending Muslims against tyrants and criminals in Somalia, Bosnia, Kosovo, Afghanistan, and Iraq, this message is neither convincingly presented nor widely understood.

(B) If the United States does not act to vigorously define its message in countries with predominantly Muslim populations, the image of the United States will be defined by Islamic extremists who seek to demonize the United States.

(C) Recognizing that many Muslim audiences rely on satellite television and radio, the United States Government has launched promising initiatives in television and radio broadcasting to the Islamic world, including Iran and Afghanistan.

(2) *Sense of Congress*. – It is the sense of Congress that –

(A) the United States must do more to defend and promote its values and ideals to the broadest possible audience in countries with predominantly Muslim populations;

(B) United States efforts to defend and promote these values and ideals are beginning to ensure that accurate expressions of these values reach large Muslim audiences and should be robustly supported;

(C) the United States Government could and should do more to engage Muslim audiences in the struggle of ideas; and

(D) the United States Government should more intensively employ existing broadcast media in the Islamic world as part of this engagement.

(b) Enhancing Free and Independent Media.-

(1) *Findings.* – Congress makes the following findings:

(A) Freedom of speech and freedom of the press are fundamental human rights.

(B) The United States has a national interest in promoting these freedoms by supporting free media abroad, which is essential to the development of free and democratic societies consistent with our own.

(C) Free media is undermined, endangered, or nonexistent in many repressive and transitional societies around the world, including in Eurasia, Africa, and the Middle East.

(D) Individuals lacking access to a plurality of free media are vulnerable to misinformation and propaganda and are potentially more likely to adopt anti-United States views.

(E) Foreign governments have a responsibility to actively and publicly discourage and rebut unprofessional and unethical media while respecting journalistic integrity and editorial independence.

(2) *Statement of policy.* – It shall be the policy of the United States, acting through the Secretary of State, to –

(A) ensure that the promotion of freedom of the press and freedom of media worldwide is a priority of United States foreign policy and an integral component of United States public diplomacy;

(B) respect the journalistic integrity and editorial independence of free media worldwide; and

(C) ensure that widely accepted standards for professional and ethical journalistic and editorial practices are employed when assessing international media.

Public diplomacy responsibilities of the Department of State
Public Law 108-468, Title VII § 7109 (2004)

(a) In General. – The State Department Basic Authorities Act of 1956 (22 U.S.C. 2651a et seq.) is amended by inserting after section 59 the following new section:

"SEC. 60. <<NOTE: 22 USC 2732.>> PUBLIC DIPLOMACY RESPONSIBILITIES OF THE DEPARTMENT OF STATE.

"(a) Integral Component. – The Secretary of State shall make public diplomacy an integral component in the planning and execution of United States foreign policy.

"(b) Coordination and Development of Strategy. – The Secretary shall make every effort to –
"(1) coordinate, subject to the direction of the President, the public diplomacy activities of Federal agencies; and
"(2) coordinate with the Broadcasting Board of Governors to –
"(A) develop a comprehensive and coherent strategy for the use of public diplomacy resources; and
"(B) develop and articulate long-term measurable objectives for United States public diplomacy.

"(c) Objectives. – The strategy developed pursuant to subsection (b) shall include public diplomacy efforts targeting developed and developing countries and select and general audiences, using appropriate media to properly explain the foreign policy of the United States to the governments and populations of such countries, with the objectives of increasing support for United States policies and providing news and information. The Secretary shall, through the most effective mechanisms, counter misinformation and propaganda concerning the United States. The Secretary shall continue to articulate the importance of freedom, democracy, and human rights as fundamental principles underlying United States foreign policy goals.

"(d) Identification of United States Foreign Assistance. – In cooperation with the United States Agency for International Development (USAID) and other public and private assistance organizations and agencies, the Secretary should ensure that information relating to foreign assistance provided by the United States, nongovernmental organizations, and private entities of the United States is disseminated widely, and particularly, to the extent practicable, within countries and regions that receive such assistance. The Secretary should ensure that, to the extent practicable, projects funded by USAID not involving commodities, including projects implemented by private voluntary organizations, are identified as provided by the people of the United States.''.

(b) Functions of the Under Secretary of State for Public Diplomacy. –

(1) Amendment. – Section 1(b)(3) of such Act (22 U.S.C. 2651a(b)(3)) is amended by adding at the end the following new sentence: "The Under Secretary for Public Diplomacy shall –

"(A) prepare an annual strategic plan for public diplomacy in collaboration with overseas posts and in consultation with the regional and functional bureaus of the Department;

"(B) ensure the design and implementation of appropriate program evaluation methodologies;

"(C) provide guidance to Department personnel in the United States and overseas who conduct or implement public diplomacy policies, programs, and activities;

"(D) assist the United States Agency for International Development and the Broadcasting Board of Governors to present the policies of the United States clearly and effectively; and

"(E) submit statements of United States policy and editorial material to the Broadcasting Board of Governors for broadcast consideration.".

(2) NOTE: 22 USC 2651a note. Consultation. - The Under Secretary of State for Public Diplomacy, in carrying out the responsibilities described in section 1(b)(3) of such Act (as amended by paragraph (1)), shall consult with public diplomacy officers operating at United States overseas posts and in the regional bureaus of the Department of State.

Public diplomacy training: A top congressional priority
Public Law 108-468, Title VII § 7110 (2004)

SEC. 7110. Public Diplomacy Training

(a) The following should be the policy of the United States:
(1) The Foreign Service should recruit individuals with expertise and professional experience in public diplomacy.

(2) United States chiefs of mission should have a prominent role in the formulation of public diplomacy strategies for the countries and regions to which they are assigned and should be accountable for the operation and success of public diplomacy efforts at their posts.

(3) Initial and subsequent training of Foreign Service officers should be enhanced to include information and training on public diplomacy and the tools and technology of mass communication.

(b) Personnel. –
(1) Qualifications. – In the recruitment, training, and assignment of members of the Foreign Service, the Secretary of State –

(A) should emphasize the importance of public diplomacy and applicable skills and techniques;

(B) should consider the priority recruitment into the Foreign Service, including at middle-level entry, of individuals with expertise and professional experience in public diplomacy, mass communications, or journalism; and

(C) shall give special consideration to individuals with language facility and experience in particular countries and regions.

(1) Personnel –
(A) In general. - The Secretary of State shall seek to increase the number of Foreign Service officers proficient in languages spoken in countries with predominantly Muslim populations. Such increase should be accomplished through the recruitment of new officers and incentives for officers in service.

(c) Public Diplomacy Suggested for Promotion in Foreign Service.
Section 603(b) of the Foreign Service Act of 1980 (22 U.S.C. 4003(b)) is amended by adding at the end the following: "The precepts for selection boards shall include, whether the member of

the Service or the member of the Senior Foreign Service, as the case may be, has demonstrated –
(1) a willingness and ability to explain United States policies in person and through the media when occupying positions for which such willingness and ability is, to any degree, an element of the member's duties, or
(2) other experience in public diplomacy.

Promotion of democracy and human rights
Public Law 108-468, Title VII § 7111 (2004)

"Promoting Democracy and Human Rights at International Organizations"

(a) Support and Expansion of Democracy Caucus. –
(1) In general. – The President, acting through the Secretary of State and the relevant United States chiefs of mission, should –
(A) continue to strongly support and seek to expand the work of the democracy caucus at the United Nations General Assembly and the United Nations Human Rights Commission; and
(B) seek to establish a democracy caucus at the United Nations Conference on Disarmament and at other broad-based international organizations.
(2) Purposes of the caucus. – A democracy caucus at an international organization should –
(A) forge common positions, including, as appropriate, at the ministerial level, on matters of concern before the organization and work within and across regional lines to promote agreed positions;
(B) work to revise an increasingly outmoded system of membership selection, regional voting, and decisionmaking; and
(C) establish a rotational leadership agreement to provide member countries an opportunity, for a set pericaucus, responsible for serving as its voice in each organization.

(b) Leadership and Membership of International Organizations. –
The President, acting through the Secretary of State, the relevant United States chiefs of mission, and, where appropriate, the

Secretary of the Treasury, should use the voice, vote, and influence of the United States to –

(1) where appropriate, reform the criteria for leadership and, in appropriate cases, for membership, at all United Nations bodies and at other international organizations and multilateral institutions to which the United States is a member so as to exclude countries that violate the principles of the specific organization;

(2) make it a policy of the United Nations and other international organizations and multilateral institutions of which the United States is a member that a member country may not stand in nomination for membership or in nomination or in rotation for a significant leadership position in such bodies if the member country is subject to sanctions imposed by the United Nations Security Council; and

(3) work to ensure that no member country stand in nomination for membership, or in nomination or in rotation for a significant leadership position in such organizations, or for membership on the United Nations Security Council, if the government of the member country has been determined by the Secretary of State to have repeatedly provided support for acts   of international terrorism.

(c) Increased Training in Multilateral Diplomacy. –

(1) *Statement of policy*. – It shall be the policy of the United States that training courses should be established for Foreign Service Officers and civil service employees of the State Department, including appropriate chiefs of mission, on the conduct of multilateral diplomacy, including the conduct of negotiations at international organizations and multilateral institutions, negotiating skills that are required at   multilateral settings, coalition-building techniques, and lessons learned from previous United States multilateral negotiations.

(2) *Personnel*. –

(A) In general. – The secretary shall ensure that the training described in paragraph (1) is provided at various stages of the career of members of the Service.

(B) Actions of the Secretary. – The Secretary shall ensure that –

(i) officers of the Service receive training on the conduct of diplomacy at international organizations and other multilateral institutions and at broad-based multilateral negotiations of international instruments as part of their training upon entry into the Service; and

(ii) officers of the Service, including chiefs of mission, who are assigned to United States missions representing the United States to international organizations and other multilateral institutions or who are assigned in Washington, D.C., to positions that have as their primary responsibility formulation of policy toward such organizations and institutions or toward participation in broad-based multilateral negotiations of international instruments, receive specialized training in the areas described in paragraph (1) prior to beginning of service for such assignment or, if receiving such training at that time is not practical, within the first year of beginning such assignment.

(3) The Secretary shall ensure that employees of the Department of State who are members of the civil service and who are assigned to positions described in paragraph (2) receive training described in paragraph (1) prior to the beginning of service for such assignment or, if receiving such training at such time is not practical, within the first year of beginning such assignment.

Expansion of Islamic scholarship and exchange programs
Public Law 108-468, Title VII § 7112 (2004)

SEC. 7112. EXPANSION OF UNITED STATES SCHOLARSHIP AND EXCHANGE PROGRAMS IN THE ISLAMIC WORLD.

(a) Findings. – Consistent with the report of the National Commission on Terrorist Attacks Upon the United States, Congress makes the following findings:

(1) Exchange, scholarship, and library programs are effective ways for the United States Government to promote internationally the values and ideals of the United States.

(2) Exchange, scholarship, and library programs can expose young people from other countries to United States values and offer them knowledge and hope.

(b) ***Declaration of Policy.*** – Consistent with the report of the National Commission on Terrorist Attacks Upon the United States, Congress declares that –

(1) the United States should commit to a long-term and sustainable investment in promoting engagement with people of all levels of society in countries with predominantly Muslim populations, particularly with youth and those who influence youth;

(2) such an investment should make use of the talents and resources in the private sector and should include programs to increase the number of people who can be exposed to the United States and its fundamental ideas and values in order to dispel misconceptions; and

(3) such programs should include youth exchange programs, young ambassadors programs, international visitor programs, academic and cultural exchange programs, American Corner programs, library programs, journalist exchange programs, sister city programs, and other programs related to people-to-people diplomacy.

(c) ***Sense of Congress.*** – It is the sense of Congress that the United States should significantly increase its investment in the people-to-people programs described in subsection (b).

(d) ***Authority To Expand Educational and Cultural Exchanges.*** – The President is authorized to substantially expand the exchange, scholarship, and library programs of the United States, especially such programs that benefit people in the Muslim world.

(e) ***Availability of Funds.*** – Of the amounts authorized to be appropriated in each of the fiscal years 2005 and 2006 for educational and cultural exchange programs, there shall be available to the Secretary of State such sums as may be necessary to carry out programs under this section, unless otherwise authorized by Congress.

Grants to U.S.-sponsored schools in Muslim countries
Public Law 108-468, Title VII § 7113 (2004)

SEC. 7113. PILOT <<NOTE: 22 USC 2452 note.>> PROGRAM
TO PROVIDE GRANTS TO AMERICAN-SPONSORED
SCHOOLS IN PREDOMINANTLY MUSLIM COUNTRIES TO
PROVIDE SCHOLARSHIPS.

(a) Findings. – Congress makes the following findings:
(1) During the 2003-2004 school year, the Office of Overseas
Schools of the Department of State is financially assisting 189
elementary and secondary schools in foreign countries.
(2) United States-sponsored elementary and secondary schools
are located in more than 20 countries with predominantly
Muslim populations in the Near East, Africa, South Asia,
Central Asia, and East Asia.
(3) United States-sponsored elementary and secondary schools
provide an American-style education in English, with curricula
that typically include an emphasis on the development of critical
thinking and analytical skills.

(b) Statement of Policy. – The United States has an interest in
increasing the level of financial support provided to United States-
sponsored elementary and secondary schools in countries with
predominantly Muslim populations in order to –

(1) increase the number of students in such countries who attend
such schools;
(2) increase the number of young people who may thereby gain
at any early age an appreciation for the culture, society, and
history of the United States; and
(3) increase the number of young people who may thereby
improve their proficiency in the English language.

(c) Pilot Program. – The Secretary of State, acting through the
Director of the Office of Overseas Schools of the Department of
State, may conduct a pilot program to make grants to United States-
sponsored elementary and secondary schools in countries with
predominantly Muslim populations for the purpose of providing full
or partial merit-based scholarships to students from lower-income
and middle-income families of such countries to attend such schools.

(d) Determination of Eligible Students. – For purposes of the pilot program, a United States-sponsored elementary and secondary school that receives a grant under the pilot program may establish criteria to be implemented by such school to determine what constitutes lower-income and middle-income families in the country (or region of the country, if regional variations in income levels in the country are significant) in which such school is located.

(e) Restriction on Use of Funds. – Amounts appropriated to the Secretary of State pursuant to the authorization of appropriations in subsection (h) shall be used for the sole purpose of making grants under this section, and may not be used for the administration of the Office of Overseas Schools of the Department of State or for any other activity of the Office.

(f) Voluntary Participation. – Nothing in this section shall be construed to require participation in the pilot program by a United States-sponsored elementary or secondary school in a predominantly Muslim country.

(g) Report. – Not later than April 15, 2006, the Secretary of State shall submit to the Committee on International Relations of the House of Representatives and the Committee on Foreign Relations of the Senate a report on the pilot program. The report shall assess the success of the program, examine any obstacles encountered in its implementation, and address whether it should be continued, and if so, provide recommendations to increase its effectiveness.

(h) Funding. – There are authorized to be appropriated to the Secretary of State for each of the fiscal years 2005 and 2006, unless otherwise authorized by Congress, such sums as necessary to implement the pilot program under this section.

International Youth Opportunity Fund
Public Law 108-468, Title VII § 7114 (2004)

SEC. 7114. INTERNATIONAL YOUTH OPPORTUNITY FUND.

(a) Findings. – Consistent with the report of the National Commission on Terrorist Attacks Upon the United States, Congress makes the following findings:

(1) Education that teaches tolerance, the dignity and value of each individual, and respect for different beliefs is a key element in any global strategy to eliminate terrorism.

(2) Education in the Middle East about the world outside that region is weak.

(3) The United Nations has rightly equated literacy with freedom.

(4) The international community is moving toward setting a concrete goal of reducing by half the illiteracy rate in the Middle East by 2010, through the implementation of education programs targeting women and girls and programs for adult literacy, and by other means.

(5) To be effective, efforts to improve education in the Middle East must also include –

(A) support for the provision of basic education tools, such as textbooks that translate more of the world's knowledge into local languages and local libraries to house such materials; and

(B) more vocational education in trades and business skills.

(6) The Middle East can benefit from some of the same programs to bridge the digital divide that already have been developed for other regions of the world.

(b) International Youth Opportunity Fund. –

(1) Establishment.–The Secretary of State is authorized to establish through an existing international organization, such as the United Nations Educational, Science and Cultural Organization (UNESCO) or other similar body, an International Youth Opportunity Fund to provide financial assistance for the improvement of public education in the Middle East and other countries of strategic interest with predominantly Muslim populations.

(2) International participation. – The Secretary should seek the cooperation of the international community in establishing and generously supporting the Fund.

The use of economic policies to combat terrorism
Public Law 108-468, Title VII § 7115 (2004)

SEC. 7115. THE USE OF ECONOMIC POLICIES TO COMBAT TERRORISM.

(a) Findings. – Consistent with the report of the National Commission on Terrorist Attacks Upon the United States, Congress makes the following findings:

(1) While terrorism is not caused by poverty, breeding grounds for terrorism are created by backward economic policies and repressive political regimes.

(2) Policies that support economic development and reform also have political implications, as economic and political liberties are often linked.

(3) The United States is working toward creating a Middle East Free Trade Area by 2013 and implementing a free trade agreement with Bahrain, and free trade agreements exist between the United States and Israel and the United States and Jordan.

(4) Existing and proposed free trade agreements between the United States and countries with predominantly Muslim populations are drawing interest from other countries in the Middle East region, and countries with predominantly Muslim populations can become full participants in the rules-based global trading system, as the United States considers lowering its barriers to trade.

(b) Sense of Congress. – It is the sense of Congress that–

(1) a comprehensive United States strategy to counter terrorism should include economic policies that encourage development, open societies, and opportunities for people to improve the lives of their families and to enhance prospects for their children's future;

(2) one element of such a strategy should encompass the lowering of trade barriers with the poorest countries that have a significant population of Muslim individuals;

(3) another element of such a strategy should encompass United States efforts to promote economic reform in countries that have a significant population of Muslim individuals, including efforts to integrate such countries into the global trading system; and

(4) given the importance of the rule of law in promoting economic development and attracting investment, the United States should devote an increased proportion of its assistance to countries in the Middle East to the promotion of the rule of law.

Middle East Partnership Initiative to promote rule of law
Public Law 108-468, Title VII § 7116 (2004)

SEC. 7116. MIDDLE EAST PARTNERSHIP INITIATIVE.

(a) Authorization of Appropriations. - There are authorized to be appropriated for each of fiscal years 2005 and 2006, (unless otherwise authorized by Congress) such sums as may be necessary for the Middle East Partnership Initiative.

(b) It is the sense of Congress that, given the importance of the rule of law and economic reform to development in the Middle East, a significant portion of the funds authorized to be appropriated under subsection (a) should be made available to promote the rule of law in the Middle East.

Toward a comprehensive global strategy against terrorism
Public Law 108-468, Title VII § 7117 (2004)

SEC. 7117. COMPREHENSIVE <<NOTE: 22 USC 2656 note.>> COALITION STRATEGY FOR FIGHTING TERRORISM.

(a) Findings. – Consistent with the report of the National Commission on Terrorist Attacks Upon the United States, Congress makes the following findings:

(1) Almost every aspect of the counterterrorism strategy of the United States relies on international cooperation.

(2) Since September 11, 2001, the number and scope of United States Government contacts with foreign governments concerning counterterrorism have expanded significantly, but such contacts have often been ad hoc and not integrated as a comprehensive and unified approach to counterterrorism.

(b) In General. – The Secretary of State is authorized in consultation with relevant United States Government agencies, to negotiate on a bilateral or multilateral basis, as appropriate, international agreements under which parties to an agreement work in partnership to address and interdict acts of international terrorism.

(c) International Contact Group on Counterterrorism. –
(1) Sense of Congress. – It is the sense of Congress that the President –
(A) should seek to engage the leaders of the governments of other countries in a process of advancing beyond separate and uncoordinated national counterterrorism strategies to develop with those other governments a comprehensive multilateral strategy to fight terrorism; and
(B) to that end, should seek to establish an international counterterrorism policy contact group with the leaders of governments providing leadership in global counterterrorism efforts and governments of countries with sizable Muslim populations, to be used as a ready and flexible international means for discussing and coordinating the development of important counterterrorism policies by the participating governments.
(2) <<NOTE: President. Establishment.>> Authority. – The President is authorized to establish an international counterterrorism policy contact group with the leaders of governments referred to in paragraph (1) for the following purposes:
(A) To meet annually, or more frequently as the President determines appropriate, to develop in common with such other governments important policies and a strategy that address the various components of international prosecution of the war on terrorism, including policies and a strategy that address military issues, law enforcement, the collection, analysis, and dissemination of intelligence, issues relating to interdiction of

travel by terrorists, counterterrorism-related customs issues, financial issues, and issues relating to terrorist sanctuaries.

(B) To address, to the extent (if any) that the President and leaders of other participating governments determine appropriate, long-term issues that can contribute to strengthening stability and security in the Middle East.

About the Editor

J. Michael Waller is the Walter and Leonore Annenberg Professor of International Communication at The Institute of World Politics in Washington, D.C., where he directs the nation's only graduate studies program in public diplomacy and political warfare.

Dr. Waller has been a participant in or practitioner in the field since he was an exchange student abroad in the late 1970s. He was a United States delegate to the United Nations International Youth Year celebrations, and represented the U.S. at various international public diplomacy and related events, as a delegate or as a journalist, in Latin America, Europe and the Middle East. He engaged in counterpropaganda work against Soviet international front organizations overseas, including infiltration and disruption of the World Peace Council; designed and implemented democratization projects in Latin America and Russia with the United States Information Agency and USAID, and was a member of the USIA International Speakers Bureau; he is a member of the USIA Alumni Association. Waller is also Vice President for Information Operations at the Center for Security Policy.

He holds a Ph.D. in international security affairs from Boston University and has been a consultant to the Senate Foreign Relations Committee, U.S. Information Agency, U.S. Agency for International Development, and the Office of the Secretary of Defense.

Dr. Waller's articles have appeared in the *Los Angeles Times*, *Readers Digest*, *USA Today*, the *Washington Times* and the *Wall Street Journal*. He is author of *Third Current of Revolution: Inside the North American Front of El Salvador's Guerrilla War* (University Press of America, 1991), *Secret Empire: The KGB In Russia Today* (Westview, 1994); and *Fighting the War of Ideas like a Real War* (IWP Press, 2007). He is co-editor of *Dismantling Tyranny: Transitioning Beyond Totalitarian Regimes* (Rowman & Littlefield, 2006) with Ilan Berman; and editor of *Strategic Influence: Public Diplomacy, Counterpropaganda and Political Warfare* (IWP Press, 2007).

About The Institute of World Politics

The Institute of World Politics is an independent, accredited graduate school of national security and international affairs. Based in Washington, D.C., the Institute is dedicated to developing leaders with a sound understanding of international realities and the ethical conduct of statecraft based on knowledge and appreciation of American political philosophy and the Western moral tradition. IWP offers Master's degrees in Statecraft and National Security, Statecraft and World Politics, and Strategic Intelligence.

IWP courses relating to the subject of this book include:

Foreign Propaganda, Perceptions and Policy

Foundations of Political and Economic Freedom

Ideas and Values in International Politics

Islam and Contemporary Global Politics

Mass Media and World Politics

Political Warfare: Past, Present and Future

Politics, Culture and Intelligence

Problems of Promoting Regime Change and Democracy

Public Diplomacy and Political Warfare

Strategic Information Warfare

THE INSTITUTE OF WORLD POLITICS
1521 16th Street NW
Washington, DC 20036 USA
(202) 462-2101

www.iwp.edu   info@iwp.edu

Sirbart Fecit

www.ingramcontent.com/pod-product-compliance
Lightning Source LLC
Chambersburg PA
CBHW020652270326
41928CB00005B/75